F
Card

24103

P9-DCI-432

## DATE DUE

| JAN 0 4 1999 | | | |
|---|---|---|---|
| MY 1 o '01 | | | |
| DE 06 '02 | | | |
| · | | | |
| | | | |
| | | | |
| | | | |
| | | | |
| | | | |
| | | | |
| | | | |
| | | | |
| | | | |
| | | | |
| | | | |
| | | | |

Demco, Inc. 38-293

# STONE TABLES

# STONE TABLES

*A Novel by*

# ORSON SCOTT CARD

*Based on the Musical Play*

*Music by Robert Stoddard*

*Script and Lyrics by Orson Scott Card*

DESERET BOOK COMPANY

SALT LAKE CITY, UTAH

BISHOP O___U LIBRARY

© 1997 Orson Scott Card

Script, music, and lyrics of the play *Stone Tables* © 1973, 1981 by Robert Stoddard and Orson Scott Card

All rights reserved. No part of this book may be reproduced in any form or by any means without permission in writing from the publisher, Deseret Book Company, P.O. Box 30178, Salt Lake City, Utah 84130. This work is not an official publication of The Church of Jesus Christ of Latter-day Saints. The views expressed herein are the responsibility of the author and do not necessarily represent the position of the Church or of Deseret Book Company.

Deseret Book is a registered trademark of Deseret Book Company.

**Library of Congress Cataloging-in-Publication Data**

Card, Orson Scott
  Stone tables / by Orson Scott Card.
    p.   cm.
  ISBN 1-57345-115-0
  1. Moses (Biblical leader) — Fiction. 2. Bible. O.T. — History of Biblical events — Fiction. I. Title.
  PS3553.A655S86   1997
  813'.54 — dc21
                        97-35881
                        CIP

Printed in the United States of America      18961

10  9  8  7  6  5  4  3  2

*To Charles Whitman,*
*believer in dreams,*
*who showed novices how to be artists*
*and boys how to be men*

# Contents

# Preface

Years ago, as a missionary in Brazil, I wrote myself to sleep many nights, composing poems, stories, anything to vent the pent-up English that I wasn't able to use during the day. I read of the *New Era*'s arts contest for young people, and on impulse I assembled some of the poems and stories I had written, added a few of my better black-and-white photographs, and entered the contest in just about every category. I think it was more the volume than the quality of my submission that induced them to award me a prize, but I used part of the prize money to buy a copy of Josephus's *Antiquities of the Jews*.

Soon afterward I was assigned to the mission office in São Paulo as the printer, which meant I spent my days in an office with a Selectric typewriter, a Xerox machine, a printing press, a light table, and a stereo. For a writer, that was like throwing Br'er Rabbit into the briar patch. Please don't make me stay here! By then I was already a few hundred lines into a verse play about Moses and Aaron, drawing upon some of what I had learned from Josephus, upon other things I had learned (and, sadly, later had to unlearn) from a well-known LDS Old Testament commentator, but mostly upon my own speculation on the convoluted relationship between Moses and Aaron.

What was it like, I wondered, for the older brother of this God-favored child, who watched his once-doomed younger brother ascend to be prince of Egypt, then fall, then return from exile as a prophet whom Aaron could only serve as a spokesman? Perhaps Aaron was like Hyrum was to Joseph Smith, an older brother whose love and faith disposed of all possible jealousies. But then how could one explain Aaron's motivation as he made a golden calf for the Israelites while Moses was up on the mount receiving the covenant from God?

Rightly or wrongly—for motivations of historical figures can only be guessed at—I thought I detected a pattern of envy, ambition, and hubris running through the life of Aaron, only broken as, shattered by self-recognition, he faced Moses before the ruined shards of stone from the broken tables of the covenant and made his unbelievably lame explanation that when he put the gold into the fire, the calf "came out"—as if his hands had not shaped it. This was no Hyrum Smith! And yet he was made the high priest of Israel, and by the time he died he had clearly become the man the Lord needed him to be.

Add to this my speculations about Moses—what it must have seemed like to him, raised in a palace and suddenly thrust out into the desert, only to find that God had been guiding his life all along—and I began to realize that out of this story, whose religious purpose is already perfectly fulfilled by the scriptural account, there was an additional purpose that might be fulfilled in the story of the relationship between the chosen man and his seemingly unchosen brother, and of the man who was driven by God until he embraced God's purpose and became the man of faith who could challenge kings and part waters.

Exploring these stories, I wrote two acts of a free-verse play I called *Stone Tables*, and then, armed with that IBM Selectric, I typed it up and sent it off to my mentor in the BYU Theatre Department, Dr. Charles Whitman, hoping for some reaction—encouragement or criticism. To my astonishment, his letter was not a critique, it was an urgent demand for the rest of the play. He had added it to that year's winter schedule of the Theatre Department! He was going to direct it on the Pardoe stage, but he needed the remaining three acts immediately so he could get the set and costume design under way.

Did he really think that, if the other three acts had existed, I would not have sent them to him?

And if that was not astonishing enough, he also told me that Robert Stoddard, who had collaborated with me on the musical *Father, Mother, Mother, and Mom* before my mission, was hard at work writing the music for the songs in *Stone Tables*.

Songs? What songs? I had written in unrhymed, anti-rhythmic verse! These were not singable lyrics—not that I was much good at writing those, either—and *Stone Tables* wasn't exactly your normal musical comedy storyline.

While fulfilling all my duties in the mission office, I used my spare time to rush through to the end of the play. Now, knowing there would be music, I included a few lines that felt singable to me and called them songs (though the best of them came straight from Exodus, in the form of the Song of Moses). Then I continued my mission as letters arrived telling me of how rehearsals were going, how wonderful Robert's music was, how controversial the play became as people started calling it a "rock musical" (even though neither the music nor the dance in *Stone Tables* had anything to do with rock and roll; this was 1973, when "rock musical" meant the scandalous *Hair* or the blasphemous *Jesus Christ, Superstar*, and evil-hunters were eagerly detecting pro-drug messages in "Puff, the Magic Dragon"), and finally how popular it was as extra performances were added to accommodate the sold-out houses.

Through all of this I heard not a note of the music and saw

the staging only in my imagination. I knew some of the leading actors because they were fellow students; I could only imagine the brilliant Mark Hopkin making Moses come to life on the stage better than my poor script deserved, and many other friends of great talent coalescing into a powerful theatrical experience while I typed up handouts for mission conferences and wrote the mission newsletter and printed it all out on an offset printer while I listened to "Horse with No Name" and "If," Joni Mitchell and Crosby, Stills, and Nash. It was so weird that at that particular moment, it was my play that was doing more direct missionary work back in Utah than I was doing on my mission assignment in Brazil.

Years passed, and Robert and I substantially revised the play twice, as our artistic growth made the weaknesses of youth too obvious for us to bear. Yet the heart of the play, and especially of the music, remained true and right for us, until finally we once again began reworking *Stone Tables* in the winter of 1996 and found support from the visionary Sheri Dew of Deseret Book for the idea of a compact disc of the *Stone Tables* music and a novel of the storyline. With the inestimable help of my younger brother, the composer Arlen Card, as orchestrator and conductor, Robert worked on creating the definitive arrangement and performance of the music while I struggled with shaping and writing the novel that you hold in your hands at this moment.

I had adapted a script to the novel form once before, with James Cameron's screenplay for the movie *The Abyss*. This time, though, it should be easier, right? After all, I wrote the play *Stone Tables*, and so I could change anything I wanted. I only had to please myself!

But nothing is ever as easy as it looks. In a play, you can skip so much of the setting and background; the audience sees the people onstage before them, and so it takes no effort to make them "real." With the novel, I actually had to do research; I had to set Moses into a particular time and place in Egypt.

No one knows exactly what part of Egyptian history the Israelites fit into. Higher critics and unbelievers, of course, are quick to assume that the Israelites don't fit there at all, that some memory perhaps of the explosion of Thera was transformed into legends of plagues and a fictitious tribal lawgiver named Moses. On the opposite extreme, literalists expect that the exact wording of the King James Version must be force-fit onto history.

I'm afraid I'm something of a pragmatist. On the one hand, I believe that Moses was a real prophet and that the story of Exodus is substantially true as written, given the vagaries of record-keeping through the centuries and the tendency to round numbers to ten or forty; and that "higher criticism" is generally of such a low level of intellectual integrity that it can excite only pity or amusement in those not predisposed to seize upon its clubhouse consensus as "truth."

On the other hand, Exodus is only one of ten thousand possible written records that *could* have been made of the events, and with Moses as the source or author of the story, much would certainly have been left out if only because of his modesty or his sense of its irrelevance to the spiritual purpose of his writing. Thus Exodus says nothing of Moses' life and achievements as a prince of Egypt, and barely includes his private life at all (and then almost always in order to teach a lesson). And yet there are no other credible sources to help us. In the years since my mission I have come to see Josephus's account as the unreliable mishmash of legend and fiction that it is, so that now I use only his account of the taking of Saba,

despite all the earmarks of romance, and his names for the
priests of Pharaoh, while I ignore his (or others') unauthorita-
tive and generally unbelievable elaborations of the life of
Moses. Likewise, after Hugh Nibley set me straight on a few
of the more obvious fallacies of the LDS commentator I had
once relied on, the material derived from that source was also
jettisoned.

In the meantime, though, I did acquire some useful speculations from the book *Return to Soдom anд Gomorrah* by Charles
Pellegrino. Since Pellegrino's book openly declares itself to be
nothing more than decently well-informed speculation, I felt
free to pick and choose what I found interesting, plausible, or
at least fictionally useful from his brief treatment of Moses.
Though his linking of Moses with Hatshepsut derives in part
from his desire to link the exodus of Israel with the explosion
of Thera, I found a completely different set of reasons. First,
Hatshepsut's story is intrinsically interesting. Second, I was
always bothered by the story of the daughter of Pharaoh being
able to take a baby out of the water and adopt him as her son.
How could such an act be politically possible in a situation
where Hebrew boy-children were being killed? As you will see
in these pages, the political life of Hatshepsut makes her completely unique — the only "daughter of Pharaoh" who would
have had the power, completely on her own, to make such an
adoption have force. Also, Hatshepsut's place as a scion of the
family that had ejected the Hyksos rulers gave a very useful
link between the story of Joseph and the story of Moses. If
Joseph arrived during the Hyksos domination of Egypt, and
was preferred by one of those Pharaohs, then after
Hatshepsut's family expelled the Hyksos invaders, wouldn't
their Israelite underlings be a hated and persecuted reminder
of Egypt's decades of shame under foreign rule?

For my purposes, at least, Hatshepsut was an open door into the novel, and while the play cannot possibly deal with her life in any serious way, in the novel I was able to develop her into a character who delighted me, if not anyone else. Her stepson, successor, and probable murderer, Tuthmose III, was also quite productive as Moses' hard-hearted adversary during the plagues. Be assured, however, that unlike some scholars, I do not regard my own speculations as if they were somehow proved by how felicitously they fit the few bits of knowledge we have. My purpose is to explore character and story. I would not be at all offended to find out that my linking of Moses to Hatshepsut and Tuthmose III is all wrong, should new evidence become available. At the same time, I also know that no one has at this time any serious evidence to disprove the story that I tell here. And that is all I need, for my speculations are clearly labeled as fiction. My readers are wise enough to know they aren't reading history.

My effort is to make sure that those who read this story emerge with an understanding of how good people struggle with each other and with their understanding of God's will as they try to make some decent use of their years of life. If in the process the book of Exodus is illuminated or enhanced for some readers, I'll be delighted; and if I have erred (and I'm sure I have) in the few alterations I have made, I am comforted by the knowledge that the book of Exodus remains, as always, untouched and unharmed by my effort to explore it fictionally. Not one word of the scripture is erased, and some words may even be highlighted by what I do in these pages.

And, of course, my retelling of the story of Moses is shaped in part by Joseph's Smith's revelation of the Book of Moses in the Pearl of Great Price. Most particularly this shows up in the explicit way characters in my novel refer to their foreknowledge of Christ. This will be surprising to non-Mormon readers of the story, who are not accustomed to thinking of Old Testament figures as having such a clear understanding of the Messiah; but *Stone Tables* is written unapologetically within the worldview of the Latter-day Saints.

I owe a great debt to many people: First to Charles Whitman, who believed in *Stone Tables* when it was still only half-created, and to whom this book is dedicated. Then to Robert Stoddard, for a collaborative relationship that is surpassed only by his friendship in the grace and joy it has brought to my life. I owe a debt also to the actors and other theatrical workers who have brought several productions of *Stone Tables* to the stage over the years, and especially to the late Mark Hopkin, who, though I never saw him perform this role, was always such a brilliant and powerful actor and singer that I feel as if my Moses were also partly his.

In my work on this novel, I must thank Sheri Dew for her patience and guidance; Robert, Arlen, and many singers, musicians, and technicians for the recordings that have inspired me as I write; my wife, Kristine, who, despite the woes of pregnancy at a not-quite-Sarah-like age, has read my chapters and guided me as she always does; Robert's wife, D'Ann, whose faith in her husband may actually exceed my own; my friend Kathy Kidd for encouragement and for catching some of my more egregious errors in Egyptian history—you'll be an egyptologist yet, Kathy!; Scott Allen and Kathleen Bellamy, who have lifted many burdens so I am free to write; and Erin and Phillip Absher, who have loved and cared for my family as if we were of their own blood, thus proving that the spirit of Ruth and Naomi is alive in the world.

*Chapter 1*

# Promises

Jochabed felt the first pain late in the afternoon. She didn't tell anyone then, because it was not a good time to try to sneak the midwife in. Besides, Miriam and Aaron had come slowly, from the first pain to the last. She had plenty of time before this new baby became urgent.

Plenty of time before she had to face the prospect of the Egyptians coming to throw the baby into the Nile.

If it was a boy. She reminded herself of that hope. It might be a girl, and if it was, they wouldn't touch her.

But Amram said it would be a boy, and surely he knew. Surely God spoke to him.

Though as long as God was taking so much interest in Jochabed's new baby, it would be convenient if he'd arrange a way for the baby to survive. Jochabed didn't know if there was some protocol for such a prayer; if there was, she surely violated it, because fifty times a day, a hundred times a day since she realized she was pregnant, she had prayed the most outrageous prayers. She couldn't even say them aloud, the way Amram always did, because she was afraid God would strike her dead. Yet she couldn't stop praying. She prayed again right now, as she thought about prayer, about God.

Do something! she demanded. Amram always names thee as the cause for everything. In the great wisdom of the Lord, the floodwater is low this year. In the great wisdom of the

Lord, the floodwater is high this year. Well, O Lord, this is a bad year for boy babies among the Israelites. Or hast thou not heard, in thy lofty place, wherever it is that thou dwellest? The Egyptians have come to hate us even though we were not part of the conquering Hyksos; they have taken away our place of honor and made us slaves, building their levees and their city walls out of mud bricks. They have forbidden us to sacrifice to thee and they fall upon us and beat us whenever they find one or two of us alone. And now Pharaoh has promised them that he will eradicate us all within a generation. If the Egyptians hear of a boychild born to an Israelite they can seize it and drown it in the river as a sacrifice; and any Israelite who resists is guilty of blasphemy against whatever bestial god it is they serve. Didst thou not know, O Lord, that they were doing this? Didst thou not *cause* them to hate us, for some great wise purpose of thine own? But tell me now, if thou wantedst us to perish here on the banks of the Nile, why not strike us all dead at once? Drown us in a flood? Cause the earth to swallow us up? Cause the crocodiles to rise up out of the river and devour us all at once? Or . . . perhaps, being merciful, merely let us fall asleep and never awaken? Why must we watch them tear our babies from us and throw them into the river to drown? What is thy great, wise plan?

By this point in her prayers she was always filled with such resentment, such rage, that she marveled God did not kill her on the spot. And her heart turned, and softened, and she wept (so many tears, all these months of her pregnancy), she wept and in her heart she prayed again and said, O Lord, forgive me, forgive me, don't punish this baby for the sinful proud wicked heart of the mother. Let me save this child alive. Let his birth not be in vain. Let him live to be a man. I dedicate him to thee, I give him to thee, I willingly say: Let him be raised in another woman's house, suck from another woman's breast, call another woman Mother, only let him live, show me a way to keep the boy alive. Keep him out of the river, O God!

And then, in tears again, in tears always, she ended her prayer and went on about her work until the next time that rage swelled up in her heart and she began again her prayer of sarcasm, then repentance, then pleading.

A pain swept over her, an insistent one. The sun was still up, but she had no choice. This baby was not going to be as slow as Aaron or Miriam were.

Three-year-old Aaron was playing with the distaff, making a tangle of the thread.

"Miriam!" called Jochabed, her voice made sharp by pain.

Miriam came indoors at once. "The water hasn't boiled yet, mother."

"I don't care about the supper," said Jochabed.

"Aaron," said Miriam, "leave the thread alone, you're undoing Mother's work!"

"I don't care about the thread," said Jochabed.

Miriam's eyes grew wide. In all her seven years of life, she had never known her mother to speak slightingly of any labor.

"Go tell . . . go to the house of Puah . . ."

"The Egyptians watch her house." Was even a child aware of the terrible things that had befallen the people of Israel? Oh, Miriam, that you should live in such a time!

"No. I know that. I meant, go to the house of . . . go find your father and whisper to him that the time of a woman has come upon me. Speak to no one else." Jochabed had meant to wait until Amram came home in the evening; she had made no plan for how to notify him before the afternoon was out. If their Egyptian neighbors got word that a midwife had been called for, they would set up a vigil outside the house, and there would be no hope then.

Not that there was hope even now. Should she wish for a mute child, so he would not cry? As well she might wish to keep him muffled up in cloth, hide him in a basket until he reached manhood. Oh, why not simply carry him to the river herself, and spare them all the agony of dread!

"Go," said Jochabed. And then: "Wait."

Miriam stopped in the doorway, confused, afraid that she had done something wrong.

"No, I just—no, don't fetch your father, no. Go instead to the boatmakers. Tell them I need pitch. A jar of hot pitch." The idea was only half-formed, but already Jochabed knew what she was going to do. A basket. Take him to the river herself. God chose to send her a boy at a time like this—well, let God find a way to save him! Jochabed knew the moment the idea came to her that it was from God. Like Noah, her baby would ride atop the flood in a boat smeared with pitch to make it watertight. Pharaoh's edict said that Israelite boy babies must be given to the river. But he never said they could not be in a boat!

A basket. One of the baskets here in the house would have to do. A new one, with a tight weave. Large enough to hold a baby.

Another pain seized her and she stopped, gasped for breath. Give me time, child! Don't be in such a hurry to get to the river that you insist on arriving there before I have your ark ready for you!

I meant it, Lord! Save this baby, and he belongs to thee. Only let me see that he's alive. Not that I insist on it—I beg it of thee as a favor, that's all. Be merciful and let me see that he's alive, let me know that he has found favor in thy sight, and then I will be content, I will bless thy name forever. Or if thou wilt not save him, then let me die in bearing him, so I never have to know of his death, or spend my life imagining those terrible moments as he drowns or is taken by a crocodile.

Jochabed slid down the rough mudbrick wall to the cold earthen floor of her house. Hurry, Miriam. My baby needs the Lord, but I need the midwife.

❖

Hatshepsut was getting ready to go down to the river when Jannes came to her. "Your father wants you," he said. And since her father was Pharaoh, there was no question but that she would go to him at once.

Hatshepsut knew something that no one else knew, however, for her father had shown it to no one else: She knew that besides being Pharaoh, he was also Tuthmose, a mere man, beset with a man's doubts and fears, a man's griefs and regrets. These days Father seemed to sink more deeply inside himself with every passing day. Hatshepsut suspected that he was preparing to die. Not that he was ill, not that he was old, but that he saw that his life had been for nothing. For Hatshepsut's two full brothers, either of whom would have been her husband and Tuthmose's successor to the double crown of Egypt, had died in their youth, and from the way the concubine Mutnefert pushed her own son forward, it was hard to doubt the gossip that Mutnefert had a hand in the convenient death of each heir. And it wasn't as if Mutnefert was subtle: Father had tried to raise two more half-brothers ahead of Mutnefert's loathsome boy, and each of them had met with an unfortunate accident.

The fact that their "accidents" had come when Mutnefert was nowhere near did not absolve her; it merely implied that she had more and more allies within the palace, who expected that when Tuthmose died it would be very, very good for their careers to be friends of Mutnefert. How many times had Hatshepsut whispered to her father that for the sake of his other children, he really ought to put Mutnefert to death? Until finally Tuthmose spoke harshly to her, despite her status as his most beloved child: "The house of Pharaoh is the house of a god," he said. "Do I publicly declare that I have unknowingly brought a snake into my house? Then I must not be a god, and the house comes down."

This had come as a shock to Hatshepsut, for she was logician enough to understand that her father was confessing a terrible secret: that he was not a god, for he *had* brought a snake into the house. And worse: that it was so important to maintain the illusion of the godhood of Pharaoh that he would sacrifice all his sons and let the twisted spawn of a monster take the crown in order to preserve it.

Since that day—and she was only twelve when it happened, not yet come into her beauty but already possessed of her wisdom and the confidence of her father—she had come to understand better that it is by illusions that men rule. The illusion of Pharaoh as all-seeing and all-powerful was necessary to allow him to govern, especially because he saw only what his aides showed him, and his power reached only as far as people were willing to obey him. The illusion of god-Pharaoh led the common people to obey him even when snakes in his own house bit his heel.

Only the gossip about Mutnefert had spread far and wide—and, more to the point, high and low. The people sensed the weakness in the king's house. They demanded a hero. They remembered the achievements of Amose and Amenhotep, Tuthmose's grandfather and father, who had driven out the Hyksos overlords and suppressed their rebellions

and restored the ancient glory and sovereignty of Egypt.
Tuthmose was weak? Then look to the past: What did
Amenhotep do that made him strong? He struck with his
armies across the borders to break the will of the enemies of
Egypt. He brought back triumph and tribute from foreign
lands.

And he executed his enemies within Egypt.

Did the people want to maintain Egypt's greatness? They
could not send out armies or bring back tribute. But they certainly *could* execute the enemies of Egypt. And now that the
Hyksos were gone for good, who was left to kill but the
Israelites, those hapless desert people who first came to Egypt
during a famine centuries before and who were raised up to
power and privilege by the Hyksos Pharaohs, who used their
loyalty, their learning, their hard work, to help them maintain
their grip on Egypt? When the Hyksos fell, the Israelites were
friendless.

The vengeance of the Egyptian people was not harsh at
first. Israelites had been their overlords, so now they became
slaves. Teachers and magistrates now made mud bricks and
built levees and walls, monuments and roads. The pleasure of
this did not last, however, especially since the Israelites continued to be more learned than the common Egyptians, as if
they thought they were all priests, and kept on with their
loathsome customs of keeping herds of animals and killing
them in bloody, smoky, stinking sacrifices to their invisible private god. More to the point, the Israelites also had far more
children than most Egyptian families, so that not only their
herds of animals but also their herds of children increased.

Not long ago the common people began to form mobs and
storm the homes of Israelite women giving birth. These inci-
dents, if allowed to flourish, would lead to anarchy. Jannes

and his son Jambres advised Tuthmose that the only way to harness the rage of the people was to make his own laws to satisfy them.

The first attempt was an order given to the Israelite midwives that they must suffocate male children as soon as they emerged from the womb, before they could ever draw breath. Thus they would never have been alive and it would not be murder. The idea was that the Egyptian people would be satisfied if they could foresee the eradication of the Israelites as a people, for within a generation the Israelites would be a nation of women, forced to turn to the Egyptians for their husbands, and within two generations Israel would cease to exist. And yet it would have been achieved without battles or bloodshed—and without public disorder.

In vain did Hatshepsut counsel with her father that to give in to the mob would weaken the crown still further. The people are not fools, she said. They'll know that you are obeying them, not ruling them.

But Jannes and Jambres were men, were priests, and Jannes had been Tuthmose's dear friend in their youth. The foolish law was announced.

Hatshepsut almost laughed aloud when Puah and Shiphrah, the leading midwives among the Israelites, were hauled into court to explain why Israelite boy children continued to be born despite the law.

"Israelite women give birth so quickly," Puah explained. "By the time we get to their houses, the babies are already breathing and they have been given names. We can't very well suffocate them *then!*"

What did Father and Jannes think, that the Israelites were so stupid they would willingly cooperate in their own eradication?

Still Father wouldn't heed Hatshepsut's advice. Instead he
followed Jannes's advice and passed a new law, that newborn
Israelite boychildren would be given to the river. Let the mobs
watch and tell the temple guards of the birth of an Israelite
baby; if the child was given to the river, it would still not be
murder but rather an act of piety. Everyone would be content,
and the Israelite threat would be eliminated in a generation.

Hatshepsut wept then, pleading with her father—in private, of course—to rescind the order. "No one is deceived!"
she cried. "Mobs have committed murder in your kingdom,
and your answer has been to commit their murders for them!
What kind of king are you! Egypt is ashamed!"

She thought her father would kill her in his rage when she
said these things. For days he did not speak to her. And now
he had sent for her—had sent Jannes to fetch her. She was
sick at heart. Would she be disowned? Set aside and banned
from the palace? Oh, please don't do it, Father! I am your last
true friend. Send me away and you are left alone with only
Mutnefert!

But she would not beg or plead with him. For the sake of
his own kingdom she would beg, but not for the sake of her
place within it.

It was a bad sign that he waited for her in open court, with
many priests and officers as witnesses. She approached him,
knelt before him, waited for her doom to be pronounced. He
told her to stand.

"For the last time my daughter stands before me," he said.

The last time. She could not stop the tears that leapt to her
eyes.

"Follow me," he said to her.

He led the way into the private room where he dressed for
ceremonies and met less formally with aides. He closed the

door. Then, to her surprise, he began to weep; he threw his arms around her and clung to her. "Oh, Hatshepsut, I have been a fool, and you were the wise one."

This was not at all how she thought the scene would go. "Father," she said, "you are never a fool."

"I have been manipulated. Jannes plots with Mutnefert — I learned of it only today. He tells me to send you away. To raise Mutnefert to the status of my wife, to make her runty little loin-goiter into my heir. Tuthmose the Second! And yet I fear that this insult is also the truth: That I have been as weak in my own way as Mutnefert's spawn would be in his. What am I now? A killer of babies, a monster, all because Mutnefert has control of . . . everything!"

"She controls nothing," said Hatshepsut.

"What do I know except what my officers tell me? Now I learn that they tell me only what *she* wants me to know. What power do I have except the obedience of my officers? Yet I discover that they are more loyal to her than to me."

"Father, think. Jannes is your friend. Isn't it just as possible that he, too, has been fooled? That his advice was wrong but sincere?"

Tuthmose heard this in silence. Because the idea comforted him? Or because he hated hearing from her, once again, that he was wrong?

"What are you planning now?" asked Hatshepsut. "Why is this the last time I will ever stand before you? How will expelling me help you with —"

"Expelling you?" Tuthmose laughed. "Don't be absurd. You were always the best of my children. Your beauty makes all men in awe of you, yes, but I know that you have always had the keenest mind in the palace. How many times have you contradicted my advisers! And yet never once have they been right, and you wrong! I have spent these last days thinking over and over again, if only Hatshepsut were my son! And then it finally dawned on me. I'm a god, aren't I? And can't a god change a girl into a boy? We Pharaohs wear these artificial beards—what's to stop me from putting such a beard on you? If I declare you to be my son, who will dare to contradict me?"

The audacity of it, the impossibility of it, left Hatshepsut speechless. And yet she also knew that it was a brilliant stroke. Mutnefert had left her alive all these years because it wasn't worth killing a girl—and because she clearly intended Tuthmose to give Hatshepsut to Mutnefert's miserable calf as his wife. But now the girl would become, not her daughter-in-law, but her Pharaoh and god. And, when Tuthmose died, her husband! The prospect of Mutnefert's reaction was so delicious that Hatshepsut laughed aloud.

"You laugh—for joy?" asked Father. "Let it be for joy, because you see the wisdom of this plan, you see that Amon has placed this idea in my head."

"Father, how can it work? Who would follow me? While you live, yes, but after you die, who would obey me?"

"You underestimate the power of the name of Pharaoh."

"You underestimate the power of resentment. You would merely create a thousand new allies for Mutnefert."

"You're smarter than she is," said Father.

"But not more ruthless," said Hatshepsut.

"Not?" he asked. "I think you are as ruthless as my father. I think you would survive, you would overmaster her, you would rule."

"Or Egypt would collapse in anarchy, in civil war as captains and aristocrats rose up in revolt against a woman Pharaoh. Do you really want me to die, torn apart by a mob or tortured by the priests for the blasphemy of wearing the beard and the crown?"

"You haven't had time to think about it," said Father. "Go, think, consider. Down to the river and while you're gone I will pray to the gods to show you that this idea is truly of divine origin. You are Pharaoh's daughter when you go to the river, but when you come back, you must be Pharaoh's son!"

"I will think and I will also pray," said Hatshepsut. "But Father, I hope the gods will show us both a better road through this swamp of treachery and decay."

With that she kissed him and embraced him and then left through the other door. She gathered her womenservants and went down the steps to the river. Let the water of the Nile wash away her confusion. She was being offered the crown of Egypt, not through her influence on a brother-husband, but in her own right, under her own name. She was also, in all likelihood, being offered a terrible death—unless she was strong and clever enough to make it work. She would have to kill so many rebels that the river would run with blood. O gods, she cried, caring not which god heard her, for any that might answer her would be her true god forever. O gods, open the door to life and close the door of death!

✳

Jochabed smeared the inside of the basket with pitch, thick and hot and gloppy; she made sure there was no break in it, no place where water could get through and drown the child. Then she covered the pitch with a blanket so it wouldn't get on the baby. She was still tamping it down when Amram came home. He brought a half-dozen elders with him. Jochabed glanced up for only a moment, but she saw at once that one—and only one—of the men was beardless and wore a hood over his hair.

"Greetings, Puah," said Jochabed. "I hope no one thought that disguise fooled anyone."

"No one took note of us," said Puah, pulling off the hood.

Amram spoke calmly. "We have nothing to fear. I hear the voice of the Lord in my heart, telling me that this boychild will do mighty works in the name of God."

"I believe you, husband," said Jochabed. "And this basket is what the Lord will use to save the baby."

Another pain swept over her. They were coming every few minutes now; she knew that she should already be squatting over the birthing straw.

"What is this basket?" asked Amram.

Miriam answered, because Jochabed could not speak. "Mother smeared it with pitch. It will float."

"Go," Jochabed said, wincing. "Miriam, go now. Down by the river. Hide in the reeds there, so no one knows you're waiting."

"What is this insane plan you've come up with?" demanded Amram.

"This insane plan was given to me by God," said Jochabed. "The command of Pharaoh is to give newborn Israelite boys to the Nile. Well, that's what we'll do — ourselves! In a basket that will float!"

"The Nile flows to the sea!" cried Amram. "Is that where our baby should go?"

"What have you done to provide for him!" demanded Jochabed. "You say that God has made you promises — but what have you done to keep them?"

"God does not need the help of man!"

"Whether he needs it or not, he's obviously not going to get it," said Jochabed sharply.

One of the old men piped up. "Is this how your wife talks to you, Amram?"

"Only when she's giving birth," Amram replied. "Women can't be blamed for how they talk then."

"My son is not going to be handed over to the Egyptians," said Jochabed. Already another pain was beginning. Had the pain before even ended?

"Come," said Puah. "You have no time for this."

Jochabed shook off the midwife's arm. "It was the midwives who saved our babies a month ago! And I'm the one today who'll save this son of ours."

"Careful how you take credit to yourself!" cried Amram.

"I take nothing for myself." Jochabed was stung by his accusation. She had only said "I'm the one" because Amram had been talking as if she were nothing. God does not need the help of man! Women can't be blamed for how they talk during childbirth! And yet that was no excuse for her trying to make *him* feel like nothing in return. Still, he should remember what was at stake here. She was a woman, yes, but in this case she was *not* just some bystander to serve the food and leave the room while the men conversed. "I'm giving my baby to the Lord," she said softly.

And he understood, because he was the kind of man who listens even through his anger. "If the baby lives," he said, "it is because the Lord has chosen to let him live. What do we care who hears the word of the Lord?"

"I believe the Lord has chosen to let him live by being floated on the Nile in this basket," said Jochabed. "And Miriam will follow along in the reeds, keeping out of sight, to watch where the basket fetches up."

"What's to stop the Egyptian mob from rushing out and filling the basket with stones?" demanded another old man.

"Why not go out and suggest it to them?" said Jochabed snidely. "As long as you're thinking up clever ways to kill Israelite babies."

The old man recoiled as if slapped. "A man could bleed to death from this woman's words!"

"Go, Miriam!" demanded Jochabed.

Amram's hand shot out and caught the girl by her shoulder. Miriam looked up into his face. "Don't you want the baby to live, Papa?" she asked.

Amram hesitated only a moment longer. "Who am I to stand in the way of the Lord?" he said.

Miriam was out the door in a moment. Little Aaron immediately began to cry. Amram picked him up and held him; the boy fell still as he began to tangle his fingers in his father's beard.

Now, at last, Jochabed let Puah draw her away into the back room of the house. She could feel the baby pushing down between her legs even before she got into place. "He's already here," she said.

"I'm not surprised," said Puah caustically. "Keep talking that way to your husband, and this will be your last baby."

"The mother of this baby needs no others," said Jochabed. And then marveled at the words God had put into her mouth.

❊

Miriam didn't like the river. Other children played there all the time, of course, no matter how the adults forbade it. And she knew that as long as you stayed close to the village and watched all the time, the crocodiles didn't pose much danger. They only got hungry now and then, and they preferred the much larger, less troublesome prey they could get when the flocks and herds came down to the river to drink. It was the river itself that Miriam didn't like, the way it moved invisibly among the reeds, tugging at her dress, first this way, then that, trying to pull her out, pull her down, drag her away. She didn't like the way the bottom disappeared sometimes, though the reeds were all the same level at the top. The river was pure treachery, so smooth on top, the water so cool on a hot day, and yet there was death in it, murder in its heart. Like the Egyptians. Such a darling child, they would say, and pat her head. And Miriam would answer in her heart: You made my father a slave. You want us all dead. You are the river, you and all of Egypt. You are the river and as long as we stay beside you we are in danger of drowning.

She said this once to her mother, but somehow the words of her mouth were never as sharp as the words of her heart. Or perhaps it was simply that Mother refused to understand her, or could not believe that Miriam, as young as she was, could see such dark truth. So Mother patted her head and said, "Don't fret about what you can't change," though Miriam had not been fretting and didn't expect to change anything. Didn't Mother understand? The Israelite people had to leave this land. The famine in Canaan was over. It had been over for generations. Miriam had listened to all the stories her father told, the tales of Joseph and Jacob, the promises made to Abraham and Isaac. She knew the truth: The Israelites had stayed in Egypt out of greed, because Joseph's accomplishments had lifted them to a lofty place. For generations they had played at magistrate and overlord, and they disdained the simple life of their ancestors. Father had said as much, hadn't he? And yet somehow he had never reached the obvious conclusion: That Egypt was not the land of Israel's inheritance. All these terrible things that were happening to Israel, they were God's way of waking up his people and telling them they must go home! If the Egyptians had not revolted, driven out the

Pharaohs who knew Joseph, made slaves of the Israelites, and now started killing their children, would Israel ever have longed to leave?

I am only a child and I see this, thought Miriam. Why can't the adults see it, too?

But they didn't, or didn't speak about it in front of her, anyway. And when Miriam let them see how she hated the river, they all assumed she was afraid of crocodiles and teased her about it, when the truth was that it was Egypt she hated. Egypt that had made Israel forget God.

Well, I remember God, I remember the land of our inheritance, I have learned the lessons God is trying to teach us, and I will teach them to Aaron—and to the new baby, too, if I have a chance. I will tell all my friends to hate Egypt, I will tell them to long for the land of our inheritance in Canaan.

In the meantime, though, she waded out among the reeds. Up to her ankles, the water still warm here in the shallows. Up to her knees, with the mud sucking at her feet, trying to lock her in place. Up to her hips, as fish and eels slithered among the reeds and brushed against her. Up to her waist, and now the currents began to reach for her, pull her this way and that, and all she had to hold onto was a handful of reeds. Here she waited, turning slowly in the water, watching for Mother to come with the basket, watching for crocodiles to come up behind her unaware. Watching the birds that came out of the sky, landed on the water, stood on tall legs, dipped sharply to catch fish and eels, rocked their heads back to swallow the wriggling captive, then took off again, flying home to their nest. We should have come to Egypt like a waterbird, to stand in the water, eat, and go away full, instead of letting the river have us.

There was a tumult from the village. As anyone could have

predicted, the Egyptian villagers were shouting, "To the river! To the river!" And there in the midst of them were Mother and Father. Mother could scarcely walk from the pain of child-bearing, yet she held the basket in her own hands. "I give the baby to the river myself!" she cried.

Some of the Egyptians shouted No, No!—not out of mercy, but because they wanted to drown the child with their own hands. But Father spoke now, his voice booming out over the water. "The law from Pharaoh is that Israelite boychildren must be given to the Nile. We obey Pharaoh! But if any one of you lays a hand on this basket, *you* are trying to take what belongs to the river, and the law will have *you* then!"

"It's a trick!" shouted someone. But no one else took up the cry. Father and Mother waded out a little way; Mother set the basket on the water. Father pushed it, farther, farther, until it was beyond the reeds, out into the slow but inexorable cur-rent. The afternoon sun beat down on the basket. It rocked from the movement of the baby inside, but only for a moment. The Egyptians shouted in anger, knowing that somehow they were being cheated. But Miriam cared nothing for them. She kept her eyes on the basket. It was moving slowly, but she could only move slowly herself. She pulled herself along among the reeds.

On the shore, the Egyptian mob walked along parallel to the ark. Miriam stayed low, so they wouldn't see her and sus-pect a trick—for of course they would assume that Miriam was there to bring the ark back to shore. The mob grew smaller and smaller as people lost interest and returned, grumbling, to their homes. But still a handful, a few, and then a pair of hate-driven Egyptians walked on, watching, watch-ing. What kind of people are you, Miriam wanted to scream at them, to seek to kill babies because you hate the parents? But she said nothing. She had more important work to do than screaming at Egyptians.

The bottom disappeared from under her feet; she held to the reeds, floating, and even though her head went under the water twice she struggled through to where the bottom was there under her feet again. On and on, following the ark among the bulrushes. It drew even with her, passed her, went on ahead of her. O Lord, whispered Miriam in her heart, if I'm to do anything for this baby, let it happen soon, because I'm getting very cold, and the ark is farther ahead of me, and soon I'll lose sight of it, and it'll be night, and I'm moving too quickly to watch for crocodiles, and I'll die here in the river. Not that it matters in thy great universe of creation whether one little girl lives or dies, but if you let me live I promise you I'll do all in my power to bring your people home to the land thou gavest them. I also promise not to pinch Aaron and make him cry when I'm angry at Mother. That's mean of me and I'll never do it again so if thou wert thinking of punishing me for it by having a crocodile catch me and pinch me to death between its great jaws here in the water, please don't.

❊

Hatshepsut walked down the stairs toward the water. Her maidservants fluttered around her like moths, each with some task of great importance, such as draping Hatshepsut's gown properly on the stairs, or arranging a stray wisp of her hair. Annoyances, really, but she couldn't tell them off for doing their work too well, could she? If they took pride in it, then one must endure the annoyance of work too thoroughly done.

She held up a foot; at once her sandal was drawn off and carried away. The other foot; and she was ready for the water. O gods, she prayed again. O gods, show me the way to preserve my father's kingdom and keep it out of the hands of evil.

Was it the cry of some waterbird that caused her to look up? She did not know what she was looking for, only that she looked, and saw, out on the water, something bobbing along, like a tiny boat, with a flash of red cloth catching the evening sun. Was this something the gods were showing her? She had to know.

She turned to the nearest of her servants. "Tawaret," she said, "do you see what's out there on the water? There, near the bulrushes."

Tawaret looked but saw nothing. "Forgive me for being stupid."

"You simply haven't seen it, that's all," said Hatshepsut. "Go fetch it."

The girl looked horrified. "Out in the water? So far?"

"It's only there, by the edge of the bulrushes."

"But the water is deep there and I can't swim."

Hatshepsut was annoyed. "Don't you know that the river will bear you up, when you go on my errand? Remember who I am, girl."

Thus encouraged, Tawaret splashed her way down the steps into deeper and deeper water. But when it was up to her waist, it got no deeper. "Oh!" cried Tawaret. "There's a smooth road under the water!"

Hatshepsut couldn't remember how far out the huge paving stones had been laid. She did know they were at a downward slope, so that no matter how high or low the water was, a boat could be drawn up to the steps. So the girl was not likely to fall off and drown. That would indeed be an annoyance if she did—Tawaret had a gentle touch with a comb, even when Hatshepsut's hair was most tangled.

The girl went toward the floating thing, as the river carried the floating thing to her. "It's a basket!" cried Tawaret.

"Bring it here!"

Tawaret drew it along behind her as she came closer and closer. A basket, yes. But there was something in it, something moving. A baby. A squalling baby. And the blanket that lined the basket was of Israelite weave.

At once it became clear to Hatshepsut what the gods were saying to her. She had asked for the river to show her what to do; instead, the river had boldly taken action and given her precisely what she most needed. Father's plan was good, but it did not begin to do what the river had set in motion.

"Look what the river has brought me!" Hatshepsut cried. "A son!"

*Moses*. The word rang out over the water.

"In fact that is his name," Hatshepsut said. "My father is Tuthmose, which means the son of Thoth. But this child is *my* son. I lift him up out of the water and place him in the royal lineage of Pharaoh!" The baby wriggled in her arms; it was all she could do not to drop it. She had never held a baby before. She had no idea they were so awkward and uncooperative.

The women listened, awestruck and—the smarter ones at least—aghast. "O Lady Hatshepsut," the oldest one finally said, "can't you see that this baby is an Israelite?"

"Of course!" cried Hatshepsut. "On this day you can see the law of Pharaoh is fulfilled! No more will Israelite boys be cast into the river, for the gods have chosen the best of them and brought him here to me!" There, thought Hatshepsut. I've ended that bloody blot on my father's record.

"But he's hungry," said Tawaret. "That's why he's crying so loudly."

"He's crying loudly because it is so painful to be born, and this is the moment of his birth," said Hatshepsut coldly. "He was born when I drew him out of the Nile the way a mother draws her baby out of the waters of her own body."

No one dared mention to her that women generally *pushed* their babies out. Hatshepsut knew, of course, how it was really done. But she was the one composing this song to be sung through the ages. She would decide how it went.

The oldest servant insisted on substance as well as style, however. "No matter why the baby cries now, neither you nor any of us has milk to give it, and I doubt it has the teeth for bread."

"Then we'll find a nurse," said Hatshepsut.

At that moment, a voice cried out from the bulrushes—the voice of a child. "O great lady!" cried the child. "I know a woman who would be the perfect nurse for the baby!"

Everyone turned to look at the reeds where the voice was coming from. A wet and shivering girl in peasant garb emerged and slowly made her way through the water toward the stone steps. "Look what else the river has produced for us," said the old servant.

"Quiet," said Hatshepsut. "This woman you know—could she begin service immediately as the baby's nurse?"

"Oh, yes," said the girl.

"Then bring her to me—not by the river, by the road." She turned to Tawaret. "You go with her, and take soldiers, so no one will dare to interfere with your errand. Tell no one where you are going—let this girl run ahead and lead you."

"Yes, Lady Hatshepsut," said Tawaret. "But the girl is wet—may we dry her first?"

"No!" cried the girl. "I mean, thank you, it's very kind of you, but the wind will dry me off as I run, and Mother—the woman I know—the nurse—she wouldn't want any delay."

"Then go," said Hatshepsut.

The Israelite girl took Tawaret's hand, and together they walked up the stairs to the palace. Hatshepsut handed the baby to the old servant.

"What do you want to bet that the nurse she's fetching just happened to give birth to a boy today?" said the old servant.

"If the gods have arranged things so kindly, so be it, and we are grateful," said Hatshepsut. "But if anyone ever says that I am not the true mother of this child, which was given to me by the river, that will be the *last* thing they ever say. You might mention this to anyone you know who might be disposed to idle gossip."

Abashed, the old servant fell silent and carried the baby up the stairs.

"Don't drop him," said Hatshepsut. "He'll be Pharaoh someday, so it would be just as well if we didn't break open his head on the first day of his life."

❊

Jochabed sat in the midst of the women, refusing to grieve. "My son is not dead," she said. "I have not lost him—God has him." But the other women chided her. "You should keen for him, silly woman. It's unnatural to be so calm."

And in the front room, surrounded by elders, Amram bore their criticism calmly. "The people are furious that you tricked them," said one. "You shamed yourself by letting your wife rule you in this," said another. "You're guilty of the baby's murder now, since you put him on the water yourselves," said a third. To all of them, Amram said nothing; and when he did speak, it was not to them, but to God. "O Great Lord of Israel, God of Abraham, Isaac, and Jacob, O Lord who preserved Joseph and raised him out of the pit and out of prison, from the hands of his brothers, from the hands of a lying woman, and from the hands of the executioners of Pharaoh, O Lord be with my son!"

This is what they were doing when the noise began in the village, first among the Egyptians, then in the streets of the Israelite quarter.

The elders leapt to their feet. "The mob is coming to kill us all! Quick, hide!"

The women clutched at Jochabed. "Oh, see what God will do now, to make you grieve!"

All were at the door in a moment. And instead of a mob, they saw a procession of Egyptian soldiers, with a finely dressed woman at their head. Behind them, Egyptian peasants came like an invading army. It took a moment to realize that running before this troop was a small Israelite girl.

"Miriam!" cried Jochabed. "Miriam, what happened!"

"Mother!" shouted Miriam. In moments she fell into her mother's arms, trembling with cold, stammering with excitement. "Mother, a great lady lifted him up out of the water and named him Moses!"

"Named him?" asked Jochabed. "Then she will save him alive?"

By now the fine lady had arrived.

"Is this the one?" asked Jochabed.

"Oh, no," said Miriam. "This is the one who got all wet bringing the basket to shore."

The fine lady spoke. "Woman, the house of Pharaoh has need of a wet-nurse. This girl says that your breasts have milk and yet you have no child to suckle. Is this true?"

Oh, yes, it was true.

"Then come with me."

"It's a trick," murmured one of the elders. "You can't trust an Egyptian," whispered another. "They'll never let your wife come back," said an old woman to Amram.

"I am this woman's husband," said Amram. "I wish you would tell me, great lady, what child it is that she would suckle. Is it yours?"

The lady laughed. "I am no great lady. I am only a slave, as you are. It is my mistress who gave birth to a child today. The river brought the baby to her, the way a rush of water brings other women's babies."

"And who is your mistress?" asked Amram.

"Who else can send soldiers for a wet-nurse?" asked the slave-lady. "Who else can bring her into Pharaoh's house? I serve Hatshepsut, the daughter of Pharaoh. The baby is her son. She calls him Moses. Someday he will be Pharaoh."

The crowd fell silent at the astonishing news.

"I will go with you," said Jochabed. "I will be proud to give milk to the son of Pharaoh's daughter." She embraced Amram, then walked stiffly toward the soldiers.

"What's wrong with you?" asked the slave-lady.

"Forgive me," said Jochabed. "It happens that I gave birth to a child today."

"But you said you had no one to suckle."

"He was given to the river, and the river carried him where it wished."

"How kind the gods are!" cried the slave-lady. "Can we be less kind ourselves? Soldiers, carry this woman gently to the palace. Let her feet not touch the ground from here to there." And though she was a slave, they obeyed her, because of the authority of her mistress.

Miriam watched as they carried her mother away. Aaron began to cry. "Don't worry," Miriam said to him. "She'll come home every day, or take you with her. Nothing bad will happen to you, because your little brother will be Pharaoh one day."

Thus she was the first to put into words what no Israelite had dared to hope. But now that it was said, Amram could say it too, and loudly. "It will be better than the days of Joseph!" he said. "For Joseph was only next to Pharaoh. Moses will *be* Pharaoh! This is why God brought us to Egypt! Because this kingdom will be ours! For one of the sons of Israel is now adopted into Pharaoh's house!"

But Miriam understood that Father was making a mistake, though she said nothing to him about it. It was Aaron who would grow up hearing the truth from her. "Canaan is the land of our inheritance, not Egypt," she said. "Your brother was lifted up by God, but not to be Pharaoh. Israel does not belong in Egypt. Israel belongs to another land." God had made promises to Abraham, Isaac, and Jacob. He would not break them now.

✼

The ceremony was not long; it did not have to be. It was enough to have Mutnefert watching from the edge of the room as Tuthmose brought his daughter Hatshepsut beside him, and beside her an Israelite nurse held Hatshepsut's newborn son in her arms. Word had already spread about Hatshepsut's bold move, and already Mutnefert's allies were plotting how to persuade Tuthmose to nullify this mad action. Give the throne to an Israelite? Unthinkable.

They had no idea what this ceremony was really for. So they remained stunned and silent as Tuthmose began the marriage of his daughter, Hatshepsut, to himself. "She is my wife now," he said, "and I adopt her child as my own. In fact, I am already father of this child, for it was I, Pharaoh, god of Egypt, who caused this baby to be placed on the Nile, and I, Pharaoh, god of Egypt, who caused my daughter-wife to recognize the child as my gift to her, as all sons are gifts of the husband to the wife, and of the wife to the husband."

Thus all the maneuvering based on Hatshepsut's lack of a husband were swept away. Pharaoh himself claimed fatherhood and took Hatshepsut into his protection as his wife. And, as his wife, she and all her offspring permanently outranked Mutnefert and her precious pathetic son.

But even this was not enough for Tuthmose. For now he took a ceremonial false beard from his steward and placed it on Hatshepsut's chin. "I also declare my daughter to be my son! Hatshepsut is a woman when she is my wife and mother of the baby Moses. But she is a man when she appears in this court and rules Egypt as Pharaoh." With that he took the double crown of Egypt from his own head and placed it on hers. "See this miracle that I, Pharaoh, god of Egypt, have performed for you today! I have made a man out of a woman! A son out of a daughter! And I have made her Pharaoh on the same day that I also made her my wife. Let anyone who speaks against this miracle be blotted out, him and all his children! Egypt, behold your Pharaoh!"

Whereupon Hatshepsut reached out and took the baby from Jochabed's arms. "Egypt, behold the son of Pharaoh!"

The court bowed down, every one of them, even Mutnefert; and Hatshepsut saw with pleasure that the old snake was smiling, pretending to be joyful. She had made her decision—she would do nothing openly against Hatshepsut now.

But she would plot, Hatshepsut knew it. Yet Mutnefert would never dream of the final move in Hatshepsut's game. For when her father died and Mutnefert began to plot again — for there was no chance that she would not—Hatshepsut would simply marry Mutnefert's miserable boy (pretentiously named Tuthmose after his father, though he resembled him in nothing but looks). She would make him co-Pharaoh—Tuthmose II—but the name was all he would get, for she would force him to adopt Moses as his heir and then lock him away in hedonistic confinement with a well-stocked household of concubines, trotting him out for ceremonies but otherwise cutting him and his mother away from all real power. Thus the integrity of Pharaoh's house would be preserved, but Mutnefert would never again have power in the kingdom.

And word had reached the palace that already the loyalty of the Israelites had been cemented. Instead of being on the verge of revolt, this skilled and educated people would be her loyal allies. It would be years before they noticed that despite the fact that Moses was an Israelite, and heir to the throne, *they* were still slaves. And even then, they would be patient in bondage, believing that someday Moses would be Pharaoh and once again prefer them above the people of Egypt.

It was Hatshepsut's job to make sure he grew up knowing how to govern—including the skill of playing one group off against another. Moses would know that the Israelites were no more his people than the Egyptians were. Pharaoh is a god, not one of the people at all; the people are his to command, and never to command him. That's the wisdom her son would grow to understand. And if he did not understand it, then he did not deserve to rule.

Hatshepsut *did* understand, and *did* deserve to rule. And if it took being turned into a man by her father, well, so be it. Her own miracle would be to turn this Israelite baby into a god. What miracles would the baby perform, when he became a man? The gods would have to show him when he came into his power. Hatshepsut could not keep any promises beyond her own lifetime, and so she would make none.

❋

After all the pain, after all the dread, after all the rage that had torn at her heart, it came to this: jostling along in a sedan chair, up the broad stairs into the royal residence, to find herself installed on cushions, where they brought her baby to her, washed and wrapped in linen, hungry for her, as she was hungry for him. As she unwrapped him and held his naked body to her breast, feeling his warmth against her, the milk flowing out of her, their hearts beating, his fast, hers slow, she kept thinking, over and over, He lives, he lives.

O God, she prayed, thou hast heard the words of thy daughter Jochabed. Thou hast seen the child that was in my womb and thou hadst mercy on him. I will bless thy name all the days of my life. My voice will be heard in all Israel, declaring that the love of God is not gone from his people. For the child of my body has been chosen, the babe at my breast has been named, and the Lord watches over him.

Sated for the moment, the baby dozed. His lips came away from her nipple, the whitish fluid still clinging to his lips. "Don't sleep yet, you lazy boy," she whispered. "You have to drink from both or mama will be uncomfortable."

Then she realized what she had said. *Mama.* She could not let him call her *mama.* Another woman would hear that name from his lips, when he first learned to talk.

For a moment it stabbed at her, a pang of regret that could so easily become resentment, anger, jealousy.

No! Though she made no sound, she shouted it in her heart. I will not be angry. I will not be ungrateful to the Lord. I asked for the life of my child, and it was given. In his mercy, God has even let me be the one whose breast he will suckle from. I will be grateful every day of my life. I will hold no anger in my heart. O Lord, help me keep all darkness from my child's life. Never let him learn of it from me.

The baby woke again, his brief nap over. She brought him to her other breast and he attached himself to it, greedy with the innocent need of infancy. What man are you, hidden in this tiny body? What have we made here, God and Amram and I? What is the path of your life? Whatever it is, God has chosen it. Walk boldly on it, my little son, when you let go of my hand and take your own steps into the world, walk boldly, for God will never let go of your hand, he will hold it always, if you only trust him.

That is what I will teach you, if I can. That is the knowledge that will flow into you with my milk. In the darkest hour, in the night of fear, the hand of God is there for you, his path is open before you, life or death, whatever gift he gives to you, step out with courage, hold to him with faith, for he will lead you to joy, and no one else knows the way.

To joy he will lead you, like my joy in this hour. Of all women, who is more blessed than Jochabed?

# B e t r a y a l s

The girl was brought to Moses in his tent overlooking the river.

"Caught her skulking," said the captain of the night's guard. "But she kept saying she had a message for the tall Egyptian in the great chariot and we figured that was you. We've made sure she doesn't have a weapon or poison on her."

Moses looked at the girl. Dressed too finely to be a common slave, but then one couldn't tell much from the clothing of the Ethiopians. They didn't dress like civilized Egyptians; they wore furs of exotic animals instead of simple linen, and bedecked themselves with gold as if they had never heard of modesty or restraint. So, what was this girl? No doubt she was angry now, if she hadn't been before, because the soldiers were unlikely to have been gentle when they searched her. The tall Egyptian in the great chariot, she called him, and not by his name. Had she been watching from the walls of Saba? Did the Ethiopians let women stand in such exposed places, when a great army was besieging them?

"What sort of message . . . do you have for me?" asked Moses.

"Are you the one?" she asked. Her Egyptian was accented but correct.

Exasperated, Moses wanted to tell the captain to take her away and include her among the captives being shipped downriver as slaves. But he paused, to keep himself from stammering. And when he had composed himself, he found he did not want her sent away. "What kind of messenger are you . . . if you don't know . . . whom the message is for?"

"My mistress doesn't know your name and didn't dare to ask. She has seen you from the city walls. She thought you might be Moses, the one they call the Monster, but to her you seemed to be no monster so she thought perhaps you were another man."

"I'm whatever man I am," said Moses. "Who is your mistress? What is her message?"

"I can speak only when we're alone."

Moses looked at the captain. "Maybe she means to . . . strangle me as soon as we're alone."

"What do you want us to do with your body when she kills you, sir?" said the captain.

"Give me back to the . . . river, which they say is my true . . . father anyway." Moses was quite aware that "they" also said many other things far less kind about his parentage. But he was not too proud to joke about the rumors with the men he might have to ask to die for him tomorrow.

"Call for help if you find she's too much for you," said the captain. He left, and Moses was alone with the girl.

At once the girl approached him and tried to put her arms around him. Moses caught her by the wrists and held her away from him. "What are you doing?" he asked.

"My mistress told me to embrace you to show what she will offer you herself if you will only be her husband."

Husband? What kind of woman sees an invading enemy outside the walls of a besieged city and sends a servant to offer him marriage? "If your mistress thinks I will lift the . . . siege in exchange for a wife —"

"She knows that you could have any woman in Egypt. If you are indeed Moses, she knows that you will be Pharaoh someday. So she must come with a dowry to give you."

"What sort of dowry?"

"Ethiopia."

"I already have Ethiopia," said Moses.

"You do not have Saba," said the servant girl. "And you will never get it."

She might well be right. The city was mostly surrounded by water, and the high walls gave bowmen plenty of time to slaughter any invader before they could get close enough to storm the walls—as if that would do any good. As for sapping, there was no way to dig through solid stone and loose sand; the stone would take too long to dig through, and even if they did, the sand would flow in and fill any tunnel they made. They could besiege the city until it ran out of food, of course, but it was just as possible that Moses' army would begin to starve first, since the land had been stripped clean by the Ethiopian army before they shut themselves up in the city.

"I will have . . . Saba whenever I want it," said Moses.

"So you simply enjoy camping outside the city, marching around and shooting arrows?" retorted the girl.

"Were you told to be . . . sarcastic with me?" asked Moses. "Or is that your own . . . flourish?"

"Do you not know who my mistress is?" asked the servant girl.

Until she asked the question, Moses had not known; but the imperious nature of the question told him the answer. "Tharbis," he said. The daughter of the king of Ethiopia.

"So you see she is herself a great dowry, for she can change war to peace just by marrying you."

"But we didn't come here . . . searching for peace," said

Moses. "We came here to . . . punish Ethiopia for raids deep into Egypt, as far down the Nile as . . . Memphis. Such audacity can't be . . . tolerated."

"We are punished now," said the girl.

"But as long as I've come this far, why not . . . conquer Ethiopia and . . . make it part of Egypt?"

The girl laughed in his face. "You have despoiled the river lands," she said. "But you have not even *seen* the heartland of Ethiopia. The high mountains, the precious hidden valleys. To conquer that land would take a thousand armies the size of this one, and as soon as you left one valley to attack the next, the one behind would rise up against you. It took a thousand years for my mistress's ancestors to conquer the land, and even now there is constant war, quelling one revolt after another. My father led one such revolt. My mistress's father pierced his belly and drew out his—"

Moses waved her to silence. He had seen the handiwork of the Ethiopian torturers. Fools—they merely guaranteed that his soldiers would not dare to desert him.

What mattered was that the girl was right. Ethiopia could be defeated and plundered, but it could not be conquered and held—not quickly enough, anyway, for Hatshepsut's position back in Egypt was always so precarious that Moses dared not be away with the army for long. Ethiopia could absorb many a blow like the one that Moses had inflicted with this punitive invasion; but Egypt could not afford to strike like this again anytime soon.

"So her father offers . . . Tharbis to me as the . . . price of abandoning the siege."

"You misunderstand. The king knows nothing of my errand."

"Then she can't offer me Ethiopia or anything at all!"

"She can offer you secret passage through the wall into the city, and from there a clever man will know how to pierce the walls and let your army in."

"She betrays her own city?"

"She hears that Moses is a man of honor," said the girl. "Give your word that you will marry her, and she knows that you will not harm her father or her family."

It saddened Moses to hear the ruthlessness of her offer. The common people of the city would, of course, be plundered and pillaged and carried off as slaves. But if the royal house was safe, that could be endured. Such an idea would be unthinkable in the house of Pharaoh. The scepters of Egypt were the crook and the flail. The flail was for discipline, for yes, the people needed to know that disobedience brought punishment. But the crook was for love: Pharaoh only had the right to be Pharaoh because he loved and protected his people, standing between them and danger, not hiding behind them. If Hatshepsut had taught him anything, it was that. Indeed, he knew perfectly well that one of the reasons why he was adopted was because Pharaoh—both his father-grandfather Tuthmose I and his mother-father Hatshepsut—wanted to find a reason to stop the murder of Israelite babies. Even a slave nation like the Israelites were under the protective arm of the shepherd.

Marriage. Hatshepsut would be furious, of course, but she would soon see that he had no choice. To come home without conquering Saba would be a thin triumph at best, and some might take it as a defeat. But to come home with the plunder of Saba and with the king's daughter as his bride—that would be a great victory indeed, and Hatshepsut would be seen as a Pharaoh who could protect upper Egypt. Word of the victory would silence enemies at home and frighten enemies abroad.

On the other hand, Moses had nothing but loathing for one who would betray her own people. Oh, perhaps she thought of this as the least bloody way of settling the war. But the fact remained that her father's power would be broken — no doubt he would spend the next ten years putting down all the rebellions that would rise as soon as word spread throughout Ethiopia of his ignominious defeat at the hands of Moses the Egyptian.

Could she really have fallen in love with him? Was it on such a silly fulcrum as this that the lever of history rested? A woman on a city wall sees a tall warrior in a chariot and betrays her people out of love for him — only barbarians did things like that.

"I have a better idea," said Moses. "You are obviously much . . . cleverer than your mistress. I will take you as my . . . wife, and free you from . . . slavery as I do. *You* show me the . . . secret way into the city."

The girl recoiled from him in horror. "And betray the trust my mistress has placed in me?"

"So you're more loyal than she is."

The slave girl rolled her eyes in exasperation. "Am I a fool? Do you think I believe you would raise me up to be your *wife?* You would take me as a concubine, perhaps, but my life would be little different from what it is now, except that you'd be the man who took me whenever he wanted, instead of it being her father."

Moses said nothing. He was Hatshepsut's best pupil, and *she* had learned the art of politics from watching the murderous Mutnefert, who was now his nominal step-grandmother, since Hatshepsut had married her cowering son and made him co-Pharaoh under the name Tuthmose II. One did what one had to do for the good of the house of Pharaoh. And so the girl was right—he would never take her as a wife, because any children she had could not be permitted to be in the line of succession. Moses' own position in that line of authority was weak, since he was adopted, while if Hatshepsut had other sons they would be of Pharaonic blood twice over, through their mother and their father. He could not afford to take a slavegirl as his wife.

"Will you marry my mistress or not?" demanded the girl.

Moses laughed at her. "You speak as . . . boldly as if you had an army at your back."

"I have a city at my back," said the girl. "I have your own self-interest." She smiled. "And even though you haven't seen her, I can assure you that my mistress is young and beautiful and a prize for such a man as you."

"Such a man as me?"

"Why, you're the son of slaves," said the girl, "and she is the daughter of a king."

Moses felt the blood rise in his neck. The girl saw, too, that she had made a mistake.

"That's the story they tell of you, in Saba," she said. "I know nothing about—"

"I'm not going to . . . kill you or even strike you because of your ignorance," said Moses. "But I am the son of the . . . Pharaoh Tuthmose I and his daughter-wife Hatshepsut."

"So the tale of your parentage as an Israelite slave is—"

"That may have been the origin of my . . . body," said Moses, "but I was given to the River and the River gave me to the . . . daughter of Pharaoh to be her son."

She looked at him with amusement. "Ah. The gods strike again."

Moses didn't like her impious tone.

"Oh, are you serious?" she said. "All this business about

Pharaoh being a god? Tharbis's father is supposed to be a god, too, and look where it's got him."

"So . . . he's a weak god."

"He's a man who is very, very sorry he didn't prevent his rebellious greedy subjects from raiding Upper Egypt."

"And Pharaoh is a man?"

"From what I hear, Pharaoh is a woman."

"Changed by her father—"

"Yes, by her father, a god—but has she fathered any children lately? Besides you?"

"Do you talk to your . . . mistress like this?" asked Moses.

"Like what? With utter honesty? Yes."

"Impudently?"

"Honesty always sounds like impudence to the vain and stupid."

Moses felt his temper flare, but he would not shame himself by striking a servant or a captive. A man's dignity is never upheld by losing his self-control; Jochabed had taught him that, and he knew it was true.

"Tell your mistress that I will marry her within the hour of our . . . taking of Saba; that her . . . father will continue to reign in Ethiopia as long as he . . . kneels to me and gives homage to my father, Pharaoh; and that I insist that you be given your . . . freedom at the same moment Tharbis becomes my wife."

"Do you hate my honesty so much?"

"I don't want my new wife to have the . . . benefit of your advice, or soon she'll be ruling Egypt in place of . . . my father."

"Your mother."

"Hatshepsut."

The slave girl laughed.

"Do you have a name?" asked Moses.

"None that you need to know," she said. "Because right

now I belong to my mistress, and the moment you marry her, I'll be free. In neither case do you have the right to ask."

"You remind me of my sister Miriam. You are so . . . careless—you seem to be free already."

"If you had slapped me the first time you thought of it, you can be sure you would never have heard another honest word from me."

"There are countless women in Egypt that I have not . . . slapped, who nevertheless . . . flatter me shamelessly."

"But would they if you were not Pharaoh's son?"

"Is your . . . mistress as honest as you?"

"No," said the girl. "But be glad of that. You find me refreshing right now, but I can assure you that no man can bear to live with a woman who speaks nothing but the truth to him. My mistress has often told me that no man could endure me for more than an hour."

"I think you underestimate the ability of some men to . . . bear the truth."

"No, *you* underestimate the ability of some men to believe that when they are told what they want to hear, it must be true."

"Why did your mistress send you, if she . . . knew you would offend me?"

"Because she knew you would try to bribe me to betray her, and she trusted me to refuse. And because if you were the kind of man who could not bear to hear me speak plainly, then you were not the kind of man she wanted to marry."

"Did she really say that?" asked Moses.

"No," said the girl. "I said it, and she said, 'You know, you may be right.'"

"Tell me how we shall go about . . . stealing this city from under the . . . king's own nose."

✳

In the event, it was pitifully simple. Moses and a company of a dozen soldiers made their way across a ford and entered a postern gate, where Tharbis, who was in fact a rather dimwitted and homely girl, kissed Moses emphatically and continuously while his men went on to take control of the gate. Within a half hour the screams of the citizens became the impossible backdrop to their idyll, and Moses had to pry her away from him in order to get to the palace doors to keep his soldiers from breaking in and capturing the royal family. As it was, he presented himself to the king of Ethiopia as his son-in-law-to-be, and the poor man, recognizing defeat and betrayal when he saw them, sanctioned the marriage on the spot. By dawn, Moses was proud owner of a treacherous wife and a pillaged city. And, true to his word, the slave girl—whose name he never again asked—was set free and sent home with part of Moses' share of the spoils and fourteen sturdy manservants to protect her—and the wealth and high station that were now restored to her and her family.

Moses, for his part, headed home to Egypt, having accomplished all that Hatshepsut needed him to do. She had her victory in Ethiopia. It would affirm her rule in the eyes of the people, proving the favor of the gods.

As for Moses' new wife, if she ever bore a child it would be proof once again of her treachery, for Moses never wanted to see her again, now that she had given him Saba without the loss of a single soldier.

The only real drawback to the entire victory was that now Moses would have to face Aaron and Miriam and Jochabed, who despite all the official declarations still believed Moses to be, first, an Israelite, and, second, their brother and son. And the unbearable thing about it was, Moses knew that they were right, even though he hated knowing it. The son and brother of slaves—and not slaves like the remarkable Ethiopian girl he had just freed. They were born into slavery, part of a nation of slaves, and Moses was one of them, not truly an Egyptian no matter what he did. That was the burden he would carry all his life, and if he failed to succeed to the double crown of Pharaoh, it would be because of the taint of Israelite blood.

*

Hatshepsut slept alone. She always did—at least in the sense that no one shared her bed. The room, however, was well guarded. Four trusted women and six trusted guards; but none so trusted that they weren't carefully watched by the others. In a world that included Mutnefert, the murderous old hag, Hatshepsut would never be completely safe—even after marrying Mutnefert's miserable weasely son Tuthmose II.

It was all such a balancing act. But it was what she was born for, and Hatshepsut loved it. Particularly because her son Moses—*her* son, not Tuthmose's!—showed every sign of being a master of political maneuvering. If she could hold on long enough for him to cement his leadership of the military, and if he could manage some victories so that he would gain the support of the people and the soldiers alike, then she could be sure that the dynasty would be carried on.

Which is why she could hardly sleep these nights, these weeks since Moses took his army up the river to punish the Ethiopians for their raids against Upper Egypt. She had little fear that he would be killed, or even that he would be defeated. The greatest danger was that he would get caught in some miserable siege or, worse yet, in an expensive, humiliating campaign chasing Ethiopian bandits all over the hills and mountains of that strange and difficult country. He could not be allowed to look like a fool, and this war could not be allowed to drain the treasury and force an increase in taxes. And none of this was under Hatshepsut's control. She hated it when important things went on beyond her reach.

She was awake, then, brooding, when she heard the tumult of horses and the clatter of chariot wheels in the courtyard. Not enough for an invasion. A messenger, then? From Moses! Victory? Or . . . not defeat. Not harm to her boy.

She rose from her bed, and at once three of her ladies were up beside her, dressing her. The guards, of course, looked away from her as soon as she stirred. By the time the messenger came to her door, she was ready to receive him.

He was not a soldier from Moses' army. Instead the messenger was from the temple at Karnak.

"What does Jannes have to tell me that couldn't wait until morning?" asked Hatshepsut.

The temple guard bowed deeply. "O gracious Pharaoh, the bitter news I bring—"

"Tell me who! Tell me what!"

"The god Pharaoh Tuthmose II is dead."

"My husband?" She was stupefied. He was younger than she was, and despite his lazy and debauched ways, he was still in good health.

More to the point, his palace was upriver, and Karnak was downriver. Why was she hearing this news from Jannes's messenger? The answer was obvious as soon as she asked it.

"Which of my husband's concubines tried to get Jannes to proclaim her little runt as Pharaoh?"

"I believe it was the boy Tuthmose who was at the temple—"

"All his sons are named Tuthmose! Except the ones named Amose, of course. Which concubine!"

"Isis, O Pharaoh!"

"Wait in the courtyard. You will ride with me."

In half an hour she had five hundred soldiers. Perhaps she was overreacting, but since she hadn't seen this coming, she had no idea how much support Isis might already have arranged. Miserable scheming viper! All these years Hatshepsut had taken such precautions against Mutnefert, her mother-in-law, making sure there was no heir born of the marriage, guarding constantly against Mutnefert's inevitable attempts to assassinate Hatshepsut so her son could rule alone. But Hatshepsut had never thought to protect Tuthmose II. Why should she? He was the one person in the palace that Mutnefert would never dream of poisoning.

And now it turned out to be one of Tuthmose II's concubines who thought of killing her husband and trying to get a share of the crown for her son. Or . . . why just a share? There were plenty of people who would far prefer to see a real Egyptian as Pharaoh after Hatshepsut, rather than the adopted Israelite, Moses. And while Hatshepsut had kept her husband under her thumb, this boy whose mother was promoting him to be Tuthmose III, Hatshepsut knew nothing of him, or how domitable he might be.

Isis. Which one of the concubines was she? They were such a weak, stupid, mousy lot that Hatshepsut never bothered to keep track of them. What a careless mistake! Mutnefert's example should have been warning enough that concubines who knew something about poison could be deadly—and the more nondescript they were, the more dangerous they could be if some kind of feral intelligence hid under their oily hair.

It would be interesting to see why this woman thought she might have success at Karnak. She had brought her son there, presumably to have the priests anoint him. Unless she was very, very stupid, she would have had something prearranged. With whom? Until Hatshepsut knew, she would keep close to these five hundred armed men who answered only to her. Moses had trained with them and vouched for them all. They were hers . . . for now.

Nothing was hers if she wasn't careful. It could all slip away, if she wasn't careful. And Moses wasn't here. Wasn't here, when the crisis came!

Well, he was only a baby the last time I dealt with a crisis, and I did all right, she reminded herself.

It was nearly dawn when they reached Karnak. Her late husband's body lay on a bier out in the open, surrounded by temple guards. Hatshepsut immediately ordered the guards disarmed, and she replaced them with a contingent of her own soldiers. But she made sure to couch her orders in the most diplomatic terms possible: "You must be tired, guarding the body of my beloved husband so many hours! Lay down your arms, and let these fresh, well-rested soldiers take your place. Immediately."

Inside the temple, it took little searching to find those she was looking for. Jannes brought the woman Isis out himself, and the boy tagged along behind. Not a boy, really, not anymore. A young man, thin and wiry. Perhaps sixteen. A child. But old enough, Hatshepsut could see that clearly—old enough that men would follow him, if the right tale were told about him.

"The grieving concubine," Hatshepsut said dryly. "How pious of you, to bring his body here to Karnak, instead of to me, his widow."

Isis said nothing.

"Pharaoh," said Jannes, "I sent word to you the moment I understood the situation."

"And what *is* the situation?" asked Hatshepsut.

The boy, incredibly enough, spoke up, even though he was within a mere gesture of having his head lopped off right here in the temple. "Don't you already know?" the boy impudently asked. "I thought you were a god."

"What a fool your son turns out to be," Hatshepsut said to Isis. "He thinks he wants to be Pharaoh, and yet he's so stupid that he actually casts doubt on Pharaoh's divinity." She turned to the boy. "You don't burn the house you want to dwell in. You don't sink the boat on which you ride."

"Thank you for the lesson," he said, still defiant. But she could see that she had wounded him. He *had* been stupid, but he was smart enough to recognize the fact. Well, what a shame, thought Hatshepsut. If he was flat-out dumb she might have a use for him. But if he was smart, well, he could not be permitted to get even a taste of power.

"I am stricken with grief for the death of my husband," said Hatshepsut. "Clearly Osiris needed him more than I. Or perhaps it is my father who called him home." She turned to the captain of her guards. "I fear that in these tumultuous times, this brave concubine and her bold son might be in danger. I order you to protect them. Take them to my palace and place the woman with Mutnefert. Let's let the grieving mother comfort the grieving concubine. As for the boy, he will be educated in the palace. I'll see what he's made of."

Apparently Isis knew enough about the lay of the land to understand that she was being imprisoned with the most murderous woman in Egypt—who also happened to be the devoted mother of the man that Isis had just murdered. There wouldn't be much sleeping in Mutnefert's room, and the way color drained from Isis's face suggested that she knew it. But after just a brief hesitation, she lashed out with words. "He's already been anointed!" she said. "He is his father's heir! Pharaoh beside you!"

"And if I ever agreed to such a ludicrous thing," said Hatshepsut, "how long would I live? Isis, I know exactly what and who you are, and I can assure you that no matter what you may have dreamed in your frenzy of grief, no actual anointing of anyone took place tonight. Isn't that so, Jannes?"

"Pharaoh has spoken the perfect truth," said Jannes. "For only I have the authority to anoint a king of Upper and Lower Egypt, and I certainly did not anoint this boy."

Isis whirled to snarl at him in turn, but the boy himself intervened. "Mother," he said, "do us no harm now."

His voice stilled her at once.

Yes, the boy was smart. Dangerous. But . . . was there some hint of the spirit of Tuthmose I in him? Yes, Hatshepsut's instinct had been right. Dangerous as he was, he was blood of her blood. And he might be useful, if she trained him properly.

"Take them to the palace," said Hatshepsut. "Clearly they are overcome by grief and weariness."

Isis and the boy Tuthmose left, surrounded by soldiers.

Alone with Jannes, Hatshepsut let some of her fury show. "All right," she said, "which of your priests will die tonight?"

Jannes shut his eyes. "Me," he said.

"Not you," she said. "But now I know who it is. Your son Jambres, wasn't it?"

"I don't believe he understood the implications of it," said Jannes.

"What, you raised him to be a fool?"

"He thought he was merely elevating the best of your father's grandsons to be Pharaoh beside you."

"No, he thought that by putting this boy in his father's place, he'd be able to cut my son Moses out of his inheritance."

Jannes said nothing.

"You know Moses," said Hatshepsut. "He is a man of strength, courage, wisdom, virtue. Has there been a better man in line for the double crown?"

"Never," said Jannes. "And when I say that, you know that I remember your father with love and respect. But Moses has one flaw, in the eyes of some men."

"So he once dwelt in an Israelite's womb. The river gave him to me."

"Hatshepsut," said Jannes, "I know. I know."

His voice calmed her. Even though she knew that he was, in effect, pleading for the life of his own son, nevertheless she forced herself to listen to him.

"I didn't say my son was right to do what he did. But I know that he was not acting against you. Nor even against Moses himself. If Moses were the *only* Israelite in Egypt, Jambres would be his strongest supporter."

"What does he fear? Haven't I kept the Israelites as slaves?"

"With lighter burdens, and many opportunities to escape service, but yes, you have," said Jannes. "The danger isn't that *you'll* favor the Israelites, or even that Moses will. The danger is the stories that the Israelites tell about him."

"What do I care what the Israelites say?"

"Ancient prophecies, supposedly made by their ancestors. Abraham, Isaac, Israel, Joseph, stories about a messiah who will return after death, on the day of judgment, and lead his chosen people to Paradise."

"What danger is there in that?"

"It makes him a god."

"If he succeeds me as Pharaoh, he will be."

"It makes him the god of the Israelites."

"They have only one god, and it's not Moses. I know enough about their beliefs to know that."

"But that's not the only version of the story that circulates. Some say his own sister has prophesied that—"

"Miriam? I think the woman is mad."

"Oh, and no king ever fell because of the words of a madman?" Jannes smiled wanly.

"What does she say?"

"That her brother is not the messiah, but he's *like* the messiah. And instead of leading the chosen people to Paradise after he dies, he'll lead them out of slavery in this life."

Hatshepsut thought about this for a moment. "It's possible that when he becomes Pharaoh, if he feels the time is right, he may liberate the Israelites. But he wouldn't be foolish enough to cause dissension in his kingdom by preferring them the way the old Hyksos pharaohs did."

"Yes, and so it also seems to me," said Jannes. "But Jambres thinks that these stories suggest something far more sinister. That Miriam is deliberately telling these stories because Moses has told her to, in order to prepare the Israelites for a bloody revolution in which he will kill you on your throne and seize power, ruling as Pharaoh himself and imposing Israelite rule over Egypt more ruthlessly than the Hyksos ever did."

"I'm sorry to learn that your son has gone mad," said Hatshepsut.

"Not mad," said Jannes. "Wrong, but still prompted by a loving desire to keep you alive and your father's dynasty on the throne."

"Am I supposed to forgive his anointing this impudent nephew of mine?"

"But that anointing never happened," said Jannes. "And if it never happened, how can you punish my son for doing it?"

Hatshepsut smiled nastily. "Do you really think that such a weak logical trap will tie my hands?"

Jannes said nothing. Because he knew that yes, that logical trap *would* bind her. That, plus several other very good reasons for inaction. It was not good to reveal dissension in the house of Pharaoh—that was why Mutnefert was still alive, and it would keep Isis and her son alive as well. That same principle also applied here, for it was plain that Jannes, whose support was vital, would not look kindly on her if she punished Jambres for his treason. Sometimes you had to sleep with crocodiles.

"Next you'll tell me that I should honor Jambres and Tuthmose for what they did," she said.

"But they did nothing," said Jannes. "Nothing happened tonight except that your husband died. And you brought his body here to Karnak to prepare for his burial as befits a Pharaoh."

"I command that your son prepare his body with his own hands. Because it was your son that killed him. If he hadn't been plotting with Isis, she would never have done it."

Jannes nodded gravely. He knew that his son deserved to die, and that Jannes had in a more subtle way betrayed Hatshepsut by shielding him. He could afford to be generous now and allow Hatshepsut some small punishment of Jambres. If it could be called a punishment, since it was a great honor to prepare the body of a dead Pharaoh.

A great honor . . . and one that by right should have gone to Jannes. Hatshepsut watched his face, looking for evidence that he realized what she had just done to *him*, how she was preparing the ground for him to be replaced as chief priest. If he recognized her first step on that road, he showed no sign of it. But then, she was not allowing herself to show her dread that Jambres might be right, that the only way for her to remain as Pharaoh was to take that impudent boy beside her as Pharaoh. It would mean a life of constant vigilance, and in the end, her probable murder as an ambitious, hate-filled young man thrust her out of the way. And yet not to raise him up might also mean her death, and all the sooner, if people like Jambres refused to be ruled by a woman alone.

More horses at a gallop. More clattering of chariot wheels on stone. What possible message could be arriving so urgently?

"Come with me," said Hatshepsut. "Let's see together what this new crisis might be."

For a moment she hoped it would be news that Isis and her son had reached the palace and Mutnefert had killed them both on the spot when she heard what they had done to Tuthmose II. But the messenger was not one of her men. He came from Moses.

"What is the word?" she demanded.

"Victory!" he cried. "Saba has fallen, and without the loss of a single Egyptian soldier!"

Hatshepsut thought her heart might burst with joy at the news. Just at the moment of crisis, her husband dead, the priests of the temple casting about for Egyptian heirs to the crown, and now the gods had given Moses a victory. He would be a hero. Her own rule would be legitimated, and all the more so because the news of the victory had arrived the very night of her husband's death. For the first time, Hatshepsut would rule alone, without either her father or her weakling husband to provide a male figure beside her. Moses had made this possible. Moses was indeed a deliverer. Just as

Miriam's prophecy had promised. Miriam's only mistake had been in the matter of who it was that Moses would save. Me, that's who he saved, you poor mad prophetess! Me, his true mother, the woman most favored by the gods.

# T r i u m p h

The people came in from the fields, rushed out of their houses, flooded the streets of the villages like the river in spring. They cried out Moses' name, calling him Conqueror, Prince of Egypt, saying he was favored by this god or that. The rich were carried out in litters or lifted up to the tops of buildings, where slaves fanned and shaded them as they shouted for Moses in relative comfort. The poor sweated and stank together in the dust of the street, the roar of the crowd filling their ears and their hearts, feeling at one with each other, with the rich, with the great Moses, with the gods.

And among them were the Israelites. Still slaves by law, in fact their lot had greatly eased since Moses was adopted as heir to Pharaoh. They worked once again as artisans, scribes, and overseers, just as they had during the reign of the Hyksos. Their slavery perhaps tempered the arrogance of those who might once have been proud, and Egyptians no longer sought to marry into the Israelite tribes or join Israelite households by adoption as they had in the old days when no Egyptian was greater than Joseph except Pharaoh himself. But the days of mobbing and massacre were over, and as for the labor required of the Israelites, many of them now hired it done, paying poorer Israelites or Egyptians or buying their own slaves to fulfill their turns at building levees, walls, and public buildings. There were Israelite children growing up who had never sloshed their feet in the wet clay in the brickyards, who had never seen or felt the lash.

Yet the Egyptians and the Israelites were not one people; indeed, the division was clearer than ever, even though both groups cheered their throats raw as Moses and his army passed in triumph down the river to Thebes. For the Egyptians were cheering Pharaoh-to-be, a god in embryo, the future personification of the glory of their great civilization. While the Israelites were cheering the successor of Joseph, who would raise his people out of the last bits of bondage and make them once again masters of the great land of Egypt. And this time they would not be dependent on a Hyksos ruler for their position of privilege. Now Israelite blood would run in the veins of the Pharaoh himself. Indeed, now that Tuthmose II was dead, many expected that Hatshepsut would name her adopted son as co-regent with her. The double crown would sit well, they thought, on an Israelite head.

And as Moses passed, the Egyptians looked at the Israelites, almost all of them standing in a separate group from them, and saw how the Israelites seemed to rejoice entirely among themselves rather than joining with the rest of the community, and they understood quite well what this meant. The Israelites expected soon to be liberated from slavery. The Israelites expected to be tax collectors and grain distributors as they had been during the years of the hated Hyksos over-lords. And the Egyptians, in whispers, in looks, in quiet conversations in their houses after the crowds dispersed, seethed with rage at the Israelites, and vowed that if Moses gave one hint, one tiny sign that he favored the Israelites over the true Egyptians, they would look to the gods to give them an Egyptian Pharaoh.

Some of them went further, whispering treason. Perhaps

that son of Tuthmose II and Isis who, it was rumored, might already have been ordained by the son of the high priest of Karnak. Tuthmose III—that was the name that began to be whispered. Moses could not be made Pharaoh because Tuthmose had already been crowned. That woman, who should not really be called Pharaoh at all, but only the Daughter of Pharaoh, she was the one who had forced this Israelite upstart on them. Tuthmose II should have been sole Pharaoh, instead of co-Pharaoh with a woman! And as for Moses' victory, he didn't actually defeat the Ethiopians, did he? He had the city given him, as everything in his life had been given him, by the trickery and treachery of a woman.

But, having said this, the whisperers looked around in fear lest anyone overheard. For the gods had clearly spoken, hadn't they? Moses had taken Saba in the name of Pharaoh Hatshepsut, and in the moment of triumph Tuthmose II had died, thus giving the triumph to Hatshepsut and Moses. If the gods had done that, then this was probably not a good time to be talking about how she shouldn't be Pharaoh. And so the treasonous words were whispered but not spoken aloud, and Isis and Tuthmose and Mutnefert all had to listen to the cheering crowds from their rooms in the palace, loathing Moses and fearing Hatshepsut. What would she do now? With this victory she could afford to have a few inconvenient relatives strangled or poisoned and mourn their deaths with a great show of grief. Mutnefert and Isis both were fasting. Only Tuthmose laughed at death and ate whatever was placed before him.

Arise, Moses, Conqueror! Rejoice! Moses! Victory! Praise the Prince of Egypt! The Gods are great! Glory to Pharaoh and Moses!

*

Hatshepsut waited for Moses at the head of the stairs leading up from the river. She wore her full regalia as Pharaoh, though the headdress alone overbalanced her so much she wore it in constant dread of toppling over. *That's* an omen the people would not need to have interpreted for them! She saw with annoyance that there were many Israelites gathered near the palace—that was the last thing she needed, to remind people that Moses wasn't really Egyptian, just when she needed them to see him as her true son and the chosen of the gods. She recognized his former kin: Jochabed, who bore him, true, and nursed him, but who was definitely *not* his mother, since any son *she* had borne was given to the river. Miriam, his half-mad sister with her prophecies and gnomic sayings.

And Aaron, that climber, who, instead of becoming a decently sycophantic courtier and capitalizing on his brother's position to become wealthy through graft and influence peddling, had decided to become the most obnoxiously Israelite of all the Israelites, wearing that uncouth wool-and-leather desert garb even though most Israelites dressed in the white linen of Egypt. Would he harangue Moses once again about how he ought to use his influence to free the Israelites so they could go back out to the desert and make their obscene animal sacrifices? Of course he would. Anything to spoil the festivities.

Hatshepsut thought briefly of having him arrested, but that was dangerous, too. It would weaken Moses' position precisely at the time when she needed him to seem strong. Worse, it might be taken as license by the people who hated and resented the Israelites more than ever. The last thing she needed was for Moses' victory over the Ethiopians to be remembered as the occasion for mobbings and massacres of Israelites. If only Aaron could understand that it was Hatshepsut's own desire for peace and decency in her kingdom that kept her from letting the Israelites' enemies destroy them. Instead, he was convinced it was Moses' influence over her that kept him safe. What a joke! If only he knew the disdain that Moses had for him.

The boats came into view, and the cries rose from thousands of throats. Hatshepsut watched as Aaron and Miriam and Jochabed wept and embraced each other at the sight of Moses, as if he belonged to them and not to the whole kingdom of Egypt. Would Moses even exist if Hatshepsut had not chosen to adopt him?

Though to be fair, it was adopting Moses that helped her secure her position at court all those years ago. Having a son and heir who was adopted by her father as well, that had been the key to everything. Hatshepsut saved Moses, and Moses, even as a baby, had saved her in return. And in the years since then he had been a true son, the joy of her heart. Hatshepsut had been the most avid student of her father's life and teachings, but in all the years of his life Moses had been a far better student, determined to learn, if it were possible, everything about everything. He studied with the priests as if he intended to become a priest; he studied with scribes as if he intended to become a scribe. The soldiers praised him as the finest of officers and the finest of fighters. And Hatshepsut herself knew that no one was a better master of statesmanship than Moses. Never mind his tendency to be a little tenderhearted sometimes when he should be ruthless, and other times too impulsive and tempestuous when he should be patient. That was to be expected of one so young and inexperienced; he would learn. No mother could ask for a better son; no ruler for a better heir. If the price for that was having to look at Aaron's and Miriam's smug, self-important faces even at her greatest moments of triumph, well, Hatshepsut would bear that small burden.

At least this time she didn't have to have that repulsive son of Mutnefert beside him, that donkey who wore the double crown only because his mother poisoned Hatshepsut's beautiful brothers.

But then she remembered how close she had come to having to share this moment with that cow-brained Isis and her snake of a son and she shuddered.

The royal boat came to the steps and the rivermen secured it. Moses descended from his high platform and stepped from the Nile to the land. The cheering doubled in volume. Other boats were brought up to the steps, and Ethiopian prizes were brought to shore. Chests filled with gold ornaments, jewelry, and figurines were brought up the steps and held high before the people. Strange animals taken from the gardens of Saba were displayed. And who was that overdecorated woman? Not a slave—this must be the daughter of the Ethiopian king, who betrayed her city in order to become Moses' wife. Hatshepsut watched with amusement as her fastidious son nodded to his beloved bride but did not touch her and certainly did not bring her forward to stand beside him. Rather she was forced to trail many paces behind him, like a captive— no, like a concubine!—as he climbed the stairs to present all his gifts to Pharaoh.

To his *mother*.

Hatshepsut raised her arms for silence. In other families, a son who came home from the wars would be embraced by his mother, covered with tears and kisses. But Hatshepsut was Pharaoh, and the scene had to be played out differently.

"Pharaoh, god of Egypt!" cried Moses. At last the crowd was still, hanging on his words. "Your ancestors stood beside me as the armies of Ethiopia melted in fear before me! Thoth entered the city before me. By magic, Thoth captured the heart of the daughter of the king. He taught her that the place of Ethiopia was in the bed of Egypt!"

Not likely that she'll ever get into the bed of Moses, though, Hatshepsut thought wryly. Sometimes she worried about him, the way he took no concubines and even seemed not to take possession of the perfectly willing slaves in the palace. When she confronted him about this, he said to her, Should I put my sons and daughters into the bodies of slaves and concubines? How could she argue with that? One thing was certain: This Ethiopian princess might be his wife in title, and to keep his word, but Moses would not let a traitor be the mother of his children.

"And when the gates of Saba fell open before me, it was Pharaoh, god of Egypt, whom I carried in my heart as I entered the city!"

A lovely speech. Unorthodox and theologically difficult, but it played well at the moment, and Hatshepsut especially enjoyed the way Aaron and Miriam were frowning. They didn't like hearing their brother talk about gods. They wanted him to believe that the *only* god was their unseen what's-his-name. As if one god should be god of river, sky, rain, and the land of the dead. As if one god would raise up different nations and have them fight each other, so that no matter which side won, the same god won, and no matter which side lost, that same god was the loser! What sort of god would fight on both sides of a battle? It was a childish, ludicrous, tribal sort of religion, invented by herdsmen so lonely that they came to believe they were the only people in the world, and so wilfully ignorant that they continued to believe it even when surrounded by the glories of Egypt and the obvious godhood of Pharaoh.

"O Pharaoh Hatshepsut!" cried Moses. "If I struck like . . . lightning, it is because . . . Pharaoh is the sky. If I flowed like a river through Ethiopia, then Pharaoh is the . . . sea to which this river flows!"

The people cheered. Hatshepsut found it so endearing, the little pauses in his speech. The onlookers had no idea that during these pauses Moses was trying to get control of his stammer. That he must have spent his whole voyage down the river memorizing these speeches so he could utter them at all. Poor boy. It was a good thing that Pharaoh used spokesmen for most public declarations. But they had agreed before he left that if he came home triumphant — *when* he came home triumphant — they would have just such a meeting in the open air, on the very steps where she had taken him out of the river.

"Pharaoh, god of Egypt, ruler of . . . Nubia, if I have glory, you gave it to me!"

And he bowed. No, laid himself out on the stairs like a slave. Well, the boy might stammer but he knew how to stage a scene as well as any of the actors in a temple pageant.

Well, she knew how to play her part in such a scene. She descended from her lofty place. At her first downward step, the crowd gasped. Pharaoh, descending to *meet* a supplicant?

"Down these steps I walked, to bathe in the holy Nile!" she cried.

They fell silent again, listening to the play she acted out for them.

"A baby rose up out of the water and into my hands. I named him Moses and took him as my son!"

She reached down, took Moses by the hand, and raised him up to his knees.

"He was adopted also by Pharaoh my father, even as my father adopted me to be his son. So Moses became son of his body, son of his daughter, and son of his son, all on the same day. Thrice the son of Pharaoh, then, is the truly-named Moses! Lifted up by the gods as now I, god of Egypt, lift him up!"

She raised him all the way to his feet. Tall! He stood two steps below her and yet they were eye to eye, and she was not a small woman. Ah, but she loved him, her beautiful boy, her creation. She had made a god of him.

❊

Moses was exhausted, but of course that would mean nothing to Aaron and Miriam. And, just as predictably, they had brought along old Jochabed. For his old nurse's sake, he couldn't make them wait until they got tired of it and went home. Even as they used their own mother to manipulate him, they still misunderstood why it worked. They thought it was because he felt filial devotion to his mother. They thought he still felt like an Israelite. But he didn't. His mother was Hatshepsut, who had taught him everything, who had lifted him up and made him great. Jochabed gave birth to his body, of course, but what did that mean? The courtesy he showed her was because she was his nurse, his childhood teacher. She was tender and kind with him and he still loved her—but one thing she had done to him that he found it hard to forgive. In his infancy she had taught him the Israelite language right along with the Egyptian, so that he thought easily in both, and passed back and forth between them with such ease that he almost didn't notice which language he was speaking.

Almost . . . and yet he had never made a mistake. Had never spoken to Hatshepsut in Hebrew, never addressed his soldiers by that barbaric language. Yet he had to stop himself and think, did I just say that in Hebrew? Was I about to speak in Hebrew? Sometimes he was quite sure it had to have been that watchfulness, that fear that had caused his stammer. He was fluent in both languages, but could not speak fluently in either without memorizing a set speech so he could *know* that he was not going to make a mistake and slip from one language into the other.

It was as Mother had told him when he was five. "You're Egyptian, not Hebrew. It's useful to know Hebrew because you will often have to give commands to Israelites, and you want your understanding to be perfect. But don't ever, ever speak Hebrew to an Egyptian. For if you give them the slightest excuse to call you an Israelite, you not only end *your* chance to be Pharaoh, you may very well destroy *me* as well."

Perhaps she didn't realize how deeply Moses took her words to heart. But he could date his stammer from that day. And his stammer weakened him. How could it not? Yet his consolation was this: Because he paused so much, spoke so slowly, framing each word, checking it and doublechecking, he always said exactly what he meant to say. Words never slipped out, the way they did with other men. Almost that made up for not being able to speak freely and easily.

He loved Jochabed, but had often thought, If only I had never learned Hebrew, how much better off I'd be. If only I hadn't had to grow up knowing I was born to slaves and foreigners.

And now my brother and sister and . . . mother . . . insist on reminding me of my low birth. Aaron will harangue me. Miriam will utter cryptic wise annoying proverbs and then smile as if she knew the secrets of all the gods. And Mother will weep to see me and embrace me with pure love and take me back to my childhood so that I'm helpless before her.

Mother—not Jochabed, *Hatshepsut*—Mother is right. I'm not ruthless enough. I could keep these people out of my life.

Just utter a word to Mother that I didn't want to see them again, and they'd never be allowed anywhere near me. But instead I continue to let them steal hours of my life in useless conversation. I do this because I am stupid and weak.

"Mother," he said, for there she was, waiting in the middle of the room for him. "Jochabed" is what he wanted to call her, but it would hurt her feelings. She embraced him, as expected; wept all over his chest, as always; kissed his cheek and said, "God has been so good to me, to let me live to see you once again."

She'd been talking that way since he was an infant. God was good to her, because he let her see Moses again. If her god was so good to her, Moses wanted to ask, why did he let her remain a slave? Why wasn't she free? For that matter, why had her second son been born under sentence of death, if her god was so good?

But he said nothing of this. He bent and kissed her, let her prate on like a baby, the words meaningless to him but the sentiment of love perfectly acceptable.

The other two were in the room, but they knew from experience that they shouldn't interrupt Moses' reunions with Jochabed. He permitted them to tag along with her, but he had warned them that if they didn't let him have time alone with his old nurse, then these visits would have no value to him at all. In short, if they intended to speak with Moses, they had to wait in silence until Jochabed had stopped weeping and relaxed her hold on him.

Finally she said, "I have to sit down, Moses. Where can I sit?"

As he led her to a bench near the wall, they pounced.

Aaron first, of course, trying to be friends. "All of Israel is proud of you, Moses. You wouldn't believe how eagerly everyone waited for the news from each messenger that came down the river."

And then Miriam, asserting her superiority. "Of course we knew you would have a victory, because God has chosen you."

He hated it when she said that, but this time, with Jochabed still resting her hand on his arm, Moses did not rise to the bait.

"I'm glad to see you're in . . . good health," he said. "You don't want for anything, do you, Mother?"

"You're such a good and careful son," said Jochabed. But there was a twinkle in her eye. That bothered him, when he saw that. As if she knew that he wasn't really half so good or half so careful as he pretended. But didn't he see to it that they had every necessity? — though not any kind of luxury that would lead people to think he was recognizing them as his family. Maybe Jochabed recognized how carefully calibrated all his gifts were.

"I wish I could stay and . . . talk with you," Moses began, but as usual his stammer made the words so slow to come out that before he could get to the next phrase — "but I must . . . bathe and sleep after my journey" — Aaron was already on him.

"I wish you could go home with us. Go to the Israelites! Meet your people, let them show you how they love you!"

"Is that what you call it?" said Moses. "Love?"

Aaron looked annoyed. "What, you think they're pretending?"

"If you would tell them the . . . truth, that I'm Egyptian and not Israelite, they'd no more . . . love me than they love any Egyptian, particularly . . . Pharaoh's son."

"*Is* that the truth?" asked Miriam.

"It's what he *thinks* is true," said Aaron.

This was unbearable. "Do you think I don't know what I am?" Moses shouted. "Do you think I don't . . . know my own heart? If I say I'm an Egyptian then I am!"

Miriam laughed. "Until the first time you do something that the Egyptians don't like."

Her laughter was as infuriating as Aaron's smugness. "Every time I let you in here to . . . talk to me, I'm doing something that Egyptians don't like."

"Oh, how brave of you," said Miriam.

Aaron added his own sneer: "You marry your way into a victory at Saba and then you whimper about letting your own family in to see you."

"You disdain my . . . victory? I have the respect of the men who . . . face death in battle."

Aaron had no answer—and what man could, who had not tasted combat? But Miriam cared nothing for the marks of courage. "You have the respect of men. It might be better if you earned the respect of God."

"You call it the respect of . . . God, but what you really mean is I should . . . do what you say."

"What God says," Miriam insisted.

"In your theology, Miriam, is there a difference?"

"Oh, be quiet, all of you," said Jochabed. "I know you didn't grow up in the same house, so you couldn't bicker and quarrel when you were little. Does that mean you have to make up for it now?"

Moses snapped back at her, "They call me a . . . coward and a liar and a fool, you treat us all as equals and think you're fair."

"I don't think I'm fair," said Jochabed. "I think I'm bored. Aren't you?"

"Come without them sometime, Mother," said Moses. "*You* I'm glad to see."

"Only because she doesn't expect anything of you," said Aaron.

Miriam was not so calm. "Do you know how Israelite women are treated, when they go anywhere alone? The insult, the danger? Is that what you want for her?"

"It wasn't my decision when she . . . moved back into the village," said Moses.

"Back to her own people," said Miriam. "Where you belong."

"No," said Aaron. "He belongs here, in the palace — where God put him."

"Can't you two even agree on what you want to . . . force me to become?" said Moses.

"And still you go on," said Jochabed.

"No, let's not go on," said Moses. "Let's finish it. Tell me what you want from me, what you . . . think you have a right to have, as my . . . birth family. I'll give it to you if I can, deny it if it's beyond my power, and then we're finished. Do you understand?"

"We'll never be finished," said Miriam.

"We already *are* finished. You'll never come to this . . . palace again. So ask for what you want and have done with it."

"We don't come here for favors, you fool," said Miriam.

"So . . . your wish is to call the . . . son of Pharaoh a fool and not be punished," said Moses. "Very well, I grant your wish. I pardon your treason. Now it's your turn, Aaron."

"We are trying to save you from destruction," said Miriam.

"I'm not," said Aaron. "I'm trying to save Israel."

"Israel's out there, scattered through the . . . villages of Egypt," said Moses. "Working as scribes and artisans all over the . . . kingdom. A few herdsmen . . . keeping up the old ways, but mostly your people are just like other Egyptians except you insist on . . . keeping your own language and you insist on . . . keeping your own . . . god. In another generation or two even those . . . differences will be gone. You're trying to save a . . . people who don't want to be saved."

Miriam and Aaron looked at each other in obvious amazement. "He's *not* a fool," said Miriam. "He understands completely."

"He misses the point," Aaron retorted. "Some Israelites are getting swallowed up in Egypt, it's true, but they're only fooling themselves. The Egyptians never allow foreigners to become Egyptian. In their eyes we're always barbarians. And we in particular are slaves and will remain slaves. Whenever they want, they'll turn on us and destroy us. They killed our babies at the time when you were born. They'll strike against us again, if they can."

"That's why we have to get Israel out of Egypt," said Miriam. "Back to Canaan where we belong."

"No," said Aaron. "God has chosen us to be the greatest nation in the world. Egypt is an unworthy, idolatrous people. Now God has raised up an Israelite to be Pharaoh someday. God has given him triumphs in battle, the acclaim of the Egyptian people. It's time for Moses to raise the Israelites out of slavery and set them in their proper place, as rulers and judges, kings and priests."

Moses burst out laughing. "You really *are* children. You have no idea of how . . . power works, or who has it, or what you can actually . . . do with it."

"I know that when Joseph was in a position of power, he raised up his brothers to share that power with him, even though they had done him wrong," said Aaron. "While you treat your family and your people with contempt, even though they have done you no harm at all."

"Joseph's brothers weren't slaves," said Moses. "And the Pharaoh of that time was not Egyptian. And there were only eleven . . . brothers, not the thousands of people who call themselves Israelites now. And Joseph wasn't . . . thrown into the river as a baby and adopted by the . . . daughter of Pharaoh and raised in the . . . palace as her son!"

Jochabed struggled to her feet, filled with rage. "How dare you! Thrown into the river!"

Moses regretted his words at once. "Forgive me, Mother, that's the way Hatshepsut speaks of it and I—"

"Does she tell you whose edict passed a sentence of death on you?"

"Her father, of course, in response to the people's—"

"In response to the people! What kind of king is that, who makes his laws to fit the most evil whims of his people?"

"The only kind of . . . king that stays in power," said Moses.

"How would you know?" said Jochabed. "You've never seen another kind. You've never seen real leadership."

"And you have?" said Moses.

"I've done it myself!" Jochabed answered. "I was pregnant with a baby that God had told my husband would be a boy. He was going to be killed if I didn't do something. So I prayed, and an idea came to me. Noah! The ark! To keep you safe from a flood of hate! I put you on the water, I trusted in the Lord. Others told me I had killed you with my own hands, but I paid no attention to them. I did what God put it in my heart to do."

"I can't see what that has to do with the . . . power of kings," said Moses.

"You see perfectly well, you just don't like it," said

Jochabed. "And you don't like it because I am holding kings to a higher standard than your precious Hatshepsut will ever even try to measure up to. I don't think she even knows the standard exists."

Moses burned with anger and part of him wanted to lash out, silence her with words. But there was another part of him, the perpetual student, the unrelenting questioner who had often reduced Hatshepsut and his teachers to consternation as they found that he could always take them to the limits of their knowledge with his demand for answers. Jochabed was saying something interesting, and he had to hear the end of it. Unlike Aaron and Miriam, who were forever singing the same tune, Jochabed rarely spoke anything but affection to him. So he did not interrupt her words, outrageous as they were.

"A true leader finds out what will be good for his people," said Jochabed, "and then shapes laws that will help achieve that good purpose. If the people don't understand what he's doing, he persuades them if he can. If they refuse to be persuaded, then he acts for their good anyway. And if doing this costs him his power, then he would rather lose his power for doing right, than keep his power by doing wrong. Because he loves his people more than he loves his office."

"If only things were ever that . . . clear," said Moses.

"Oh, I know where the problems are," said Jochabed. "Most of the time you *don't* know what's good for the people. You make your best guess, but you know you might be wrong. But there are times when you *do* know, as I knew what God expected me to do for you, and then I bent for no one, not my husband, not the elders, not even my own heart that could hardly bear to put you out on the water and let you drift away."

"Miriam and Aaron are . . . telling me God's will?" asked

Moses. "They can't even agree . . . between them what I ought
to do. Send Israel out of Egypt or raise them up to be over-
lords over the Egyptians! Both of these are . . . foolish dreams.
To attempt even to free Israel from . . . slavery would mean the
end of Hatshepsut's reign as Pharaoh. Don't you understand
how . . . precarious her position is? The priests of Karnak
would . . . cease to stand with her. She would have to bring a
man onto the . . . throne beside her. The most likely . . . candi-
date for that role is a conniving little snake named Tuthmose,
who showed a talent for war when I was . . . teaching him as a
child. The soldiers . . . love him but he grew up nursing a deep
. . . loathing for me precisely because I am an Israelite. If
Hatshepsut weakens enough that she has to . . . share her
throne with him, I will no longer be heir. If I'm not strangled
or . . . poisoned, I'll become a . . . servant of the household, and
when Hatshepsut . . . dies I'll be lucky if I'm allowed to go on
living as a . . . slave."

He could see from their faces that Aaron and Miriam
weren't hearing a word he said. But Jochabed was listening,
because Jochabed actually cared whether Moses lived or died.

"You think Hatshepsut's manner of ruling is weak and
cowardly?" Moses went on. "That all she cares about is hanging on to . . . power for herself? You're wrong. What she cares
about is Egypt. She even cares about the Israelites in Egypt.
Because she's Pharaoh, Israel's slavery is bearable. Because
I'm the heir, because I'm . . . victorious in battle, the mobs
aren't killing Israelites anymore. *That's* the truth about how
. . . power works in Egypt, and why your fine talk about a
'higher standard' is just another recipe for . . . destroying
Israel, while Mother's supposedly cowardly way, her 'selfish-
ness' as you call it, is what keeps every single one of us alive
and . . . free enough to have this argument!"

Jochabed looked at him with icy eyes and said, "You call *her* 'Mother'?"

So she hadn't understood him, either. "You . . . taught me to . . . call her that yourself," said Moses.

"When you were little, and I feared she might change her mind and toss you back into the river," said Jochabed.

"You never knew her, you still don't understand her, none of you. Israel has no better . . . friend than Hatshepsut."

"God is a better friend than any Pharaoh," said Miriam.

"Yes, look how excellent his record is so far," said Moses.

Miriam ran to him, tried to slap him; he caught her arm.

"Don't you know that it's . . . death to raise your hand against me?" said Moses. "If anyone saw you! If you . . . struck me and left a . . . mark that I couldn't hide! —"

"Don't you know that it's death to speak blasphemy against God?" she cried.

"You're the one with power," said Aaron. "You come down the river in triumph as your people live in shame and subjection on either hand. This could be the hour! Even you can see that, if you'd only open your eyes! Raise your hand and set your people free!"

"Raise my hand and set them free?" Moses laughed scornfully. "They *are* free. Slaves in Egypt are . . . better off than free men anywhere else. And as for Israel . . . being 'my' people, they all look like . . . strangers to me."

"If you ever walked among them, instead of hiding here in the palace!" cried Miriam.

"Israel is your mother, your brother, your sister!" said Aaron. "It's time to show Israel that you know who you are."

"The moment I show myself as an Israelite, I will no longer be the . . . son of Pharaoh and then who would . . . follow me, Egyptian or Israelite?"

"You are the chosen leader of Israel," Aaron insisted.

"No, you are," said Moses. "Or doesn't God accept . . . volunteers? This is *your* obsession, he's *your* God, you do it."

"Who's talking nonsense now?" said Aaron.

"Do you really think I don't understand you? You want to use me in order to make Israel . . . master of Egypt, yourself master of Israel, and then Egypt, under you, master of the world. You're every bit as ambitious as . . ." But he chose not to mention Isis and her treason, or her son Tuthmose whose ordained head should, by rights, be on display somewhere.

Even without the mention of treason, Moses' words struck home. "Maybe I am ambitious," said Aaron. "Growing up a slave, growing up hearing Mother and Father and Miriam talk all the time about how *you* were the chosen one, *you* were the hope of Israel, yes, I did, I wanted to be the one, I prayed to God to let me be the one to set Israel free. But I grew up, Moses, something you might want to try, and I realized that I wasn't the chosen one and so all I could do was try my best to get *you* to do what God has prepared you to do."

"Well, if God's been . . . preparing me to free Israel, I can't wait for him to tell one of you his plan. I don't start any . . . campaign without knowing precisely how I intend to win it."

"You were planning on that traitorous princess giving you Saba?" said Miriam scornfully.

"I *had* a plan. But that didn't bar me from . . . seizing opportunity when it came."

"You cannot resist the will of God," said Miriam. "You think you understand everything, how power works, what you can and can't do, but I tell you that God is God! You're a man. His plans are known to him—why should he consult with *you?* Do you tell your common soldiers your whole strategy?"

"At least they know that I exist," said Moses mildly. "And

now, please, let's have done with this. You've told me what you want, and I've told you why it's impossible. If I tried to do these things my power would . . . disappear, and Hatshepsut would be weakened, and in all . . . likelihood Israel would end up far worse off than it is now. The subject is closed. Go away."

Moses bent over and kissed Jochabed on the cheek. "I'm glad to come home to you."

"Do I get to meet my daughter-in-law?" asked Jochabed.

Moses winced. "It wouldn't be a . . . good meeting, Mother. I couldn't explain to her who you are."

Jochabed sighed.

"Marriage in the palace isn't like marriage in the . . . village, Mother."

"How would you know?" murmured Miriam.

Moses ignored her, or tried to. "I married her because I gave my word, and I gave my word . . . because it would open the . . . gates of Saba without any of my men dying."

"So you're not going to give her any babies?"

"I never promised she'd be the . . . mother of a Pharaoh," said Moses.

"How canny you are," said Miriam. "How clever."

"Amram never promised me that *I'd* be mother of a Pharaoh, either," said Jochabed.

"You have two wonderful Israelite . . . children who will probably get themselves killed someday," said Moses, "but in the meantime, don't they make a . . . mother proud?"

"Yes," said Jochabed.

"But not as proud as *you* make her, Moses," said Miriam. "The boy who conquers women from afar with his pretty looks. The boy who will face Ethiopian armies, but shrinks in terror from walking the streets of an Egyptian village as an Israelite."

"I walk the streets of . . . countless villages every year."

"But as Pharaoh's Israelite son, *not* as a common Israelite." Miriam's eyes danced with the challenge.

"I don't have the . . . costume in my wardrobe," said Moses.

"Aaron will gladly change clothes with you, won't you, Aaron?"

Aaron looked with distaste at Moses' Egyptian garb. "I'd be ashamed to be seen in public half-naked like that."

Miriam sneered at him. "Oh, you used to wear linens all the time, until you decided it was an un-Israelitish thing to do."

"It doesn't matter," said Moses.

"But you said you'd do what we asked, if it was in your power," said Miriam.

"You already asked for . . . things I couldn't do."

"Ah, I see," said Miriam. "It was a trick—the first request out of our mouths was also the last. You're too clever for us, Moses."

"Moses wouldn't last two minutes in a village," said Aaron, "not without his name and reputation, his soldiers and his station in life."

Moses knew they were goading him, and it was tempting to refuse their request just to stymie them. But he also found his curiosity piqued. Again, the student in him wanted to know: What was it like to be an ordinary Israelite in Egypt?

"It's nice to see you show your . . . true feelings, Aaron," said Moses. "It's my name, my reputation, my soldiers, and my . . . station in life that you resent. Tell me, will it be enough for you to . . . bring me as low as you? Or do you also have to be lifted up above me . . . before you can be happy?"

"Not everyone is driven by pure ambition," said Aaron. "You pretend to care for Egypt, but all your actions are designed to protect your own position. While I have put everything on the line for the sake of Israel."

"Admit it, Aaron," said Moses. "We're two of a kind. We both think we're . . . leader of a mighty nation." And with that Moses left, feeling rather good, though he couldn't think why.

※

Jochabed watched Moses leave, watched Aaron and Miriam as they ranted to each other about how selfish and blind Moses was, and all she could think of was what might have been, if Moses had been able to grow up in her house in the village. He would have been one of those tag-along brothers, following Aaron everywhere, and gradually earning his own way into the games of the boys. Both of them studying together at their father's knee, learning to read and write, learning the writings of Abraham—of the stars, of creation, of the goodness of God.

If only she had the power to heal them as if they were truly brothers and sister, so their children could grow up around her. But it wouldn't happen. Her children were afflicted with greatness. Great ability, great ambition. It would be a miracle if they *did* get along.

How could she explain it to them? In the end, after all the arguing and quarreling, after all the loving and embracing in life, we're alone, each one of us, alone without any true friend who really understands us. All strangers to each other. All we want is for someone else to truly know us. Aaron longing to have Moses see how true and noble his cause is; Moses longing to have Aaron understand that he is already doing all he can to be a good ruler. Each incapable of knowing the other's virtue, because like all children they only wanted to be known, and cared little about giving that gift to others.

I can't give them that gift either, thought Jochabed. Old as I am, I know what it is they need, but I can't give it. I can love them, but I don't truly know them either. Only God knows. Only God can understand their hearts.

O Father of their souls, O Maker of earth and heaven, lightning and river, I know thy great works will come to pass without need of any prayer or plea from me. But if my years and deeds on this earth have earned me the right to one more blessing from thee, let it be this: Somehow, in all the twisting pathways of their lives, for my sake let them twine together, let their lives converge, and when at last they face thee, let them do it as brothers and sister, trusting each other, loving each other, as if they had grown up as close as flowers growing from the same seed. Even if I'm dead by then, thou wilt be alive, and where my love hasn't even the power to make them polite to each other, thy love will give them the power to be one, three yarns braided into one stout rope in thy hand.

Hast thou ever had a son? Does God contain within his infinite wisdom the knowledge of how it feels to cast a son upon the waters, to set children free into the terrible heat of the sun? Be merciful with my children, as thou wouldst be with thine own most beloved child.

# I s r a e l i t e

M oses felt drained by his meeting with Aaron and Miriam, but he always did. It took more energy to deal with them than it did to conquer Ethiopia, or at least so it seemed right now. But he also knew that they were merely an annoyance, the bite of a flea compared to the danger posed by the young upstart who had got himself consecrated as Pharaoh when Isis poisoned Tuthmose II.

This young Tuthmose was imprisoned quite comfortably — a couch for sleeping and reclining and a high table for spreading out scrolls and reading to his heart's content. And Moses knew that the boy was a good student, for at times Moses had taught him along with the sons of the other concubines of Tuthmose II. Many of them were named Tuthmose, but even among the rival boys it was well known that *this* Tuthmose was *the* Tuthmose of his generation, for he had the force of will and the quick grasp of tactics that would make him a powerful Pharaoh. He was also, however, stubborn beyond the point of foolishness, and his vanity and ambition drove him more than his reason or even his heart. The boy loved his father, and so he hated Hatshepsut for the way she made her husband a mere figurehead and hated Moses for being Hatshepsut's favorite. Yet this boy was ready to step into his father's place the moment his mother arranged his death.

"All I want to know from you," said Moses, "is whether

you knew your . . . mother was going to poison your father before she did it, or merely . . . took advantage of it after the fact."

Tuthmose looked up from the scroll he was reading, regarded Moses for a long moment, and then looked back down.

"Is that your refuge," asked Moses, "to become a scholar now that your hopes of becoming Pharaoh have been dashed?"

This time Tuthmose did not look up.

"I see," said Moses. "You believe you already *are* Pharaoh, and that it is only an evil . . . conspiracy by Hatshepsut and me that keeps you from your rightful place. So you cannot speak without . . . lying or raging or otherwise doing things beneath the . . . dignity of Pharaoh. Therefore you will keep . . . silence, hoping that this will allow you to . . . survive until you figure out a way to . . . kill me and Mother."

Tuthmose languidly rolled up one end of the scroll a little way, slid the whole assemblage over, and unrolled a few new columns of text.

"Mother and I are trying to . . . decide whether you should be imprisoned here for the rest of your . . . life, or whether you should . . . tragically die of an illness."

"The gods curse the one who raises his hand against the consecrated head," said Tuthmose.

"Interesting. That doesn't . . . bode well for your mother."

"Father died of an illness."

"A very sudden illness. Very much like the illnesses that your . . . grandmother, Mutnefert, caused to happen to Hatshepsut's . . . brothers in hopes of making her son Pharaoh."

"People get sick sometimes."

"Your mother killed your father," said Moses, "and your grandmother killed your uncles. If I were you, I'd be . . . very watchful of the women you take as concubines."

"You will never be Pharaoh," said Tuthmose.

"On the contrary," said Moses. "It is very likely that after a decent interval, I will take your . . . father's place as Pharaoh beside Hatshepsut."

"As long as Hatshepsut is in power, Egypt has no Pharaoh," said Tuthmose.

"That in itself is . . . grounds for you to die," said Moses.

"But you don't dare kill me for it," said Tuthmose, "because you know that half of Egypt, including most of the army, feels the same way."

"As long as we care how the army . . . feels, perhaps you should take into account the . . . fact that the army holds me in very high esteem right now, and doesn't know you at all."

Tuthmose laughed. "You're a fool if you believe that, Moses. You're an Israelite. The army despises you and would love to see you toppled."

"They have followed me to war and . . . found victory."

"The victory belonged to Egypt. To them. Not to you. Not to your . . . *mother.*"

Moses couldn't help admiring the way that Tuthmose was maintaining his pride, even at the risk of his life. He also understood that this made Tuthmose all the more dangerous, and his advice to his mother would be to have Tuthmose quietly executed for his treason, as the law demanded, for as long as he was alive he would plot, and as long as he plotted there would be those in Egypt who would join with him and help him.

"You've decided to have me killed, of course," said Tuthmose.

"Wouldn't you?" asked Moses.

"I think I've made it clear what *I* would do with me."

"I meant, wouldn't you have a . . . traitor like yourself executed, if you were in my place?"

"I could never be in your place," said Tuthmose. "I have the blood of Pharaohs in my veins. While you have the blood of slaves."

"My Israelite blood is the . . . blood of prophets," said Moses.

Tuthmose laughed aloud. And Moses himself was shocked by his own words. Since when did he care about prophets? Since when did he defend Israelite blood?

"At least you didn't answer me with some mumbo-jumbo about how the Nile is your father and you have the water of the sacred river in your veins," said Tuthmose. "I appreciate your showing me that much respect."

"I have no respect for you," said Moses, "except the respect a . . . barefooted man has for a snake."

"That's the respect you *should* have," said Tuthmose. "But it doesn't matter whether you kill me or not, Moses. You'll never be Pharaoh. The people can bear Hatshepsut for her father's sake, and because she is of Pharaonic descent. But you—you would be unbearable."

"That's the difference between us, Tuthmose," said Moses. "You want to be Pharaoh at any cost, even the . . . life of your father. While all I care about is the . . . good of Egypt."

Tuthmose blushed. "I love Egypt. I loved my father."

"Yet you would gladly let either of them suffer whatever . . . torment was necessary to let you become Pharaoh."

Tuthmose whispered his reply. "I didn't know."

"I didn't think you did," said Moses. "But now my question is, what do *you,* the man who wishes to be the . . . supreme judge of Egypt, what do *you* think should be . . . done to the concubine Isis?"

"I think she should be honored as queen and mother of Pharaoh," said Tuthmose.

"There are worse things than an Israelite that . . . could come into the house of Pharaoh," said Moses. And he left.

Behind him, Tuthmose, his eyes filled with tears of impotent rage, whispered, "I *did* know. The gods will justify me. Father was weak, and it will take a strong Pharaoh to get rid of Hatshepsut and her slaveboy."

Moses didn't need to hear these words. He already knew the truth. He would counsel Hatshepsut to have the boy killed immediately. But she would not do it. She claimed that she never acted against Mutnefert because it would create turmoil and weakness in the house of Pharaoh, but the truth was that Hatshepsut hadn't the heart for killing, and that would be her downfall someday, unless Moses was there to protect her.

❈

As slavery went, Nun had rather the best of it. No one supervised him because he had no betters to correct him. He arose in the morning because he couldn't wait to get to his work. He dined with his family and there was always plenty to eat, enough that guests were welcome at his table, because the work of a painter of glyphs was well-rewarded. He had to have the talent of a painter, with the same knowledge of colors on stone and colors on plaster; and yet he had to be able to read and form words as well as any scribe—better, since his work would be seen by thousands at once, and any error would be visible for decades, perhaps centuries. Nun was well-regarded for he made no mistakes and his glyphs were gracefully shaped and he worked at a good speed. Surely if there was any Israelite who had reason to love Egypt it was Nun.

And yet his heart seethed as he walked the streets of his village of artisans, for even though he received deference himself, he saw how his fellow Israelites were despised, ordered about, jostled, insulted, and set to foolish tasks by Egyptians who fancied themselves their superiors. Their masters.

If I lost a finger and could not properly hold a brush, he thought, if my eyes failed me and I could not see, how would they treat me then? One fallen stone on my hand, one fleck of sand in my eye and that would be me shoved against the wall by passing Egyptian youths, me set to carrying water even though I was done with my labor for the day, merely because to resist the order of an Egyptian meant a certain beating.

They valued him, they paid him well, they left him alone, but as he often said, a valued slave is still a slave.

A few days ago, Nun had heard the tumult when Moses passed down the river. Nun paid no heed. He bade his eldest son Joshua good-bye and set out for work. "But papa," said Joshua, "Moses is coming down the river!"

"Moses can fly overhead like a flock of birds for all I care," said Nun.

"He's the general of the armies, and he's one of us!"

"He's one of us," said Nun, "and that means that he's a slave."

"He's son of Pharaoh!" cried Joshua.

"Don't argue with your father," said Anna, Nun's wife, Joshua's mother.

"He'll be Pharaoh himself someday!"

Nun laughed bitterly. "Joshua, he will never be Pharaoh."

"Why not, Papa?"

"Because a valued slave is still a slave." And then he took his paintpot up to the top of the scaffolding and in the most dizzying place he wrote the words of triumph. The name of

Moses was written there, and the name of Hatshepsut, but Nun had seen the places where once the names of Hyksos Pharaohs were written, and then were chiseled and rubbed smooth again as if they had never borne writing. Moses, I put your name here in paint; the chisel will someday tear it out, because no slave's name will be on the monuments of Egypt. And as for your mother, how long will her name last as Pharaoh, once a man again rules this land? All her deeds will be ascribed to her father or her husband or her successor, and she'll be counted as the mere daughter of Pharaoh once again. You are temporary, Moses and Hatshepsut. But I put your names here in my most enduring paint because that is what puts food on the table in my house.

In fifty years, a hundred years, a thousand years, the desert sand will eat away all my painting. So what will it matter if my work gets undone in five years, or ten? Five years or five centuries, the acts of men will not last. Only God will remain, and the works of God, and of man only his soul will withstand the worms to stand before God, and I will stand there and God will say, "What did you do with your life, Nun of the tribe of Ephraim!" And I will say, "I worshiped the Lord God from my first word of the day until my last." And he will say, "What did you paint upon the stone?" And I will say, "Nothing, for all the works of man are nothing." And he will say, "Were you a slave in Egypt?" and I will say, "I was a servant in Egypt, as I would have been a servant in any other land, for a true man of Israel is a servant of God. Who then will make a slave of him who serves God of his own free will?"

Such was the comfort Nun took, such were his thoughts as he painted.

Today he went too long, and it was nearly dark when he came down the scaffolding. All the other artisans had left, and now he remembered that some had called out to him and asked if he was going to keep painting in the dark. Did I answer? he wondered. He could not remember. The moon lighted the path down from the monument, lighted it well enough that he hardly walked more slowly than he did in broad daylight, though darkness and shadow did change the shape of things.

A man fell in step behind him on the path.

"If you're a robber," Nun said, "you're wasting your time. I'm an Israelite and a slave and I carry nothing of value except this paintpot."

"I'm not a robber," said the man. He spoke Hebrew, and Nun relaxed.

"What brings you here so late at night?" Nun asked.

"Going home," said the man.

"What a pointless lie," said Nun.

The man stiffened.

"You obviously live in the palace, and you're going the wrong way."

"Perhaps I'm lost."

"Perhaps you're sneaking out at night, in which case your clothing will give you away." The man was wearing perfect white linens like a servant in the palace.

"Then . . . trade me . . . your clothing," said the man.

Nun stared into the shadow where the man stood and laughed. "My clothing is smudged and filthy with work. There are flecks of paint all over me, and where I sit is covered with dust."

"That's what I want," said the man. "The clothes . . . of a common . . . Israelite."

Nun laughed. "I'm a painter of glyphs. Dirty as they are,

my clothes are far finer than most Israelites can wear. Find a shabbier man."

The man was silent for a moment. "You're here . . . and not a shabbier man."

"Your clothing is too fine for *me*," said Nun.

"Too fine for me . . . to pass through this . . . village . . . unobserved," said the man. "Come, do it quickly."

Nun noticed how he paused, searched for a word. Slow. Strange. From his speech, he might even be a fool, halting, staggering through his sentences. And yet he spoke with authority, as if he were used to command. Who that spoke Hebrew had such a ready sense of his own authority? This could be no one else but Moses himself, slipping out of the palace to move among the Israelites in secret. Well, I'll keep your secret, thought Nun. I'll keep it so well that even *you* don't know that I know it.

"I have a better plan," said Nun. "Let me take you to where the common workmen keep coats against the cold air of the desert night. True slaves' clothing, if that's what you want."

Moses—if that's who it was—followed him to a shed where many old and cast-off things were kept; the leavings of slaves, so valueless that the doorway stood open at all times. In the darkness, the man stripped off his fine linen and put on a tattered tunic and a filthy coat and laughed. "It feels strange on my skin," he said.

"You should have left your linens on under it," said Nun. "Wool itches, when it chafes your skin." Which you'd already know, if you weren't royal.

"Then I should learn what it . . . feels like," said Moses.

"Go where God leads you, then, my friend," said Nun. And silently he added: O God, please stop this poor fool from using that tone of authority when he speaks to Egyptians, for they'll see the clothes, not the man, and this poor fellow's proud bearing cries out for a beating. "Be meek," he said. "Obey everyone."

The man was in such a deep shadow that Nun could not see his face.

"Why is that?" asked Moses.

"You're used to the palace and its ways," said Nun. "Or perhaps the temple, though I've heard of no Israelites serving *there.*"

"The palace," the man grudgingly confirmed.

"Out here, you'll get no deference, now that you've shed that spotless white linen."

"I appreciate the advice," said Moses.

"May it not lead you to destruction," said Nun softly.

"What?"

"A prayer," said Nun. "I prayed for your safety."

A pause. "Thank you."

"Go where God leads you."

Nun walked from the shed and back onto the path. The moon's position meant that he had to pass through a long stretch of shadow. He had to stop and think where the path went, lest he step from it in the darkness and plunge down some cliff or break his leg on some stone.

"You can follow me through here," Nun said. "I think I know my way in the darkness."

Moses laughed. "I memorized the path when it was still light. You, who walk through here every day, you're unsure of how it goes?"

Nun was offended. "I have other things on my mind."

"A man should watch where he's going," said Moses, "so he doesn't . . . bark his shin." Then Moses took Nun by the arm and led *him* through the deep shadows and back out into the moonlight. Not one false step, not even a pause, though they walked with some deliberation.

"You have good eyes and good memory," said Nun.

"I've trained them," said Moses.

"But only God sees far and true, and only God remembers all that should be remembered."

"I'm sure you're right," said Moses.

"You say that but you don't believe it. You're not sure at all."

"I'm sure you . . . believe you're right," said Moses.

"Even when you think you choose for yourself, you still walk the path that God has chosen for you," said Nun. "That's what I teach my son."

"You have a son?" asked Moses. Nun saw with amusement how he kept his face averted. As if it had been his face that gave him away.

"I named him Joshua."

"Deliverer. From what will he . . . deliver you?"

"It's not for me to choose how he'll fulfill his name," said Nun. "Perhaps he'll earn it by delivering *you* out of danger."

Moses laughed again. "Perhaps he might, when I'm old, and he's still young and strong."

"May you live to be old," murmured Nun.

"Another prayer?"

"I pray always," said Nun.

"No wonder the world is so rife with . . . misfortune," said Moses. "God is busy . . . listening to you."

Nun shuddered with the cold that ran through his heart at such casual blasphemy. This man does not know God, thought Nun. Lifted up as you were, Moses, don't you know yet how powerful God is, when he takes hold of the brush of your life? He will make the lines, and your life will flow into the glyphs he makes with you. Until you run dry of ink, until your bristles clot and the painter throws you away. Let some good glyphs come out of you before then, my friend, so God will feel good about the work he did with you in his hand.

※

Moses knew that the painter recognized him, but he couldn't figure out how. Perhaps it was simply a good guess. He meets a Hebrew-speaking man in clothes of perfect whiteness and fine weave and cut — who else could it be but Moses?

Nonsense. That description fit a good number of slaves in the palace. There must be other clues to who he was that he hadn't anticipated. Things that gave him away, that showed he had spent his life in Pharaoh's house. Just because he went on campaign and saw the common people's houses as they were getting pillaged didn't mean that he understood what it felt like, how a peasant might act, the words he might say. Moses was probably speaking in too educated a manner. Or too confidently. Though, now that he thought about it, this man who just helped him find clothing wasn't exactly diffident. If anything, he spoke more boldly than Moses did, and his Hebrew was quite elevated. And if he painted glyphs on stone, he must also be educated in the Egyptian language. What is it about me that makes it so obvious I'm not like him?

So he would keep to the shadows, avoid speaking to anyone. The point was not to prove that he could pass for a common Israelite — why should he? He wasn't Israelite at all, except by accident of birth. No, what mattered was for him to learn what the experience of the Israelites was, to see if Aaron and Miriam actually knew what they were talking about. No, to prove that they were wrong.

But why did he care about that? Why prove them wrong? Why did he let them irritate him and goad him into doing truly stupid things like this? He should give up this mad charade and go back to the palace at once.

"You! Israelite!"

An Egyptian man called out to him. Then he turned and leaned into a doorway and spoke loudly to someone else. "There's a big strong one right here." He turned to Moses again. "Come here! Why should I have to tell you twice?"

Moses answered in Egyptian. "You didn't . . . tell me . . . before." And he didn't come.

The Egyptian looked almost pleased, though there was rage in his eyes as well. "Ah, he thinks he's too big. What is it, Moses comes down the river and suddenly Israelites think they're *all* princes? Well, let me give you a bit of information. If Moses ever left the palace he wouldn't last two minutes, there are plenty of us who'd be glad to finish what the river left undone."

It was only a fleeting temptation for Moses to tell him who he was and watch him cower. Because it occurred to Moses now that he didn't have soldiers at his back or a sword in his hand. He could certainly defeat this Egyptian scoundrel in single combat—but this fellow lived here, and how long would combat between him and an Israelite remain single? They wouldn't believe Moses was really Moses, and even if he did, his boast might be true.

Indeed, the man's remark had already made Moses' venture worthwhile. Despite all the rituals and assurances and declarations, in the eyes of at least some ordinary Egyptians, Moses was still just a jumped-up Israelite.

The man had pulled a stout walking stick from inside his house.

If he lays a hand on me I'll kill him.

Moses immediately repented of the thought. It was Moses

himself who had chosen to come here incognito. This man was showing him what he wanted to learn—that any Egyptian could accost any Israelite and expect obedience. If Moses resisted, not only did he risk his own life, he also risked provoking more hatred and ill-treatment of the Israelite slaves, and that would be wrong. If he was going to be Pharaoh some-day, he had to care more for the people than he did for him-self.

"Sir," said Moses, "forgive me. I . . . didn't hear you and all I . . . meant was . . . I didn't understand your . . . command. Whether you . . . wanted me . . . to come or go."

"Whether you. Wanted me. To come or go!" The Egyptian mocked his halting speech. "Kneel where you are, mudhen."

Moses sank to his knees.

The man raised his walking stick and struck Moses across the shoulders. Again. The pain was sharp and hard, but Moses was well-conditioned and proud and would not bend or show that it hurt. Until it occurred to him that the man was waiting for a sign of capitulation, and if Moses didn't give him one, the beating wasn't going to stop.

"Sir," said Moses. "Please." It hurt him worse to beg than it did to bear the blows of a man who was clearly not as strong as peasants were reputed to be.

The man's wife poked her head out the door. "Oh, you're the bright one, beating him when we need him to carry water."

"I'm not hitting him that hard," said the man. "And you should have seen his eyes! He doesn't know his place."

"He's a dimwit," said the woman. "Didn't you hear the way he talked? He doesn't know what he's doing. Now are you fetching me water or not?"

"Get up," the man said to Moses. And in a few moments Moses found himself being driven to the edge of the river like a beast, and like a beast he was burdened with two heavy jugs of water hanging from a yoke. Moses was strong, but his muscles were trained for battle, not bearing, and in a surprisingly short time the weight overbalanced him and made him stumble.

At once the Egyptian was screaming at him, hitting at his shoulders with his stick. "You clumsy fool! Are you trying to break my water jars? Where am I going to get another?"

"You're going to break them with your own stick, you bonehead!" shouted Moses in reply. He didn't stammer when he spoke in warning.

Moses' daring in calling him a name stopped the man long enough for him to realize that Moses was right, not a drop of water had been spilled but the stick was in danger of breaking a pot.

"Stand up and carry it. You'll pay for those words when we get home."

Moses marveled at the man's stupidity. Did Egyptians really think an Israelite would carry water for them, knowing he'd be beaten when they arrived home?

And then it dawned on him just how humiliated and despairing the Israelites must be, that even knowing they would be punished, they continued to obey and serve, knowing that resistance led to much worse.

There were onlookers now, of course, even though it was dark. Egyptians stood in their doorways, laughing and goading the man on. "Break his leg when you get him home!" "Stripe him good!" "Break your stick on him!" "He's not from around here, who *is* he?"

In other doorways, though, the people were silent. Moses noticed that the silent observers lived in the smaller, shabbier houses. The Israelites, living cheek-by-jowl with the

Egyptians, and yet helpless to help one of their own. Not that Moses needed their help.

Not that he was really one of their own.

I won't come back and get vengeance here, thought Moses. That would be petulant of me. This man is actually helping me to learn what I came out here to learn.

At the house, Moses walked sideways through the door and carefully lowered the yoke until the jars sat on the floor. Only when he got the yoke off his shoulders did the man raise the stick again. But now they were indoors, and Moses *was* trained in combat. He caught the walking stick in one hand and tore it out of the Egyptian's grasp.

The man's wife screeched in fear. The Egyptian himself was slower to understand what had happened, but gradually he realized that a tall, strong Israelite that had just suffered a beating now stood before him with his own heavy walking stick in his hand. Moses could kill him with a blow, the man knew it.

But Moses grasped the walking stick in both hands and broke it across his knee. He had done the same with javelins and lances, stouter weapons than this. Then he handed both halves to the cowering Egyptian. "You can tell your neighbors," said Moses, "that you broke it . . . on my back."

Moses saw understanding finally reach the man's face. Angry as he was, the Egyptian wouldn't dare tell his neighbors that a slave had disarmed him in his own house. He would rather lie and have others think him master of his own house. The Egyptian backed away, holding the two halves of his walking stick, and said, "Get out of here."

"May the Nile bless this house," said Moses, invoking the standard water prayer. "May Anubis pick up someone else's scent."

Apparently they weren't used to having Israelites offer prayers in the Egyptian language—or parodies of prayers, like his Anubis remark. They retreated even farther from him.

"Get out," the woman pleaded. "Please, we're sorry. My husband never meant to hurt you."

"He never . . . cared whether he . . . hurt me or not," said Moses. Then he slipped out into the darkness of the street, stooping over and scurrying away as he imagined a man might do who had just had a walking stick broken across his shoulders.

In the night there wasn't much else to see. People were inside their homes, except for those who were at taverns, or were slipping home from visits—not much traffic, just a few people who regarded him with suspicion, mostly because of his height and obvious strength. The woolen clothing itched maddeningly, especially as the night breeze cooled the sweat he had worked up, carrying the water from the river. He wanted to get rid of it and run home, naked if he had to, run home and put back on the white clean linens that he was entitled to as Pharaoh's son. He had never known how much those linens were like armor, protecting him from blows.

Coward, he told himself. You came to learn and you're learning. Hatshepsut stopped the Egyptians from killing Israelites at birth, but Aaron and Miriam were right this far: The bondage of Israel was still real and hard to bear. They were right to wish for freedom.

So . . . I've learned that, and now I should go home.

You've learned nothing, he told himself. A little touch of helplessness. Does Aaron have some different way of walking and talking when he's out here among the people? In the palace he puts on arrogance as if it were his own skin; but out here, surely that attitude would earn him many a beating! No,

Aaron must also have learned some style of cringing that would persuade surly Egyptians not to beat him.

But instead of gloating, instead of wishing to see Aaron humiliated like that, Moses was glad he had never seen it. Only a few hours ago in the palace Moses would have laughed at the thought of Aaron being put in his place. Now, though, Moses had a different perspective. He wasn't an Egyptian out here, dressed like this. He wasn't an Egyptian at all, in the eyes of the Egyptians.

I can never be Pharaoh, he realized. Mother's as foolish as I have been, to think we could bring it off. They're already restive under the rule of a woman. Give the double crown to an Israelite, and there'll be mutiny, revolt . . . bloodshed. Moses might put down such revolts, but at what cost? Egypt had suffered under the Hyksos rulers. They would believe that through sheer trickery it had happened to them again. They would not bear being ruled by a slave, and that's how they would see Moses' ascension to the throne.

He found a heap of straw behind a stable. It seemed clean enough, by moonlight. He lay down on it, pulled some over his legs and body for warmth, and lay there thinking about how he could tell this to Hatshepsut, and what they might do. Tuthmose had to die at once, of course. He was too dangerous to leave alive. One of the other sons. But how galling, to let any of Mutnefert's grandchildren ascend the throne.

No other choice, thought Moses. For the good of Egypt, for Mother's good, I have to step aside and let someone else be named heir. I can teach him, perhaps. Train him to be the Pharaoh Mother always meant me to be.

Feeling noble, wise, and self-sacrificing, Moses went to sleep.

And woke, still in darkness, though the first greying of dawn was visible in the east. What had wakened him?

"You broke my eggs!" came the cry again. "They were worth more than your life, you filthy old slave!"

Moses rose quickly from his bed of straw and saw an old Israelite man on his knees, a basket of eggs spilled at his feet. Why so many eggs?

"What will I feed my guests?" demanded the Egyptian. A tavern owner.

The old man mumbled something, a plea for forgiveness. No, a prayer.

"Hear, O Israel," he murmured.

Another blow fell.

"The Lord our God."

Another.

"The Lord is one."

He fell over onto the ground, barely able to curl himself into a ball. It wouldn't help him, for Moses could see that the Egyptian was poised to land the next blow hard on the old man's bald head.

It couldn't be borne. Moses took the cudgel from the man's hand as easily as he had taken the walking stick the night before.

But this man didn't shrink away. He bulled right into Moses and knocked him down, sending the cudgel flying.

It took only a moment for Moses to recover, and before the tavernkeeper could get to his feet to fetch the cudgel, Moses tripped him and then leapt upon him, covered his mouth with his hand. "Make no sound," said Moses, "and I'll let you live."

But the man wasn't a screamer. His hand came up with a knife in it. Moses was trained for this. It took no thought at all. As the man stabbed at him, Moses caught his hand and drove it downward into the man's own heart. He died in a moment, having never made a sound.

Moses didn't mean to kill him. He was a soldier, one who fought with his own hands and trained hard with his men, and his reflexes had taken over.

But he didn't have any reflexes for this situation. One night living as an Israelite and he had killed somebody. What would be the consequences? If Moses ran away, the fact would remain that an Egyptian had been killed while beating an Israelite. The old man that Moses had tried to save might be blamed for it. Worse, it might trigger a riot, with Egyptians killing their helpless Israelite neighbors.

It's a good thing I wasn't named Joshua! Look at the sort of deliverance I've brought to Israel.

The body had to be hidden. Let them think he had wandered off and fallen in the river.

Moses hoisted the body up onto his back, hooking the dead man's arms with his own arms so the blood would run down the corpse and none of it would get on Moses beyond what was already on his hands. The river wasn't far. Moses' first thought was to take him there. But no, that would be insane, the body would float and be found. Instead Moses carried him the other way, toward the desert. No one saw him, he was sure of that. The farmland was only a narrow strip near the water; he reached desert sand very soon. With his bare hands Moses dug furiously down into the base of a low dune, then rolled the body into the depression he had made. It was a simple matter to pull down sand from the dune to cover him. The prevailing winds blew from the west. The dune would keep shifting over the body and bury it under tons of sand. By the time the body emerged from the other side of the dune, no one would remember that the tavernkeeper had ever lived, or even have a guess as to whose the body was or how he died.

It was sunrise when Moses got to the river to wash the blood off his hands and lose the knife in the water.

I've learned enough, Moses thought. A man has died. Perhaps I saved the old Israelite's life in the process, but that doesn't change the fact that my being here is a mistake. I'm an oaf out here, I don't know how to survive as an Israelite.

He took off his sandals and began to jog along the road toward the palace.

"You keep your wife's nose out of my wife's business and I'll *leave* her alone!"

Moses heard the argument before he rounded the corner.

"It's everybody's business!" came the answer. "I think it should be *your* business, the things your wife is doing!"

Moses arrived at the scene just as one man roared, picked up a much smaller man, and hurled him against the rough brick wall of an Israelite hovel. A woman screamed and ran to cover him with her body.

"Nobody calls my wife an adulteress and—"

Moses shoved him and sent him sprawling before he could lay a hand on the woman.

"Doesn't Israel . . . have enough enemies, without . . . fighting each other?" Moses demanded.

The man picked himself up off the ground, sizing Moses up as he did.

"What, Moses, are you going to kill me like you did that Egyptian?"

Moses was stunned. Who could have seen him? Who could have known who he was? And how could word have spread so quickly?

He knew the answers as soon as he thought of the questions. The old man who was being beaten must have seen Moses kill the tavernkeeper. And the glyph-painter who gave him these clothes last night, he knew who Moses was, and word would have spread, at least among the Israelites, that Moses was abroad that night, along with a description of exactly how he was dressed. So when a tall stranger, dressed as he was reported to be dressed, did the unthinkable and fought with an Egyptian and killed him, there would be no question it was him.

The real issue now was whether he could trust Israelites to keep his secret.

"You aren't fit to judge me," the man said scornfully. "You're an Egyptian, not an Israelite. Go back to your palace and sleep with that Ethiopian whore you brought back with you."

And that was his answer. There were doubtless plenty of Israelites who didn't think they owed Moses any loyalty at all.

Without another halting word, Moses returned to the road and kept on running. The taunts of the Israelite filled his ears long after he couldn't possibly still be hearing his actual voice.

❋

The story reached the house of Aaron before he could leave for the day's work. He laughed aloud in triumph when he heard it.

But Miriam soon came from Mother's house and she wasn't laughing. "We're all in danger now," she said.

"We're always in danger," Aaron said. "But now Moses has cast his lot with us! I knew if we could provoke him into coming out among the people, he'd remember who he really is!"

"And what is he really?" asked Miriam.

"An Israelite!"

"Aaron, you poor goat-brained boy," she said, "he doesn't even know what an Israelite is."

"He killed an Egyptian who was beating an Israelite. It's the beginning of our resistance, the beginning of our revolt!"

"Hold off on your war plans," said Miriam. "This is the opposite of the right way for your revolt to begin. Who will be Moses' army? Who will obey him, when he's now proven himself to be one of us?"

"We will!"

"Yes, there are so many trained Israelite soldiers. And we have so many bows and arrows, so many trained spearmen."

Aaron looked at her with consternation. "Then why did God make this happen? What was this morning all about?"

"It was the first step," said Miriam. "God has a lot of work to do with that boy before Moses is truly useful."

# S a n d

Hatshepsut heard Moses' story without letting herself show any emotion. He told his tale the same way. Wanting to observe the people — no, he said *his* people, she noticed that, it stung her — he borrowed Israelite clothing and wandered out among them, passing for a slave. An old man being beaten, Moses had to intervene, though he had no soldiers behind him, no visible authority. Had he come back later, he could have punished the wrongdoer, but no, he had to act in the moment, had to stop that moment of mistreatment as if that one slave had some particular value. Oh, stupid, stupid, the whole venture from the beginning. Pharaohs are not prepared to be common men.

She heard him out. She kept her silence. Even when he was done with his sorry confession, she kept still.

"Mother," he whispered.

"Am I?" she asked.

"Are you what?"

"Your mother?"

"You are my Pharaoh," he said. "And my mother. You lifted me out of the water."

"But you plunged back into it today."

"It was sand I was into, up to my armpits."

She was not amused. "You killed one of my people," she said.

"He was about to kill another of your people."

"No, of *your* people."

He did not protest, he did not deny. He only looked away, ashamed.

"Yes," she said, "today you chose. Today they took my son away from me."

"I was your true son," he said.

I *was* your son, he said. I *was*.

"You taught me not to . . . tolerate injustice," said Moses. "Didn't you?"

"I taught you that it was vital to preserve your own position first, so you would have the power to help others later."

"But if I always . . . preserve myself first, when will I ever dare to act?"

"So. You acted."

Again silence filled them and spilled over into the room.

She saw him now as if for the first time. Not the child anymore, so bright, so eager to talk to her after a day of the business of government, asking about this, commenting about that. Not the adolescent, either, fierce in his weapons practice, sweating from exercise in the blazing sun, smelling more like a man than poor Tuthmose II ever had, and yet she didn't send him away to bathe, indeed wouldn't let him go, she made him stay and talk to her about what he was learning as a warrior, things she had never learned herself. But neither of those sons of hers was there, they were gone, not dead but buried anyway, lost within the body of this man who, though stricken with grief and fear and remorse nevertheless stood tall and unbending, unwilling to mourn for what he could not alter. Or perhaps not mourning. Perhaps not remorseful, either. He had made his choice. He had been her son, but was no longer. The Israelites had kidnapped her little boy, her strong young warrior, and in their place left this changeling. They were his people now, not Egypt.

Nonsense. She refused to accept such a ludicrous notion. He was young. He had been overcome by the romantic notion of going out among the people in disguise. He had cast himself in the hero role and now wanted to play it to the hilt, the way young men always did, but if she took charge of this, she could bring him back to his senses. She did not have to surrender so easily. He was still her Moses, once he woke up to how irrevocably his future would be decided today.

"What I must do," Hatshepsut said, "is declare you to be Pharaoh right now, today. The way my father did with me. Raise you up beside me. Affirm that you were doing my will when you went out among the people. That you did justice in my name."

"No," said Moses.

"Why not?" she said.

As if it were a lesson, as if he were the child again, trying to prove what he had learned, he recited his answer. "Your position is already weak. A woman as Pharaoh. And waiting for his moment is a son of a male Pharaoh who has already been consecrated."

"I'll have him strangled at once."

"Strangle an Egyptian Pharaoh in order to . . . protect an Israelite? Yes, that will . . . firm up your position, won't it."

"Don't be sarcastic with me."

"Mother, it was already impossible. That's what neither of us understood. Even before I . . . dodged out of the palace, the Egyptian people had . . . made up their mind. If I ever became Pharaoh, they would regard me as a hated enemy, an overseer from . . . foreign lands. You, your father, and the . . . gods might regard me as a true son of Pharaoh, but the . . . people don't. I'm still a son of slaves to them. That's why I call the Israelites my . . . people—because *your* people have . . . determined that that's all I can ever be."

She shook her head. "It was a change inside *you*. It was a choice *you* made."

He said nothing. This stubborn stranger. Who was he, and what had he done with her child?

"You've walked away from injustice before, when it served no purpose to intervene," she said. "When you raised your hand to save that old man, you chose him to be your father instead of your subject."

"I never meant to hurt you," said Moses.

She laughed at him. "Hurt me? You have no power to hurt a god."

"Then it won't hurt you when I leave."

The words cut her so deeply she couldn't breathe.

"Where?" she whispered.

"Exile. I won't tell you where because it's your . . . duty as Pharaoh to hunt down a slave who . . . killed an Egyptian."

"I never said that! Such a law could never apply to you!"

"Either I was the son of Pharaoh or I was the . . . son of slaves. If you affirm me as a son of Pharaoh, you'll fall. If you declare me to be the son of slaves, by my own choice, by my own act, then you'll . . . show yourself to be the true Pharaoh, loving Egypt more than your own son."

"You are my general," she said. "You are my right hand. You have cut off my hand."

"You'll find another."

"The only other man who can fill that role is Tuthmose, and he can only do it if I affirm his consecration and raise him to his father's place."

"Then do it."

"He'll betray me."

"Not tomorrow, and not next week. You'll have time."

"Time will work for him, not for me."

"I can't help that, Mother! Do you think I don't want to undo what I did today? But I can't. I've already . . . betrayed you. If you try to save me you'll . . . destroy yourself now."

"The law obliges me to have you killed," she said.

"Do you think I haven't . . . considered that?" said Moses. "If that's your . . . decision, I'll make no effort to resist you. Do your will with me."

"Tell me why Pharaoh shouldn't execute justice upon you."

"Because I just got home from Ethiopia. Did the gods give me . . . victory there or not?"

"I would have to accuse you of plotting directly against me."

"No doubt Tuthmose and Isis would be happy to . . . tell the world how I conspired to . . . kill their beloved father and husband and arranged for his . . . murder while I was still coming down the river from Ethiopia."

"I don't need their perjury!" cried Hatshepsut. "It's me you killed! My body you buried there in the sand! I won't last ten years, five years with you gone! You fool! You disloyal, selfish, slave-hearted, ungrateful, *stupid* . . ." Hatshepsut was shocked to find so much rage in her own heart. She was about to lose the only person she had ever loved besides her father and brothers. Only this time it wasn't the gods taking him, or a murderous concubine. The boy had done it to himself, had done it to her, and it infuriated her. "Take a chariot to whatever border fort you choose. Take a letter with you, giving orders for your own execution if you attempt to return, but forbidding them to pursue you into the desert. Give it to the captain of the border guard as you leave. I'll put my seal on it."

"You'll let me write the orders for my own . . . banish-
ment?"

"Aren't you listening? You'll write the order for your death.
That's the sentence I pass on you. Death. For treason. You
deserve it."

"I know."

"You have killed me, Moses. I raised you up and saved
your life, and you—"

"You shouldn't have."

She burst into tears. "Yes, I should! I would never have
been Pharaoh without you. The gods gave you to me and gave
me a kingdom in the same moment. Because I had you I had
a son and so I could be Pharaoh. The gods put me in this place,
and now they take it all away from me, they take you away
from me."

"It isn't the gods, Mother. I did it."

"You—oh, yes, you planned it this way from the start, is
that it? Your spies told you that a tavernkeeper would be beating an old Israelite before dawn this morning and you chose to
be there alone in time to kill him with your bare hands—"

"The gods do not . . . control my life!"

"And you paraded in front of the walls of Saba in order to
provoke that poor foolish girl into betraying her family, her
kingdom, out of love for you—the gods had no hand in that,
either!"

"My choices, my . . . mistakes, Mother."

"No, Moses. It took the rage of a god to make a mess this
terrible."

Again Moses looked away from her.

"What!" she demanded. "What is it you're not saying,
when you avert your eyes that way!"

"Miriam told me that the Israelite . . . God was controlling my destiny."

"Oh, now, *there's* a powerful god, every single person in the world who worships him is a slave, you know *he's* the mighty one."

Moses turned to her with anguish in his eyes. "Set them free, Mother."

"What!"

"Get them out of Egypt."

"Who?" Tuthmose? Isis? What was he saying?

"The Israelites, of course! It's *their* god who's doing all this. Get them out of here and he'll . . . leave you alone. Maybe even reward you by . . . protecting your throne."

His words astonished her. "When did you become a believer in this barbaric tribal superstition?"

He looked embarrassed. "If it isn't the Israelite god, then what . . . god is it that's . . . taken control of my . . . life?"

So he wasn't serious about the Israelite deity. She was relieved. "You know I can't get rid of the Israelites," she said. "I thought of it myself before you learned to speak, and my father explained it to me, and I taught it to you. The labor that they do can't be replaced. Every Israelite laborer frees an Egyptian to be a soldier. Besides, the people wouldn't stand for letting them out of their bondage."

He turned and looked her in the eye, and his voice was suddenly different, stronger. "Mother, Egypt will recover from the . . . loss of the Israelites more easily than it will recover from . . . keeping them."

His tone frightened her. The change in him. Was he in fact possessed by some god? "What kind of nonsense is this? Where do you get such foolish notions?"

It seemed that Moses only then realized what he had just

said. "I don't know," he said. "I just . . . it just came . . . to me."
He laughed nervously. "My brother . . . thinks he's a revolu-
tionary, my . . . sister thinks she's a prophet. Madness runs in
my . . . family."

"When I die," said Hatshepsut, "it won't be the Israelite
god who kills me. It'll be Tuthmose III."

Moses shuddered. "Don't call him that."

"By this time tomorrow it will be his name," she said.
"After what you've done, I'll be so discredited that I'll have no
choice, you know that. I'll need him to legitimize my own rule.
And then it's just a matter of time." She looked at the pain in
this beautiful stranger's face and it broke her heart. For there
was no sign of remorse now. He pitied her, but he would do
nothing to help her. "Get out!" she cried. "Don't make me look
at you!"

He took a few steps away from her, then rushed to her,
knelt before the throne, clung to her legs, laid his head on her
lap, and wept as he murmured, "Mother, Mother, I'm so
sorry." For a few moments she petted his cheek, his hair,
remembering the child, remembering the joy of having him
around her always, the symbol of her power, yes, but more
than that, the gift of the gods to him, the child who could
extend her rule of Egypt beyond her own death, and now he's
ruining everything, the stupid, stupid . . ."

"Get out!" she wailed again.

He rose to his feet.

"I sentence you to death!" she whispered furiously. "Let
your chariot *fly* if you want to live!"

He bowed to her; tears dropped from his eyes as he did.
Then he turned and strode on those mighty legs that had once
toddled along these halls as she held his hand. On those legs
he walked to the door and out of her life.

"You've murdered me!" she wailed after him. And she felt that it was already true. Not some future event, not some day when Tuthmose III would decide he was strong enough and strangle her—poison would not be *his* way—but now, right now, she was dead, her heart was dead within her because her Moses, her true son was gone.

❀

Moses took a charioteer with him because without one he would look like a man of no rank, and for the sake of a swift journey he needed to look like what he was, the leader of the armies of Egypt on an urgent errand. He had to race faster than any other messenger so that the news of his crime and his exile could not possibly precede him. He could not stop to sleep. Last night when he pulled straw over himself to stay warm, he had never imagined that it would be the last night of sleep he ever had in Egypt.

His one consolation as his chariot flew over the road toward the head of the gulf of Suez was this: At least Aaron and Miriam wouldn't get their way, either. If he couldn't fulfil Hatshepsut's dreams, at least he'd have the satisfaction of knowing he wouldn't help Aaron or Miriam fulfil their mad plans, either.

"Is there to be a battle at the Red Sea?" asked his charioteer. "Are the people of Canaan attacking us?"

But Moses explained nothing, just stood behind the driver, holding on to the sides of the chariot so he didn't fall as it bounced along the smooth royal road.

❀

"The fool!" shouted Aaron. "He saves one old man's life and gives up the chance to free a nation! He flees into the desert when he should have led a revolution!"

Miriam and Jochabed let him rage. He ranted so loudly
that soon half the Israelites in the village were gathered around
their house, some of them remonstrating with him to be careful, careful, lest the rage of Hatshepsut descend on his house,
on their village. It took hours but at last his rage spent itself.
His clothing torn—for he tore it in his grief at the news of
Moses' exile—he finally staggered away from his mother's
house, the people clearing a path for him, for fear that if they
touched a man of such fire their hands would burn.

"He's so selfish," said Miriam, when the last echoes of
Aaron's voice finally left the corners of the house. "All he
thinks about is the collapse of his own foolish plans, when his
own mother weeps because she'll never see her younger son
again."

Only then did Miriam realize that Jochabed, though
weeping, was not grieving. No, she was *smiling.*

"Mother, have you gone mad?"

"Not today," said Jochabed. "Give me a few more years of
scenes like this, and I'm sure I will be, but for today, no, not
mad at all."

"Why are you smiling?"

"Why shouldn't I be?" said Jochabed.

"Because your younger son is now in exile!"

"How can he be in exile, when God is with him? God is his
native country, Miriam, and as long as God goes with him he is
home everywhere."

"But you won't see him," said Miriam.

"Ah, but you forget, *we're* the ones in exile, not Moses.
*We're* the ones who are servants in another people's homeland."

"No, I haven't forgotten that," said Miriam. "Are you really
*that* faithful, Mother, that you can be *happy* when your son
loses his high station and becomes a fugitive?"

"High station?" said Jochabed. "I never cared about his high station. I put him on the water to save his life, not to make him Pharaoh. That was *God's* plan, and I'm sure God is simply taking the next step."

"The next step to where? Moses is *gone.*"

"What a foolish question!" said Jochabed. "You really are a foolish girl, Miriam."

Stung, Miriam started to leave the room. She stopped when her mother started saying something. Only Mother wasn't speaking to her. She was murmuring as if comforting a baby in a cradle. She was talking to Moses.

"God's hand is strange to us, Moses," she said. "He cares nothing for the moment, nothing for the feeble ambitions of men and women. He sees the road that flows onward forever."

She was almost chanting. Her words ebbed and flowed like the songs the old men sang, tales of Abram and Sarai, of the father at Mount Moriah preparing to sacrifice his son, of the servant of Abraham meeting Rebecca at the well, of the rivals Jacob and Esau and the seven years of service, of Joseph the dreamer and his many-colored coat. The words came out of her with the same holiness. Miriam's eyes were opened. A woman could find a song of God in her heart.

"You'll be driven until you learn to freely reach for his hand," said Jochabed. "God has shaped you to the man you are. He made you choose which people yours would be. But you yourself chose to keep the covenant."

Was that what Moses did this morning, when he killed a man and buried his body in the sand, thinking no one saw? Was he somehow choosing? Or was he merely driven by accident and impulse? Miriam tried to understand.

"And now God's hand will make you the man of God to set this people free."

Miriam shuddered with a thrill of joy. Ah, Lord, is this prophecy coming through my mother's lips?

"Look for his hand in the road behind," said Jochabed. "And when you've learned to see it, then look for his hand in the road ahead. Take his hand, follow his hand. Only in his hand will you be free."

And then her chanting stopped and Mother broke down and wept. "Only God will bring you back to me," she said. "O Lord, bring him back to me."

I fear that's a prayer that God won't grant you, Mother. When Moses returns, you won't be here to see it.

But *I* will.

Miriam knew this with her whole heart. She wasn't sure whether it was God promising it to her, or her promising it to God, but she knew that it would come true. Moses would return, and Miriam would be there to greet him.

"I'll be ready," she whispered to God. "As far as my voice will reach, people will hear it every day, every day from now until he comes again. God will not forget his people. He will send someone to save us from bondage and take us to the land that was promised to our fathers. We'll *all* be ready for him when he comes."

＊

The wind was rising when Moses reached the border fort. An east wind, a storm wind, raising sand into roiling clouds, into a fog of sharp, cutting grains.

"What are you thinking of, Great One?" asked the poor confused captain of the border guard. He had only seen Moses once, in a parade several years ago, but he knew his reputation, knew of the triumph in Ethiopia. "There's nothing so urgent out there that you have to risk death by traveling into that sand!"

"You think not?" asked Moses. For a moment he thought of giving the man his orders now—but he didn't know this captain and wasn't sure how he'd react if he knew that Moses had fallen from power. Some men would think that they might curry favor with Pharaoh by killing Pharaoh's fleeing enemy. And despite all that had happened, Moses was determined not to get himself killed. His life might have no value to the gods—to God, if that's who was destroying him—but it still had value to Moses, if only to keep God from having the satisfaction of breaking his pride.

What was this god, anyway, this God of Abraham, Isaac, and Jacob? Nothing like the gods of Egypt, that was certain. No majesty like Horus in flight, no grace of life-giving Isis, no resurrecting power like Osiris in the underworld, no light like Amon. This god was more like the madcap gods of the Cretans, who had built their city in the Nile delta under the protection of the Pharaohs and there worshiped a bizarre pantheon of feuding adolescents that they called gods. Such disorder! If those gods were real, it was a wonder mountains weren't shifting in waves like the sea, a wonder that down didn't switch places with up three times a day. That sort of primitive, uncivilized god was as barbaric as the people who worshiped him. The gods of Egypt had dignity and well-ordered kingdoms. They did not quarrel among themselves. Those who studied the Book of the Dead knew the orderly passage into the next life. Egypt's gods asked little and gave much: order, safety, predictability.

The Israelite god didn't even have the passion and fire of the golden calf that had won a devoted following during the Hyksos domination—including more than a few Israelites, who envied the divine madness of those who danced before the calf. No, the Israelite god did nothing but reach out and

make bizarre, pointless changes in Moses' life. Including forcing him to flee into a sandstorm.

If you meant to swallow me up in the sand, why wasn't I
the one to die this morning, and let that tavernkeeper bury me
instead of the other way around? The gods are all tricksters,
bringing up winds out of strange quarters, sometimes warm
and sweet, sometimes filled with rain, sometimes filled with
sand like a billion knives. Abraham was promised that his
descendants would be like sand. But which sand? The inert
sand by the water, moving only when the sea roiled it in the
turbulent belly of the wave? The dry sand of the desert, life-
less and sterile until the wind picked it up and hurled it at
stone with such force that the stone gave way, bit by bit, before
the onslaught? It hardly mattered either way. Gods had their
way with men.

A day ago, a year ago, Moses would have laughed at such
thoughts. He thought he could build walls so strong that the
wind of change could never get in at him. He let them fly
wherever they'd blow. He was like a stone, which the wind
could never pick up and move. Others ran around, panicking
whenever change came upon them. But Moses was unmoved.
Immovable.

And now he had become a grain of sand himself, picked up
and hurled wherever the wind of God chose. Hatshepsut and
Jochabed had both taught him that he was destined for greatness. But no, he was just another grain of sand among the billion grains, to be flung against stone whenever some god or
another decided. He had no destiny. Only the whims of the
gods. Or of God. Did it matter to the sand which breeze
picked it up?

Well, here's some news for you, God, or gods: You can kill
me, but until you do, you don't own me. I make my own

choices, go my own way. The storm will pass. The sand drops back down to the floor of the desert. And then you'll find out I was never sand at all, but a seed, and out of death I'll make life. You can't break me. And whatever plan you have in mind, you can't make me.

❁

Nun came down from his scaffolding, the paint still wet on the stone behind him. As soon as he reached the bottom, the stonecutters climbed up to where he had been, and began chiseling off the inscription he had been painting. The account of Moses' "birth" from the river, a gift of the gods to Hatshepsut: the story, no longer true, had to be expunged from memory. What did it matter that the people of this time knew the truth, that an Israelite had lived to adulthood as a son of Pharaoh, that he had conquered Ethiopia? In a generation it would be gossip; in two generations, legend; in three, myth; and in four, forgotten. Only what was on the stone would last, and so Moses had to be erased, if not from this time, then from eternity.

This meant nothing to Nun, for even though he stirred the paintpot and plied the brush, he despised the illusions of the Egyptians. They thought they could touch eternity with inscriptions on stone, but what man chiseled off in a day, God would chisel off in a hundred thousand days, using the irresistible chisel of sand in the wind. But what God engraved in the hearts of his chosen people, that would *never* be forgotten.

At home that night, Nun took his little Joshua on his knee and had him recite again the words from the stone. Joshua had it like a song. And other songs, too, the tale of the garden, the tale of Abraham and Isaac, Lot and the angels in Sodom, Noah and the ark. And in other houses, those tales were also known and told, perhaps in slightly different words, perhaps including some different passages, mixing things up a little (or was Nun's version mixed up?), but substantially the same tale. Including the tale of Moses, who proved that, once redeemed from bondage, a son of Abraham could be the greatest of princes. Pharaoh, angry or fearful, cut the name of Moses from the stone, but this only engraved his name deeper in the hearts of Israel.

"I will grow up and kill Egyptians the way Moses did!" cried Joshua.

"No!" said Nun sharply. "Be wise! When Moses killed an Egyptian, God abandoned him and let him be driven out. If Egyptians are to die, God can kill them. What God needs from us is to keep the covenant of Abraham."

Joshua, who had seen the circumcision of his baby brother, looked at his father with wide eyes, and his hand drifted inadvertently below his waist.

"That is only the beginning of obedience," said Nun. "As Jacob obeyed, we must obey. Did he kill his father-in-law when he kept him unfairly in bondage? No, he labored more, and won two wives and a dozen sons. When Joseph saw visions, did he conceal them from his brothers to save his own life? No, he spoke boldly what God gave him to say, and lived a life of marvels."

"Did Moses disobey God?" said Joshua.

"Who knows?" said Nun. "What God sends into the desert, God can bring back from the desert."

# S h e e p

When Zeforah and her sisters were younger, it used to take three of them at least to move the stone cap off the well. Now any but Keturah could do it alone, if they had to, and if sheer stubbornness could move rock, Keturah could probably open the well without using her hands.

Still, though she was fully grown now, Zeforah didn't enjoy moving the capstone. Despite the calluses on her hands, it was rough work, and she often scraped herself till her fingers bled. But that was why she insisted on moving the stone herself, and without help. No reason for the others to get scraped up before they had to. Soon enough Father would bow to the inevitable and find some miserable specimen of masculinity for her to marry. A few sheep for a dowry. Standards were low in this clan of the Midianites. There were so few women that Zeforah could almost pass for a beauty. But no matter how few men there were, not a one of them could pass for a wit.

And when Zeforah said things like this, Father always said, "Well, who's telling you to get married? It'll cost me a ram and several ewes, and after the wedding I'll have one less daughter to help me."

"One less mouth to feed," someone else would say—usually Sarah. And Keturah would leap to Zeforah's defense until there was a pile of sisters on the rugs fighting with each other like swarming bees. In vain did Zeforah explain to Keturah that those smart remarks of Sarah's meant nothing. "Why get upset when it doesn't bother me?" To which Keturah would reply, "That's why." Neither of them seemed able to get the other to comprehend what she was talking about.

It was an odd combination—Zeforah, the eldest, and, as her constant companion, Keturah, the youngest, a sweet ten-year-old who had a mouth that could provoke an angel to rage, Zeforah was sure of it. Hadn't she spent Keturah's entire life getting her out of trouble with the other girls? And yet it wasn't because Keturah meant to be provocative. She just had a way of saying exactly the thing that would get a rise out of Hamar or Sarah, and then Zeforah would have to intervene. "Try to curb your tongue around the prickly ones," Zeforah insisted, "so they won't kill you. It would confuse Father terribly, old as he is, if he had to learn to count to some number other than seven."

"Then does that mean you'll never marry?" asked Keturah.

"I didn't say that."

"Then Father will have to learn to count to six, after your husband takes you away."

"My plan is to take my husband away from wherever he was and get him started working with me as a shepherd."

"It won't be the same," said Keturah.

To which Zeforah had no reassuring answer. When she married, there would be a separate household, and Keturah wouldn't find Zeforah so ready to talk to her. Especially if she were to be married to someone from another clan, which Father kept threatening to do whenever Zeforah argued with him.

Marriage. Zeforah refused to think any more about it today. Instead she put her energy into moving the capstone off the well and drawing up water for the sheep. The other girls were keeping the flock nearby, not that it took much effort. Even sheep were clever enough to know when they were thirsty and to realize that only water would satisfy them.

But not clever enough to line up nicely and take turns. It could be quite a job making sure each animal got plenty to drink. As Zeforah and her sisters threaded their way among the jostling sheep, Keturah began to chatter. "Sheep are stupid!"

"It took you this long to realize it?" said Sarah. Of course it was Sarah.

"Well, if sheep are stupid then lambs must be stupider because they have to grow up to be sheep, right?" said Keturah, oblivious to Sarah's snideness.

Hamar started talking in baby talk to a lamb which was not really a baby anymore. "Does this poor little lambkin need to cry now? Did mean old Keturah hurt his little feelings?"

"Am I the only one who's insulted by this?" said Keturah, addressing the others as if she were trying to make a point at a village council.

"Hamar's just making a joke," said Zeforah.

"Not Hamar, who listens to *her?*" said Keturah. "I mean Father."

The others were baffled now. "When did Father insult anybody?" Zeforah asked.

"Today, when we left! Every day! Every morning, every night! He calls us his little *lambs.*"

The others burst out laughing. "He's always done that," said Hamar.

"But why?" said Keturah. "Sheep are stupid, smelly, filthy, clumsy—"

"Oh," said Sarah, "*that* part only started after you were born."

"What does Father *mean?*" Keturah insisted.

Zeforah didn't answer, though she had had precisely this conversation with Father many years ago and knew what his response would be. She wanted to hear what the others would come up with.

"Look at Zeforah being wise," said Sarah. "She thinks she knows the right answer and wants us to make fools of ourselves before she makes a speech out of it."

As always, Sarah found exactly the thing to say that would leave Zeforah completely flummoxed.

"Well, am I right or what?" said Sarah.

"I really *do* want to know what you think," said Zeforah.

"Come on," said Sarah. "Here, I'll help you start: 'Father says. . . . ' Now you go on from there."

Keturah, who had endured Sarah's sneers as if she didn't hear them, now sprang hotly to Zeforah's defense. "If Zeforah tells us what Father says it's because she sees us forgetting the rules. And because she's too modest to speak as if the ideas came from her."

"Someone has a little disciple," said Hamar.

"Water the sheep," said Zeforah. "I didn't ask the questions and I didn't offer any answers, so I don't know why we're arguing about the way I boss you all around since I hadn't even gotten started."

"All I want," said Keturah, "is to know why Father calls us sheep!"

"Because Father *likes* sheep!" Hamar said. "And Father likes them because he doesn't come out here and watch them every day, he sits home in the shade copying those scrolls, over and over again. So for him sheep are just something he shears and occasionally butchers or sells. The stink of them isn't in his nose all the time."

Zeforah, already stung, kept her silence despite how angry she was at Hamar's diatribe. Besides, Hamar was looking at her, waiting for a retort, which made it almost fun to smile benignly and say nothing.

"He doesn't shear *us*," said Keturah. "He doesn't butcher us either."

"But he'd sell us off one by one, if he could only find a taker for Zeforah," said Sarah sweetly.

"A blind man whose first three wives are all old," suggested Asa. "Because Zeforah is so handy with the chores."

"Another bird chirps," said Hamar.

"Don't tell me you're criticizing Asa because she doesn't talk as much as you, Hamar," said Zeforah.

"Nobody talks as much as Hamar," said Sarah.

"Except you," said Asa.

"All right, who taught the younger ones to talk!" said Sarah. "Why can't they all be more like—sheep!"

"I didn't say a thing," said Dinah.

"You never do," said Hamar. "You don't think of anything to say until you're falling asleep at night. I hear you murmuring all the clever things you didn't think of during the day."

"Enough," said Zeforah.

"Watch out, everybody!" cried Sarah. "Here it comes! 'Father says. . . .'"

Zeforah had to bite her lip to keep from saying what she had been about to say. For it did, indeed, begin with "Father says."

"I wish I were as smart as Zeforah," said Hamar, her voice drippingly sweet. "She always knows just how much is enough."

And then, as always, when Zeforah was just on the verge of losing her temper, she felt something give way inside her and the anger just flowed away. She looked at her sisters, saw that Hamar was cross and Sarah never really felt in good health, so that every day was hard for her, and the younger girls were trying to decide whether being grown up meant acting like Hamar or acting like Zeforah and—and Zeforah loved them anyway. It was better sometimes to be alone than to be with them, true enough, but with a job like this, watering the sheep, it took all their hands, and if being snippy was how they entertained themselves, Zeforah could endure it.

"Oh, look. Now Zeforah is going to be *sweet*," said Hamar nastily.

Zeforah only smiled and looked away. Looked, in fact, for Keturah, who was angrily—but silently—untangling a bramble bush from a lamb's wool. "You see how the sheep follow each other along a path," said Zeforah.

"I think a lesson is coming!" cried Sarah.

Keturah was listening, though.

"Father wants us to follow him that way. He steps here, so . . ."

"So I step there," said Keturah.

And at the sound of Keturah's voice, the others fell silent, for they did, in fact, love their baby sister and didn't want to make her feel bad. Zeforah sometimes envied Keturah the comfort of being youngest. Everyone had held her as a baby and loved her; nobody had ever felt that way toward Zeforah, except Mother, and she was gone.

"How can I follow Father on the path of life?" said Keturah earnestly. "He's a man, a reader of books, a leader, a ruler, a judge, and I'm only a girl and the best I can ever be is—"

"Is a daughter of God," said Zeforah. "Father can teach you, but he can't save you if you don't keep the commandments yourself. It's between you and God. Between me and God."

Keturah smiled and turned away.

"Was that wrong?" asked Zeforah.

"It just—all the commandments have to do with how we treat other people."

"Not all of them," said Zeforah.

"But the hard ones," said Keturah. "It's between me and God, but what God wants me to do is *not* pitch a stone at some village boy when he makes a crude remark. So at that moment, it's between me and that boy."

"What does she think she is, a prophet?" asked Sarah. But her mockery was affectionate, and Keturah laughed.

"Oh, was I being deep?" asked Keturah.

"You sounded like Father, that's all," said Asa. "Always thinking about things the next layer deeper. You should have been a boy, except that would have ruined everything."

They all looked at her in surprise. "Having a brother would ruin everything?" said Keturah.

"He'd be the boss of everything, then, even if he was the youngest, wouldn't he? Because someday he'd be the owner of Father's flocks, and we wouldn't. So it wouldn't be just the sisters."

"Maybe that would be better," grumbled Hamar. But nobody agreed, not even her. And the thought of how a brother would have changed things—happiness for Mother and Father, but a loss for the sisters—made them solemn and, for a while at least, less grumpy with each other.

The sun beat down, and the sheep drank as the sisters took turns drawing from the well.

And then, as the routine was at its most peaceful, a man leapt from behind an outcropping of rock and ran at the sheep, screaming, flailing about with a stick, scattering the animals and shocking the girls into screaming.

He wasn't alone, either. There were four of them, not villagers, but rough men living wild who had probably heard that in Midian there was a flock tended only by women. Zeforah took up her cudgel and she saw that the other older girls had kept theirs close at hand as well, but what could they do? The men weren't after them, they were after a couple of lambs they could run off with and butcher and live for a few weeks.

Hamar was thinking the same way. "Zeforah, don't hit them, if we leave them alone they'll take a sheep and—"

"And be back again and again," said Zeforah grimly. "I'll break their heads in!"

"They'll kill you!" screamed Keturah.

But Zeforah was not going to let that tall one get away with a yearling like that, or any sheep at all. "Put it down!" she screamed as she ran at him. He paid no attention to her until she landed a blow with her her cudgel in the small of his back.

He bellowed, dropped the lamb, and fell to the ground. "She broke my back!" he cried.

The others stopped their pursuit of various lambs and gathered around their fallen comrade, helping him to his feet. He was still in pain, but she hadn't broken anything, much as she might have wished to. They looked at her with cold anger and now she was really afraid.

"All we come for is meat," said the oldest of them. "But if we have to teach a lesson, we can do that too."

And now Zeforah realized what she had done, exposing not just herself but all her sisters to immediate vengeance. Only Hamar and Sarah were big enough to make any kind of stand, and already they were standing beside her, Hamar giving orders to the younger girls to run back home to tell Father what was happening. But Dinah and Asa were too frightened to do anything but cower.

At once one of the men ran to block their path down the valley. "No need to worry your papa," said the leader. "Half a dozen daughters? I bet he'd be glad if we took four of you to marry with. Take a couple of sheep each as a dowry and bring you on home to do for us." He smiled. "Without those big old sticks though. Why don't you just put them down before you get your arms broken?"

Zeforah was about to answer—bravely, but in a conciliatory tone, if she could figure out how to do all that while her voice trembled and her knees shook—when there came another voice from behind her. A man's voice, and with a strange accent and a very formal, educated tone.

"You've had your . . . fun for the . . . day," said the man. "Now put down the . . . sheep and . . . leave."

"We aren't . . . here for . . . fun," said the leader, mocking the way the stranger hesitated as he spoke. "And we aren't af-f-f-fraid of you, either."

Zeforah didn't take her eyes off the enemy, even as the stranger gently threaded his way between them to take his place at the forefront. He wore a sword at his waist. A beautiful, polished sword. Because he was so finely armed, it took a moment for Zeforah to realize what he wanted as he reached one hand behind him and waggled his fingers, clearly asking them to give him—what?

It was Hamar who understood, and put her cudgel into his hand.

"You picked the wrong people to rescue," said the leader. "We got to eat and there was no call for her to go breaking a man's back with that stick, was there?" His tone was mild, but Zeforah could see how he crouched, ready to spring; how the men spread out, inviting the stranger to come closer and be surrounded. She wanted to tell the man to watch out, to be careful. Only he didn't walk into the middle. Instead he sidled around by the rock, so they were only on one side of him. And they responded by trying to maneuver around him.

In the process, the ruffians began to get rather close to the girls, and Zeforah, seeing the danger, herded them back out of the way, keeping her own cudgel ready in case they tried to attack their weaker opponents.

Suddenly the stranger darted forward—it seemed to be a single leaping step, like a cat pouncing—and struck the leader a sharp, hard blow just below his right shoulder. The man howled and dropped his stick. "It's broken!" he cried. And it was true. The arm hung useless, and Zeforah could see from the rubbery way it dangled that there was a new, painful joint between shoulder and elbow. One blow, and his arm was broken? What kind of man was this!

"If I have to . . . hurt you all, you'll . . . starve," said the stranger.

"Kill him!" cried the leader, even as tears of pain ran down his cheeks.

The others moved forward, but with far more caution than before. They seemed about to give each other a signal to rush the stranger when he leapt again, not in the direction he was looking, and swept the legs right out from under the youngest and smallest of them, who was no bigger than Zeforah herself. The boy rolled on the ground, howling and grabbing at his ankle.

"Half done," said the stranger. "Just the right number of

healthy . . . men to help the . . . broken ones . . . get away from here."

They did the arithmetic in their heads and, after a while, mathematics prevailed. The two unbroken ones helped the others limp and stagger off into the rocks.

Now, the fight over, the younger girls began to whimper or wail. Hamar and Sarah comforted them but the stranger paid no attention to them. At first he seemed to be following the men, but there was no fight left in them, and so the stranger turned at once to gathering the scattered sheep. He wasn't terribly good at it, and the sheep could tell that he was inexperienced and took merciless advantage of him, so it took him twice as long to round up the few sheep he was able to bring in. Zeforah set the girls to gathering the rest; work calmed them more than words of comfort ever could.

Zeforah was astonished when even now, having just been saved by what could only be divine intervention, Hamar found something to grumble about. "Father says we're supposed to solve our differences by talking."

Before Zeforah could answer her, the stranger himself spoke up. "That's what I did," he said. "But I had to . . . try several . . . languages before they understood."

Sarah giggled, and Hamar smiled in spite of her surly mood. Still, Zeforah could not leave this man with the impression that they were ungrateful. "Sir," she said, "decency says we may not speak to you, for you are not known to our father. But gratitude has the better claim on all of us, and we thank you."

Emboldened by the fact that Zeforah had spoken, Keturah bounded right up to the man. "You speak very high Hebrew," she said. "Like Father, not like the villagers. But why do you keep . . . pausing . . . like . . . that?" Her own pauses were a perfect mockery of the stranger's speech, and the younger girls laughed; this time, though, Hamar and Sarah seemed to recognize that this might be taken as a grave insult.

"Hebrew is not my . . . native tongue," said the man. "I . . . search for words."

But Zeforah knew enough to guess that this was, at best, only partly true. This man's speech was blocked by something other than foreignness. Yet she did not begrudge him the untruth, if such it was, for might a man not have a small story to save his pride from the shame of halting speech, or any other such lameness?

The sheep were gathered now, and had their fill of water. "Sir," said Zeforah. "Let us cover the well, and then come with us to our father's house, where he will know how to thank you most graciously."

"What I did was not for the sake of thanks," said the man.

"You're a traveler in need of a roof and a meal, from the look of you," said Zeforah. "Why not accept them from those who are most eager to give them to you?"

He smiled. His dust-caked face seemed to crack at the unaccustomed expression. "I'll accept your . . . kind offer. Let me make another. I'll move the . . . stone over the well for you, if you'll . . . let me have a . . . drink first."

"A drink!" cried Zeforah. "Of course you're thirsty!"

Immediately she lowered the waterbag into the well, then drew it up and dipped her own cup into it to serve him. He drank carefully, spilling nothing, and without slurping. But he also did it boldly, not turning away, so he clearly thought of himself as her equal. Or her better.

"As far as I'm concerned," he said, returning the cup, "any debt you owed me is . . . satisfied."

"By a cup of water?" she laughed. "Water has great value, but life still means more."

"But for me, water *is* . . . life."

Keturah piped up. "Father could make a whole sermon out of that."

"Then your . . . father must be a wise man."

"He's a priest of the most high God," said Zeforah. "He serves the Midianites in the valley."

"The most high . . . God has . . . blessed him . . . with six beautiful daughters."

Hamar hooted. "I wonder which one is the ugly one!"

"There are seven of us," said Zeforah. "But Rachel is at home, preparing supper."

"She's the prettiest," said Keturah. "All the men in the village think so."

"And that's enough now," said Zeforah. "Let's cover the well and take this stranger home to meet Father."

"No, that's for me to do," he insisted, but now his weariness seemed too much for him, for the lid of the well didn't yield to his will the way the ruffians had. Zeforah wordlessly joined in beside him, and then Keturah and Asa, before the stone budged.

"I'm weak," said the man when the stone was in place.

"Only weary," said Zeforah. "Please, follow me." She set out on the path down the canyon. He put one foot before the other so ploddingly that she wanted to offer to let him lean on her. But she knew that his pride had already been injured by his inability to cover the well by himself. So she would let him do his own walking, and only lead the way.

❉

Jethro heard them calling, the younger girls, and felt relief and annoyance, both. Annoyance, because he had done so little today, despite all his hours of work on copying the book of Abraham. Relief, because his eyes were bleary and his back ached. He was getting old, no doubt of it, and that was not a happy thought. What if he died before he had made a complete copy of all the holy books he had? Some were getting old indeed. Worse yet, what if he died before one of his daughters married and had a son to whom he could give the scriptures? A son whom he could ordain a priest? Sometimes he despaired of *that* desire, for unless God wrought a miracle, his daughters would end up marrying one of the ignorant clods from the village, or, worse yet, from one of the other villages that didn't even bother to bring their sacrifices to a priest, they had fallen so far from Father Abraham's religion. Uncircumcised, unlettered—even if one of his daughters, in desperation no doubt, took such a one as husband, their sons would be hard-pressed to grow up to be anything other than oafs.

No, no, no. Everyone is teachable. Or if they're not, then God in his wisdom wishes for all my life's labor to be for nought.

"Father!" It was Keturah who burst into his tent, and right on through the veil into the inner room.

"Keturah!" he said sternly.

"Oh! I forgot!" She scooted back out into the outer room. "Father, forgive me, did I get dust into the room?"

"No, no." He laid his pen aside, and, leaving the precious papyrus scroll open for the ink to dry, he emerged from the inner room. "What brings you scampering home like a rabbit? Are boys with stones chasing you?"

"You should have *seen* what was chasing us! Four big men, trying to steal the sheep! Trying to run them off, and they threatened to do terrible things, but the stranger broke them into pieces like *crackers* and he's so thirsty and Zeforah spoke to him and offered him hospitality here but she told me not to tell you that because she wasn't supposed to speak to him so now she'll be mad at me."

Keturah looked so dismayed that Jethro had to laugh. "Keturah, of course I won't be angry with Zeforah, and she won't be angry with you. If a stranger saved my daughters and my sheep, do you think I'd deny him the hospitality of my home, or be offended because my daughter spoke to him? If I know Zeforah, she spoke to him only to thank him."

"That's right!" said Keturah.

"Then she did well. Let's go meet this stranger."

Keturah ran out of the tent, then ran back to clutch at his robe, at his hand. "Come on, he's so tired he's almost falling down."

"Did he have a long journey, then? Or was he injured in the confrontation with those four big men?"

"They didn't lay a hand on him," said Keturah. "He must be a soldier. Or a hero!"

"Heros are all myths," said Jethro. "There are only men, and God, and men of God."

"Then he's a man of God!"

Keturah was jumping around him. "Am I a sacred calf, and you a pagan to dance around me?" asked Jethro.

At once she calmed down. "I'm no pagan, Papa," she said. "I'm just . . . exuberant."

"I should never have taught Zeforah to read, if she's going to teach you words that the village boys don't understand."

"The stranger talks funny," said Keturah. "Bookish. But he . . . pauses . . . all . . . the . . . time."

"Interesting," said Jethro. Clearly this stranger was the most interesting thing that had happened to Keturah in her entire life.

Keturah went on, telling about the stranger over and over again, until at last the running commentary could end for there he was in the flesh. He *did* look weary. And the other girls seemed almost as insane with curiosity about him as Keturah. They could hardly walk without stumbling, their eyes were so focused on his every movement. And yet none of them was speaking to him; Jethro was pleased that their training in modesty had managed to hold even in the face of such temptation. Their mother would be proud.

"Sir!" cried Jethro. "My name is Jethro! Welcome to my tent! This is your home!"

The stranger looked at him blankly. "Sir, I owe it to you to . . . give you my . . . name in return. But if I say that . . . name, I bring . . . danger to you and your house."

"You can trust the discretion of my daughters," said Jethro. "Think of how much they clearly want to ask, and haven't."

The stranger looked away, embarrassed, because he still did not intend to comply, but was also reluctant to make up a name.

"I'll spare you the effort of lying. Your name is Moses, you are no longer Hatshepsut's heir, and you fear that the mighty arm of Egypt will seek you out in these miserable Midianite villages here in the Sinai."

The stranger—Moses—looked stricken. "How could word of this arrive . . . before me?"

Jethro laughed. "No word has reached me. I looked at your clothing. Egyptian. Very high-born Egyptian. And yet you speak Hebrew fluently, with the accents of an educated man. Keturah told me you defeated four men easily, breaking bones. Yet you didn't have the strength to move the capstone over the well, so you were trained as a soldier but aren't used to manual labor. There's only one Israelite in Egypt who could fit that description. Yet here you are, alone, filthy from crossing the desert on foot, without supplies, and hiding your name. So clearly you've fallen from power and fear retribution from Egypt. All this is obvious. Is there something I've missed?"

Still not looking at him, Moses replied, "I . . . killed a man."

"You're a soldier. You've killed many men, or had them killed."

"I . . . killed an Egyptian innkeeper who was . . . beating an Israelite servant."

Jethro laughed. "And this is what you tell me when you want me to take you into my tent?"

"I . . . might as well. If I . . . didn't, you'd . . . guess it anyway."

"Rachel has kept things baking and boiling all day. As long as you don't have a habit of killing cooks, you're welcome to dine with us."

"I started smelling the food halfway down the . . . canyon."

"And you kept coming! This is a compliment that I'm sure my little Rachel will cherish."

It took a moment, but the stranger finally understood the layers of irony and affection in Jethro's remark, and smiled. Indulgently, perhaps, but Jethro was willing to be indulged. From all reports, this Moses was a great man, a commander whose men generally lived through his campaigns, a governor whose people rejoiced in their government. But then, this might be merely the legend that would accrete to any prominent son of Abraham, risen to such a lofty place. Even Midianites, who were only sons of Abraham by adoption — more like great-nephews of Abraham, if one wished to be precise — took pride in the stories of Moses, so it was unlikely that if he were an arrogant oaf the word of it would have reached the nether regions of Sinai.

The girls outdid themselves at dinner, falling all over each other in their eagerness to serve the stranger. It seemed that every dish required at least two girls to bring it in, and two more to carry it away, while others hovered nearby with towels and finger bowls, wine flagons and fresh cups. Every dish they owned had surely been used and scrubbed twice before the meal was half done. And it seemed to Jethro that twice the normal amount of seasoning had been dumped into every food at the last moment, so that everything was spicy. More than once his eyes widened at the first taste of a dish . . . but his guest seemed not to notice, and ate with perfect manners and self-restraint, despite the fact that he must be famished.

The only daughter who seemed not to come in at all during the meal was Zeforah. Of course, the perverse child. Here was the most marriageable Hebrew in the known world, and Zeforah insisted on hanging back. Well, her modesty was commendable. It would recommend her to this man of manners and subtlety. Because this Moses was not leaving here without a daughter of Jethro as his wife. One of his girls, at least, had to be married to something other than a village clown, and there was no other conceivable reason that God would have led such a man to Jethro's home. No, God had led him direct to Jethro's daughters! The Lord's intentions could not be clearer, and who was Jethro to attempt to thwart the will of the Lord?

Jethro beckoned to Sarah, who at once rushed over with the wine flagon. He whispered to her, "From now on I expect this level of service when I dine alone."

She gave him a thin little smile, which brightened to a

toothy grin as soon as she remembered that Moses might be watching. Her teeth were fine and white, her best asset.

"Tell Zeforah that I want her to bring in the fig cakes herself," he whispered.

"She won't," said Sarah softly. "We've tried."

"Tell her if she doesn't, I'll send him outside to fetch the cakes himself."

Sarah's expression at first was doubtful—would Father do such a horrible thing? Such a breach of all decorum? And then she realized that, yes, he would. She rushed outside to the kitchen.

A few moments later, Zeforah came in with a tray of cakes. She shot an evil glance at her father, which he answered with a smile. Then she knelt before Moses and presented the cakes.

Jethro saw, with satisfaction, that it took a moment for Moses to notice the cakes at all, because he was busy greeting Zeforah with a grin.

"Beautiful, isn't she?" said Jethro.

A blush leapt to Zeforah's face. Modestly she looked down at the cakes.

"Trouble is, she thinks she should have been my eldest son. God gave me gems, and she thinks I want a stone."

"I've wished for soldiers with her . . . courage," said Moses. "She struck one and nearly . . . broke his back."

"Zeforah struck the first blow? Why am I not surprised?"

"I suspect they would have won the battle without my help," said Moses, "but I hope I spared them a bruise or two."

"It's hard to imagine what's happening in the modern world, when a man's flocks aren't safe from mountain bandits." Jethro sighed, long and mournfully.

Zeforah made a move as if to set down the tray of cakes.

"You haven't tasted the fig cakes yet," said Jethro.

Moses reached down to take the smallest one.

"Not that one! Not that measly rat-sized bite! Not that deformed half-cousin of a fig cake! You are my guest, and you must take the best my humble household has to offer."

Laughing, Moses took the biggest of the cakes. Zeforah at once came to offer the tray to her father.

"I suppose that now I'll have to go myself to tend the flocks, which will put an end to my real labor. Oh, if only I had a man in my household, who could be guardian of my herds and protector of my daughters!" Jethro sighed again.

Zeforah glared again at her father. Apparently she thought his hint was too broad.

It hardly mattered. Moses seemed oblivious. "What's your real work, then? If not shepherding?"

"My real work is to serve God."

"Oh, yes, your daughters mentioned that you served the villages here as a priest of . . . God."

"Of the only true and living God," said Jethro. "But these bumpkins can't tell a real God from the carven pretenders. They pray to an idol for the sun to shine, and then it shines, and they think it proves something—they live in a dry land, what should the sun do if not to shine? And then they come to *me* to offer sacrifice to the true God when their child has fallen down the well and drowned, and they think it proves I'm a bad priest that their baby doesn't get raised from the dead! A perverse and ignorant people who try the patience of God."

"Did they really think a god could raise the dead?"

"Because I teach them that God will resurrect the dead, when the last trumpet sounds over the Earth, they think it means that God will also do it now, at their convenience. In vain do I try to explain that God means this life to be a trial, of our faithfulness, our obedience, and so things must happen which are hard to bear."

"Theological subtleties are always wasted on the ignorant."

"Now that, my friend, is a foolish thing to say," said Jethro.

Moses raised his eyebrows. Apparently no one had called a statement of his foolish for a long time.

"The ignorant," explained Jethro, "are the only people who *can* be taught. You, for instance, fancy yourself an educated man. That means that you would never dream of learning anything from a desert herdsman who calls himself a priest. You'll eat my food, you'll sleep in my tent, you'll contemplate my daughters, but as for actually learning anything from me, the thought would not cross your mind."

It amused Jethro to see the horror in Zeforah's eyes. She could pretend that she didn't want him to tout her charms to this man, but when she thought he was insulting Moses, that he might be driving the man away, she was just as annoyed as any of the other girls would be.

"You're mistaken, sir," said Moses. "I saw your household as an island of . . . peace, and I wanted very much to learn how you . . . created such a place."

"An island of peace! What, did my girls actually refrain from quarreling among themselves while you were with them? Then you are indeed a miracle worker."

"I had all the education that Egypt has to offer. I learned of war from the warriors, of . . . gods from the priests, and of . . . government from my mother. I learned of the Israelite God from my Israelite . . . mother, and on my own I learned all I could about . . . farming, architecture, astronomy. . . . But in the end, what was any of it worth? I let my . . . temper throw me from the . . . pinnacle of power."

"This man you killed, was he defenseless?"

"No. If he hadn't fought me, I wouldn't have . . . killed him."

"So you didn't mean to kill him."

"No, of course not. But that doesn't . . . change the fact that if I had . . . kept my temper, that man would be alive, and I would still . . . be the son of Pharaoh."

"Would you? Would he? Are you a prophet, then?"

"I don't understand your . . . question."

"How can you know what *would* have happened? All we ever know is what *did* happen. Even then, we scarcely know why. What plan is God working out in the world? Tell me the truth, Moses. Did you really think that you would ever inherit the double crown of Egypt?"

"It would have been hard."

"It would have meant civil war. It would have meant the rampant slaughter of the Israelite people if you had even tried."

Moses' eyes flashed. "You seem oddly expert on the affairs of Egypt, especially for a man who says that one can't know what *would* have happened." Jethro noticed, too, that when he was angry, Moses didn't stammer.

"You see?" said Jethro. "You won't let me get away with pretending to such knowledge, but you are willing to consume yourself with guilt about things you understand even less. How did you know that God didn't arrange all of this in answer to my prayers that he bring a suitable husband for my brilliant eldest daughter?"

Zeforah gasped and dropped the tray of cakes.

"My brilliant, beautiful, *clumsy* eldest daughter," Jethro corrected himself. "Fortunately, fig cakes taste even better with a bit of carpet fiber in them."

"Sir, you are . . . generous indeed," said Moses. "But I'm

not a . . . fit man to be any woman's husband. If I'm . . . found, I will be . . . killed."

"You'll be found when God wants you found, and you'll die when God wants you dead. Not before, not after."

"Why do you even think that a . . . god would notice me?"

"Not *a* god. God. The Lord. The one whose name we do not speak. The God of Abraham, Isaac, and Jacob."

"In Egypt, we know who the one . . . god is, the first god, . . . Ptah, the maker of heaven and earth, the . . . creator of all the gods. Is this the one you will not . . . name?"

"What the Egyptians know of God is the rumor of a memory of a legend of a dream." Jethro grinned his best grin. "*I* have the words of Abraham himself. Of Enoch. Of Adam, when he first prayed to the Lord God at the altar he built in the dreary world, after he was cast out of the garden."

Moses cocked his head. "You have such things memorized?"

"Written down. Did you think that only Egyptians knew how to write? That only papyrus could hold words? Abraham had writing, too. On the parched skin of lambs we write, and copy it again, generation after generation. And not in the inconvenient elaborate temple writing of the Egyptians that takes forever to copy out. But . . . what do you care? You're an educated man. What could you learn from a priest in the desert?"

Moses grimaced. "How did I . . . give you offense? I hope I haven't been . . . proud in such a . . . generous house."

"You've been the soul of modesty," said Jethro. "I'm the rude one."

Zeforah's quick, nasty smile showed that she agreed.

"Have another fig cake now that my beautiful eldest

daughter has gathered them up like rose petals from the carpet."

She rolled her eyes and carried the tray back to Moses. This time he didn't hesitate to take the best of them, and Jethro saw with pleasure that he gave Zeforah a little smile, as if to say, I'm sorry your father is being so embarrassingly open about his ambition for you, but I like you anyway. Or was he reading too much into his glance? Give him time, the boy would come around.

"Would you imagine learning a whole new way of writing?" said Jethro. "So that you could read the very words that Abraham wrote?"

"If you . . . kept me here, I'd have to labor to earn my . . . keep," said Moses. "What I was . . . doesn't matter. What I am now is a man of no . . . property and no . . . prospects. And no experience or useful skill. All I'm . . . good for is . . . plain labor. The lowest servant in your house."

"That's what we'll call you," said Jethro. "So people don't start guessing who you really are. A desert wanderer that I took in because God told me to."

"Did he?" asked Moses.

"He didn't have to send an angel, if that's what you're asking," said Jethro. "The fact that you're here at all made the message clear enough."

"What message?"

"Think, man! What is your name, if not the Egyptian word for 'son.'"

Moses blushed. "Do I get . . . claimed again?"

"No, no, I'm not saying son-in-law—that's for you and my daughter to work out—whichever daughter you fancy, if any at all, but you'd be a fool to look at any of them as long as Zeforah's available, the rest are either children or shameless scolds, God bless their hearts—I'm saying you are named *son*, which is the name of the anointed one."

"Who is that?" Moses looked sick. "I know of a . . . son who was anointed—he . . . conspired with his mother to . . . kill his own father and take his place."

"Then he's no son at all, is he?" said Jethro. "The true Son is the one anointed by God. He will come to deliver Israel from bondage."

"If you think that . . . just because Hatshepsut named me . . ."

"Not you! Not the bondage of mere slavery. A man can be a slave and still serve God. It's the bondage of sin I'm talking about, and you're already too impure to be *that* Son. Oh, to have a year in which to relieve your ignorance. Better yet, five years!"

"If you can . . . teach me what . . . God is doing to me, if you can make me understand why I was raised up only to be thrown down . . ."

"Oh, that's the most important thing you can learn? The meaning of your own life? When I can unfold the universe of God's creations to you, all you wonder about is why you aren't still wearing fine linens in a stone house in Egypt?"

Moses looked stricken. "I must have offended you, sir, but I don't know how. I beg your forgiveness, and I'll be on my way."

"What! You think I'm angry? This isn't angry! This is excited! I have someone who knows all that the wisest nation in the world can teach, and now you're here and ready to learn something *true* for a change. Leave here? I'd like to see you try! And go where? God gave you the name Moses because that's what you are supposed to be. Not a king, but a child of God, always following him your whole life. Only when you are a true son to God will you be fit to lead, and then it will not be *you* that people follow, it will be God."

"Are you that kind of son of God?"

"As best I can. Which is why I'm not afraid to speak bold truth to you. Because a true heart does not run from the truth, or fear it, or become angry."

"But I am angry. And a- . . . a- . . . fraid."

"But you're not going to run, are you?"

"I've already made my run. Across the desert. To this . . . place."

"Stay with me, Moses. Let me make a true son of you. Learn my learning. Labor at my labors."

"I know . . . nothing about being a . . . shepherd."

"What's to know? You sit and watch the sheep! Moses, be a brother to my daughters."

"All this you offer me," said Moses, "and the . . . sun has not yet risen on me in your house?"

"I already know who you are," said Jethro. "Not your legend—what is *that* worth? I know your heart."

"*I* don't, and you do?"

"Of course," said Jethro. "I'm an old man. I've seen everything. It's all familiar to me now." Jethro rose up from his seat. "Stand up and let's make this place over into a bedroom. Half the pillows are yours."

"If I'm to be a . . . servant in your house," said Moses, "it's not right for me to share your . . . bed."

"I told you," said Jethro. "You're to sleep where my son would sleep—at my side."

"You do me . . . too much honor."

"It is God who honors *me*," said Jethro. "By entrusting you to my care." Impulsively he strode to Moses and embraced him. "Sleep and be at peace, Moses. You may not know it yet, but God has rescued you from Egypt, and you come to this place like a shipwrecked sailor cast upon a friendly shore."

"I do know that much, sir," said Moses. "And if it's . . . God who made you such a . . . kind man, then I thank God for you."

"There. That was almost a prayer. You're already waking up." And with that, Jethro began tossing pillows around. The girls scurried out of the tent, off to find their own beds in the other tent.

But Moses simply stood there, looking embarrassed.

"What is it?" asked Jethro.

"I'm filthy from traveling, sir," said Moses. "Before I sleep on your pillows, shouldn't I bathe?"

Jethro laughed. "This isn't Egypt," he said. "We don't have a huge river of water flowing past our houses. Fresh water is for drinking. As for bathing, well, it's a long hike down to the sea, and you're only filthy and sweaty again by the time you get home. We're not offended by dirt and a little bit of stink here."

"But I offend myself," said Moses.

"Live with it," said Jethro. "Until the sheep object, we haven't water enough to waste it on baths." He stretched himself out on half the accustomed number of pillows. "I'm an old man. I probably snore hideously, so you'd better get to sleep fast before I start in and keep you awake all night."

Moses lay down on his own pillows, but in a few moments tossed them aside and lay directly on the carpet. "I'm not used to soft sleeping," he said.

"I am," said Jethro, gathering the discarded pillows and making up his bed the way he usually did. "When you get old, you'll see."

Moses was asleep before Jethro could lie down again. He

blew out the lamps and in the darkness listened to the man's breathing. "O God, blessed be thy name," Jethro murmured. "O God, thou hast given me a son."

*Chapter 7*

# Words

Moses did not take well to the numbing routine of the pastoral life. Every day the sheep needed water. Every day one of Jethro's daughters led him on the search for new pasture, or taught him how to herd the stupid animals — couldn't they train a dog for this? — or tried to teach him the silly country songs that they used to pass the time. All the while, Moses could not drive Egypt from his thoughts. Mother — Hatshepsut — what was she going through? How was she dealing with the crippling blow that his exile caused her? Was she able to keep the boy Tuthmose from combining with the priests to oust her? No doubt by giving him exactly what he wanted, his own throne. She would be able to rule over and around and even through him for a time, because he was still young. But he would work at soldiering — he had a gift for it, Moses knew that from his own days teaching the boy — and in due time he would have his own following among the soldiers, who would long for him to lead them instead of a woman.

As for the priests, well, that was Tuthmose's deepest weakness, that he was already beholden to them. Was he stupid enough to use them again? Didn't he understand the constant danger that the priests posed to Pharaoh? Why else did Pharaoh have to become a god? It was so he could outrank the priests in their own hierarchy. Priests had meddled in government before, and it was always extremely difficult to get them out again, because any action taken against a priest was immediately portrayed by them as an attack on the gods. If Tuthmose went to them again, if he admitted them to the inner ring of government, there would be no expelling them. Maybe he would have the strength to keep them under his control during his own lifetime, but sooner or later there would be a weak pharaoh and the priests would seize power for themselves.

The worst thing was that Tuthmose was not the sort of man who would take the long view, who would care even a bit about the rulers who would come after him. Let them solve the problems of their own time. Tuthmose would do what was needful now. That kind of pharaoh was the reason Egypt had fallen under the sway of the Hyksos invaders from Canaan. Weak without knowing he was weak. Weak because he inherited weakness from his father and never suspected it. Tuthmose would be ambitious, bold, triumphant no doubt, but he would leave Egypt weaker than he found it. That's why he was unfit to rule, and now he would rule, and it was Moses' fault. Because he couldn't control himself, because he had to help one slave, and now a whole kingdom would pay.

And what was happening to the Israelites now? Because he killed an Egyptian to save a single Israelite, what punishment was being visited upon them all? What was Jochabed suffering now? How were Miriam and Aaron cursing him? Or were they—yes, certainly they were—gloating, knowing they had driven him to a commitment to them and their people. Though they would insist that it was their God that had driven him. . . .

"What were you thinking?" Keturah demanded. Small as

she was, her voice penetrated, echoed from the cliffs. A few of
the other girls were near enough to hear and look up.

Moses looked around, tried to remember what he was supposed to be doing. Oh, yes. A simple job. Watching the nursing ewes and their lambs. But where were they? Oh, only a
few yards off. "There they are," said Moses.

"Look at what you're letting them eat!" Keturah grabbed
him by the hand and dragged him over to where the ewes were
gathered. As they walked, Moses could see that the ewes were
unsteady on their feet. One of them took a couple of steps and
fell over.

"Oh no," said Moses. "Is it dead?"

"Drunk. Drunk as one of the village men at a festival. This
plant makes them dizzy. Now we won't be able to get them to
do anything for hours."

"I didn't know."

"I *told* you there was a patch nearby and you had to watch
to keep them out of it!"

"I'm sorry," said Moses.

She pulled up one of the plants and waved it right in
Moses' face. "There it is! It doesn't look like anything else. I
pointed it out to you before!"

"I'm sorry," said Moses again.

"Well what's the matter with you anyway?" demanded
Keturah. "It's not like this is hard! *I've* been doing it since I was
four!"

Moses was beginning to get annoyed. "I said, I'm sorry."

Keturah might have launched into yet another diatribe—
certainly she was ready for one—but Zeforah arrived right
then and cut her off. "That's enough, Keturah. He gets the
point."

"But he doesn't listen!"

"We were patient with you when you were starting out, Keturah."

"I was four!"

"Keturah, teach with patience, not with anger."

Disgusted, Keturah stalked away. "*You* can get the ewes away from here, then."

"I'm truly sorry," said Moses. "My mind wandered. She was right to reprimand me."

"She's good at starting reprimands," said Zeforah. "She has plenty of teachers to help her learn *that*. The hard thing is knowing when to stop."

"Many a junior officer has the same problem," said Moses. "He keeps ragging at the offender, waiting until he feels satisfied. But anger only feeds on itself, so the more you rag, the less satisfied you are. It leads to deadly insult, or to blows, or both."

"Fortunately," said Zeforah, "my sisters aren't soldiers. The insults may be deadly, but the blows are light."

He tried to mimic her deft way of helping the drunken ewes stagger away from the plant, but no matter what he did, he kept knocking them over, sending their lambs away bleating, while Zeforah's ewes never fell at all. She ended up herding five for every one he managed to get back to the safe pasture.

"I'll never be good at this," he said.

"God will give you the skills you need," said Zeforah.

"It's God's fault that I need these skills in the first place."

"But at least you're not hesitating," said Zeforah.

"What do you mean?"

"When you speak. You don't take those little . . . pauses."

He looked at her in mortified surprise. "No one has ever . . . spoken to me about that . . . before."

"Oh, no. There you're doing it again. I never should have mentioned it."

"I just . . . you don't . . ." and he gave up, speechless. Had he really stopped hesitating for a while?

"Father said that you hesitate because Hebrew isn't your first language," said Zeforah.

"That's how it . . . began."

"And because you spend your life balanced between two nations, two mothers, two languages, two roles."

"An interesting analysis."

"But I think it's because you're proud and don't want to get caught making a mistake."

Did she dislike him? Was that why she delighted in striking right at the heart of his vanity? The other girls seemed to be on their best behavior around him—except Keturah, who spoke her mind no matter what. Zeforah, however, seemed to go out of her way to be completely oblivious to the fact that her father had as much as offered her to him. But of course—she didn't want to marry him, and so she was as unsubservient, as self-willed as possible.

"No doubt you're right," said Moses.

"Which means that when you *don't* hesitate, it's because you're *not* being proud. And that's a good thing."

"I'm . . . capable of a . . . good thing?" said Moses. "What a . . . surprise."

She seemed to recoil as if slapped. "What did I do to deserve that?"

"What?"

"Sarcasm. Nastiness."

"I assure you I was . . . mocking only . . . myself."

"You were putting me in my place," she said. "Only I was *in* my place. I'm your teacher here."

"Yes, you are," said Moses.

"I didn't ask for the job, you know," she said.

"True."

"And you're not trying very hard."

"I do everything I'm told," he said. He couldn't quite keep all the bitterness out of his voice.

"No, you don't. Shepherding is boring work, but you have to remain alert all the time. Imagine if you left a soldier on watch and he did as badly as you did today!"

"He'd be hanged from the prow of my boat."

She looked horrified. "No! Please tell me you're not so barbaric!"

"Not if he's new. If he's in training, he gets a taste of the lash. But a *soldier* doesn't betray his men. Are these sheep my men?"

"They are," said Zeforah. "Or at least, you can think of them that way if it helps you."

"Fat ewes with nursing lambs. Well, they're like soldiers this far—they get drunk every chance they get."

She laughed. And so did he. For a moment, at least, it felt as though they were on the same side.

The same side of what?

"Suddenly you look so sad," she said.

The words surprised him. No, not the words, but real concern in her voice, and the ache that struck his heart, the feeling that tears would come to his eyes if he let them. He turned away from her.

"What's wrong?" she said.

I don't know, he thought. Am I so weak that even the slightest sympathy stabs me to the heart? In Egypt, I wasn't surrounded by affection—it was honor I had there, and obedience. Why should I miss it so much now?

"I didn't mean to make you angry," she said.

"I'm not," he said. "I'm not used to. . . ."

She waited but he couldn't think what it was he wasn't used to so he never finished the sentence. He returned to herding the last of the drunken ewes back to the meadow where the rest were gathered.

He saw how desperately the lambs lunged for the teat, nearly knocking over their unsteady mothers. That's me, he thought. That's the pain that I didn't expect. Neither of my mothers was ever allowed to be mine the way these ewes belong to their lambs. I grew up with plenty of people telling me how to be a man, how to be strong and wise and good. But that tone of voice, gentle, concerned, and those words, Suddenly you look so sad, as if it mattered to someone how I felt.

What a baby I am. Cut off from Egypt, I've come here to the desert to become, not even a shepherd, but a lamb.

"All done," said Zeforah.

"All that work because I couldn't get my mind off. . . ."

She waited a moment, then laughed. "Is this going to be another of those sentences that remains a mystery? 'I'm not used to . . .' and now 'I couldn't get my mind off. . . .' Or are you just . . . hesitating extra long?"

For a moment anger flashed within him. She was jeering at him! Nobody mocked his stammering!

But these girls all teased each other. It was their primary manner of conversation. The same attitude that let her speak to him with warmth and sympathy also let her tease him. An attitude of . . . intimacy. Like a sister with her brother. That's why it hurt so much when she was so readily kind. He had plenty of sisters and brothers. Not just the ones by blood, Miriam and Aaron, but also his adopted brothers and sisters in Pharaoh's house—the children of Tuthmose II by his concubines. He had been teacher and taskmaster to the children of Pharaoh's house; he had been lectured and whined to by Miriam and Aaron. But no one had been like *this* with him.

Except his fellow soldiers. The boys who trained with him when he was a child. Of course they knew who he was, but they were freer with him than anyone else ever was, before or since, and he missed it. That's why it hurt, because he had lost that when he became a ruler of men. The closest he had ever come to having a family was in the exercise yard with a wooden sword in his hand. And now, helping drunken ewes regain their balance. With a young woman who would never have earned a second glance from him in his previous life.

More fool I, if that were so, he thought. Because *she* is real, more real than any of the daughters and sisters and mothers and wives of noblemen, always trying to impress me. She really doesn't care whether I approve of her or not, because she has nothing to gain from me. She just . . . likes me.

"Now I've offended you," she said.

"I wasn't sure how to answer you," he said. "Tease you back, or finish those sentences."

"Are you giving me a choice?" she said.

"I think so," he said. "I'm not good at either one, though. Out of practice with teasing, and I've spent my whole life learning how to speak carefully instead of candidly. You can see how much I'm slipping—because I spoke the beginnings of those sentences aloud."

"What was it," she said, "that you weren't used to?"

"Affection," he said, for now he was sure that was what it was.

But it was the wrong word. Her eyes went wide. "Thank heaven my sisters couldn't hear you say that!"

So *affection* was too strong a word for her. This was becoming more and more like a negotiation between ambassadors. "What should I call it then? The way you spoke to me? Friendship. Brotherhood."

"I wouldn't know about brotherhood. I just spoke to you . . . like a person."

"Now who's hesitating?"

She slapped at him playfully. He laughed. She slapped again, and this time caught him a glancing blow across the cheek. His hand, by reflex, lashed out and caught her wrist in a hard grip. At once the smile left her face and her body froze. Just a moment too late he let go of her arm. Her skin had been cool and warm, both at once, in his hand.

"Sorry," he said. "Soldier's training."

"All right," she said. "No hitting. I've learned that rule."

"Anyway, you see what happens when I finish my sentences? I was right to leave it as a mystery."

"What was it you couldn't get your mind off?" she said.

"That's easy. I was sitting there thinking through all the awful things that were bound to be happening in Egypt because I went into exile. How my mother—the Pharaoh, Hatshepsut—how she would be crippled, forced to take an obnoxious boy and give him the double crown. And the Israelites—it's bound to go worse with them, now that I've proven myself to be disloyal to Egypt after having the best that Egypt can give a man."

"What a heavy burden to bear," she said.

"Heaviest because there's nothing I can do."

"Then it's not your burden, is it?" she said.

"The opposite is true. The burden is heavier precisely because I can't do anything about it."

"The guilt is heavier," she said. "But think about it, Moses.

None of the bad things that you've mentioned are *caused* by your leaving. They were always there, waiting to happen. That boy you don't like —"

"Tuthmose the *third*."

"Did you conjure him into being? I thought I heard you telling Father that he had already been conspiring with the priests. Had already been anointed."

"Well, yes."

"And as for the Israelites, they were already slaves, weren't they?"

"There's slavery and then there's slavery."

"I'm sure that's true," she said, "but it still seems to me that you didn't *cause* any of these bad things. It seems to me that you were preventing them as long as you were there, but one way or another, they were going to get rid of you someday anyway, and those same things would have happened, only maybe worse."

He could only stare at her in astonishment. She was more like Hatshepsut or Miriam than he could have imagined, for her analysis, though based on only the most rudimentary understanding, was correct. He laughed.

"Oh, now I've made a fool of myself."

"The opposite, the opposite," he said. "You've made a fool out of *me*." He shook his head. "No, that's not it either. You've made me wise, that's what you've done."

"Well, now that I've solved your stupidity problem, what's next?"

"I wasn't being stupid. I was being vain. Thinking that I caused things that have always been there. Pharaoh's house has been plagued with politics since before I was born. The very idea of having a woman as Pharaoh is shocking enough — I'm the least of her problems. I helped her last as long as she has, and with the priests conniving against her she couldn't last forever anyway. And when I was born they were *killing* Israelite babies."

She looked shocked. "Oh! They won't start that again now, will they?"

"I doubt it. The ones who hate Israelites didn't much like what came of that the last time."

"What came of it?"

He laughed wryly. "Me."

"You were supposed to be killed?"

"My mother put me in a basket lined with pitch and set me afloat on the Nile. I could have been tipped out by a crocodile or taken in by some poor family and raised, or caught by the mob and drowned. Instead . . . Pharaoh's daughter took me out of the water and named me 'Son.'"

"What a magical story."

"A true one, anyway."

"So why are you sad?" she said. "Why do you spend your days mourning whenever we aren't actually throwing lambs at you?"

"Is that what I do?" he asked.

"Everyone is trying to be nice to you because of all that you've lost."

"How kind." He didn't know whether he liked having their pity.

"All but Keturah. She says that you're being childish about it because you grew up having more than anybody has any right to expect, and when it ended you could have been killed in Egypt or died on the desert but you're still alive so it's like you have a second chance on life if you'd just stop sitting around feeling sorry for yourself."

"She said such a long speech? Practically an oration."

"Word for word."

"And you memorized it."

"She said it often enough, I couldn't help it." Suddenly she burst into laughter. "Look at you! Taking me so seriously!"

"I don't know how else to take you."

"Not seriously."

"Why not? Aren't you serious?"

Now it was her turn to look flustered. "I meant. . . . I mean, yes, I'm serious, but not grim. You're supposed to . . . I don't know . . . laugh and pretend you think I'm joking but then really hear what I said and think about it."

"Ha ha," he said, voice flat, as if he were reading badly, like a schoolboy. "What a tease you are."

She laughed again. "There. That's it. Now I don't feel like I've offended you."

"You've never offended me."

"Then what were all those silences about?"

"I wasn't offended."

"Don't lie," she said.

"I wasn't offended. I was . . . surprised."

"Don't fib, either."

"Embarrassed."

"Now we have at least the shadow of truth."

"As if you knew what really happened in my heart."

"I do know," she said. "Your face is so easy to read."

"Is it? A woman who thinks reading is easy?"

"It is easy. And reading faces is easier yet. Men's faces, at least. Father's and yours, anyway."

"Then why do you need me to tell you why I fell silent?"

"Because I want to be the kind of friend you tell the truth to."

He thought about that for a moment. Why should he be so afraid of this? "I was hurt," he said. "I was . . . grieving."

Suddenly the playfulness left her face. "I know," she said.

"Not for Egypt," he said. "That was earlier. When you spoke to me, I was grieving because. . . ."

"And again his voice is lost amid the bleating of the sheep."

"Because I wished someone had spoken to me like that all my life."

"I would have, but you never invited me over to your house." She smiled.

He wanted to ask her, Did God take me out of Egypt so I could find you? Did he see what was missing in my life and force me to go to the one place where I could find it?

Instead, being foolish and timid, he didn't say those things. Instead he teased her back. "Well, if your father has his way, we'll have our whole lives together for you to make up for it."

But it didn't work as he had thought it would. There was no answering laugh, no playful slap. Instead her face froze and she turned away from him. "You may be sure that you'll have no such burden added to those you already carry, sir."

"What's wrong?" he said. "What did I say?"

"Nothing, sir," she answered.

"What's this 'sir'? Am I supposed to pretend he didn't as much as offer you to me the first night I got here?"

She turned around to him with fire in her eyes. "Father can offer all he likes," she said, "but he offered what wasn't his to give." And she stalked away from him.

Almost at once the other girls emerged as if from hiding. Not "as if"—they were hiding, of course, quite aware that some kind of scene was being played out, and now that Zeforah had clearly put an end to it, they had to know what it was he said or did to make her walk off in such a sulk. She was rejecting their inquiries, of course, but he could only imagine what report might make its way to Jethro.

One thing he had learned: It wasn't just former sons of Pharaoh who didn't like to have their pride nicked.

*

On the surface it was a celebration — Tuthmose's investiture as Pharaoh. To the people it made no difference that because the new Pharaoh was so young, Hatshepsut would continue to guide the kingdom in his name. What mattered was the spectacle, the majesty of gods made flesh among men. What did they know of this boy? The man they knew, Moses, turned out to be an Israelite after all, treacherous, slaveborn; Tuthmose III was of the house of Pharaoh by blood, and now the kingdom was in order again. So the people gladly cheered the processions on land and down the river. Gladly they joined in the prayers and rituals, and gladly they received the extra portions of grain distributed for the grand occasion.

As for Tuthmose himself, the spectacle meant little. He did his part, making sure the people got their view of majesty. Those in the know were aware that he had very little power, was virtually a prisoner in that he could only go where Hatshepsut gave him permission to go, could only see those she wanted him to see. Only he, Hatshepsut, and — if he still lived — Moses knew that Tuthmose had a bit more going for him than appearances would suggest. He had clout enough even now to insist that his mother be allowed the freedom to come and go from him as she liked, and he insisted as well that the priests Jannes and Jambres be permitted to minister to his spiritual needs. To these requests Hatshepsut acceded, but only after Tuthmose made it a life-or-death ultimatum: Let him have free access to these three, or the only way he'd go through the public investiture was as a corpse. No matter that he had to fight to win even these pathetic concessions. What mattered was that Hatshepsut didn't want him to have his way, and she had given in.

What a weak and womanly thing to do! If she had any brains at all, she would have had Tuthmose killed the moment Moses fled into exile, and claim that Moses murdered him. Then she would have had no rival to share the throne with her, and Moses' exile would have done her some good. Instead, she nattered on about how one must act for the good of Pharaoh's house, and since, loathsome as he was, he was the only credible heir, she had to leave him alive. Why? An heir became important only when the king died. Why should the king, being dead, care who came after him, unless it were his own child? She had none; therefore *her* line ended with her. Yet she still acted as if she had some obligation.

Well, she had one duty, and one alone: To die, not today, but when Tuthmose was old enough to take the reigns of power without the risk of civil war. If she happened to die naturally, that would do; but die she would, and it would be called natural, for what was nature but the will of the gods? And Pharaoh was one of them.

Pharaoh. That is who I am, thought Tuthmose. Pharaoh after my father. *He* might have been weak enough to let a woman rule above him; so am I, now, while I'm still a child. But he was content to live in shameful submission throughout his adult life. Not that he held it against Hatshepsut for humiliating his father. If Hatshepsut was the stronger, the more ruthless, the more innately gifted by the gods, then she *should* rule; if Tuthmose II could be dominated, then he was no Pharaoh.

But I am not my father, he thought as the double crown was lowered onto his head by the hands of the woman he would someday bury. I will *seem* to be just like him, weak and compliant, until Hatshepsut dies or my position is strong enough with the army and the priests to make my move.

His only sorrow was the Moses was not here to see his triumph. Moses, the very model of a man, the perfect son, the perfect teacher, the perfect heir. It was against Moses that Tuthmose always measured himself—his strength, his beauty, his magnanimity, his leadership in battle, his cleverness in tactics, his smoothness in judgment. From earliest childhood Tuthmose had known that he must learn to be everything that Moses was, with one exception: He would not have that fatal sentimentality that made him hold back from the brutality of power. He would not have let the treacherous princess of Saba live! Her disloyalty would have been punished by bringing her dead body home, hanging from the prow of his river barge. Nor would he have restrained himself from killing a young rival who dared to let a priest anoint him as Pharaoh. Oh, it would have been such a pleasure to have Moses there on the day of Hatshepsut's death, so that he could see how well his student learned from him. He had pictured it so often: Moses on his knees, too proud to beg or weep or even tremble in fear, looking into the eyes of his master Tuthmose III as the man behind him twisted the cord around his neck and strangled the life out of him. Now Tuthmose would have to forego the sweetest fruit of triumph—proving to Moses on his very body which of them was the stronger man.

Down the river in glory rode Tuthmose III, still a child in the eyes of the people cheering on both banks of the Nile, clearly under the power of Hatshepsut. But he knew their eyes saw something else as well: That she was a woman and should never have shamed the crown by wearing it; that he was young and would outlive her. How soon that day would come, they couldn't guess.

Only a few weeks ago, Moses came down this same river. The cheers *he* heard were full of genuine love and admiration. Someday, so would the cheers for Tuthmose. But one aspect of Moses' triumph would remain unmatched: There would never be Israelites lining the banks of the river to cheer for Tuthmose III. On the contrary, the Israelites were too useful for any Pharaoh to waste them by letting them have such freedom. They were the enemy that the people could hate, so they would not resist the Pharaoh's tax collectors; they were the slaves that the people could despise, so they would not resent their own poverty. Any kingdom that did not have Israelites would have to invent them, they were so useful. Hatshepsut had been wasting them, but that, too, would change.

For now, though, Tuthmose was merely another boy, dependent like every child on whatever he could persuade adults to let him have or do. He might be dressed up in the regalia of Pharaoh and have thousands cheer, but the heat of the sun-god, Amon, still beat down on him as on anyone, and he still had to paint his eyes to prevent damage from the unrelenting brightness of his light. Pharaoh might be a god by title; it would take a little while before the title became the truth.

*

Moses could never get used to the custom of women and men eating separately. Not that Jethro wasn't charming company, for he was a man of great wisdom, who knew lore of all the desert tribes and wasn't wholly ignorant of Egypt, which he had visited several times in his youth. But night after night without the company of women, without the relaxed conversation of the table. Here there wasn't even the table, and the women ate out by the fire, as they cooked. Though he knew it was bad manners to question the local customs, tonight Moses was especially frustrated by his inability to converse with Zeforah, who still seemed to be avoiding him because of that one foolish joke this afternoon.

"Why do . . . people of the . . . desert . . . dine separately?" asked Moses.

Jethro raised an eyebrow. "Why do the people of Egypt shame themselves by eating together? Don't hold up the customs of Egypt to me as a model, Moses. People there think nothing of traipsing about with no clothes on."

"Only the lower . . . classes, and then only in the . . . fields."

"Come now, I've seen rich women in gowns of linen so diaphanous that you saw their nakedness as clearly as if they stood in a hot bath surrounded by a bit of steam."

"Nakedness isn't an offense to the Egyptians. It's one of the ways the Israelites . . . make themselves annoying, wearing heavy . . . clothing even during the . . . sweatiest labor." Moses paused to take another bite. "But this . . . criticism of Egypt seems like a poor . . . substitute for an answer to my . . . question."

"You asked a question?"

"Why don't women and . . . men dine together?"

Jethro shrugged. "I *did* answer. It's a custom. We grow up this way, so eating together seems about as immodest as if we bathed together."

"Now that you mention it . . ."

"No, please, no more accounts of how easy and natural the Egyptians are."

"So if it's just a . . . custom, Jethro, why couldn't you change it?"

"And bathe naked with women? My own daughters? Do you want God to strike me dead?"

"Who said anything about . . . bathing? I was talking about *eating* together."

"Moses, there'd be no conversation from them because they'd spend the whole time giggling and whispering and being shy and embarrassed or even outraged and offended that you made them do something so crude and ill-mannered. Just because it's a mere custom doesn't mean that it has no power. Once you grow up with a custom it's very hard to change. Even the most reasonable changes can be very disruptive."

Moses knew that Jethro was right. "I know," said Moses. "I'm a . . . stranger in a strange land here, and it's wrong of me even to wish for the . . . customs here to adapt to me. I'm the one who must adapt."

"Oh, but we *are* adapting to you."

"I hope I'm not too much of an inconvenience."

"Not at all. Your manners are so refined that even my most ill-mannered children are on their best behavior around you."

"Refined!"

"The way you persist in cleaning yourself all the time. Don't think I haven't heard of how you use the trough water to wash your face and hands."

"The sheep don't mind . . . drinking it, so it's not as if it goes to waste," said Moses.

"But now you've got my daughters doing it. How did Hamar say it? 'Moses is prettier than we are.' How's *that!*"

"Untrue."

"So what did you and Zeforah quarrel about?"

Moses was so surprised he had to laugh. "Quarrel!"

"You've been avoiding each other. You can't take your eyes off her, but she won't even look at you. A reversal of the normal situation, I might add."

"I offended her. Not . . . meaning to."

"Nothing to do with offensive Egyptian customs, I hope."

"I thought we were . . . brother and sister. So I tried to . . . tease her as a brother might."

"Brother and sister! What a silly thought! Not a one of them wants you for a brother, though I dare say at least six of them will have to."

"That's part of what . . . bothered her," said Moses. "Your assumption that I'll . . . marry one of your daughters."

"Why not? Somebody's got to."

"Zeforah says she'll make up her own mind."

"Well, that's the truth," said Jethro. "Ever since she was a baby, she obeys only because she understands and agrees with the rule. A swat on the behind meant nothing to her. Shaming her, lecturing her, nothing worked. Only persuasion. Like an adult. The time-wasting tedium of it! The man who has an intelligent child is doomed to spend his life justifying every decision he makes."

"I can see that you're . . . proud of her."

"I didn't set out to teach my girls to read, you know. What would be the point? There probably won't be any scrolls in their husbands' houses. But . . . Zeforah saw me reading, day after day, and there was nothing for it till I taught her how to read."

"She really can? How recently did she learn?"

"Before she was six. Amazing, isn't it?"

"Six! Six-year-olds are still . . . trying to make up stories from the . . . pictures instead of reading the hieroglyphs as syllables."

"Different language, different writing," said Jethro.

"You don't write as the Egyptians do?"

"I don't have a lifetime to waste making all those pretty pictures," said Jethro. "I tried to learn hieroglyphics when I was

in Egypt, but my sheep would grow old and die waiting for me
to memorize all those characters."

"How *do* you write, then?"

"Letters."

"I don't know what you mean."

"You just ignore the vowels. Instead of writing different
characters for ta, te, ti, to, you just write the 'tuh' sound."

"But there are plenty of words that would be written
exactly alike."

"True, but it's always easy to tell, in the context, which
word was intended."

"So you have fewer . . . glyphs to memorize."

"Letters. And they're simpler to draw. Not pictures at all.
Maybe they once were, but I can't begin to guess what the
original picture was."

"You have to show me."

Jethro beamed. "I thought you'd never ask. Have you
eaten all you want? I won't have food around my scrolls. I
spend my lifetime copying them, then somebody spills wine
and there I am, having to start over."

"I'm through eating and . . . drinking," said Moses. "I
haven't read anything the whole . . . time I've been here."

"You won't read this right away, either."

"Oh, of course not, I know. . . ."

Within moments the food was cleared away and Jethro
had the scrolls stacked up on the carpet in front of Moses.
"These are my copies, not the originals. Those are old and precious. Someday they'll fade completely or rot or something, I
know that, but in the meantime, they may very well be the
very originals that Abraham wrote with his own hand."

"Abraham! Knew this alphabet?"

"I asked my father if it was Abraham or Lot who made up

these letters, and he just laughed and said that the prophets were writing down records of what God said to human beings, right from the beginning of time."

"Who made up the letters, then?"

"Either God or Adam."

From the tent door came another voice. "Or Eve." It was Zeforah. Moses was relieved to see her. While she was talking mostly to Jethro, she included Moses in the conversation. The avoidance was over. It hadn't really lasted all that long. Either he was forgiven now, or she didn't want to give Jethro an excuse to say something about how it was good for a man to quarrel with the woman he plans to marry, so he can see if he can bear to live with her sharp tongue.

"Come in," said Jethro. "I want Moses to see how well you read."

"I don't want to be the reader," she said.

"Nonsense," said Jethro. "If you didn't want to read you wouldn't have come in. Here, the book of Enoch."

"Who's Enoch?" asked Moses.

"From before the flood. You know about the flood?"

"There's one every year."

"A flood that swept away the corruption of the children of men."

"The Nile does its share of . . . sweeping."

"It wasn't the Nile," said Jethro. "You really are ignorant, aren't you?"

"All I know of Israelite . . . teachings was what my . . . birth mother taught me. A few stories. The idea of one God over all."

"Not one God *over* all the other gods. One God that really exists, while all the other gods are merely imagined beings that never lived."

"Yes, well, my . . . brother and sister tried to explain all this to me, but I can't help but think that it's a . . . foolish idea. All the . . . prayers going to the same god! And there are a lot of Israelites . . . praying to him—not to mention Midianites like you, and those others. The Edomites, right?"

Jethro smiled. "Zeforah knows the answer to that prayer question."

Zeforah rolled her eyes. "I was a child then. Do you still hold it against me?"

"Not against you!" Jethro insisted. "*For* you!"

"God's capacity to love his children and hear their prayers is infinite," said Zeforah. "He listens to us much better than most of us listen to him!"

"I take it you asked the same . . . question when you were little," said Moses.

"I knew that the village children talked of many gods," said Zeforah, "but at home we talked of only one—a god so sacred no one can even speak his name. So yes, I had to know why we had only one God, invisible, nameless. I thought we were being cheated." Zeforah smiled ruefully. "If it had been a mortal sin, Father would never dream of bringing it up. But because he thought I was *cute,* asking all those questions in my lisping child-voice, he doesn't hide my shame."

Jethro scoffed openly. "You weren't that cute as a baby, I'll have you know!"

"I was as darling as they come," said Zeforah, "or you'd never have been able to persuade Mother to have the other six after me."

"We were just trying to get it right," said Jethro. "We kept coming closer and closer, and finally—Keturah."

Moses noticed that neither one said what had to be the truth—that Jethro and his wife were hoping for a son. Not that they didn't know it. They had spoken of it openly before. But in this game, the teasing didn't strike at the hard truth, that might have hurt Zeforah's feelings or shamed Jethro. That's what I did wrong, Moses realized. The teasing has to take place within safe boundaries. I crossed those bounds.

"The scrolls," said Zeforah pointedly.

Jethro grinned like a foolish boy and carefully unrolled the book of Enoch.

The letters were strange. Small and meaningless. "This isn't even writing," said Moses. "It's as if you . . . dipped a bird's feet in ink and made it run in rows."

Jethro looked at him in consternation. "Just because *you* can't read it, it isn't writing?"

"No, I . . . didn't mean it that way," said Moses. "It just surprised me that it wasn't . . . pictures. How can you remember them?"

"Because there are fewer letters to remember," said Jethro. "So the shape comes to *mean* the sound. You look at it and immediately your mind forms the letter."

"Is it written in Hebrew?" asked Moses.

"What use would it be to me if it were not?" asked Jethro.

"I just never thought of Hebrew as a language that . . . could be written."

Jethro shook his head. "Before the Egyptians had stopped running from the crocodiles long enough to scratch pictures on boulders, the servants of God were writing books."

Moses couldn't hide his skepticism.

"He doesn't believe you," said Zeforah.

"No, he just doesn't think that anything is older than Egypt," said Jethro. "Egyptians believe that at the core of their being. But God is older than Egypt, and it wasn't in Egypt that he first spoke to men."

"Where was it?" said Moses.

"God spoke to the first man and the first woman when they were first sent out into the lone and dreary world," said Jethro. "And he commanded them to keep a book of remembrance, so their children could learn the words of God, and their children's children, forever. Writing is as old as the human race."

"Then why are there so many . . . people who have no writing?"

"Adam was a godly man, but the evil one, the enemy fallen from heaven, the one we call Satan, tempted his children and grandchildren, and many of them rebelled. When they rejected Adam, they rejected his book. They refused to learn to read it. But they always remembered the idea of writing. They knew it was something holy men did. They just didn't know any more which men who *claimed* to be holy really talked to God. So their false holy men, who didn't really know anything about the true and living God, came up with silly picture writing just as they came up with silly religions." Jethro grinned. "You should see the way they write in Chaldea and Assyria. Pressing squared-off sticks in clay. A whole book would be a brick wall! You could build a house out of a scroll!"

It was Moses' turn to laugh. "So now who is it who's making fun of other people just because they do things differently?"

"Ah, but *you* were making fun of something that was *better*. You have to admit that there is no standard of judgment by which those shards of clay are better than writing with ink on scrolls."

Moses took the challenge. "A man of Akkad would . . . doubtless tell you that as long as he keeps his writings dry, they'll last forever and don't have to be . . . copied out by hand every . . . generation."

"True," said Jethro ruefully. "But then, no one reads a book as carefully as the man who's writing it out by hand."

"I've done my share of . . . copying, as a schoolboy," said Moses. "You just write it down, glyph by glyph."

"That's because Egyptian writing is done with little pictures. So you're thinking, draw a bird, draw an arrow, without regard for the sense. But with Hebrew, you make the sounds in your mind because the letter doesn't look like anything but the sound."

But Moses had already thought beyond this playful contest. "Jethro, are you telling me that what you have here on this scroll is an exact copy of the book of remembrance written by the first man?"

Jethro hesitated. "No, not at all. I'd give my life for one look at that book."

"But it was written in Hebrew? Hebrew is the oldest language?"

Again, Jethro hesitated. "I doubt it," he said. "Who knows what language Adam spoke? No, if that book is still on the earth, and if that language is still spoken, I don't know who reads the book, I don't know who speaks that tongue."

"And yet you know it once existed?"

"I do know it," said Jethro. "Because I know that God still lives."

"And how do you know that?" said Moses. "Every . . . priest can point to things that happen in the world around him and say, 'God did that.' And what is his . . . proof? Why, the thing happened, didn't it? Therefore . . . God did it. Therefore . . . God lives!"

"By that judgment," said Jethro, "there are no gods at all."

"No," said Moses. "I say only that men have no way of knowing what was done by the . . . gods, or what they meant by it. Does a hawk fall from the sky before a . . . battle? Then the . . . priest will say, Look, Horus shows you how you will fall upon your enemies! Then you lose the . . . battle, and the . . . priest goes home and says, 'Horus warned us that we would fail, for didn't we see a hawk leave the sky rather than look upon our defeat?'"

"An interesting observation," said Jethro. "If you ever get tired of shepherding, you would no doubt make some chieftain or king a fine omen-reader. As long as you learn to get away before your prediction comes out wrong."

"Oh, even that's easy. You learn to say, 'Look, a hawk! Horus is watching us!' And the . . . king says, 'Is that a . . . good omen?' And the . . . priest says, 'If you have been faithful to Horus in your offerings, and have not offended him, then it is . . . good.'"

Zeforah laughed. "Are kings such fools, then, to believe in priests who say such nonsense?"

"Why not?" said Moses. "The . . . king is brought up to believe in it from childhood on. Besides, it throws the . . . burden back on him. He has to search his heart and . . . decide if he's been pure in his devotion to the . . . god."

"So if he wins, he was faithful, and if he loses, he was unrighteous?" said Zeforah. "So every battle becomes a judgment of the king."

"That's what it means to be a king," said Moses. "With or without the . . . priest, everything is a test of the . . . king's worthiness. Good harvest? Good king. Bad harvest? Wicked king."

"Now, now, Moses, don't fib," said Jethro. "Bad harvest, wicked *people*."

Moses looked at him sharply, then smiled in defeat. "You're right, of course. Kings are as good as . . . priests at the game of . . . putting blame on others."

"The true God," said Jethro, "holds men responsible for what they choose. Not for the outcome, but for the intent."

"That's the mercy of God," said Zeforah. "For men are weak, and fail, but God judges us by our will to obey."

"So then if a man does . . . good, but his intention was to . . . deceive his enemy. . . ."

"Then God counts the goodness as a sin, because it was a lie."

"But how does a man tell the difference?" asked Moses.

"A man doesn't," said Jethro. "God judges."

"Men have to judge, too," said Moses. "I sat in judgment . . . day after day. Especially in . . . command of an army. Two men have a . . . dispute, they lay it before me. I have to . . . decide."

"But your judgment is imperfect. Sometimes you're wrong. God is never wrong."

"Then it would be . . . kind of him to . . . give us hints."

"That's what was written in the book of remembrance!" cried Jethro. "God's teachings! God's *hints*."

Moses shook his head. "But that book is lost."

"Lost to *us*," said Jethro. "Not to God! He remembers. Every word we write down is written in the mind of God. If all my scrolls were burnt today, if every copy of these books were lost, God could put the words into the mind of a prophet whenever he chose, and have the book written down again."

"So why write it at all?"

"Because not all men are prophets," said Jethro, "but all men need to hear the word of God."

"Are you a . . . prophet?" asked Moses.

The silence in the tent was painful. Tears came to Jethro's eyes, and slipped down his cheeks. Moses was appalled that his simple question should bring such ready emotion. He was about to apologize, when Zeforah intervened.

"Moses," she said, "my father is not grieving. He weeps for the love of God in him, for he's about to tell you something sacred."

Jethro smiled and touched his daughter's hand, drew her down to kneel beside him. "I'm not a prophet, my boy," said Jethro, "because God doesn't need a prophet for these people—a priest is enough. But from time to time, I have felt the presence of God in my heart. I'm reading, and a passage from the scripture lights up in my mind as if I heard a voice speaking it. Prophets hear the voice of God, full and loud. But a man like me—I hear the whisper of God. He is alive, not made up by priests or kings to serve their purposes, but alive and guiding his children."

"Who are his children?" asked Moses.

"Whoever will follow him," said Jethro. "Abraham was promised that his descendants would be the children of God. We men of Midian take that to include us, for our ancestor, Lot, was Abraham's adopted son and heir during all the long years before Abraham finally had sons of his body."

"The adopted son was then . . . cast aside?" asked Moses. The question was pathetic, he knew that, since the central fact of his life was his own adoption by Pharaoh's daughter. But he could say it in front of this man and this woman, because . . . why? Because there was no shame in showing weakness in front of them.

"The adopted son was wealthy in his own right," said Jethro. "But Abraham assured Lot that his children, too, could partake of the promise if we lived in obedience to God."

"Are the Israelites the . . . children of God as well?"

Jethro nodded. "If they'll obey God, then yes, they are."

"Yet the children of . . . God are slaves in Egypt."

"The children of God are in school," said Jethro.

"I grieve for how they must be suffering, now that I've . . . brought shame on them."

"I thought they weren't really your people," said Jethro. "I thought you were Egyptian."

"I didn't choose to be one of them," said Moses.

"You did when you killed an Egyptian rather than let him kill an Israelite."

"I saved a helpless old man from a . . . cruel lout of a . . . taskmaster. I acted as Pharaoh's . . . son, not as an Israelite."

Jethro shook his head. "Deceive yourself if you want, but you don't deceive me."

"I spoke from my heart."

"You acted as a son of God," said Jethro. "Pharaoh's sons have done all kinds of abominations over the generations. The man who is being made Pharaoh even now, you said he was involved in poisoning his own father."

"He wasn't . . . taught to act that way by Pharaoh," said Moses.

"Wasn't he?" said Jethro. "Didn't you tell me that *his* father became Pharaoh because his mother poisoned the true sons of Pharaoh, the sons of his queen? Sounds to me as if *that's* the way the sons of Pharaoh act, killing for their own advantage, or at least taking advantage of killings done for their sake. While you acted very differently, killing a man for the sake of justice and mercy rather than advantage and ambition."

"Those men and their mothers were . . . corrupt," said Moses, "but the ideal of Pharaoh's house is pure."

"The ideal of Pharaoh's house is but a pale shadow of what it means to be in the house of God," said Jethro.

Moses looked at the tent walls around him. "Is this the house of God? Does he dwell in a tent?"

"If the children of God dwell in tents, then God would not be ashamed to dwell in one," said Jethro. "I know his spirit has been here." Again tears flowed down his cheeks. "Oh, Moses, let it be true that God thinks of this as his house."

Moses did not look away, for Jethro did not seem ashamed to weep. Nor was he proud of it. He didn't even seem to notice that he was weeping. Rather the man was filled with joy, and his body could not contain it.

"Do the words in these scrolls teach a man to be as good and happy as you are?" asked Moses.

"Yes," said Zeforah. "They do."

"Teach me to read them," said Moses. "I would like to be happy. I would like to be such a man as you."

Jethro took his hands, drew him into an embrace. "As I said when you first came here, Moses—God has given me a son."

"People keep saying that when they meet me," said Moses. "They aren't always glad of it later."

＊

Young Joshua couldn't understand why the family was leaving their home near Karnak. "How can we move when you aren't done with the writing?" he asked his father.

Nun tried to explain. "They don't need me to write on the stone anymore."

"But you're the best."

"I'm the best, but I'm an Israelite, and all the Israelites have to move to Lower Egypt and make bricks."

"But anybody can make bricks," said Joshua. "Only a few people can write."

"Pharaoh has decided that Israelites are brickmakers now."

"Are you sad, Papa?"

"Not really," said Nun. "If I stayed, they'd make me write lies. I'd rather make true bricks than write false words."

When Joshua remembered the move later, he could barely picture their old house or the village by the Nile or the great buildings. What he remembered was his father's face, and the words: I'd rather make true bricks than write false words.

*

Zeforah watched Moses with fascination, and not just because she knew that Father intended her to marry him. Moses was interesting for his own sake. The body and bearing of a captain of thousands, but the stammer and eagerness of a child. He showed no shame at ignorance, no resentment that Zeforah could read the scrolls easily while he still made them out word by word, guessing often at what vowels should be understood among the letters, struggling to learn nuances of words, or words that weren't in Hebrew any more at all, so their meaning was lost. He was willing to learn from her, a woman—though the one time she asked about this, he looked at her as if she were insane for asking.

"Why shouldn't I?" he said. "My . . . mother was a woman. I understand that everyone's . . . mother is."

"You speak as if it's natural for a man to learn from his mother," said Zeforah. "You need to look at some of the village boys. They don't think there's anything they need to learn from women."

"Then the . . . shame is theirs. And their . . . fathers'."

"You have to admit that your mother wasn't typical, either. She taught you skills most women don't have."

"Not that these are useful skills to me now," he said, laughing. "Unless you think the villagers would like to have a . . . king. A sort of . . . toy Pharaoh. I could make them . . . take turns at being ambassadors to the next village to negotiate . . . treaties." Though he was mocking himself, she could see a glimpse of the life he had expected to lead, and realized that he was probably very good at it, that Egypt could have done much worse than to be governed by this man.

And yet God had brought him here. To Zeforah, this seemed to be proof that God had not struck Moses down from a high place, but had rather turned him away from a wrong road. So God was not punishing him for his sins, but rather giving him another school to learn in. And this was the school! Here in the shadows of the craggy mountains, in the upland meadows where sheep were more plentiful than men, and snakes more plentiful than sheep. A man great in the eyes of the world, but now he must become great in the eyes of God. And it was to my father that God brought him!

She tried saying these things to Sarah, but Sarah only looked at her as if she had lost her mind. "You cannot possibly know or even guess what God is doing," said Sarah. "You don't even know what *Father* is doing from day to day."

"He's teaching this man the holy books," said Zeforah.

"It would be more helpful if somebody would teach him a little more about sheep."

"He won't be a shepherd all his life, Sarah."

"No, not at this rate. You can't be a shepherd when all the sheep are dead!"

"He hasn't killed a single one."

"Because we're always watching him. He's more trouble than twenty sheep."

"No!" cried Zeforah. "He's being prepared for greatness. I think he might even . . ."

But she couldn't say it. Not to Sarah, not to this practical, sharp-tongued girl who would laugh at the thought and throw it back at her endlessly.

"He might even what?" Sarah asked.

"I don't know what I was going to say."

"Liar," said Sarah, and the accusation could not be denied. "You're just not going to tell me."

"That's right," said Zeforah.

"He might even . . . be your husband!" said Sarah.

"That's *not* what I was going to say."

"He might even . . . get bitten by a snake one of these days if he keeps walking around muttering to himself like a madman."

"I was definitely not going to say that, though he really should be more watchful—"

"He might even be crazier than Father," said Sarah.

This was beyond joking. "That's not funny," said Zeforah.

"It's what they say in the village."

"They wouldn't know wisdom or holiness if it was announced by fifty angels."

"Oh, fifty? I think they'd know it with fifty." Sarah laughed. "Oh, Zeforah, why must you be so solemn all the time?"

"I laugh as much as anyone."

"You laugh sometimes, yes, but *not* as much as anyone, and it doesn't last long, and there's always something solemn inside you watching everybody laugh and not taking part in it, not really."

The accusation stung, though perhaps it wasn't an accusation at all, but rather a mere observation. Sarah couldn't help it that everything she said sounded just a little snide.

"I was just trying to tell you what I was thinking about," said Zeforah.

"And I was telling you what I thought of what you think," said Sarah.

And that was that. Zeforah told no one her speculation. But she knew Father had to be thinking it, too. Some of the more obscure passages in a scroll that had no name because the first few columns were missing—how many, no one could guess. Father got it from his great uncle along with some books in much better condition, and when Zeforah asked why it was so much older and in so much worse condition than the other scrolls, Father showed her how difficult the language was. "I don't know a lot of these words," he said. "And the letters have changed form. I don't even know what this one *is*. Do I sound it? Or not? This word might be the word for angel, but it might not."

"What language is it?" Zeforah asked.

"Hebrew, I think, or I couldn't read it at all," said Father. "But not Hebrew the way we speak it now. A very *old* Hebrew, or a version of the language as it's spoken and written in a far-away country. Or both. So I'm never sure if I've read it right. But look, there are sections that tell some of the same stories in the book of Abraham. And some things that might be from the prophecies of Enoch. And see where it ends—when Noah comes out of the ark. Yet it isn't a history at all. It's more like a series of songs. But the songs have stories hidden in them. But are the stories of the future or the past? The language is so different that I can't be sure if words that seem the same have the same meaning at all. So I don't think it's worth your while wasting time trying to read *this* one."

Father might as well have smeared it with honey in order to keep flies away—it was the only book Zeforah could read for weeks. Father was right, of course, it was unreadable, or at least it was impossible to be sure whether she had read it aright. But there were tantalizing glimpses in it, hints of great knowledge that had been lost.

"Whatever was in there is lost, all right," said Father. "But whether it was *great* knowledge is hard to say. The previous possessors didn't value it enough to preserve it or copy it."

"But only because they couldn't read it easily," said Zeforah.

"Whoever made *this* copy understood it."

"How do you know that? Maybe they copied it letter by letter, and never understood it at all."

"And you'll succeed where they failed?" asked Father.

Stubbornly she continued to read it and it was plain to her that Father was rather proud of her for trying. He enjoyed discussing it with her, too, and that's how they emerged with the idea that whoever the writer of the scroll might be—and she speculated that it might have been Noah himself, though Father told her not to guess because it might just as easily have been some lonely shepherd with poor spelling and a penchant for writing down his incoherent dreams—whoever the author might be, he had clearly believed that there was a figure of prophecy who would come someday, and he would be known as the Son, and the power of God would be in him, and he would deliver the people of God from their most awful enemy. The writer even said that the Son stood between men and God, protecting men from God's wrath, and trying to teach men to be worthy of God's love. Only if he carries them will the words of our prayers be heard in heaven, the writer wrote. So we must pray to God in the name of the Son, as if it were

the Son speaking for us . . . or so Zeforah thought the scripture said.

Father told her she was wrong to reach conclusions when
the book was so unclear. But ever since then, she had surrep-
titiously murmured the words "in the name of the Son" or "let
the Son carry these words" before she uttered her closing
*amen.* If the others noticed her extra mumbling they never
spoke of it. She was sure Father must know what she was
doing. If he thought she was definitely wrong, he would stop
her. So she took that as a sign that he did not think her understanding of the nameless book was completely wrong.

Moses had only been here a few days before it occurred to
her for the first time that perhaps the fulfilment of that
prophecy was happening before her eyes. Didn't his name, in
Egyptian, mean "son"? And it wasn't just a part of his name,
the way "mose" was a part of the name of Tuthmose. It was his
whole name. And more than that: God had been guiding his
life from the beginning, had seen to it that he was born of
Abraham's lineage, and yet was given great power in the most
ancient of kingdoms, and had learned all its learning. When he
had received all that Egypt had to offer him, Moses was
removed from his lofty place in a matter of hours. And where
did God send him? To a desert where there just happened to
be the perfect man to teach Moses about God. That was why
Moses had been given the chance to learn Hebrew as well as
Egyptian, so that he could speak to Father and, when he came
to the holy books, he could learn to read them relatively
quickly.

Everything pointed to the idea that God had a great purpose for this man. And Zeforah could guess what that purpose
might be. Wouldn't the prophecy be fulfilled if Moses went
back to Egypt at the head of a mighty army and delivered the

children of Israel from slavery? The Israelites were groaning and praying in their bondage, but only when Moses—Son—carried their words to God would they at last be heard and a deliverer sent to them. Oh, it was so plain to her, so plain. Moses was the fulfilment of prophecy!

But she dared not say this; even her halting, hinting comments to Sarah had come to nothing. Father rebuffed her the moment she started trying to ask him about it—she had only to mention the nameless book and he jumped all over her. "Don't try to distract Moses with that book now! He's like a baby, just learning the simplest ideas, still struggling with his letters! Why give him a puzzle that even great scholars like you and me can't figure out?"

Great scholars indeed! Father didn't realize how it stung her when he teased that way. He thought he was including himself in the joke, but of course she knew that he really was a great scholar, while she . . . if she went to any gathering of wise and learned men, and tried to open her mouth and say, "When I was reading in the book of Abraham," they would scorn her as an imposter. Reading! What kind of fool does this maiden take us for? So Father's little joke had too much sting to it.

He was right, though. Without even knowing what she was going to say, he was right. Moses had no need to know of these prophecies now, especially if he were the fulfilment of them. What *he* needed was to learn to pray and hear the answer of God in his heart. There would be time enough for *him* to learn about the prophecies after they had all been fulfilled. For the prophecies weren't clear, and it would only confuse matters if Moses spent all his time trying to decode the nameless book instead of turning his heart to the Lord. She could not help thinking, though, that someday he would open the nameless book and recognize himself in the man of prophecy.

And this man is to be my husband.

No! She tried to strangle that thought before it even entered her mind. It would only set her up for disappointment, to think that way. Moses' wife would be a queen, if not of Egypt, then of some great kingdom. The best she could hope for was to be treated as a friend. But a wife? She could honor him and help him, and serve God by doing both. But she had better not let herself love him, for it was Moses that God had great plans for, not Zeforah, not the eldest of the seven girls of a shepherd priest. Moses would leave again to fulfil his prophetic destiny, and she was determined to remember him with fondness, not with regret and grief.

That is why Zeforah was fascinated with Moses. Not, as her sisters supposed, because she expected to marry him, but precisely because she did not, and therefore had to watch him and memorize everything he did and said so that she could treasure the memory when he was gone. She would bring out the nameless book and read it again and say, Yes, now I understand this part, and Yes, that obscure word is now clear, for I have seen him do these things, the Son who was foretold. His hand touched mine as we covered the well on the day we met. . . .

So she knew the first time he tried to pray. It was a warm afternoon, the deceptive kind of day when you think you don't need to come inside because it will be hot all night; but Zeforah knew, as Moses could not, that in late autumn the night would turn cold very quickly, bitterly cold, dangerously cold. She saw how he helped them finish the chores but then slipped away when they were walking home, and withdrew himself into the rocks.

Of course there were a thousand reasons why a man might part with the company of women and hide himself among the rocks of the mountain, and there was not a one of them that Zeforah would not be wrong to interrupt. But what if he lingered too long, and it got cold, and he took sick? She had to stay and wait for him, so that if he delayed too long she could warn him, call out to him to come home now before the night's chill came. And she could help him find his way home in the dark, for there wouldn't be much moonlight tonight.

Keturah noticed she was hanging back. "Tell the others to go on without me," said Zeforah. "I'm waiting for Moses. But don't tell them that, they'll only make crude jokes."

"They'll make them anyway," said Keturah. "You keep promising to explain to me what they mean."

"And I'll keep that promise. When you're older."

"I'm not completely ignorant, you know. I know what sheep do."

"Well, I can assure you that Moses and I will *never* do what sheep do. Now go!"

"Sheep *eat.* Aren't you going to eat?"

"Go!" Zeforah said, pretending to be pretending to be annoyed. Keturah must have noticed the edge in her voice, for she stopped herself before her next jest could come out of her mouth, and then hurried away down the mountain.

With the girls gone, it became very quiet. Zeforah did not walk around looking for Moses, for she did not want to interrupt his solitude. Instead she sat very still, resting on a sunwarmed rock, lying back and looking at the stars. In that stillness, she could not help overhearing him, even though he spoke quietly. She wasn't eavesdropping, or at least that wasn't her intent. But she heard him.

"O G-g-g-g. . . ."

This was not his normal hesitation. Instead of a pause, the word he was trying to say seemed to be hung up in his mouth like cloth on a bramble bush.

"O G-g-g-g. . . . Hear the words of my. . . ."

It was the word *God* that he could not say. Why? Yes, he was slow and halting of speech, but it was as if speaking the common name of God would tear something inside him.

And well it might. To speak to God might very well require him to tear something deep and strong and well-beloved out of his heart. His love of Egyptian learning, or the arrogance he sometimes put on as a tool to overawe and command others. Or it might be some secret sins that she knew nothing about, perhaps even the killing that had toppled him from power. Or it might be the enemy, the evil one, Satan, tying up his tongue so he could not speak. She wanted to run to him, or even to speak out—in this still evening air she knew he would hear her if she spoke in the mildest of voices—she wanted to tell him that he did not have to speak the words aloud, that if Satan blocks the tongue, God can also hear the thoughts of the heart.

But she said nothing. After a while, Moses' voice fell silent. A long while later, she heard his footsteps on the path down the canyon. There was still some pink-edged daylight left, so he had no need of her. He would never know she was there, that she had heard him, had violated his solitude at such a fragile time as his first uttered prayer to the Lord.

She lay on the rock and waited until his footsteps faded and she could hear him no longer. Then she opened her own mouth, and whispered her prayer. "O God," she said. "O Father, open his mouth, ease his heart, give him peace." And then she added, as she always did these days, "Let my prayer be borne to you in the name of the Son."

At that moment she almost laughed aloud at her own

absurdity. If Moses *were* the man of prophecy, then she was praying to God in his name to help the very man in whose name she prayed! No, it was too absurd. How could a mere man, like Moses, be at the same time the ambassador between men and God? She must have misunderstood the prophecy. Moses was simply an interesting man with an unusual past and a strange name. The nameless book was not speaking of him; indeed, she had almost certainly misunderstood it in the first place, and anyway, if the book had any value people would have taken better care of it, Moses is a waste of my time and . . .

And she knew where these thoughts were coming from.

"I want nothing to do with you, Satan," Zeforah whispered fiercely. "I won't listen to you."

With that she slid down from her perch and walked home. It was nearly dark now, for night fell quickly in the desert, especially in the craggy shadows of the mountain, but she knew the way, as sure-footed as an old sheep. When she came home supper was already being served, and Hamar told her off for worrying them all, most of all Keturah, who nevertheless insisted that she had been waiting to talk to Moses about something. "But when Moses came home without you and didn't even know where you were —"

"I was fine," said Zeforah. "I didn't stay to talk to Moses."

Strictly speaking, it was true. She had stayed to listen, though that was not her original purpose. She had stayed to listen, and she had heard — the scriptures weren't just an interesting project to him. He was taking them to heart. He wanted to pray. He wanted to feel the spirit of God in his heart.

And he had failed. That's what kept her awake that night, praying again, praying herself to sleep. O God, have mercy on Moses. Even if he isn't a man of prophecy, he's a good man who has lost everything. Let him find thee, O Lord, and then he will have everything again, only this time what he'll have is that which can never be lost, can never be torn from his grasp by those who hate or envy him. For the love of God cannot be interfered with. Let him feel thy love, O Lord.

Just as she drifted off to sleep, she heard the words as if someone spoke them softly into her ear. "He will be your husband," the voice said. "He will love you, and he will lead a mighty nation in the service of God."

She must have imagined it. It must have been the secret wish of her heart speaking. It must have. . . .

Why bother coming up with more excuses when she knew the truth: That God had answered her prayer, not with the thing she asked for, but rather the thing she wanted most in her heart. To know that he would be her husband. That he would love her. That he would lead a mighty nation — those were the questions that she really wanted to ask. And yet her prayer had not been a lie. She knew, though not because of words invisibly spoken in the darkness, that if she had not been praying for Moses, God would not have answered her unspoken wishes. It was just as Father said: God hears the words that we're too proud or too ashamed to say.

Oddly enough, instead of flustering her, instead of making her even more shy in front of Moses, her new sureness of a future connection with this man made her more relaxed and confident in front of him. Her marriage, when it came, would come because God or Moses had decided on it, and either way she would be content. She wasn't the sort of woman who could ever be a queen, but she would certainly do her best to give him children, and to train them up to be true sons and daughters of this kingly man that God had brought to her. That was all she could do, but if he loved her, then it would be enough.

Hatshepsut stood in her chariot, wearing her regalia, striking the pose that her father had told her looked most mannish. She knew that it fooled no one, and outraged some; but she also knew that if she did not strike such poses, affirming her will to rule as a man, then resentment would turn to ambition, and someone, fancying her to be weak and womanly, would strike out to try to take her place.

There were no crowds around her this time, and Tuthmose was in the custody of the teachers she had hand-picked for him because they had the essential qualification: They loathed Tuthmose as a patricide and hated having to associate with him. There was no chance of him charming them, winning them to his side. But even without the crowds and without her dangerous rival, the poses were still necessary, for with Moses gone she was utterly alone. There was no one whose love and loyalty she could trust, for it was in the best interest of the disloyal to behave exactly as loyal men would. She knew that not all the people around her were hypocrites, but she had to act as if they were, for to trust any of them was to open herself up to betrayal. So the poses never ended, even here, surrounded by a few of her most intimate counselors. For all she knew, every single one of them was ready to leap to Tuthmose's side the moment he called them to act. Every single one of them might have a knife he longed to plunge into her heart.

She stood in her chariot and inspected the carvings in the ravine. Scribes had stood on scaffolding to write the exploits of her reign on the smoothed stone walls, where there was hope that the wind would not scour the words away too soon. Then, in the past few weeks, they had ground away the old writing and replaced it with new, for the name of Moses had to be utterly expunged. Now there was no story of Hatshepsut pulling a child out of the Nile; now it was Hatshepsut herself who conquered the Ethiopians and took Saba by force of arms.

When I am dead, she thought, Tuthmose will do the same to me. I removed Moses' name because he represents a dangerous mistake that threatens my authority; he will remove my name because he hates me. What will he write? That far from being Pharaoh, I was a usurper. No doubt he'll declare that his father was the true Pharaoh and not a mere puppet that I controlled. He'll say that I was his sister-wife, and only when he died with Tuthmose III still a child did I seize power. I'll be painted as a traitor, when he was the traitor. I'll be painted as the illegitimate ruler, while he is the son of a son of a concubine in whom the blood of the Pharaohs runs so thin as to be nonexistent. History will believe his lies, and claim that my true history is only propaganda.

Well, it's what I deserve. As I expunged Moses' name, so will my name be scoured off the stone.

She wanted to weep for him, could feel the tears welling up inside her. But she refused to let them show. She did not come this far to have it all erased. Whether it was the wind or Tuthmose's artisans, this writing on the wall was in vain. It would disappear. The stone would become raw stone again. She would be forgotten. She would be denied. She would be vilified after her death, and her great achievement in maintaining Pharaoh's house and Pharaoh's kingdom, despite all the disadvantages of being a woman, would be turned into a crime instead of a credit. It galled her. It made her angry. She would shed no tears today.

There had to be a way to cheat them. To send her story forward into the future so they would have at least the chance to know some truth about her. Moses would be forgotten, of

course, but that couldn't be helped, he made that choice himself when he killed the Egyptian for an Israelite's sake.
Hatshepsut, however, would be remembered.

"Bury it," she said.

The chief of the stonecutters looked at her in confusion. He
must have heard her wrong, but it was not his place to question Pharaoh. Seeing his hesitation, she had mercy on him, and
made her instruction clear. "Take all the rubble you have
cleared away and fill the ravine. As high as you can fill it, cov-
ering these inscriptions."

"But then no one can see them," said the chief of the
scribes, who, being more educated, apparently felt he could
speak boldly to Pharaoh.

She looked at him coldly, to let him know that she did not
need a fool like him to tell her something so obvious.

"We will fill it," said the chief of the stonecutters. "We will
fill it and cover everything."

Someday, thought Hatshepsut, someone will be digging
here and will discover these inscriptions. It will be long after
Tuthmose III is dead, hundreds of years from now. My story
will be there for all to read, to tell the truth about my reign.

Of course, it will be a man who discovers it, and men who
read it, and so they will probably doubt my story, and believe his.
But what they believe is their business. The truth will be told. I
will not be slandered without giving my answer to the ages.

If only Moses could have the same power, to write down
his story, to tell his life. Oh, my son, my son, why, after a life
of such iron self-control, did you have to have such a lapse as
that, to let a moment's compassion throw you into the river of
history to be swallowed up and carried out to the sea of forgotten men? You had the seeds of greatness in you, but when

they list the names of the great Pharaohs of Egypt, your name will not be there, my lost son, my lost joy, my lost hope.

As she rode away in her chariot, the driver keeping the horse at a stately pace, a dreadful thought came to her. What was to stop Tuthmose from digging up these inscriptions to destroy them?

But then she remembered the kind of man she was dealing with. He had no forethought. He cared nothing about the future, only about his own time, obtaining a kingdom and holding it for himself. What she buried would stay buried while he was Pharaoh. Having her story out of sight was good enough for him. If he had the will to be great, to create something for the ages, she would not despise him, and they would not be at war. But he was a small-hearted man, and so he was her enemy. He would win in the end, but defeating her would not make him great, it would just make Egypt smaller, too.

※

Moses worked hard at learning all the new things in his life. The shepherding was hard, and some of Jethro's daughters were anything but patient with him, making it clear how stupid they thought he was that he didn't know the things that any shepherd's child knew from the cradle up. He never answered harshly, though, and over the weeks and months their scorn became teasing, and now and then even a moment of grudging respect, as he showed that he could, indeed, master at least some parts of their art. The sheep no longer sensed his awkwardness, and would obey him and submit to his care. The girls did not obey him, of course, but they finally treated him as an equal. As a brother.

The other part of his education was more enjoyable but also less important. To help with the sheep was the duty he owed to Jethro for his extraordinary hospitality. To read

Jethro's books was a pleasure for its own sake, and Moses felt guilty for how many hours he pored over the strange Hebrew writing by the light of a floating wick in a lamp of oil.

Why was he so fascinated? The Hebrew language was strange enough to him that he couldn't hear the nuances in it the way he could in Egyptian; he had no idea if the writing was elegant or plain. The books were so different from the holy writing of the Egyptians. There was no attempt to glorify the men and women in the stories they told. They were shown plain, sins and stupidities along with their moments of godliness. A small mind and a great heart could exist in the same man. How refreshing, to read such plain, believable tales! How it inspired trust, to know that the prophet did not always paint himself as a perfect man. How could the story of Jacob be known, if it had not been told by him? True, there were different accounts, some in which he had a perfect right to the inheritance because he was truly the firstborn, others in which he was the pure trickster, setting out to take the inheritance because his brother was such an oaf and Jacob resented the way Isaac favored the red-haired one. There was no reason, however, why these tales could not all be true. Why shouldn't the same man be both an ambitious trickster and yet have right on his side? Why shouldn't God send a vision to the exiled Jacob, showing him heaven and letting him choose? Jacob paid in years of service for his sins—how could he damn Laban for tricking him, when he himself had tricked his father to win his blessing? So he bore the life God gave him, and served him humbly, and in the end he got his beloved Rachel, and his sons. And if the sons in turn caused him grief, they also brought him joy in the end. It was a believable life, not one made pretty for the admiration of others. It was not a hero story. It was a story of a man made good by God. Or rather, of a man who chose to be good when taught by God.

Of course Moses saw himself in all these men. In Abram, laid under the knife in Chaldea, saved from becoming a human sacrifice himself by the intervention of an angel; then, his name changed to Abraham, holding a sacrificial knife himself as he almost, almost gave his own beloved son to God. Lying and putting his wife in great jeopardy, though one account said it was Pharaoh who wanted her and another account said it was another man; and yet a third story said that it was Isaac who lied about his wife. For all Moses knew, the same thing happened three times, for surely God was not afraid to repeat history. Having great wisdom and hearing the voice of God in their ears did not turn these men into something other than men. They could still be unwise sometimes. But their unwisdom did not trouble them: They wrote it down right along with the stories of the goodness and majesty of God. They were not afraid of truth.

And it *was* true, Moses knew that. Now that the word of God was not being flung at him by Aaron and Miriam in the effort to bend him to their will, he could see that the God of Abraham, Isaac, and Jacob was different from all the gods of Egypt, and that the faith required to believe in him was different from the faith he had grown up with. In Egypt, the gods were given credit for everything, but in fact one could never see them doing anything. Moses had realized at an early age that it was the priests and the Pharaohs who decided what it was the gods had meant by what they did. If there were no gods it would not change what was written about them.

But the God of Abraham was not to be tamed by scribes or rulers. His intentions were not invented by men to give divine sanction to their own actions. He spoke his own mind,

and it was often at odds with the will of the men who served
him, and they had to change their course to fit what he
designed. Sometimes they obeyed when he spoke to them;
other times he had to shape events against the will of the men
who either did not understand him or opposed him openly.
This was a God who was alive. This was a wild God, in that
no man could ride him; rather it was the men themselves who
had to be broken to the will of God, so he could ride in their
hearts and guide them as a man guides his chariot.

"Is the age of . . . prophets over?" Moses asked Jethro one
night, as Jethro copied a manuscript and Moses studied what
was written on another scroll. "Did it end with Joseph? And
why are there no . . . prophets of Midian?"

"The age of prophets is never over," said Jethro. "But
sometimes the prophets fall silent because there is no people
willing to listen to them."

"The . . . people of Midian aren't willing?"

"They don't listen to the scripture that they have. Why do
you think it was Isaac and Jacob through whom the line of
prophets descended, and not Ishmael and Esau? My fore-
father Midian knew of God, but did not devote his life to serving him. Even Lot, who was nephew, brother, and son to
Abraham, was no prophet. He tried to be a good man, a decent
man, but he was a man of the world. Abraham could never
have lived in Sodom, but Lot could, because that's what his
business required of him. That is the lineage through which I
come. That's why the scrolls I copy hold the tales of Abraham,
Isaac, and Jacob, of Joseph and his brothers, and not of
Midian, Esau, and Ishmael."

"So why did the . . . prophecies stop? Why didn't Joseph's
sons, Ephraim and . . . Manasseh, . . . carry on in their father's
work?"

Jethro shrugged. "How can I judge men I never met? Of individuals I can say nothing—they might have talked to God, and God may have told them to keep their mouths shut. But as for why Israel didn't listen, I can tell you that: Egypt did it to them. Power and prestige did it to them. Civilization did it to them."

"Took away the voice of . . . God?"

"Took away the will to listen to that voice. Egypt had so much wisdom, the Israelites became ashamed of their own. They despised the lore of their fathers because the Egyptians were so rich and so refined. So the Israelites became scribes and rulers, and fancied that they were as Egyptian as the Egyptians. Not until they lost their wealth and power did they remember God. And by then, these books were lost to them."

"Lost? But I heard some of these stories from . . . Jochabed and Miriam, and heaven knows Aaron spoke of the . . . promises of Abraham until I thought I had them . . . memorized."

"They pass on their corrupted stories, yes, by word of mouth," said Jethro. "But no one ever laid out a scroll like this for you. You didn't even know that Hebrew could be written down, did you?"

"Some . . . tried to write it in hieroglyphs, but the sounds didn't . . . fit right, and it was a mess, unreadable by Egyptians or Hebrews."

"You see how Satan works on people," said Jethro. "He doesn't tell them there is no God. He doesn't fight openly. He just makes them ashamed of themselves. He makes them admire the world. He makes them trust in the learning of the world and despise the primitive myths of their ancestors. And even when they reached out to try to recover those old tales, did they really understand them?"

Moses shook his head. "No, they just . . . picked and chose

the . . . parts that were useful to them. Aaron was full of stories of the . . . destiny of the children of Israel, but I never heard him speak of the . . . covenants and . . . commandments. He kept telling me to submit to the will of . . . God, but he never taught me to . . . pray."

"So it was his own will, not God's, he wanted you to submit to?"

Moses smiled. "I don't think it ever occurred to him that there might be a . . . difference between the two."

"So. Do you?"

"Do I what?"

"Pray?"

"I've tried."

"And?"

"God knows the feelings of my heart, doesn't he?"

Jethro shook his head sadly. "My son, *you* don't know the feelings of your heart until you discover them by praying. You have to ask. You have to *choose* to speak to God, not just expect him to do what's right for you. After all, every man has every possible desire. What if God granted all our wishes? Our path would be strewn with dead enemies. The weather would be a nightmare, as one man's healing rain was another man's disastrous flood. We have to choose which desires are the ones we want to act upon. Then we put those choices into words and pray them to God."

"I have no words."

"I doubt that."

"I have no choices."

"And that one I know is false."

"Jethro, the only life I have is one that's . . . borrowed from you."

"Not borrowed, given. And not given, either—I still have

it. It isn't gone. So what you really mean is that the only life you have is the one you *learned* from me, and I'm telling you that my life is a life of prayer, and you aren't praying."

"Teach me how."

"You hear my prayers."

"But you . . . pray for your daughters, for the villagers. I'm not a . . . father, and I'm not a . . . priest."

"Both shortcomings are remediable, but that's another matter."

"Why should . . . God hear me, Jethro? He already closed every . . . door in my life. I think what he wants of me now is a life without . . . choices. A life of humility. To be reconciled to my losses until I think of them as . . . gains."

"Very good. Very plausible. But are you right?"

"I don't know."

"And you never will until you ask. Right now you're just like those priests you talk about in Egypt, always able to invent a story to explain the meaning of omens, to show what the gods meant by everything. You're inventing your own story of what God wants for you, and acting on it, but I'm telling you again as I've told you before, God will not open the next door for you until you choose to knock on it!"

Moses smiled wanly. "Jethro, I'll . . . try again."

"Do. And again after that!"

❉

Jochabed was too old for these changes. It was a bitter new life that was beginning for the Israelites now. Aaron was all for starting a revolution, but cooler heads prevailed, and instead Aaron submitted, as they all submitted, moving from their homes, scattered throughout the Egypt, and gathering in the wet clay brickmaking lands along the swampy edges of the Nile in the edges of the delta. Miriam was the one who claimed it was the mercy of God. "After Moses fled, the Egyptians were ready to start murdering Israelites again. So gathering us together and separating us from the Egyptians is saving our lives."

But when Jochabed's back ached from bending over to pack and smooth the mud in the forms, or from laying out straw on the endless acres of wet bricks to help them dry faster, she did not feel her life was saved. She felt as if the Lord was punishing her and all of Israel, though for what she did not know. Oh, Moses, what were you born for, why did I suffer such pains for you, why was I shown the way to put you in the river, why were you lifted up, when your whole life came to this: False hopes, now dashed, and your people restored to bondage?

And then, when she was feeling most embittered, she would remember that the Lord's love for Israel was like a parent's love: Sometimes children had to be set to tasks they hated because the work needed doing, or because it was good for the children even though they didn't understand. God's hand has been in our lives, doing extraordinary things, so why should I doubt him now? Somewhere Moses is alive. Somewhere God is working with him, shaping him as I shape these bricks. Moses was simply in the wrong mold here. He had to be cast from it, then kneaded and remade in a new shape. God's hand is here as well. I'll certainly be dead before his work is finished, but I have no doubt that from my womb came the Lord's true servant.

Moses, wherever you are, look for God's hand in the road behind you — it is so clear, so obvious how God has chosen you. And when you've learned to see his hand, look for it in the road ahead. Take his hand, follow where he leads you, for only in God's hand will you be free. Only God can bring you back to Egypt, to your people. To me.

# F i r e

It was the end of the day, and it was spring, and the new grass was so sweetly green that Moses wanted to gambol like the lambs in the meadows. The sun's ruddy slanted light brought the rocks to blazing life, and the girls were all happy and frolicking, and there were village boys with their hearts set on Hamar and Asa and Sarah and they rather liked the attention and even liked the boys, a little. So there was joy in Jethro's household from morning to night, and laughter and teasing and fun. And here in the uplands where the sheep nibbled on the new grass, there was joy in Moses' heart as well. In all his years in Egypt, the seasons had come and gone with no meaning except a change in his duties. In the time of flood, the business of the government was distributing the stores of grain; when the flood subsided, there was planting; when the harvest came, there was gathering and storing. All these things he saw, but his own connection to them was to hear reports of how the harvest went, and what the surpluses were, and where the excess grain might be shipped and sold.

Here, though, he felt the grass beneath his feet, felt the blood and slime of the newborn lambs on his hands as he helped with the hard deliveries. He had felt the trembling flesh of the sheep under his hand as he held them to be sheared by those with some skill at cutting wool without cutting skin. He had smelled the stink of life in his nostrils, and now the freshness of spring came to him with such power that for the first time since coming to Midian he did not miss his old life in Egypt. Indeed, he felt that for the first decades of his life he had been cheated, because he lived a life of words in which his only physical labor was in learning how to fight and kill for the kingdom. Now, though words still filled his mind and heart, his hands were strong in the business of life. The sun beat down on a back that was bent in labor.

In Egypt the rich despise manual labor, he thought, yet they are the ones who are poor because they make nothing with their bodies, but only please themselves. The rich are poor; the poor are rich, the world tells its lies, and the wrong people are envied for all the wrong reasons.

The day's work was done, but Moses did not want to go back down the mountain to the tents of Jethro, for even though he was caught up in the book of Enoch, that great prophet who led his people to such perfection that God removed them from the world and took them to himself—even though he was eager to read more of that prophet's words and works, his body could not bear to leave the cool grass. So as the girls put on their sandals for the rocky trek, Moses left his off. "I want to stay till dark," he said. "I know the way by now."

"But you *must* go down," said Zeforah.

Sarah made a hooting noise, and Hamar laughed.

"Why?" asked Moses.

Zeforah was silent, unwilling or unable to explain.

"Oh, this is stupid," said Sarah. "Zeforah has always stayed up the mountain after dark on these first green nights of spring. She makes us leave and keeps the meadows for herself."

Zeforah's lips were set—she hated Sarah's tone, but it was clear that what Sarah had said was true.

"Isn't there room enough for me here, too?" said Moses.

Zeforah rolled her eyes. "Of course. I just didn't want you thinking I was staying up here to be with you."

Again, hoots and derision from her sisters.

"Then I'll go down," said Moses. "I'm not here to take your customary pleasures away from you, and I understand about the need for solitude."

"I think the meadow is large enough for the two of us," said Zeforah.

That had the other girls so amused they could hardly breathe for laughing.

"Do you sometimes think," said Moses, "that your sisters are insane?"

But after a while the girls left, driving the sheep before them. And Moses and Zeforah were alone. He made as if to walk to the far end of the meadow, but she caught his arm. "No," she said. "I don't want you far away from me. I'm here because I love this place in springtime. I wouldn't make my sisters leave, except they get so silly it spoils the mood. *You* won't be silly, I think."

So she didn't mind him being there. Like Hebrew letters, her moods were so hard to read. They meant nothing except themselves. They could not be compared to anything. Zeforah was Zeforah.

Moses knew that Jethro wanted him to marry her. But what did *she* want? He didn't want a wife who married him out of filial duty. He wanted what he had always wanted, a marriage between equals, the kind of marriage that Hatshepsut should have had but didn't. He had nothing but contempt for the marriages he had seen, in which middle-aged men married young girls, to father children on them but treat them otherwise as servants or children themselves. It took a weak man to prefer a wife like that, who wouldn't dare to answer back when he was foolish, or to insist when he had neglected a duty. Zeforah would certainly not be one of those child-wives. Talking about the scriptures with her was often as invigorating and challenging as talking to Jethro. And she was the only one of the girls who was patient with him as she taught him about shepherding—and so he learned more from her than from any of the others. And she was lovely, especially now that she had joined him in his custom of washing his face and hands every day in the sheep's drinking water. She was not so stubborn that she would not let him teach her, too. He liked her. He could easily love her. If they were supposed to marry, it would be a good marriage, and he would love the children she gave him.

Furthermore, the time of decision was coming near. He had come in autumn, and now it was spring. Through these seasons that sheep were always close enough to be herded home every night. But during the summer they had to take them up to the highest meadows, out of the killing sun, and in those days they would not come home at night. He could hardly sleep up there, night after night, without being married to one of them. The scandal in the village would be impossible. There would have to be a wedding, or Moses would have to stop working at shepherding. Well, that would be fine with Moses.

But what did *she* want? Each of the other girls—even Keturah!—had gone through a flirty stage with him, trying to catch his eye. But not Zeforah. She was all cool business with him, talking about the question or problem at hand, and when she joked with him, it was like a brother. He did not want to be her brother. But that distance remained between them. That sense that he could stand outside the door but was not quite welcome yet inside. He did not know what the barrier was. But he did know that Zeforah was the only one of the daughters that he could happily marry; and she was the only one who had never given him even a hint that she wanted him as a husband.

Until now. Was this a hint, letting him remain with her in this meadow? Letting him share her ritual of springtime?

And what was that ritual? Did she lie in the cool of evening and count stars overhead? Did she sing with her voice echoing among the stony canyon walls? Did she shed her clothes and prance like a lamb in the grass? That idea had some appeal for him, he could not deny. But no, she would hardly have invited him to stay for that.

So he sat down in the meadow and looked at the sunset. And she came and sat beside him, and watched it, too.

"All that color in the sky," she said. "And the green of the grass. Why green? Why red?"

Moses was taken aback. "Why not?"

"Exactly," she said. "God could have made it any way he wanted. He didn't have to put such fire in the sky."

Moses pulled a blade of grass and held it up. "The beauty of variety," he said. "And the beauty of the familiar. This green must come every year."

"And yet it never grows old."

Her smile, the tenderness of her voice. How he wanted to take her in his arms. Did she want that, too? Was that why she stayed?

Just as he was about to test the theory with the touch of his hand on hers, she drew herself up to her knees, facing the sunset. Out of reach. Had she sensed his desire and wanted to avoid the awkwardness of refusing him? Or was it pure chance, and she had no idea of what was in his heart?

Even as he thought these thoughts, he babbled something about the sunset. "Of course these colors probably come by necessity. Dust low in the sky turns red when the sun shines through it. The green of living plants is probably part of what makes them alive, and we find it beautiful because we love life. Or because it's familiar."

She looked at him with benign pity. "Does anything beautiful come by accident? Toss some stones—will they come up a temple? God made a garden world for us to tend, and then he stepped away to watch and wait. Someday he'll come to harvest. To weed. But look at the sky tonight. You can't tell me that all that grace and glory is undesigned and undesired chance."

"And this is what you stay for?" he asked.

"We sing our hymns to God," she said. "But on these nights, I hear him singing back to me."

She turned again to face the sky and when she spoke, her voice was different. Tender, loving. The voice she might be saving to speak to her children. Perhaps the voice she had used with her mother when she was dying. The voice she might be reserving for only her husband to hear. The voice with no hard edge to it, no wariness, just warmth and trust.

"O Father, thank you for the sky tonight," she said. "The way the sun is red and gold like fire, the silver in the clouds, the bursts of light and the shining rocks of the hills. And for my eyes so I could see it, and for love and peace that fill my life, so I can recognize the white that's hiding in the dusty fleece. And thank you for the cool of the gathering night." Then, more softly, she added the words that he had seen her murmuring at the end of every prayer in Jethro's house, only this time he heard her, this time the words were clear. "In the name of the Son. Amen."

This was her ritual, then. What she stayed for, by herself. To pray. And she had let him keep this vigil with her, and had let him hear this most private prayer. She did love him, he saw that now; and he also saw what the barrier between them was. She could not wholly give herself to him until he wholly gave himself to God. He was a student of the scripture, but not yet a servant of the Lord. Before she could take him as her husband, she had to know that he could also pray.

And it was not enough, he knew, for him to murmur an *amen* at the close of her prayer. She heard him, and she smiled a little, but it was not enough.

If only he could pray. If only he could get the words out. But the fear and confusion that made him hesitate in his normal speech had become a terrifying, choking stammer when he tried to pray. Her words flowed so gracefully and naturally—how could she understand how much even the attempt to pray cost him? He knew it was his own unworthiness. He could not utter a word to God; his mouth was shut when he tried.

She turned to him, reached out to him, touched his cheek with her gentle hand. "You haven't stammered once today," she said. Then she rose to her feet and walked away from him, along the meadow to the path leading down to Jethro's tent.

What did she mean by that? Perhaps it was true, perhaps he was confident enough that he no longer hesitated to choose his words when he was with Jethro's daughters. But no, she meant more by it. It was as if she knew that he longed to pray, but that his stammering blocked the words. It was as if she had heard him struggle. She wanted him to pray. She wanted him to be worthy to marry her. She knew what he had only just realized, that it was the silence between him and God that stood between him and Zeforah.

That was why she had shown him a prayer, and then left him alone to pray himself.

For a moment he wanted to rebel against the assignment, to refuse to obey. But he recognized that as pure foolishness and put it aside. He wanted exactly what she wanted, and if she was trying to help he would have to be a dolt not to accept it gratefully.

He knelt, as she had knelt. He looked at the sunset, as she had looked, though the color was waning fast as darkness came on.

"Oh G-g-g-g . . ."

He bowed over in despair. He could say the word *God* in conversation, but he could not say it when he tried to speak to God. Why? What was it? The evil in his own heart? Was it God himself who silenced him, forbidding him to speak? Or was it his own fear?

She had used the word *Father* when she prayed. To her, the word had meaning, for she knew her father, was close to him. What did *Father* mean to Moses? Stories of Amram, but he never knew the man. Stories also of Tuthmose I, Hatshepsut's father and first husband, before she took on her weakling half-brother, but all these fathers were only rumor to him.

But he knew what *Zeforah* meant by saying "Father," and loved the idea that God might be toward human beings as Jethro was toward his daughters. It was a clear and lovely image, to think of God that way, only even wiser, even more loving, even sterner when the occasion demanded it. That's who he must speak to. A God who was like Jethro.

"Oh F-f-f-f . . ."

No. He would *not* be stopped. Not this time, not when he

knew his hope of life with Zeforah was on the line. "O F-f-f-f-fa . . ."

Not even his love of Zeforah could bring words to his mouth. Who had the power to open his mouth and let him speak? Only God himself could do that, and how could he ask God to help him ask God to help him?

Why not? Just because his prayer was circular, why not?

"O F-f-f-father give me s-s-s-s-speech!" he cried. "O Father, give me . . . give me . . ."

And then he realized that in the process of asking, his prayer was answered. The realization rushed through his body like fire. When he prayed for the power to pray, it was given to him. God heard him. God was listening!

But now that he was given speech, what should he say? There would be no meaning in repeating Zeforah's prayer. There was only joy and gratitude in her heart. But Moses' heart was filled with darker and more complicated things.

"O Father, I didn't kneel to thank you for the sky. Though I do thank you for it. The sky, the grass, the spring lambs. For these people, these good, kind people. Jethro. Zeforah. Zeforah."

So there *was* joy in him, after all. He *could* pray with gratitude, as she had.

"And for the time to see the world clearly, I thank you for that," he said. "I never saw anything in Egypt, I never knew anything . . ."

But even as he spoke, he knew that he was pretending. Not lying to God, but to himself. For he did not hate Egypt, did not despise what he had learned there. God must not have despised it, either, if Jochabed and Hatshepsut were right and it was divine intervention that put him in Pharaoh's house to begin with. So he would not pray his first prayer without speaking his mind; now that God was listening to him, he had some things to say.

"Why did all this happen to me! What was it for, all this lifting me up and knocking me down! Was it you doing it? Or was it my own mistakes? Or was it chance? Bad luck?"

The anger in his own voice surprised him.

"Or maybe it was good luck," he whispered. "There's peace here. But I'm not at peace. There must be something more for me to do than sit on rocks and tend sheep! And yet there are times when I think there's no more important labor in the world. Sometimes I feel that I've lost everything that mattered in my life. And then other times, all I want is here, all I want to do is lose myself in the love here. But you know all this. You know all my feelings and I have no choices that are in my power, so why do I bother even praying! Why did you loose my tongue when I have nothing to say! You're the wind and I'm the grain of sand, you're the mill and I'm the barleycorn. Well while you're busy grinding me, you might at least give a hint of what I'm being ground up *for!*"

His anger surprised him. He had hidden it from himself for so long that the dark power of it was frightening, and he forced himself to be calm. He didn't know much about praying, but he knew that yelling at God was probably not the best approach.

"I don't even know if you're there," he said. "I'm probably talking to empty air."

But he did not believe it.

"I hope you're there," he said. "I want you to be there, because then there's a hope that my life and all the million lives before and around me have some purpose to them. If you aren't real, then life is a cruel joke that's played on us by a vicious child, and the only way to get the better of it is to die!"

Again, the pent-up rage had found a way out, and again he calmed himself.

"Help me to be patient, Father," he said. "Whatever you're doing with my life, I can wait. That's a choice, isn't it? To wait. To live in each good moment."

He wondered when the answers might come. And then realized that perhaps the answers were coming from his own lips. He spoke his rage, and then for some reason it occurred to him to speak of patience. Was that how God answered his prayer, by putting words into his own mouth?

"I don't know how this is done," he said. "Is this the way to pray? Did I offend you? Help me not to feel like a fool tonight for having shouted at the sky like this."

He bowed his head. The sky was dark. The stars were out. He rose to his feet, but then had the nagging feeling that he wasn't done. "Father," he whispered, "I know the miracle that came tonight. My mouth, opened. The gift of speech. The gift of Zeforah's example, her kindness. Thank you."

It was all he could think of to say, and yet he still didn't feel that he was done. Then he remembered. Zeforah's little ritual still waited for him.

"In the name of the Son," he said, not knowing what it meant, or why she said it. But now the prayer was finished. "Amen."

❋

Jethro was worried. Again Moses and Zeforah had lingered on the mountain, and again they came down separately. The only difference was that this time it was Zeforah who returned first. Did they think he wouldn't notice that his daughter was alone with a man? He knew Zeforah well enough to know that nothing improper had happened. Indeed, he thought he knew Moses that well, too, and could trust him.

But if all was so innocent, why did they return separately? Why did they act as if they hadn't seen each other on the hill?

Tonight in particular, Moses was almost giddy, garrulous through dinner, talking of nothing, everything, anything, and yet never quite listening to his own words, sometimes saying the same thing twice. Finally, fed up with whatever evasion was going on, Jethro asked him point blank. "What is it!"

"What is what?" asked Moses. Oh, such calculated innocence.

"The thing you're not telling me. The reason you and Zeforah stayed up in the meadow tonight and neither of you got back till after dark!"

Someone outside the tent dropped a dish. Well, that's what the girls got for eavesdropping. Let them clean up the mess and pretend they weren't listening.

"We . . . she wanted to show me . . . the way she celebrates spring. The sunset on a warm day."

"And did she show you?"

"Yes."

"And what happened?"

"Isn't that for her to tell?" said Moses. "It was a private thing, and I don't know that it's my place to talk about it."

"I'm her father!"

"And yet she never told you? Then who am I to presume?"

Jethro leaned close to him, letting a little of his annoyance show. "So you, only six months in my household, are shown what I can't see?"

Zeforah was standing in the doorway, holding a platter. "I prayed, Father. I never thought to tell you because . . ."

"Because why?"

"Because you know I pray every day. I don't tell you when I breathe, either. Will you let poor Moses alone? Nothing happened up the mountain today that's worth making such a fuss over." She looked at Moses in annoyance. "It was kind of you to be careful, Moses, but I don't have any secrets from my father."

Jethro looked suspiciously at the plate of sliced sausages. "How many of these fell in the dirt when that dish broke outside?"

"None of them," said Zeforah. "It was Moses' bowl of soup that broke, and we're getting him another."

"Well, I'm glad Moses will get his soup, and I'm glad the sausages are clean, and I'm glad that you prayed up on the mountain, and I'm glad that Moses is so careful of your feelings. It's astonishing how glad I am tonight."

Moses smiled. Zeforah did not. "I'm sorry you're annoyed, Father."

"I'm not annoyed. I'm glad."

"Father, I didn't ask Moses to stay with me, he was going to stay anyway to look at the sunset. We are not conspiring behind your back. We did not discuss marriage, and we didn't talk about you. We talked about the sunset and then I said my evening prayer and I came home. I have done nothing to deserve your suspicions and so I resent it."

"I wasn't suspicious."

"I'm *glad* to hear it." She stalked out of the tent.

"Isn't it nice everyone's so glad tonight?" said Jethro.

Moses smiled. "We didn't discuss marriage, Jethro, because I know the custom here is for a man to discuss it with the father first."

"We've already discussed it. I already gave you permission to court her before you even thought of it yourself. I'm *not* suspicious."

"I *do* think of marrying her, Jethro. But until now I knew

better than to talk of it with her, because I knew she wouldn't have me."

"Wouldn't have you?"

"Wouldn't have me."

"She never said any such thing to me."

"Why should she? I never asked her, so it didn't come up."

"Oh, don't be foolish, Moses. She likes you."

"Jethro, I know she likes me, and she knows I like her. We're good friends. She's my teacher, my fellow reader, we work together by day and study together by night. I never much liked my brother and my sister because they were always demanding something from me, but Zeforah is brother and sister, friend and teacher, all at once. But she wouldn't marry me till now, and you know why."

For the life of him Jethro had no idea what Moses was talking about.

"She won't marry a man who doesn't measure up to you, Jethro."

"But there's not a man alive who can meet *that* high standard," he retorted.

"You think I don't know that?"

"I was joking."

"A man jokes by telling the truth lightly. You're a man of God, Jethro. Do you think Zeforah would consent to have the father of her children be anything less than that?"

"So be a man of God," said Jethro. "It isn't hard, if your heart is good."

"I study, Jethro. I learn all that I can about the Lord and his dealings with his people. I believe that it's true, all this scripture, at least as far as I haven't misunderstood it. But that isn't enough."

"No?"

"I tried to pray, Jethro, and I couldn't."

"Couldn't? What do you mean, couldn't? Your tongue stopped working?"

Moses answered cheerfully, "Yes. Exactly. I couldn't speak. Couldn't get a word out, if I was talking to the Lord."

"You mean you were shy about it?"

"I mean I opened my mouth and nearly choked on my tongue. I could not speak. Until tonight. Until I heard her prayer, and I wanted so badly to be like her, to be able to pour out my heart to the Lord. So when she left, I tried again, and this time. . . ."

"This time the Lord opened your mouth."

"Yes."

"That's obvious," said Jethro. "I've been listening to you all through supper. Not once did you hesitate."

"Didn't I?" said Moses.

"So you prayed."

"Yes."

"And?"

"And what?"

"What happened when you prayed?"

Moses looked at him quizzically. "I spoke to God."

"And that was all?"

"Yes," said Moses. "I guess that was all."

"He didn't answer?"

"Jethro, I opened my mouth in prayer and words came out. *That* was the answer to my prayer. To pray at all was the answer to my prayer."

Jethro nodded. "Well, I'm glad to hear it. So now you'll marry her?"

"Now I've taken the first step on the road to becoming the sort of man that she might consider marrying."

"Come on now, Moses! Look at the plate she has to choose from! You've seen the village clowns! Even if you had a four-pound goiter you'd be at the top of the list."

"She doesn't have a list, Jethro. She has a heart."

"So you'd be at the top of her heart. Or the center of it. Whatever."

"Just be patient with us, Jethro."

"I want grandchildren. Preferably including the occasional boy. I'm not a young man!"

"Jethro, I'll admit that part of the reason I wanted to pray was in order to begin to become the kind of man that Zeforah would be glad to marry. I don't think the Lord holds that motive against me. Why shouldn't a man turn to God in order to become worthy of the love of a godly woman? But even if Zeforah still refused me, I would stay on this road for its own sake. God waits for me at the end of the road. I would like to walk the whole way with Zeforah beside me, but I'll walk the road for its own sake. For God's sake. Even if I have to walk it alone."

Jethro smiled broadly and leaned back upon his pillows. "That's what I needed to hear," he said.

"What was?"

"That you seek God for his own sake."

"Well of course."

"There's no of course about it. Until this moment, if you had actually asked me for Zeforah's hand, I would have turned you down flat."

Moses looked at him in utter exasperation. "You've practically thrown us at each other!"

"To see what kind of man you were. Never laid a hand on her, never took advantage, it was as if I had forbidden you even to think of marrying her. I like that trait in you—that you saw what Zeforah needed and knew it wasn't you. Yet."

"What, you mean all your marriage talk was a test?"

"Why not?" said Jethro. "Zeforah is the light of my life. You think I'd even consider letting her marry a man who might take the joy out of her?"

"Were you tempting me?"

"Of course not. I knew you had proper manners, and I knew she'd never encourage any liberties. I was tempting you to become your best self."

"Jethro, are all priests of the Most High God as devious as you?"

"Moses, I'm not devious at all. I speak my feelings."

"Then wait until the Lord gets used to the sound of my voice. Wait until I've had a chance to become more like the man that she deserves to marry."

"I'll wait as long as you want," said Jethro.

"Well," said Zeforah from the door, "I *won't.*"

"Zeforah," said Jethro. "When did *you* come back?"

"When Keturah ran and told me you were talking marriage, right out in the open."

"That little scamp was eavesdropping?" asked Jethro.

"When you're talking about marriage?" said Zeforah. "When you're deciding our future? You'll never have a private discussion of *that* subject, if we can help it."

Moses rose to his feet. "Jethro, didn't you hear what she just said?"

"Yes! She and her sisters plan to spy on me!"

Moses turned to Zeforah. "Won't you wait for me to become ready?"

"And when will that be? When you're perfect? When I'm long past child-bearing?"

"Well, that didn't stop Sarah and Abraham," said Moses.

"Ask father for my hand," said Zeforah.

"I want to marry your daughter," said Moses.

"Do you love her?" asked Jethro.

"At first I admired her, and then I desired her, and then I was in awe of her, and then I honored her, and then I longed for her good opinion of me, and then I wanted to have what she had, which is to have a heart perfect before the Lord."

"Think again," said Zeforah.

"You didn't answer my question," said Jethro.

"I passed through each of these stages, and every single one of them is a part of love. Better than I loved either of my mothers. Better than I loved any of my friends, better than I love even you, Jethro, I love your daughter."

"But do you love her as much as you love God?" asked Jethro.

Zeforah rolled her eyes impatiently. "Father."

"Sir," said Moses, "I don't know God that well yet. I really only know that part of him that shines from your life, and from Zeforah's. How can I love God more than you, when part of what I love about the two of you is God in you, and in your lives?"

Jethro turned to Zeforah. "Well, what do you think? Will he do?"

Tears were streaming down Zeforah's cheeks. "This is the beginning of my marriage, Father. Couldn't you have handled it *normally?*"

"What?" said Jethro. "What did I do?"

Moses walked to her then. "I never knew my father, Zeforah. May I have yours?"

"Gladly," she said.

He reached out to her, a tentative hand, toward her cheek.

She let him touch her, to wipe away her tears; then she turned her face to meet his hand, kissed his palm. "I never had anything like a normal family, either," said Moses. "But will you help me make one, even though I don't know how?"

"I don't have a normal family either," said Zeforah. She put her hands on his chest. He hadn't realized until that moment how much he longed for her touch.

"I know why I need you, the thousand reasons why my life could never be complete without you," said Moses. "You are your own best dowry. But I have nothing to offer you in return, except my love and honor, and all my hope of joy in this life and in the life to come."

"That will do," she said.

"Stop talking and kiss her, Moses," said Jethro.

"With all due respect, Jethro, that's not for you to decide."

"Stop talking," said Zeforah, "and kiss me."

"Now *you*, you get a vote."

With a growl of frustration she flung both arms around his neck, pulled him down, and kissed him firmly on the lips.

"I hear there's a priest nearby," said Moses, when the kiss was done. "Let's see if he'll marry us right away."

"Took you long enough," said Jethro. "Now if you two don't mind, I'd like to finish my supper."

They laughed, they embraced him, and then they left together, to walk and talk for another hour in the moonlight. Jethro found he wasn't hungry after all, and when the other girls, all aflutter with excitement about the first betrothal in the family, finally cleared the supper dishes away, Jethro fell to his knees and wrestled with the Lord about Moses. The gist of his prayer was this: Whatever you have planned for this boy, Lord, don't let it interfere with my daughter's happiness. Don't make a widow of her, don't make her a lonely woman, don't break her heart. No daughter of yours or of mine has ever deserved better from you than Zeforah does. I'm not telling you what to do, Lord, but let Zeforah have her time of joy with him, before you call him away to do whatever it is you plan for him.

The Lord didn't strike him dead for his audaciousness in praying such a prayer. Jethro took this as a good sign, and went to bed.

❉

Hatshepsut was not expecting any visitors, but there were footsteps in the corridor. And they were not the quiet padding steps of a barefoot servant. They had the clipped sound of the hard military sandal.

Hatshepsut rose at once from her bed and gathered a robe around her body. She could feel the stiffness in her joints that told her every night and every morning that she was getting old. But she cared little for such minor pains. What mattered was the sound she was *not* hearing—the soldiers on guard, asking her if she needed something, where she was going, whom she wanted to summon. Therefore she knew there were no soldiers on guard, even though with no moon and no lamps lit, she could not see their places by the walls. And if there were no guards to protect her, it meant that her reign was over.

She had kept Tuthmose carefully pinned down for years beyond his maturity, for she knew he was too young and angry and immature to rule. But this strategy only worked because the others around her—the military leaders, the high priests at Karnak—agreed that Tuthmose III would not make a good ruler. Not that they discussed it. She knew they agreed because her orders continued to be obeyed, and Tuthmose's were not.

But someone had decided that tonight would mark the

change. Tuthmose III was ready to rule. Unfortunately, there could be no sharing of power. Tuthmose would not allow Hatshepsut even to be a figurehead. His hatred of her was unabated, however it might be hidden behind studied courtesy. To decide that Tuthmose no longer needed to be restrained was to decide that it was time for Hatshepsut to die.

Were you in such a hurry, Anubis, to lead me to my father? She could almost hear the breath of the jackal god in the doorway of her room.

But it was no jackal god. It was a mere jackal.

"Hatshepsut," he whispered.

"Tuthmose," she said. "So you came to do your murder by your own hand?"

He took the cover off the lamp, and now instead of a faint ruddy glow there was a flickering yellow light that framed his face. A tall man now, taller than his father. And with a pretty face — another legacy of his father's penchant for bedding only pretty concubines. No political marriages for him! Nor bedtime conversation, either. And this was the result. The murderer standing in the doorway, bearing a lamp in one hand, and in the other . . .

Not a sword or a knife, as Hatshepsut had expected. Rather he held a platter of fruit.

"Hungry?" she asked him. "Come to share?"

"There are two ways we can handle this," said Tuthmose. "You can eat a few of these very bad figs and die of their unfortunate aftereffects. Or you can be condemned for treasonously usurping the throne of Pharaoh, and be publicly executed."

"Which would *you* rather I did?" said Hatshepsut.

"I only care that you die," said Tuthmose. "I've had your talons around my throat long enough."

"Years. But not enough years for you to learn decency."

"Are you going to criticize me even now?" said Tuthmose. "Or is this a prelude to appealing to my better nature?"

"Oh, my dear boy, I am well aware that this *is* your better nature. Your ill nature would be to hire someone to slit my throat in the night. So I'm proud of you for coming to do this yourself."

He sighed. "Choose, Hatshepsut."

"What do you *think* I'll choose?" she asked.

"More teaching?" he said. "All right, I think you'll choose the fruit."

"And why?" she said. "Let's see how well you understand your enemy."

"Whatever I say, you'll tell me I was wrong."

"Now, Tuthmose, be fair. I've never lied to you."

"I know you're not afraid of pain, or of death either. Nor are you willing to die, so you won't see the fruit as a welcome way to end this life. You care about history: You'll choose the fruit so that your name won't be shamed by your public execution as a traitor."

"Perhaps I do care about history," said Hatshepsut, "but not enough to die for it. No, you still don't understand me."

"It won't matter when you're dead."

"It will matter that you couldn't even comprehend the enemy who was closest to you. How will you do at seeing into the heart of enemies you've never even met? I tremble for Egypt with you to protect her."

He strode to her and thrust the platter toward her. "Just eat the figs."

"How many?" she said.

"A couple should do it. The more you eat, the faster it will go, and so the shorter the time you'll go through excruciating abdominal pain."

"How kind of you to choose a painful one."

"Even if we handle this privately," he said, "you *are* being punished for your crimes. It shouldn't be painless."

She took a fig from the plate and popped it into her mouth. It had a bitter taste. "Oh, this is a subtle one," she said. "Don't use this one again unless you find a better way to disguise the flavor."

"Yes, well, Mutnefert died before I could learn the really devious methods of the poisoner's art."

"I don't even like figs," she said.

"I know."

"Do you know why I'm eating them?"

"Because you wanted to pretend that you died by your own choice instead of mine," said Tuthmose.

"No, Tuthmose. I choose this death because . . ."

"Is the pain starting?"

"Of course." She took another fig. "If you execute me, you would bring turmoil to the house of Pharaoh. It would weaken you and every ruler after you. Once the killing came out into the open, there would be no stopping it. You'd have to kill any potential heir—including sons—that appeared to be vying for power. Your eventual successor would have to kill all his brothers and cousins and nephews. The Nile would run with blood."

"Why should you care?"

"I think you'll be a very bad king, Tuthmose. You want power and glory, but glory above all. You'll plunge Egypt into stupid wars."

"I'll win my wars."

"Perhaps you will, but you'll end up with conquests you haven't the firmness or strength to hold. And you'll never have the wit to yield when it might look like defeat. You would rather bring Egypt to ruin than to humble yourself even a little."

"Pharaoh does not have to yield to any man."

"And yet I yield to you."

"You were never Pharaoh."

"Even now, I care more for Egypt than you ever have or ever will. I eat these figs because I know that the house of Pharaoh must be very strong to survive your foolish reign. Therefore I will choose a manner of dying that will not weaken the house of Pharaoh. This gives me hope that after you, better Pharaohs will inherit a kingdom that is still governable."

"I'm really surprised you're still talking. But I suppose your will to talk is even stronger than your will to live."

She ate another fig. And another. And another. The pain was terrible, but she did her best to show none of it.

"I have done nothing in my life that I'm ashamed of," she said. "I'm not even ashamed that you are my heir, for I chose and raised and taught and trained a better man than you, and it was not my fault that he did not last."

Hatred flamed up in Tuthmose's face. "You dare to speak of him even now?"

"He was a man, Tuthmose," said Hatshepsut. "Unlike your father. Unlike you."

He lost his temper then, and struck her a brutal blow across the face. She crumpled to the floor, and for a moment the pain in her jaw made her forget the agony in her belly. She wondered if the pain of this poison was anything like the pain of child-bearing. That was something she had never experienced. She had had one son, but not from her body. How symmetrical, to feel the birth pangs now, just before her death.

Her jaw did not work. She had to open it with her fingers; the pain shot through her head and made her gasp. But now she could speak, mumbling, barely intelligible, but it was speech, and he would listen, because, despite his hate, he knew that she was Pharaoh.

"Moses fought a strong man with his bare hands, and killed him," she said.

She wanted to finish by saying, *You* can only strike a dying old woman. But she hadn't the strength for speech now. No matter. He knew without her having to say the words.

"You'll be nothing," said Tuthmose. "When the history is written, it will call you a usurper who stole my rightful place from me."

Let him babble. She didn't care. She had done as well as she could with the time she had as a god upon the land. It was time for her to ascend to the realm of the gods.

Now, Anubis. I'm finished here. Take me to my father.

❋

Even the married daughters came home for this. Asa and Hamar both found husbands who turned out not to be village bumpkins after all, but men who could read and write, one a man of trade, the other a stonecutter who was often called upon to carve inscriptions in stone. They were there, with their husbands and their children; Jethro's other daughters fussed over the little ones until Zeforah's younger children were quite jealous. But Zeforah's oldest boy, Gershom, the firstborn, cared nothing for what the younger ones were doing. He thought himself a man now, and to Zeforah's unaccustomed eye he could well be a man; what was the dividing line, she wondered? If it was character, then he had the character of a good man. If it was size and strength, well, he had a ways to go. Clearly he meant to be worthy of his father. So Zeforah charged the boy with no duties today. Let him give his full attention to his father, to his grandfather.

Jethro looked at his grandchildren scampering around, made his normal pointed remarks to the unmarried daughters, as if it were their fault and not his that they hadn't married yet. "Look at these children the Lord has given me!" he said proudly.

"*We're* your children, Father," said Dinah. "Those belong to Zeforah and Asa and Hamar."

Jethro continued, undistracted. "I raised you up, with the help of your mother for a while, and then with the help of God. I prayed you to adulthood, and now look at you, raising your own flocks. I have every intention of sharing all my wisdom and experience with you at every opportunity!" He pointed to Gershom. "This boy! How can I teach him?" And to Asa's oldest girl. "This girl! I must gather her in. That's what a father does, and that's what I am, a father. No matter how old you are, I am still a father."

"If my children learn from you," said Moses, "then they can have no better teacher."

"Of all my sons-in-law, Moses," said Jethro, "you're the one who stayed around in hopes of inheriting my secret fortune. Today you'll have the only treasure I have truly valued."

Moses stepped forward and knelt before the old man. Zeforah rested her hand on Gershom's shoulder; she felt Keturah take her other hand.

Jethro laid his hands upon Moses' head and spoke words that Zeforah had never heard before, for Jethro had been ordained to his priesthood before Zeforah was born, and he had trained no other priests until Moses came. Now Jethro had decided it was time to give Moses not only the priesthood, but also his own new copies of the scrolls. The fading, aging copies that Jethro had collected all his life would stay with the old man—but his copying work was done. It was for Moses, now, to make new copies and pass them on.

It was a simple ritual, the words gentle as birdsong in the still air of the summer morning. They were in a high meadow where the heat did not come so insistently, and where no curious onlookers would come by. Because they were shepherds, even their moments of holiness took place in the presence of the sheep. But the herd was quiet, too, as if they were also reverent before the power of the Lord as it was given from one trusted servant to another.

And then it was done. Moses rose to his feet, embraced his father-in-law, and then came to Zeforah and embraced her, too. "Why am I afraid?" she whispered to him.

"I feel it too," said Moses softly. "But it isn't really fear."

"Moses," said Jethro. "I dreamed a dream last night. I saw you walking on Mount Sinai."

"What happened there?" asked Moses.

"In the dream, nothing. But I awoke knowing that this was a dream you should fulfill. Wasn't it the wind that blew you here? That same wind has come again."

"It's time to divide the flock for the heat of summer. I'll take a portion to the summer meadows on the slopes of Sinai. But why does the Lord want me there?"

"I don't know," said Jethro. "God often whispers in the hearts of men."

"I have felt his presence in my heart," said Moses.

"But now and then," said Jethro, "he feels the need to shout. Go and hear him."

For a moment, Zeforah's fear seized her. She wanted to cry out to him, Don't go! I'll lose you if you go! Our mornings of prayer, our days of labor, our evenings of peaceful study, our nights of talk and dreams and ardor, all will be finished if you go up to the mountain of the Lord.

She forced herself to stay silent. I knew from the start that he belonged to God, and God would someday claim him. I had more years than I ever hoped for. I have these children. I have a place in his heart. And maybe it's nothing. Maybe he'll go up the mountain and pray and the Lord will show him that the life of a village priest in Midian is the great calling he was prepared for, that the simple duties here are greater than all the majesty of Egypt.

She knew that if this was the message from the Lord, Moses would be content. But she knew that would not be the Lord's message.

Moses kissed her, kissed his two sons, Gershom and Eliezer, and gathered the younger children, all girls, into a single vast hug, which left them screaming with laughter. Then he walked off across the meadow, deftly gathering a portion of the flock and guiding them toward the path that would take them along the ridge to the shoulder of Sinai itself.

"Watch for snakes!" Gershom cried out.

"I'll be watching!" Moses called back to him.

"I want to follow him, Mother," Gershom said.

"You *are* following him," said Zeforah. "That is your life's work."

"No, I mean I want to follow him *now*."

"It was your father who was called to the mountain," said Zeforah. "Bide your time. The Lord knows where you live."

"Oh, Mother," he said. "You always say that."

"And it's always true," she said. "Come, we have a feast. Time to celebrate!"

"Father took no food with him," said Eliezer, the younger boy.

"He's on the Lord's errand," Zeforah said.

"But he ate nothing all day yesterday," Gershom pointed out.

"The Lord will give him strength."

"It's dangerous out in the rocks, up on the mountain!" Eliezer had a couple of bad falls that had taught him that lesson.

"Nothing will happen but what the Lord intends. That has to be enough for you, Eliezer, Gershom.

"Is it enough for you, Mother?" asked Gershom.

She laughed then. "No. But I pretend that it is."

He thought about this for a moment. "Then I will, too. As long as *you* know how worried I am."

But Zeforah was not worried for Moses' safety. The Lord didn't bring him this far to let him perish in the rocks of Sinai. She had different fears that Gershom and Eliezer could not understand. It didn't matter. She would be strong to help her fretting boys, and that would help her also.

"Oh Lord," she prayed quietly, "let him come back to me. Let him still be mine. Yours too. Yours first. But also mine."

❖

The mud huts of the Israelites, hundreds of them, thousands, spread like a rash across the clay flats of the delta. All around them and among them were the fields of brick molds, the ones filled with clay and strewn with straw, drying in the sun; the empty forms stacked and waiting to be filled with river mud. And during the day, the people swarming like termites on the face of a hill, carrying sledges of river mud, bags of water, empty molds, ricks of straw.

Then came evening, and the people returned to their squalid temporary hovels, built in a few hours, to be torn down eventually by the annual flood of the Nile, then built again.

Slaves in name and law ever since the Hyksos rulers were driven from Egypt, the Israelites were slaves now in daily, hourly fact, slaves like the prisoners of war who were worked to death, to help defray the cost of capturing them. There were few Israelites alive who could even remember the days of the Hyksos Pharaohs, the glory days when the children of Israel helped rule over the land. Nor were there many Egyptians who had ever seen an Israelite being proud, or exercising any kind of authority. Yet the passion for vengeance was kept alive in the Egyptians' hearts, not least by the priests who still told their stories of how the gods delivered Egypt from the foreign oppressors. To see the Israelites slaving in the brickyards by the river, that was proof to the Egyptians of the power of their gods and the greatness of their kingdom.

But a strange thing happened among the Israelites. A generation before, their desert roots had been almost forgotten. They dressed like Egyptians, or undressed like them; the Egyptian language was more and more the first language of the children growing up; Israelites married Egyptians, and taught them in Egyptian schools; and Israelites, even while claiming still to serve the God of Abraham, Isaac, and Jacob, attended the public rituals and knew the names of all the Egyptian gods.

Now, in slavery, without even deciding openly, the Israelites did not strip off all their clothing as an Egyptian would, to work in the sun; instead they covered themselves as desert people did, even though their light but voluminous clothing was stained with mud by day's end. The women modestly hooded their heads in defiant contrast to the way the Egyptian women brazenly showed their faces to any man. The names of Egyptian gods stopped being uttered in oaths or figures of speech; the Egyptian language was hardly spoken in the brickyards, except when an Egyptian overseer was making his inspection. Even then, Israelites who were probably more educated in Egyptian than their masters pretended not to understand them when they spoke.

And Miriam saw these things, and rejoiced.

"It really annoys people to have you go about smiling and telling them you told them so," Aaron said to her. But she only smiled at him and said, "I don't rejoice at our suffering. But God will cause us to suffer if that's what we require to remember him."

Now they stood beside each other, with several of the other prominent leaders of the tribe of Levi. No one questioned Miriam's right to stand among them. They might resent the presence of a woman, but they knew she had foretold all this. They knew that the light of God was in her, and they clung to whatever light they had, even in the form of this most obnoxious and outspoken woman. They looked out over the river, as they had been commanded to do, to watch as Tuthmose's barge came down the river.

"It is unseemly," said one man. "He does not mourn Hatshepsut's death, but acts as if her dying were a triumph of his own."

"He probably killed her," said another.

"Keep that thought to yourself in the future, please, unless you want us all killed."

"What troubles me," said Aaron, "is that he particularly wanted us Israelites to line the riverbanks to watch him pass. I'm not sure how much worse our lives could get, but I imagine he'll find a way."

"Not necessarily," said a man. "If we cheer him enough, perhaps he'll take pity on us."

"Cheer him?" said Aaron. "I think he wants to see us sullen and miserable."

"Sullen and miserable would look like proud and stubborn to him," said Miriam. "But if we cheer, he'll see that we have lost all pride and are utterly submissive."

"So you think we should?" asked Aaron, shocked.

"I think we should turn our backs to him," said Miriam. "And I will do exactly that, though I know none of you will have the courage to do it."

"Are you mad?" asked a man.

"The oppression of Egypt is making Israel remember their God."

"But if Egypt kills us all, who will be left to remember him then?" demanded another.

"If we are all gathered around father Abraham, rejoicing, what will we care what happens in Egypt?"

"She wants to die, Aaron. Please try to constrain her so she doesn't take the rest of us with her."

"I don't want to die!" said Miriam. "I want to live in freedom, like any of you! But fools that you were, you *thought* you were free when you were completely ensnared in the ways of the Egyptians. It took slavery to make us all see that Egypt was not beautiful or admirable. It took suffering to show us that the learning of the Egyptians was foolishness compared to the wisdom of the Lord."

They seethed, but one of them said what they all knew was true. "You were right, Miriam, all along you were right. We never belonged here. I would to God Jacob had seen Egypt, turned around, and gone home."

"No!" cried Miriam. "That was God's plan as well! We have become a mighty nation here in Egypt. In Canaan among the dozens of tribes, who would we be? Here we have learned

all the skills of civilization, and our numbers have increased as
we ate the corn of this rich land. We had generations of shelter
here, and that was what God wanted for us. If only we had
remembered who we were. I tell you that the day is not far off
when God will lead us out of Egypt and return us to the land
he promised to Abraham and Isaac and Jacob. We'll carry the
bones of father Jacob back to Canaan, and the nation of Israel
will rise in that promised land."

They heard her reverently, and believed her. "The problem," said Aaron, "is how to train our men in the use of the
sword, without the Egyptians seeing."

"The sword!" said Miriam.

"Keep your voice down," said Aaron. "Of course the
sword. Do you think they'll let us walk out of here? We have
to be ready to fight. We vastly outnumber any army the
Egyptians can bring against us, but numbers are nothing if we
have only our hands and bodies to thrust onto the swords and
spears of the soldiers."

"God does not need armies to bring about his will!" said
Miriam.

"The barge is coming!" cried someone farther up the riverbank. The cry was carried downstream by voice after voice.
Of course, the same thing had happened all morning, since the
cry moved much faster than the barge, and it only meant that
somewhere many miles upstream, the barge had been seen.
This time, though, it turned out to be true for this place, for
there shining in the sun was the great barge of Pharaoh.

Miriam and Aaron withdrew from the other men. Miriam
climbed up onto the highest point she could find — only a few
cubits above the level of the river — and pointedly turned her
back to the water.

"Aren't you even curious to see?" said Aaron.

"I saw when Moses came down the river in triumph, after his victory at Saba."

Aaron's face grew grave. "We harmed him, pushing him to go out among the people."

"He was in God's hand, not ours," said Miriam. "We did him nothing but good, helping him remember who he was."

"I thought it would be so easy for him to rally the people. But he knew," said Aaron. "He had actually been a leader of armies, and he knew that it could not be done so easily."

"God is doing it."

"Yes, we are becoming more unified as we become less capable of doing anything *with* that unity."

Miriam laughed. "Don't you see that it's when we're utterly helpless that we'll turn to the Lord and he alone, by his power alone, will save us?"

"An interesting idea, and if it's ever put to the test I hope you're right," said Aaron.

"I dreamed of Moses last night," said Miriam.

"Oh?"

She knew he did not like hearing her dreams. It annoyed him that the Lord showed her things that were kept hidden from him. Or else it annoyed him that she *claimed* to see these things, for sometimes he asked her pointed questions as if he thought she made up these dreams. Aaron was a jealous man, and hated the idea that someone else knew things he didn't know.

"I dreamed of Moses dressed like a man of the desert, walking among stones. Then a great fire came and swallowed him up. And he came out of the fire all ablaze, but he wasn't burned. It was as if he had become the sun, and wherever he went there were no shadows, and every corner and crevice of the rocks was illuminated."

"No doubt you're going to tell me what it means." There it was, that skeptical tone.

"I would but I don't know," said Miriam. "I only know that I dreamed of Moses filled with light, and then today we stand by these dark waters and watch this evil son of Satan come down the river to gloat over us in our captivity and I can't help but think God was showing me some portion of his plan."

"Moses is dead, Miriam," said Aaron.

"If God wills it so," said Miriam.

"He went out into the desert in the midst of a storm with scarcely any food or water. No one lives through that."

"They do if God wills it so."

"You and Mother," said Aaron. "She died believing in him."

"In God? Or Moses?"

"It's hard to know whom she worshiped more," said Aaron.

"So Moses lived in Pharaoh's house and you never had a chance to be great and famous," said Miriam. "He's been gone all these years and I haven't seen that you suddenly blossomed outside of his shadow."

Aaron glared at her. "I was never jealous of Moses."

"Self-knowledge can be painful," said Miriam, "but not half so damaging as self-ignorance."

"You don't know everything," said Aaron.

"I don't have to know everything to know more than you," she said. "Moses was a great general so you think you have to be a great general, too. But he studied war, and you never did. He had well-trained armies, and you don't know how to begin training one. Don't try to become Moses. The only result will be slaughter."

"I'm not trying to become Moses! I'm preparing to lead Israel to freedom."

"Hear yourself: *I'm* preparing to *lead*."

"I know we can't win by the strength of our own arms. God will give us the victory."

"God will give us freedom in his own time, in his own way. Instead of making your own foolish plans and then demanding that God fit in with your schedule, why don't you submit yourself to *his* will?"

"I don't know what his will is!" cried Aaron.

People turned to look. They lowered their voices.

"Turn around," some of them said. "Don't make trouble for us!"

But Miriam did not turn around. Quietly she said to Aaron, "If you don't know what the Lord's will is, why not try asking?"

"He doesn't speak to me."

"You don't speak to him!"

"I pray all day in my heart," said Aaron.

"You never pray. You just complain and make demands."

"You don't know how my heart breaks when I bow before God," said Aaron.

Maybe it was true, thought Miriam. "No, I don't know. I'm sorry. I judge you too harshly, because you're my brother."

"Because I'm the brother who's still alive," said Aaron. "That's what you won't forgive me for. Wonderful Moses is dead, and all that's left is Aaron."

"Moses wasn't wonderful," said Miriam. "He was confused, just as you are, and the Lord has chastened him and brought him low, just as he has done with all of Israel. He does it with all men and women, one way or another—we face our wickedness and weakness. What matters is, do we despair or rage or fight? Do we surrender to our wickedness and fear? Or do we turn to God to put strength and goodness into us?"

"What you mean is, do we turn to Miriam and let *her* tell us what to do."

His snideness infuriated her. He still had that knack. "I've never asked anyone to do what I want," she said. "But since no one has ever followed my advice, we have no idea whether things might have worked out better, do we?"

"Moses followed your advice once," said Aaron.

"Yes. Your advice, too," she answered. "We were wrong in every detail, both of us, but we were right about the most important things, and we still are. We're still on the same side, Aaron. God's side."

"If only he'd tell us where his side is."

"It's not to take swords into our hands," said Miriam.

"You don't know that."

"Yes I do! If you led an Israelite army to victory, the temptation would be too great for you. The story would be told that King Aaron won the freedom of the Israelites."

"I have no intention of being king of anything!" he snapped.

"When Israel leaves Egypt," said Miriam, "it will be in such a way that everyone will say, Look what a miracle has happened here. The Lord God of Israel freed his people from bondage in Egypt."

"That's what we'll say when we win," said Aaron. "Our victory will *be* a miracle."

"And thus my brother continues to earn his place at the head of the long line of people who completely ignore me."

The people around them were becoming quite agitated. "Turn around! Don't make trouble! Don't shame us! Don't make him angry!"

Finally hands were laid on Miriam and Aaron both, Miriam to turn her around to face the water, Aaron to keep him from springing to his sister's defense. Forced now to face the water, Miriam threw back her head and cried out at the top of her voice, "Tuthmose! God sees your wickedness!"

Thus it was that Miriam watched the passing of Pharaoh imprisoned by many hands, with a rag stuffed in her mouth. But she exulted in the moment, for there she stood, the perfect symbol of her people—bound and silenced, but still defiant. Look at me now and see Israel, ready for the Lord to come and redeem us from captivity.

*

For Moses, tending sheep had now become second nature. He watched them all without even thinking, herded those that strayed without losing the train of his own thoughts. He could sing softly to them, utter a sharp command, touch one with his staff to get its attention, and through it all his thoughts remained his own.

The Lord's call had come, not to Moses directly, but to Jethro; yet Moses did not mind, his pride was not hurt because he had no pride before God. This time, he obeyed, not because he had no choice, but because he had already made the choice. He knew that whatever God required of him, he would give, if not gladly, then at least willingly, for God would not require of him anything which was not intended, in the long run, to bring joy to the children of men. The only problem was how desperately uncomfortable it could be in the short run, to those who obeyed the Lord.

In his years among the Midianites, Moses had been purged of ambition. All that was left was a heartfelt wish to remain with his family, raising his children, loving his wife, studying the scriptures, ministering to the villagers, and tending the sheep. But he knew that was not what his life pointed to. God did not give him this impossible life in order for him to spend

his last years quietly. This call to the mountain meant the end
of his peace.

I will give all you ask of me, Lord, but please, please don't
take from me all that I love.

Was this what Abraham said, going up the slope of Mount
Moriah? Why am I complaining—has God asked me to slay
my boy Gershom?

He found a meadow in a sheltered vale on the mountain's
slope. He labored several hours pulling brush and stones
together to make a fence to keep the sheep from straying away
from the grassy place. He knelt among the animals and prayed
for God to lead him where he was supposed to go. Then he
began climbing, through ever steeper, ever stonier terrain, until
he was clambering by hands and toes, knees and elbows, up
small cliffs, along narrow ledges, going wherever the mountain
seemed to be leading him, going ever higher into the mountain.

He should have been weak from fasting, but his hands still
had their grip, and he watched his own body as if it were
another animal, climbing mindlessly on. He was thirsty and his
mouth was dry, his lips cracked with the dust of the climb, but
the dryness in his mouth and the soreness of his lips were only
interesting facts that he took note of, but cared little about.

The ground leveled out on a shelf of land perhaps six paces
wide. The air was cooler here, he had climbed so high, and the
leaves on the bushes were green even though it was high summer. Life grew from every crevice in the rock. He stopped and
looked around him. Below him the rocky land spread out like
a carpet carelessly thrown, looking softer from this distance
than it ever did close up. The air was so clear that he could see
the blue water of the arm of the Red Sea that separated this
land of Sinai from the true land of Midian across the water.
Somewhere on the other side of the mountain, across another

arm of the Red Sea, lay the land of Egypt. He did not want to look that way. He felt no nostalgia for the place, or for the prideful, fearful, arrogant, stammering man he was when he lived there.

He felt something behind him. Warmth, perhaps, or just a presence. He turned. Far along the ledge there was a bloom of fire enveloping a green bush.

"It burns, and yet it lives," he said. "Lord, is this the thing you brought me here to see?"

A voice came to him then, though he wasn't sure he was hearing with the ears of his body, for the sound seemed to come from all around him, from inside him, making him tremble throughout his body, dropping him to his knees. And yet he was not afraid. The voice was not violent. The opposite: It was gentle, yet so strong, so irresistible, that it weakened his body just to hear it. He knew that if the voice were not restrained so tightly, his body would die from the sound of it, for this voice, if it ever shouted, would shiver the stones of this mountain into dust.

"Moses," the voice said, and his own name sounded strange to him, hearing it spoken by the voice of God. "Moses," God said again.

"Here I am." His own words sounded weak and foolish, like the shoddy imitation of a voice, for he had heard what a voice could be, and now his own was nothing.

He tried to rise from his knees and walk toward the burning bush, but the voice came again and stopped him. "Come no closer. Take the sandals from your feet, for the place where you are standing is holy ground."

Moses sat in the grass and unlaced his sandals. The silence while he did so was overpowering. God was waiting for him to take off his shoes.

At last he was done, and knelt again, so weak he had to lean on his staff, hardly daring to look at the bush, hardly daring to look away.

"I am the God of your fathers, the God of Abraham, of Isaac, and of Jacob. I have seen the misery of captive Israel, I've heard them crying to me under the whip, I know their grief, and I'll deliver them. I'll bring them to a land that flows with milk, that runs with honey, to Canaan, broad and fine. For they are mine, and you, my son, are mine."

In his heart, Moses heard these words with rejoicing and with dread: rejoicing, because the longed-for day of deliverance was now at hand; dread, because the Lord would not be telling him if he were not expected to do something to help bring it about.

"Go to Pharaoh," said the Lord, "and bring my people out."

Not me, he wanted to cry out. "Will Pharaoh let them go for the asking?" he said.

"He will stand against the will of God, but he will break."

*He*, the Lord said. So Pharaoh was a man. Hatshepsut was dead. Moses felt a pang of regret, but then relief as well. She had lasted for many years after Moses went into exile — or came out of exile, as he thought of it now. He hoped her death, when it came, was not bitter to her.

"I'll stretch forth my hand," said the Lord, "to strike down Egypt with my wonders, and you will leave with the wealth of Egypt, not stolen, but freely given to you by the Egyptian people, if only you will leave and take the anger of God away from them. It will not be the hand of men that delivers Egypt, but *my* hand, and all the world will say, The Lord God remembered Israel."

He wanted to say, You can do this without me, Lord. With

all your power, what am I needed for? But what he said was, "I've been gone so long, the Israelites won't know me. They never knew me, I was never a man of faith among them, they'll ask me, Who are you, that the Lord would speak to you?"

"What's that in your hand?"

Moses had to look. "A staff."

"Throw it to the ground."

With so little strength, Moses could only let it drop. At once it turned into a snake, a large one of the most poisonous kind. Fear gave him strength he hadn't thought he had, as he scrambled crabwise away from it.

"Take it by the tail."

It took a moment, but he conquered the fear. If the Lord told him to take hold of the tail, then either no harm would come of it, or it was the Lord's will that he should be bitten, and it would not be harm in that case, either. So he got back on hands and knees, approached the snake warily, reached out to its tail and took hold.

It was his staff again, the cool smooth wood that he had polished himself.

"Put your hand inside your robe, to touch the skin of your chest."

When Moses drew his hand out, it was white and scaly. Leprosy. He held the hand away from him, knowing that what the Lord had done to him the Lord could heal, but still frightened by the numbness in his arm. It was as if the hand he saw were someone else's, because he could not feel it.

"Put it back in your robe."

At first he was reluctant to touch himself with the unclean hand, but then, knowing that this was how it would be healed, he moved eagerly, and when his hand emerged again the skin was clean.

"If these two signs don't convince them that you come from me, then take up the water of the Nile and pour it on the ground, and it will turn to blood."

But it would not be enough to overawe them. They had to know that he came in fulfilment of their faith, not as a new prophet wiping away all that had been taught before. "The elders will ask me, If you have spoken to God, what is his name? I don't know how to answer them, Lord."

"I am that I Am," said the Lord. "Tell them that I Am sent you to them."

Moses had no idea what these words would mean to the Israelites. Such a phrase did not exist in the scripture Jethro had. But then, if it were written down, it would not be secret.

Moses knew that he would obey, if the Lord really wanted him. But there were so many men whose whole lives had been dedicated to serving the Lord, committed to freeing Israel. Compared to them, Moses was a latecomer. They would resent his being placed ahead of them. "Lord, you could give these powers to any man. I'm not the one to send. You want a prophet, a man of mighty words, an eloquent man! When I speak to strangers I stammer, I'm slow and hesitant. People grow impatient listening to me. How will Pharaoh hearken to the Lord if his messenger is ridiculous?"

"Who made man's mouth? Who can heal the dumb or the deaf? Who makes some men see, and some blind? Go and my voice will go with you and give you words when you need them."

Moses knew that the Lord could open his mouth and give him speech—hadn't he done it before? Wasn't it already a gift of God that he no longer stammered when he spoke to his family? He didn't doubt God's ability to give him words; but why not send one who wouldn't need such help?

"Send someone else, Lord. My brother Aaron wanted to be the savior of Israel! Or anyone else, anyone—whoever you want, you can make him your messenger. I'm the last man who should show his face before Pharaoh. He'll refuse most adamantly because I'm the one speaking for Israel."

Only then did it occur to him that this, too, might be part of the Lord's plan, for Pharaoh to humble himself before the man he had resented and envied all through his childhood.

"I'll bring you your brother Aaron to be your spokesman," said the Lord. "You'll give him words to say, as I give those words to you, so that you will be to your brother as I am to you."

Moses saw at once that having Aaron speak for him as if Moses were God and Aaron the prophet would make it even more galling to Pharaoh. Well, it was the Lord's errand. And it would indeed be a miracle if Pharaoh didn't have Moses and Aaron dismembered the first time they even attempted to enter his palace.

But the first miracle would be persuading Aaron to take a role subservient to his younger brother.

"What should I say to Pharaoh? How will I even get to see him? Tuthmose hated me before I left."

"Why do you fear for your life, Moses? No one can raise a hand against you while I am with you. Say to Pharaoh, The Lord God says, Israel is my son, even my firstborn. Let my son go, that he may serve me. If you refuse to let him go, then I will slay your own son, your firstborn."

Moses imagined himself standing before Tuthmose and saying to the man with all the power of Egypt in his hands that if he didn't obey God, his firstborn son would die.

To his own surprise, once he imagined himself doing it, the last fear fled from him. For it would not be Moses challenging

Pharaoh, it would be the Lord God of heaven and earth commanding Pharaoh, and if there was a quarrel it was between them. As long as he remembered that he was God's servant in this, God's messenger, and not speaking for himself, then there was nothing to fear. All would happen according to God's will. Moses might never see his children again, but that also lay in the hands of God: the children were God's gift to him in the first place, as was Zeforah, and what God gave him so bountifully, the Lord could take away if it were his will that Moses' life should end.

Though he did not say it aloud, the Lord heard the thoughts of his heart, and answered him. "Let this be an assurance to you: You will come here again, with the host of Israel, and serve me together upon this mount."

And with that, the voice let go of him, and left him empty, and the fire surrounding the bush faded, leaving it vibrant and green. Only when the fire left the bush did he realize that what he was looking at was more than fire, was not fire at all, but was the presence of the Lord, if only his eyes had been pure enough to see. Yet burned into his heart was the afterimage of the face of God. Moses felt as if all liquid had been drained out of his flesh, leaving only a dry husk, weightless as chaff. Yet he felt as if the fire from the bush burned inside him, sustaining him, filling him up with light instead of water, instead of blood. He went so easily back down the mountain, for his body had no weight, he had no fear of falling, he moved as gently among the rocks as goosedown gusting in the wind.

He would do what the Lord commanded him to do.

The sheep waited patiently for him, and when he walked among them, they gathered around him. He did not need to speak to them, or drive them. Rather they followed his footsteps wherever he walked. They knew, he was sure of it, they knew whose voice had filled him today, and they followed him as if he were the Lord.

He spoke to the sheep as he led them along the ridge, back toward home. "Now I know that man is nothing, which I never had supposed. I have seen the Lord in glory, I've had his glory in me, and the Lord did not despise me." And the final realization, that he had been given the gift of the prophets — with joy he announced it to the flock: "I have seen his face."

# Chapter 9

# R e u n i o n s

It was only a dream. Aaron wouldn't even have mentioned it
to Miriam, except that he thought she might find it amusing. "I'm dreaming of Moses now, too," he said.

"Oh." She didn't seem all that interested. "What was he
doing in *your* dream?"

"He came out of a sandstorm in the desert. His face was so
covered with sand that I couldn't see who it was. I gave him
water, and he washed his face, and it was Moses."

"Then you must go meet him." Just like that, from his
dream to her assumption that he must go off on some mad
errand. But Miriam was sure that it was a true dream, given
by the Lord. "It was too clear," she said. "It couldn't have been
one of the normal dreams of sleep. God is bringing Moses
back out of the desert, out of obscurity, and it is you who must
meet him and reveal him to the rest of Israel."

"How am I supposed to find him?" asked Aaron. "There's a
lot of desert, and since I'm an Israelite slave, I probably can't
even *get* to the desert."

"Don't be absurd. As long as we meet our quota, they don't
mind if one Israelite or another goes off on errands here and
there."

*Insane* errands, he wanted to add. Except that the dream
*was* different. She might be right. "That doesn't change the fact
that Moses could be anywhere."

"Aaron. You're deliberately trying to be stupid. He went *into* the desert from the border outpost at the head of the Red Sea. Where else would he come back?"

"So I go there and sit around for a week and finally give up and come home."

"A week? You'll wait until he comes," said Miriam. "When God gives you an errand, you don't decide it's over until you've completed it."

"If you've misunderstood my dream, that could be a long wait," he said. "I have a wife and children, you know. Elisheba doesn't like it when I'm gone too long. I have responsibilities."

"Then don't go," said Miriam. "All these years, you tell me you wish God would speak to you the way he speaks to me, show you things, give you something to do. All these years, you plot to raise an army to overthrow Pharaoh, you devise these elaborate plans that would only end up getting somewhere between a hundred and a hundred thousand people killed. And now God actually calls you to act, and you remember you have responsibilities."

The scorn in her voice stung him, but that wasn't what made him go. It had been an extraordinarily clear and memorable dream, and he wanted it to be from God. Besides, it made a kind of sense. Moses' name might have been expunged from every monument and every book, but he was well-remembered by Israelite and Egyptian alike. If God wanted to liberate Israel, he could do worse than bringing Moses back from exile. No one could galvanize Israel more quickly, unify all the tribes, and strike fear into the hearts of the Egyptians.

Not that Moses would want Aaron's counsel—he never had before—but it had to mean something that God sent Aaron to meet Moses. Aaron wouldn't have to wait for Moses to invite him to take part—he had his own call from the Lord.

So after two days of walking, Aaron showed up at the caravanserai near the desert outpost where Moses had taken his leave of Egypt. Most caravans came through the northern border outpost, the one at the Sea of Reeds, the marshy land on the Mediterranean shore. That was the best route into Egypt if you came from Canaan, and most people did. This southern entry served only the caravans from deepest Arabia, south where the frankincense was harvested. Thus there was little traffic, and the soldiers soon noticed Aaron and asked his business.

Waiting, that's what he told them his business was. Waiting for my brother to come through.

Are you sure he's coming this way? What did he say in his letter?

He didn't send a letter.

Oh. Someone came ahead of him, then. What did his messenger say?

And what, exactly, could Aaron say to that? He wasn't sure at all that he was waiting in the right place. Nor was he sure that he had understood the message, or that it even was one. So he shrugged at the soldiers' questions and, when he ran out of food, he began working for them, doing chores in exchange for meals. At home he would have been making bricks all day; here, he was digging whatever they wanted dug, and building whatever they wanted built. It made no difference to him. He was waiting for Moses. Or despair.

Moses came first. One day a caravan was sighted in the distance, and the soldiers made ready. Aaron worked beside them, taking orders from everyone; the soldiers offered him encouragement. "Maybe your brother will be with this one."

The dromedaries, loaded with bags of precious spices, came through at their stately pace. Aaron looked at the men who walked along beside the animals. As desert travelers did, they all had their heads covered, and all the men of any age had long, full beards. When Aaron saw him last, Moses had been clean shaven. Would Aaron recognize him if he saw him face to face?

It turned out that he recognized Moses before his face was visible. Though Moses was still many rods off, a bearded man dressed in wool homespun bringing up the rear of the caravan, Aaron recognized his bearing, his stride. Moses walked with the strength and vigor of a soldier, and with the boldness of a man who does not think anyone is his superior. All these years gone, and nothing changes.

Aaron strode out to greet him. "My brother! My brother, is it you?"

Moses smiled, threw wide his arms, and when they reached each other, Aaron found himself folded in a vast embrace. Moses must have been this tall and strong when he left — Aaron hadn't known because they had never embraced as adult men.

"So the Lord found you and brought you here," said Moses.

"I could say the same to you," said Aaron.

"I'm not the man I was, Aaron," said Moses. "Now I know that you were right — I'm a man of Israel, not of Egypt. Nor of Midian, where I've lived these past few years."

"Are you married? Do you have a family?"

"God gave me a splendid wife who is my teacher in everything, and we have two sons and three daughters. My wife and children came as far as the last caravanserai with me, but I sent them home to my father-in-law."

Aaron lowered his voice into a conspiratorial hush. "I've

been careful not to tell anyone the name of the brother I was waiting for."

"Thank you, but that won't be necessary. I'm entering Egypt as Moses ben Amram. I'm here as myself, on the Lord's errand."

"I had a dream from God that brought me here," said Aaron. "Was it the same with you?"

"Not a dream," said Moses. "A vision. God came to me on the mountain, in a fire that burned in a green bush but didn't harm it. He spoke to me in a voice—oh, Aaron, when you hear his voice—but you must know what I mean. Have you felt how the voice of God fills your body so you hardly need to breathe? It becomes your life while he speaks to you, and when he left me I was so weak I could hardly walk, and yet so light I thought I could fly."

As Moses went on and on about his vision, Aaron felt something break inside him. He should have known. Moses left as an unbeliever, but of course he would come back as a prophet, a greater prophet than any that Aaron had heard of— for which of them ever had the experience Moses was telling about? Aaron had his little dream, but Moses had a great vision.

That's the story of my life, thought Aaron. I'm the one who feels the pain of Israel, but Moses is the one the Lord chose. From the cradle on. What was I? A spoiled brick, to be tossed back into the river and become mud again? I was invisible to God. Now that he finally notices me, I'm still only a faint shadow in the blinding light that Moses has in him.

They came at last to the checkpoint, where the soldiers greeted Aaron with a smile. "Here at last, eh? Well, we'll miss your help, Aaron!"

They almost passed Moses through without even asking

his name, but the duty sergeant remembered at the last moment. "We need to have your name for the records," he said.

"Moses," answered Moses.

Aaron shriveled with fear, but tried to show none of it. It was impossible that the soldiers wouldn't know his name.

The sergeant laughed. "Moses! There was another Moses, you know. Went out into the desert from this very outpost, in the middle of a storm. He used to be the son of Pharaoh, till he killed somebody and had to flee. We figure the desert got him. The sand, the wind."

"No, he lived," said Moses.

"Well, listen to that! Boys, did you hear what he said? This man knows something about what happened to Moses, the general who—"

And then, suddenly, he remembered that it was forbidden to mention Moses by name.

"That is to say, the former son of Pharaoh, whose name we've all forgotten."

The other men laughed.

"So what happened to him? How do former sons of Pharaoh live, when they get out into the desert?"

Several of the other soldiers had gathered around now, and were making mock bets about whether Moses had been sold into slavery or merely forced to marry some toothless desert maiden.

"Actually, he's become a fairly good shepherd," said Moses. "And he would have been happy to remain at that labor, but the Lord God of Israel appeared to him and sent him back to Egypt."

"Sent him back!" The sergeant laughed. "Oh, I'd like to see him dare to show his face here again!"

"Would you?" said Moses. "Then open your eyes, soldier. I'm the one who passed through here all those years ago. I'm the one who's been tending sheep. And I'm the one who's here with a message to Pharaoh from the Lord God of Israel."

The soldiers fell still. They had no idea what to do now.

"I suppose we should arrest you," said the sergeant, making it sound halfway joking, just in case Moses was only having a jest at their expense. It would be too embarrassing to claim to his superiors that he had arrested Moses, only to have it discovered that it was only some desert rat with a sense of humor.

"Arrest me or not," said Moses. "Either way I'll see Pharaoh soon enough. As you can see, I'm not trying to sneak in secretly. Send word to him that I passed through here and that I'm on my way to speak to him, as soon as I visit with my brother and sister. Pharaoh is not afraid of me. If you arrest me, it will look as if he is."

Aaron had to admire the bold, cool way Moses addressed the soldiers. He spoke to them as an officer, and they were properly subservient. When it was clear that they had no intention of arresting him or interfering with him in any way, Moses bade them farewell and stepped out smartly, with Aaron hurrying a little to keep up. Moses did not look back. They were well out on the road, with Moses trying to learn everything he could about events in Egypt since he left, when a chariot came clattering up behind them. Moses did not so much as glance at it, just stepped out of the road and kept on walking. Aaron forced himself to pretend to be as nonchalant. It turned out Moses was right—the chariot was *not* coming to arrest them. But could it be that he really didn't care?

"There went the messenger to report that I've entered Egypt," said Moses.

"The Lord must have shown you everything, for you to know that there was nothing to fear from the soldiers."

"On the contrary," said Moses. "The Lord gave me only a few general predictions—that Pharaoh will not let Israel go until he has suffered greatly under the hands of God. And that the children of Israel and I will gather at the mountain of the Lord, after Egypt has let them go."

"But that conversation with the guards—you can't tell me you didn't know it would turn out well."

"I knew it would turn out as the Lord wished," said Moses. "Come now, you and Miriam were telling me these things when we were all young. The Lord gives us commandments, but expects us to be resourceful in carrying them out."

"But you were so confident. Not showing the slightest doubt."

"I was confident in the Lord," said Moses. "But I had no idea whether I would come before Pharaoh as a free man or in chains."

"Well, if it *had* been the chains," Aaron pointed out, "they would have arrested me, too. You might have thought of that."

"I would have, if you had come here at my command," said Moses. "But it was the Lord who sent you the dream that brought you here, and you came here in obedience to him, not me. If you're with me, then we must face Pharaoh together. So if one of us is in chains, or both, is up to the Lord."

"Couldn't you have discussed it with me first?"

"Aaron, I asked the Lord to send you instead of me. I knew that you were the one who dreamed of leading Israel out of captivity, and I knew you had the abilities that would be needed. But the Lord didn't take my advice. Instead, he charged me with the task, and gave me a companion—you.

You're to be my spokesman in dealing both with Pharaoh and with the Israelites."

"It makes sense for me to speak for you among the Israelites, where I know all the leaders of every tribe," said Aaron, "but I don't know anyone in the palace. I think you could guess that once you left, we were no longer welcome at Pharaoh's house. So I can't think how I'd be helpful there."

"You are to be my spokesman," said Moses. "Those were the Lord's instructions. He said that I would give you words to say as God gives words to me. I was to be to you like God, he said."

Aaron stopped walking. "Are you *trying* to hurt me?"

"Why should you be hurt?" said Moses. "I'm telling you what the Lord said. It has nothing to do with *us* or our feelings. We'll be meeting with Pharaoh, and Pharaoh's a god, remember? I come as the ambassador from the most high God, who is king of heaven and earth, and so I will not deign to speak to Tuthmose directly. He'll have a dozen, a hundred courtiers there who all treat him like a god. I will have only you."

"I'm a proud man," said Aaron. "But if it's the Lord's will, I'll serve as your spokesman. To have Israel free, I'd gladly die—so why should I let a little humiliation bother me?"

"We're brothers, Aaron, as we've always been. Back when I was in Pharaoh's house I was too proud or fearful or— what?—too Egyptian to accept you as I should have. But I know you now as my brother, and you know me. I don't know how the Lord will bring Israel out of Egypt, but I know he will. I was *not* glad to be the one called to speak to Pharaoh. I *was* glad to find out that you would be with me. You have always had courage, Aaron. Boldness that I didn't have. You have never been afraid to speak your mind, even in Pharaoh's house, where others were so obsequious and eloquent in their flattery that I could barely comprehend their messages."

"Yes, I imagine *my* messages were always clear," said Aaron, with a laugh. "When I think of the things that Miriam and I said to you. . . ."

"I was relieved to find out that the two of you were still alive. I was afraid that some vengeance might have been taken against you. Hatshepsut knew that you were urging me to act like an Israelite, and mothers are very resentful of those who get their children into trouble."

Aaron stiffened. "Even now, you refer to that woman lying in her huge stone tomb as your mother, when your *true* mother lies buried in a grave that no Egyptian will ever tend, and no Israelite will ever visit?"

Moses looked genuinely surprised. "Aaron, do we need to visit that old question? I was told from infancy that Hatshepsut was my mother. I lived in her house. I grew up as her son. Now that she's been murdered and put in her grave, must I repudiate her in order to keep you content?"

Aaron was startled. "The Lord told you, then, that she was definitely killed?"

Moses laughed. "No, no, the Lord didn't tell me any such thing. I just know the way that Pharaoh's house works. Pharaohs who die of sudden illnesses caused by eating bad fruit—that was the official rumor, wasn't it?—let's just say that Hatshepsut is the most recent in a long line of sudden deaths in Pharaoh's house. My only consolation is that those who use poison as a political instrument never eat a meal in peace. Every bout with indigestion will cause Tuthmose to fear that justice has come to him at last. And it *will* come—but from God, not from poison."

"Speaking of things that come from God," said Aaron, "it's

going to take some planning to figure out how to convince the elders of the tribes that you are indeed the Lord's prophet. They don't know you as an Israelite, and—"

Moses held up his hand for silence. "The Lord has already provided us with all the persuasion we'll need. Take your walking staff, Aaron, and throw it to the ground."

Moses seemed to be amused at Aaron's fear of the snake, his reluctance to pick it up again by the tail. "No, Aaron, I'm not laughing at you. I'm laughing to remember how I did exactly the same thing—and I was in the presence of the burning bush. Now, for the second sign the Lord gave us. Put your hand into the bosom of your robe."

Fearfully, Aaron did so; when it came out leprous, he cried out in horror. "Have I failed a test?"

"No test, Aaron. Just put your hand back into your robe."

Aaron did, and kissed his own hand when it came out clean. "To be cut off from the land of the living, and yet not be dead," he said. "How could I bear that?"

Moses shook his head. "That's how most men live, and don't even know it."

"Will that happen every time I put my hand in my robe? Do I get a snake every time I drop my staff?"

"Only when I command you to do it, Aaron. It's not something you can do whenever you feel like it. The elders will see that it's not some trick I do, like the priests with their carefully staged miracles. I have only to command, and nature obeys— and power like that comes only from the Lord."

And only to you, thought Aaron.

At once he was ashamed of his resentment. How could he not be glad? Miracles had been done using his own staff, his own *body*. The Lord was moving to free Israel, and the power of God had flowed through him. If Aaron had power only when Moses commanded him, well, that was better than not having the power of God at all.

"Pharaoh might well try to forbid a gathering of elders," said Moses.

"He might also forbid the wind from blowing," said Aaron, "but as the wind blows, so also do the elders gather." He grinned. "They don't watch us that closely. As long as we live in desperate poverty, and as long as we labor, all of us, even our wives and children, to meet their tally of bricks, then they're content to let us govern ourselves how we will."

Moses nodded, his expression grim. "Governing ourselves—that's the problem that the Lord will leave to us. When the Lord succeeds in bringing Israel out of Egypt, we have to turn these tribes—half Egyptian in their thoughts and habits—into a single nation that respects and obeys the Lord. I know what it took to prepare *me* to serve God. I hope they'll be easier to teach."

"Nothing's easy with Israelites," said Aaron, thinking of the endless quarreling. The saying was that wherever you had two Israelites, you had three opinions—each man's true opinion, and an opinion exactly opposite to whichever one was stated first, which the second man will immediately adopt as if he had believed it all his life.

"What do we do when someone decides that you and I are not really the ones God wants to rule that nation? What if we face a rebellion? Do we become tyrants in order to hold Israel together as one nation? The Lord will free us from Egypt, but who will keep us at peace with each other?"

"The danger isn't rebellion so much as division," said Aaron. "The one thing Israel has maintained far better than our religion is the separate identity of the twelve tribes. Thirteen, really, since Ephraim and Manasseh act as if they were still carrying on their old foolish rivalry and they won't allow anyone to combine them as the tribe of Joseph. Each tribe has its own leaders, and each one will be afraid that some other tribe will have the ascendancy."

"So they'll assume we intend to have our tribe of Levi rule over all the others," said Moses.

"That's why I never have a council of fewer than thirteen members," said Aaron. "I can never afford to let any tribe feel left out, or that tribe will be my enemy."

"I'm glad to see you've already had experience with this," said Moses. "Governing people is hard enough when they are used to being a nation, and are accustomed to the way government works in their lives. Every person will have his own idea of what freedom means. Most will recognize that we still must have laws and judges, to keep the peace and to protect our nation from enemies. But it'll take time to bind these tribes into one nation, the children of Israel, the servants of God. A nation of priests and prophets, Aaron, that's what we must become. When the people all have the spirit of God in their hearts, then we'll be like the people of Zion or Salem, and without war our enemies will be driven away by the power of God, and without animosity all disagreements will be settled with the love of God in our hearts." Moses sighed. "In the meantime, I'll have to rely on your intimate knowledge of the leaders of the tribes."

Aaron felt his heart racing, to think of the kind of nation that Moses envisioned. He had never heard of Zion or Salem, but he had some notion of what it might mean to be a nation of priests and prophets. To get to that condition, though, they had so far to go. "Now I'm gladder than ever that I've worked to make friends with the leaders of every tribe," said Aaron.

"There is none that has cause to hate me, and I think there's none that does."

"When they see the power of God flow from your hand," said Moses, "some of them will remember old offenses that didn't even bother them at the time, and they'll say, Who is he, that the Lord has given him power like that? Wasn't he the one who used to quarrel with me as a child? Didn't I hear that his own children misbehave? Why did the Lord choose him and not me?"

Aaron flushed with embarrassment. Had Moses read his mind?

But Moses went on as if his words had no application to Aaron at all, and they spent the next several hours' journey with Aaron telling Moses about all the elders of all the tribes. Whether Moses could possibly remember all this information, Aaron had no idea. But he was glad to have the chance to show how well he knew the leaders of the people. If Moses had some notion that Aaron resented him, Aaron was determined that he would never have cause to think such a thing again. It was the Lord they served, and the Lord's people. Both of them were called by prophecy, however different their experience might have been. If the Lord had need of any man, he should be glad to serve, no matter how high or low his office might seem in the eyes of others. For in the service of God all offices were made noble by the nobility of their master, and all yet all officers were lowly servants compared to the one they obeyed.

Besides, even though Moses was ahead of him and always would be, Aaron couldn't help but notice that being second in the eyes of the Lord put him well ahead of everyone else.

❧

Jannes and Jambres came to Tuthmose as soon as they

were summoned. If they thought of themselves as kingmakers for having helped Tuthmose gain sole possession of the crown, they never showed it. If anything, they were more obedient and subservient than they had ever been with Hatshepsut. This wise humility was an attribute he appreciated in his priests. That way he didn't have to kill them.

"What service can we perform for our god Pharaoh?" asked Jannes. Jambres, though he was now a man of middle age, still let his father do the talking on public occasions. This was an illusion, of course. In private, it was Jambres whose keen mind was worth consulting. And Tuthmose knew perfectly well that it was to Jambres that Tuthmose owed the support of the priesthood. Jannes was old, just going through the motions.

"Do you remember a slave who pretended to be a son in Pharaoh's house?" asked Tuthmose.

"Wasn't that during the time that a woman was pretending to be Pharaoh in Pharaoh's house?" asked Jambres.

Jannes glowered at his son. "I was commanded to forget any such slave who went into exile some years ago."

"Now I command you to remember again," said Tuthmose. "He's back."

"We know," said Jambres. "Our informers among the Israelites told us of a meeting last night on the banks of the Nile. Some magic tricks were done. The bumpkins were impressed."

"The staff into a snake," said Jannes, "I've been doing that one for years. The snake back into a staff, that's harder, but. . . ." His voice trailed off.

"I assume," said Tuthmose," that you're speaking of the power of the gods."

"If the slaves are going to start showing off what their

nameless invisible desert god can do, we plan to match them trick for trick," said Jambres. "My father is an expert at helping the gods show their . . . presence."

"So you know that Moses has announced his intention of coming to see me."

"We were surprised that you didn't have him killed," said Jannes. "Isn't he under sentence of death?"

"Yes, well. . . ." Tuthmose stared off into space. "It's not as if he poses any danger. The army is ready to slaughter Israelites should there be any rebellion. But *my* observers didn't mention anything about the Israelites arming themselves."

"No," said Jambres. "Incredible as it may sound, my informers insisted that Moses and his hot-headed brother Aaron utterly refused any idea of armed rebellion. They are going to let their god persuade you to let them go. In fact, Moses and Aaron told the tribal chieftains that you will *beg* them to go, and the people of Egypt will thrust gold and jewels upon the Israelites as gifts when they depart."

"Moses was a better general than he is a prophet," said Tuthmose. "There'll be begging, but it won't be from any Egyptian."

Jambres made as if to speak, then said nothing.

"The priest of Amon is shy before the god Pharaoh," said Tuthmose.

"Does a man counsel a god?" said Jambres.

"You shouldn't," said Jannes. "The gods don't need counsel."

"I take counsel all the time," said Tuthmose.

"But this is personal," said Jambres.

"I forgive you before you speak," said Tuthmose.

"Kill him now," said Jambres. "Whatever game playing is too dangerous."

"Dangerous? What, do you think the military will t an Israelite traitor who's been tending sheep in the wilde all these years? Do you think I can't crush any revolt he m raise? Do you think my guards won't stand ready to stop attempt at assassination?"

Jambres nodded and looked at the floor.

"Answer me!" said Tuthmose.

Jambres sighed.

His ancient father laughed. "I told you not to try," said the old man.

"Try what?" said Tuthmose.

"To persuade you when your mind is already made up," said Jannes.

"Persuade me not to see Moses? Why! Do you think I don't know the man, every corner of his mind? I was his best student. *He* didn't know that — I pretended to be dimwitted, not to understand half what he said, so he wouldn't see the danger that I posed. But I learned everything he had to teach. Do you think he can surprise me now?"

"Of course not, Pharaoh," said Jambres. "Thank you for forgiving me."

"No, I want your warning! I want to hear it so I can laugh at you later."

"But you have already answered my fears. I have no more. I am at peace with the wisdom of Pharaoh."

"Do you know what I think, Jambres? I think that whatever it was Moses did at that meeting, the sticks-and-snakes thing, you don't believe it was a trick, the way your little demonstrations are. I think you're afraid his god is more powerful than yours."

"God is God," said Jambres. "Amon is the name for him here, and Ptah is also his name; he wears many faces in many lands. But behind all images and dreams and tales and powers of the gods there is the same creator god, the father of all. We know that this creator has stepped away, and left this world to the lesser gods. This nameless Israelite god might be one of those, or might be a name for the first God of gods. But the underlying power is the same. Can God be more powerful than God?"

"Am I supposed to make any sense of this priestly nattering?" said Tuthmose.

"You admired Moses as a child," said Jambres. "You said so to me, even as you told me how you hated him."

"What I said then, I said as a little boy, not as a man, and certainly not as Pharaoh."

"But it is on the head of the little boy, and the man, and the Pharaoh, that the crown was set."

"You think I still admire Moses? He turned out to be weak. Soft-hearted. A follower, like one of those poor little calves or lambs the Israelites cut open and let bleed to death on their altars, back when they were still allowed to do that."

"I think you want him to admire you," said Jambres.

"Wrong," said Tuthmose angrily. "I want him to see me where he thought to be! I want him to see all his ambitions fulfilled—but by me, while he's a rustic, a pastoral clown. Admire me? No, I want him to see what he lost! I want to fill his heart with regret! I only wish he had come back before Hatshepsut died. He missed her by only a few weeks, isn't that amusing? I wish he could have been here to see her, and then the next day, see her dead. But this is the next best thing. To see me in my glory, and know that he is nothing!"

Tuthmose was standing now, roaring, his voice filling the

empty hall. The last echo rang through the room after he stopped speaking. When it was still, Jannes bowed low, and Jambres bowed, if possible, even lower. "We must make ready," said Jannes, "to match him power for power, to show him that Amon is as capable as his nameless god."

"Go on, get out," said Tuthmose. "I wish I had been upriver at the palace in Thebes instead of down here in Memphis, so near to where the Israelites do their labor in the lowland mud. The stink is in my nostrils day and night."

They were already at the door, but Jambres turned and spoke. "Then why not let them go, when Moses asks?"

"Hush," said Jannes, looking terrified.

"Because he is the one asking me," said Tuthmose. "Is that what you expect me to say? Is that the kind of Pharaoh you think I am? Well, I am the god of Egypt, caretaker of this land. Do you think I don't feel that as surely as that sanctimonious Hatshepsut ever did? I will keep the Israelites here because there are hundreds of thousands of them, and if we let them go, they would immediately be an enemy outside of Egypt, an enemy that knows every road, every city, every treasure house, every granary, and every military outpost in the Two Kingdoms. They will *never* leave Egypt. Egypt didn't invite them here, but Egypt nurtured them and taught them and fed them and helped them become numerous, and Egypt will not let them go to stand outside our borders and spit on us."

The priests left, father and son. Feeble Jannes leaned on Jambres's arm. When Tuthmose was young, he had envied them their closeness. A father training his son to become his replacement. Tuthmose's father barely knew he existed. At first this hurt Tuthmose, for he was sure that this meant his father did not mean him to be Pharaoh. Later, he understood that what his father did required no training—play with the trappings of power, indulge the appetites of your body, and let usurpers do the real business of government and military leadership. His father's every breath was a waste of air. That was why Tuthmose had arranged for his mother to learn the poisoner's art from Mutnefert, and to use the knowledge to strike his father down. A bad father is a bad Pharaoh, that's what Tuthmose understood. Jambres had a good father, who did his work well and taught his son with love and rigor. So he could honor the old man until his natural death.

That was why Tuthmose had been so eager for his queen Sakhmet to bear him a son, which she did on the first try. Little Ptahmose had been a squalling nuisance for the first while, loud when he wasn't inert. But gradually he became more like a human being, learning to smile, to play with his hands, to laugh. Then to walk, to speak a few words. A miracle every day, and every day Tuthmose went to him. No one but Isite ever saw how Tuthmose got down on his hands and knees to romp with the child. And not even Isite knew that when Tuthmose watched the baby nursing, he sometimes felt so bitter, for the more Tuthmose gave to his own child, the more he realized how easy it would have been for his father to do the same for him.

The only one who ever showed any interest in him, who ever demanded that he become something, that he make use of his mind, that he meet some standard of achievement, that he obey any kind of rule, was a certain Israelite interloper who had no right to be in the house of Pharaoh in the first place.

I will be the father I wish I had, that was Tuthmose's iron resolve. My son will grow up knowing that the gods have smiled on him by giving him to me.

As for Moses, I'll show him that I learned all his lessons well. Every move he makes, I'll counter exactly as he taught me to. I'll cut his support out from under him. By the time I'm through with him, the Israelites will be eager to drive him back out of Egypt into exile—if they don't kill him themselves. Let him see what a *real* son of Pharaoh can do with power.

❊

In the morning Moses and Aaron set out together, staves in hand, to make the trek to the palace at Memphis. It was to be a journey of several hours, and they had to carry their dinner with them, since there would be no friendly house to take them in, and no innkeeper that would dare have them under his roof. Miriam saw them off from the door of her hut, laughing and singing as they departed. Neighbors looked on in awe, and Moses suspected that it was because they had never seen Miriam happy before.

As they passed along the sledge road where the brick forms were hauled, the people looked up from their labors. There were no cheers, as there had been when Moses returned in triumph from Saba. Instead there were isolated cries: Go with God! God protect you! Let God deliver us from bondage! God is merciful!

Moses stopped only once, where the workers were especially numerous, and murmured words to Aaron. Aaron stretched forth his arms and addressed them all in a booming voice. "Hear, O Israel! The Lord our God, the Lord is one!"

They repeated the phrase. Repeated it, chanted it behind them as they walked on toward the house of Pharaoh. Hear, O Israel! The Lord our God, the Lord is one.

❊

Pharaoh sat on his throne, but he did not even look up when Aaron preceded Moses into the hall. The old priest Jannes stood a few yards in front of Pharaoh.

"The name of Moses was once familiar here. A common murderer, I think he was, who ran away to escape justice."

Moses murmured to Aaron, "Don't play this game. We have a message."

"The Lord God of Israel," said Aaron, "has sent his prophet Moses with a message for Pharaoh."

"Ah, yes," said Jannes. "I heard of this god. I never quite understood—does he love his people, but hasn't the power to free them? Or is he powerful, but hates Israel so much that he leaves them in bondage?"

"Is Pharaoh ill," said Aaron, "that he must send an old frog to croak for him?"

All the assembled priests, officers, and courtiers went still as stone. Apparently no one had ever spoken to Jannes so rudely. Aaron worried that perhaps he had gone too far—but Moses had told him that he was to be scornful of everyone but Pharaoh himself, and was to speak to Pharaoh as an equal, not a superior. "You can handle scorn, can't you?" Moses had asked. "I was born for this," Aaron had replied. Now Aaron was having second thoughts. But he knew not to turn around and look at Moses—that would show weakness. If Moses wanted him to tone down the arrogance, he had only to ask.

Pharaoh lifted his head and looked at Moses and Aaron for the first time. Aaron had not realized how young a man he was. He still had his youthful slenderness, and there was a sadness and a hunger in his eyes—just what Aaron would expect from someone so consumed with ambition that he had killed for it.

"Pharaoh is a god," said Jannes. "Why should *he* speak to *you?*"

"Moses has heard the voice of the living God," said Aaron. "There is no one else worth hearing."

Pharaoh spoke softly. Jannes turned and knelt to him as he listened to Pharaoh's instructions. Then he arose and turned to the court. "In his magnanimity, Pharaoh is willing to hear your god's petition."

That little show could not go unanswered, Aaron decided. He turned and knelt to Moses.

"What are you doing?" asked Moses softly.

"If Jannes kneels to Pharaoh, I kneel to the prophet."

Moses did not smile, but Aaron could see that he wanted to. So my little brother likes how I've gotten into the spirit of this. Aaron couldn't help but be pleased, and he ignored the tiny stirrings of resentment at the thought of Moses condescending to him. Remember, Moses, Aaron said inwardly, I'm doing this for show.

"You know the message," Moses murmured.

Aaron arose and, as he had done out in the brickyards that morning, he spread wide his arms and spoke loudly. "The Lord God of Israel has said, My people will have a feast to honor me!"

Jannes replied at once. "If the slaves are planning a feast, clearly we have been giving them too much grain."

Aaron ignored the interruption. "Let my people go, the Lord has said, three days' journey into the wilderness to offer sacrifice before the Lord."

Jannes turned and knelt again to Pharaoh. His answer, when it came, was intoned in the same declamatory style he had used before, but Aaron could hear the smug delight in his voice. "It is well known that Israelites are thieves and idlers, and Pharaoh knows that this is just a trick to get away from work. Pharaoh has been too generous and lenient with you. Since you have food to waste on feasts, your ration will be reduced, and you can eat those extra animals to keep up your strength. Since you have time to waste on sacrifices, you will no longer have straw delivered to you to help in the drying of the bricks. You must send men to fetch it yourselves. But your daily tally of bricks will stay the same. You can come present your petition again, if there are any Israelites left who still want to sacrifice."

Pharaoh arose from his chair and left the room.

Immediately Moses whispered, "Let's go." Aaron followed him as he walked boldly but unhurriedly out of the hall.

"How did I do?" asked Aaron, when they were outside.

"Fine," said Moses. "You have a flair for this."

"What now?" said Aaron. "They didn't even try to negotiate."

"This *is* negotiation," said Moses. "He's trying to cut off our support. The plan is to get the Israelites so upset by the new rules that they send us back to beg Pharaoh to remove the extra burden. Or—and this is what he'd prefer—they repudiate us entirely and send other emissaries to beg forgiveness. Then, when we've lost all support or have abandoned our mission, he sends soldiers to arrest us and kill us. When we're dead, Pharaoh mercifully restores the old work rules and he emerges stronger than ever."

"How do you know that's his plan?" asked Aaron.

"Because I taught him that myself. When faced with a rebellion, don't attack the leader—that makes a martyr of him. Instead bring harm to the people he represents, and blame their own leader for it. Get them to turn against him, discredit the leader completely, and you don't have to use a single soldier to bring down the rebellion. They'll beg you to forgive them and take them back."

Aaron thought about this for a moment. "Explain to me now what *our* plan is."

"I don't know," said Moses.

"You know *his* plan, and you don't know ours?"

"I'm just guessing, mind you, but I think that this is the part where you hold the Israelites together in spite of Pharaoh's harassment."

"Me!"

"You're the one who understands the Israelites," said Moses. "We have to get them to trust in God and stand firm with us."

"If I'd ever been able to get them to stand firm on anything, we'd be free already," said Aaron.

"This time it's the Lord who's leading them. If they won't stand with the Lord today, they aren't worthy to be free."

"But what can I promise them? If they stand firm now, things will get better?"

"In all likelihood, they'll get worse," said Moses. "But they'll see the hand of God reveal itself in due time. After they've proven their faith in God."

"It's possible to have faith in God," said Aaron, "and not have much faith in us."

"We're the ones that God chose to do this," said Moses. "If they repudiate us, they repudiate God."

"You don't expect me to *say* that to them, do you?"

"Why not?" said Moses. "It's the truth. And even when it's offensive, the truth still sounds good to godly men. If you try to deceive them or bribe them or threaten them or shame them, some will stand with you and some against you, just as they would with any other man. But if you tell them God's plain truth, Aaron, they'll feel it confirmed in their hearts by the spirit of God, and if they love God they'll follow us."

"You're sure of that?"

"Aaron, God promised me that I would celebrate with the children of Israel at the mountain of the Lord."

"Yes, but did he specify that you'd be doing this in the flesh? Or in the spirit, having died first?"

Moses laughed. "Aaron, you're the spokesman. Speak boldly."

＊

Miriam was used to people whining and complaining and doubting and raging, so as they began to gather around her house when at the end of the day's work, she was not at all surprised to hear every possible nasty comment about those meddlesome fools, her brothers. Why did Moses return to Egypt, to make their lives even more miserable? To take away the last scraps of leisure in their lives? To make their children hungry? On and on and on. The choir of complaint. Someone bring a zither, we need to get everyone on the same note.

By the time Moses and Aaron themselves returned, the crowd was surly and very large. The leaders of the other tribes were notable for their absence. Clearly they didn't want to be around to face the outcry.

So it was amusing to see how jaunty Moses and Aaron were as they strode along the road, planting their staves and pushing off with every other step. Hadn't they heard what Pharaoh's messengers had declared? About having to procure the straw instead of having it delivered? About the shorter rations?

"I'm glad you're here," cried Aaron to the crowd, smiling broadly. "You should have been there! Pharaoh's lackey, Jannes, the priest of that false god Amon, almost croaked when I called him an old frog!"

A few laughed, but one cry from the crowd silenced them.

"That insult cost us hours of extra work every day!" Cries of angry assent swept the crowd.

Aaron laughed and shook his head. "Don't you see that God is showing all the people of Egypt how weak and ineffective Pharaoh is? He thinks that he can come between the children of Israel and the prophet the Lord has sent to them. On the contrary! God will come between Pharaoh and *his* people, until they groan for him to let Israel go. Israel will stand together! But Egypt will fall apart."

"What's going to make them hate Pharaoh!" demanded a woman.

"The power of God," said Aaron. "Stand firm, and let the Lord work his will."

"In the meantime we work ourselves to death!"

"For a few days we work harder," said Aaron. "Is that too high a price to pay for freedom? I've heard many a man among you say he'd gladly die to win our freedom from bondage. Is death so easy? The extra bricks you make will show your faith in God! Every brick is a gift to God!"

"It'll go into Egyptian buildings all the same," someone called.

"Egyptian buildings that your children will never have to look at, because they'll be in the promised land! Moses knows that you're suffering! That's why the Lord sent him here—to change that suffering to joy. Be joyful as you work now, for you are not working as slaves! Pharaoh is no longer in control of you. He can only respond now, to what the Lord says to him. God rules in Egypt now!"

The hecklers were still there, but now the bulk of the crowd was with Aaron. Miriam had to admire how smoothly Aaron handled it, turning Pharaoh's punishment into a heroic burden borne for God's sake. This is fine today, she thought.

But what speech will you give the next time, when Pharaoh makes it even worse?

"I look out upon the people," cried Aaron, "and I see the children of Israel, men and women of every tribe. But where are your leaders? Why are they hiding? Why do they not stand beside the prophet of the Lord? The day will come when every man will claim that he stood beside Moses the whole way. But you are my witnesses—they were not here today!"

"Not true!" cried a man.

"Ephraim is here!" cried another.

The first man came forward. "I'm Caleb, and I stand here for Judah."

"Caleb," said Aaron, "I should have known that of all the elders of Judah, you would be the one to stand with us."

The man from Ephraim also came forward. He was painfully young, hardly more than a boy.

"I don't know you," said Aaron. "You weren't at the meeting of the elders."

The young man nodded. "My father was, and told me all that took place. Today he was plagued with pain in his knees and elbows and fingers, so he couldn't walk, but he sent me in his place. My name is Joshua. My father is Nun."

"That grand old man!" cried Aaron. "Israel, do you hear? Joshua stands up for his father Nun, an elder of Ephraim. And Caleb stands up for Judah. Men of Judah! Men of Ephraim! Your tribes are known to have faith in God! And I stand here for Levi. But you men of other tribes, where are your elders? When God brings Israel out of Egypt, do you want your tribe to be left behind because you repudiated the prophet instead of trusting in the Lord?"

At once there was a flurry as men ran off in search of their tribal elders. Miriam caught Aaron's eye and smiled at him. Well done, brother.

The meeting lasted an hour, as each of the tribal elders arrived and tried to outdo the others in affirming how loyal they were to Moses, and how firmly they would all endure Pharaoh's persecution without complaint, because they trusted in the Lord to deliver them.

Miriam did her part. She refrained from laughing in their faces. Weak and frightened men — soon enough new leaders would emerge from the tribes, while the timid old ones drifted off into meaninglessness. That elder of Judah, Caleb, he was a good one, Miriam knew he had a name for courage. And the young one, the boy Joshua — what a surprise he turned out to be. A son of Nun was bound to be bookish and quiet, she would have thought. Instead, he outdid Aaron in fervency until Moses had to silence him by gathering him into his embrace and taking him aside to talk in private.

Afterward, when the three of them were alone in the moonlight, sitting on the ground outside Miriam's hut, she asked Moses what he said to the boy.

"Not a boy, Miriam," said Moses. "A man. I told him Aaron mentioned that his father, Nun, was a painter, writing inscriptions on stone. I asked if he had learned to read and write, and he said yes. I've made him my scribe."

"A mere child!" said Miriam.

"Why, did *you* want the job?" said Aaron.

"I wanted *your* job," said Miriam. "I never would have thought you had it in you, Aaron. Standing up to all that heckling without letting them bully you."

"I don't let people bully me," said Aaron.

"Not anymore, anyway," said Miriam. "I'm praising you, Aaron, so please don't argue with me about this."

"Sorry," said Aaron. "I didn't know what praise sounded like, coming from you."

"I was just as surprised to see courage and vigor coming from *you*," said Miriam.

Moses roared with laughter. "Nothing changes! Gone for all these years, and nothing changes!" He threw his arms around Miriam. "Have I ever told you how I honor you, for speaking honestly when no one wanted to hear? The Lord's will has not been forgotten in Israel, not by anyone within the sound of your voice."

Miriam was taken aback. No one ever embraced her, not since she started speaking so boldly in the name of the Lord. But startled as she was, she rather regretted it when he released her. And his praise brought tears to her eyes. No one had ever thanked her or honored her—they had only avoided her or tried to get her to hold her peace, or at least speak more tactfully.

But then she realized: He was handling her, dealing with her. "I think you're flattering me, Moses," she said acidly. "I don't do what I do to be praised."

Moses smiled, a little sadly. "Can't trust anyone, can you?"

"You're still the same man you were when you left, Moses," said Miriam. "Look what happened today—it was Aaron who saved the situation with the crowd. You didn't even raise your voice."

"The Lord gave me Aaron to be my spokesman," said Moses. "It would be foolish of me, then, not to let him speak."

"You're so complacent," said Miriam. "You have nothing at stake here. Your family is in Midian, safely out of harm's way. While we have everything on the line!"

Moses shook his head. "My life is on the line, Miriam. If I seem complacent, it's because I believe the Lord's promise, spoken to me in his own voice. Why should I be afraid? And you, Miriam, haven't you known from childhood on that God would do the things that he's doing now?"

"Yes!" she cried. "I loved the Lord and I loved Israel when you were playing at being Pharaoh's son in the palace!"

Moses regarded her in silence for a few minutes. "And now the Lord has shown himself to me, and called Aaron in a dream. We're the ones who were called, and not you. Which is it that galls you more, that God chose us for the job, or that we're doing it better than you thought we could?"

"I don't know how you could do it worse!" said Miriam. "There isn't even a glimmer of a plan in what you're doing. Despite Aaron's fine words, it's Pharaoh who's in control of the situation."

"I've spent years of study and prayer, learning how to turn my life over to God, without trying to make plans of my own," said Moses. "As for Pharaoh, he's in control of nothing. God rules Egypt as he rules all lands. Generally he doesn't interfere, letting the fools be foolish while the wicked do their worst. Miriam, God called me and Aaron because he wanted us to do something different from what we were doing before. You, however, have been serving him exactly as he wished, from childhood on—from the day you spoke boldly to Hatshepsut and brought our mother into the palace to be my wet-nurse. Why should the Lord call you again, when you're already on the right road?"

Miriam glared at him. "More flattery."

"More truth," said Moses. "We need you to listen to the complaints of the people, and assure them that their suffering is worthwhile because God is turning all their pain and grief into a miracle."

"That's fine for you to say," said Miriam. "But when does the miracle start?"

Moses sighed. "Some people can't see miracles when they're right in the middle of them."

"Better than seeing miracles where they don't exist," said Miriam.

"You're determined to stand entirely alone, aren't you," said Moses.

"That's where I've always stood," said Miriam. "And isn't it just typical that when you decided to turn to the Lord's way, you couldn't come stand *beside* me, you had to leap on ahead and play the prophet as if you were the first person ever to speak the words of the Lord to this people."

"What you don't understand," said Moses, "is that if they're the words of the Lord, what does it matter who says them? I *am* standing beside you. So stop trying to elbow me off. There's room for all of us in the Lord's service, not just us three but every man and woman of Israel."

"Is that what you think? That you can turn Israel into a nation of prophets? Go back to Midian, Moses, but stay in the shade, the sun has been cooking your brains."

Moses patted her hand. "Stay alone, then, if you want."

"I don't want to be alone, I *am* alone, and I always have been."

"That's how it feels," said Moses, "to everyone who hasn't found the Lord."

"I'm alone *because* I found the Lord."

"That's why you're *not* alone. But if you insist, we'll all be very quiet and pretend not to be here, so you can go on believing in your own isolation. In the meantime, I hope you'll help us with the people."

"I'll help the *Lord*."

"Good," said Moses. "He loves you even more than I do."

With that, Moses got up and went inside the house.

"Well," said Aaron, "that was as childish as I've ever seen you act."

"Shut up," said Miriam.

"Envy is so ugly, especially when it's so nakedly expressed."

"While *your* envy is all dressed up as loyalty," said Miriam. "But some of us see through the costume."

"Aren't *we* the complicated family," said Aaron. "We chased Moses all those years, and now that we've finally caught him, we don't want him."

"But we've got him anyway," said Miriam.

"The truth is, Miriam, that Moses is not the same man he was. None of that I-know-everything attitude. He really does live for the Lord now. He's humbled himself. I'm trying to do the same."

"I live for the Lord, too."

"I know," said Aaron.

"I did sound envious, didn't I. But that wasn't how I really feel. I'm tired. I can't believe I said the things I said."

"Miriam, everyone who knows you often has said the same thing: I can't believe Miriam said the things she said." Aaron laughed and gripped her hand a moment, then got up. "I hope Elisheba has heard the rumor that I got back from the palace alive. She was worried when I left her this morning, and so were the children."

"I know," said Miriam. "I helped her care for your children half the day. Nadab and Abihu are useful at making bricks, but the younger boys can't stop scampering right through the bricks before they're dry, leaving little footprints."

"Thank you for watching out for my family," said Aaron.

"Your family is my family."

"Do you think we'll ever meet Moses' wife and children?"

asked Aaron. "Or even that father-in-law he can't stop talking about? The one who taught him to read Hebrew?"

"Didn't you hear the prophet? We'll all be together to serve God at the holy mountain."

"Or die trying," said Aaron.

"Do you think he really saw the Lord? Or just a bush on fire on a hot day?" Without meaning to, Miriam had blurted her own worst doubts.

But Aaron only chuckled. "It's not the way I would have done it, but Miriam, he got us in to see Pharaoh, we spoke boldly to him — it was exhilarating. Why shouldn't it be true? Maybe my dream was just a dream and Moses only happened to be returning to Egypt while I was there waiting for him. But I think God's hand is guiding him. If I'm wrong, you'll be burying me quite soon."

"If I'm not also dead because of Moses."

"Good night, Miriam," said Aaron. "I have to hike all the way to the palace again tomorrow."

"What, aren't you going to haul straw for us?"

"I'm a talker these days, Miriam, not a doer."

"In other words, you haven't changed a bit," she retorted.

He laughed, kissed her on the cheek, and went back to his own hut, leaving her alone as always.

But no, not alone. Moses was asleep inside her house.

The Lord's prophet — and he told her that the Lord chose her, that she had done well, that he loved her, that the Lord's cause needed her.

Maybe it was all flattery to try to persuade her to help him keep the people calm. But she knew in her heart that it wasn't flattery, it was the truth. God *did* love her. God *had* noticed her, and all her faithful service.

# Chapter 10

# B l o o d

It was the younger priest, Jambres, who spoke for Pharaoh this time, greeting Moses and Aaron with a bright, cheerful smile. Pharaoh, too, seemed in good spirits as he gazed at them.

"I'm happy to tell you that we are getting remarkable savings from the changes you encouraged us to introduce," said Jambres. "Are you here to tell us that you've found even more leisure time, so that we can get the tally of bricks for even less expense?"

"The Lord God is angry at your rebellious spirit," said Aaron. "The Lord has said to Moses, Tell Pharaoh he has one last chance to let the children of Israel go."

"Is this a threat?" asked Jambres. "The god whose people don't even know his name is going to do what, exactly? No doubt you're going to tell me that *your* god is so powerful he holds the clouds up in the sky! Your god makes it rain! Your god makes the wind blow!" He laughed. "I'm sure he does all those things. Now, if you can speak a word and get him to *stop*." Jambres laughed. "Do you think you can frighten us with threats of what your god will do?"

Moses whispered to Aaron for a moment. "We don't want you to obey out of fear," said Aaron. "We want you to obey because what God commands is right and good. But if you do not choose to do what is right for its own sake, then fear will have to do."

"Throw your staff to the floor," said Moses.

Aaron obeyed, and it turned into a hissing serpent.

Jambres laughed again. "Any god can do that," he said. He and Jannes stepped forward, brandishing rods of their own. They spun around and threw down their rods and they, too, were snakes.

Aaron was startled, but Moses whispered to him, "They made the switch while they were spinning around. They were already holding snakes before they threw them down."

Aaron was relieved—he had never expected the priests to match what God had given them power to do. He was about to reach down and take his serpent by the tail when it slithered away, rushing toward the priests' snakes. In moments it had seized one by the head, and then, in a few writhes and twists, it swallowed the whole thing. It did the same with the other snake. Then Aaron picked it up, and it became a rod again in his hand.

It was Aaron's turn to laugh. "Did you think you could fool God?" he asked. "You know that what you do is only illusion. But what God does is real."

Jambres was putting a good face on it, though. "So far all I've seen is that your snake was hungrier than ours. In Egypt the gods with power are Egyptian gods."

Moses whispered to Aaron.

"Moses is grieved that you don't care about the welfare of your people," said Aaron. "The Lord God told us to demonstrate his power in this harmless way, so you would have the chance to repent of the evil you have done to the chosen people of the Lord, without bringing harm upon your people. Instead you answer him with these childish illusions. Very well, Pharaoh. Tomorrow you will see the power of the Lord stretched out over Egypt."

"If you're thinking of rebellion, Moses," Jambres began.

But Jannes touched his arm, interrupting him. The two priests turned and conferred with Pharaoh.

"No straw at all," said Jannes. "Let the bricks dry by themselves in the sun. The Israelites will be told that this was because you continued your insulting ingratitude, instead of doing homage to Pharaoh for his great mercy in allowing the Israelites so much leniency and freedom."

Moses and Aaron wordlessly turned their backs and left.

❉

At dawn, Pharaoh and his wife and son went down to the river to drink, to pray. Soldiers stood guard nearby, but as always many people were gathered to present petitions on the riverbank. Tuthmose found these intrusions tiresome, but it was good for Ptahmose to see his father being magnanimous to the common people. It set a good example.

He should have expected that among the petitioners were Moses and Aaron. To the captain of the guard he said, "Those two—why were they allowed here?"

"We inspected them for weapons," said the captain. "You've been seeing him in court, so I thought . . ."

"No, you did well," said Tuthmose. "It's good for my son to see this, as well."

Tuthmose took his son up onto his shoulder and walked to the petitioners. "I see that two slaves have come here, perhaps to apologize for their foolishness yesterday. Pharaoh is a forgiving god. I will hear their petition."

Aaron's voice rang out. "The Lord God of Israel says, Let my people go."

Pharaoh shook his head sadly. "How much must your people suffer, before you learn?" he asked.

"That is the question God asks of you," said Aaron.

Moses spoke loudly to Aaron, this time intending for all to hear. "Aaron, the Lord God commands that you stretch out your hand over the waters of Egypt. By the command of God, all the water of Egypt, in all the channels of the Nile, in every pool and pond, in every jar and vessel, every font and cup, will turn to blood."

Aaron thrust out his arm over the water of the river. Then, pulling a cup from his shoulder bag, he reached down and scooped water from the river. When he poured it out, the other petitioners gasped, and one cried out. For in the first light of dawn, the liquid was bright red, like blood from a fresh wound.

At once the petitioners knelt on the steps and touched the water, cupping it in their hands, tasting it on the tips of their fingers. "It's blood!" they cried. "It's all blood!"

"Blood," said Ptahmose.

Tuthmose was filled with loathing. Moses and Aaron had done this in the sight of his beloved son. His first instinct was to order them arrested. But that would look like weakness. It would look as if he believed in this trick of theirs.

"Your petition is not granted," said Tuthmose. "I'm not impressed by these foolish tricks."

"For seven days," said Aaron, "the Nile will run with blood."

Ignoring Aaron, Tuthmose carried Ptahmose back up the steps to the palace. Sakhmet, the queen, followed him, wisely refraining from any comment.

Throughout the land there was no water, and within hours the clamor became desperate. Only when someone noticed that water seeping into a deep hole was pure enough to drink did the complaints give way to a plan. All through Egypt, wells were dug, and water was hauled with desperate haste to the places where people could not find new water no matter how deep they dug.

And the story spread that the god of the Israelites had done this, because Pharaoh refused to let them go out into the desert to offer sacrifices.

Jannes and Jambres made a great show of turning water into blood in front of hundreds of witnesses in the great hall that afternoon, and the official line was that once again, the god of the Israelites had done nothing that Egyptian gods couldn't do. But when Tuthmose was alone with the two priests, he had a very different opinion. "Are you trying to make me look stupid?" he demanded. "What good is it to prove that you can also turn water to blood, if you don't have the power that I *need*, which is to turn blood back into water!"

To that, Jambres and Jannes had nothing to say.

"No more of these demonstrations," said Tuthmose. "I'm sure you can come up with convincing illusions every time, but as long as you don't have the power I need, I don't want to see you showing off a power that no one wants. It makes me look pathetic."

The priests bowed.

"Moses thinks I'm going to send for him and ask him to remove this curse. But the people are getting water by digging holes. He can make blood rain out of the sky for all I care. The Israelites will stay in Egypt. He's lucky I don't start killing a hundred Israelites a day until he stops this nonsense."

"Why don't you?" asked Jambres.

"Because I'd be making a hundred martyrs," said Tuthmose, "and even if Moses complied, it would only demonstrate that he was the one with the power, while all I could do was kill."

"Very wise," said Jambres.

When the priests had left the palace, though, Jambres had a different opinion. "Tuthmose is confused. It bothers him that Moses' god has such power."

"I'm not sure," said Jannes. "I think it's not the Israelite god that Pharaoh fears, but the Israelite himself. Moses is the one who is driving us all before him, and Pharaoh hates that. No matter what he does, he'll look weaker than Moses. In front of another man, Pharaoh might humble himself. But he would rather die than humble himself in front of Moses."

"Then the Israelites have made a mistake, choosing Moses as their prophet," said Jambres.

"He was chosen by their god," said Jannes. "And who knows what their god intends? As long as it's Moses who faces Pharaoh, Pharaoh's heart will remain hardened against all pleas or demands. What I fear is that this god *wants* Pharaoh to refuse, so that the power of the god will be shown at its fullest."

"Father," said Jambres, startled. "You believe in this Israelite god, then?"

"Haven't you tasted the river?" said Jannes. "It's blood. Pure blood. The fish have died because they can't live in it. Their corpses line the river's edge and the stink is already rising. This is not trickery."

"But the Israelites are suffering right along with our people," said Jambres. "They're out there digging wells like anyone else."

"Digging wells," said Jannes, "but not making bricks."

"Ah," said Jambres. "Not meeting their tally. Shall we remind Pharaoh of this?"

"What can he do about it? Being harsh with the Israelites has brought this plague on us. I don't think he's willing to face the consequences of being harsher still."

"And what do *we* do?" said Jambres. "This is making us look weak and ineffectual, too."

"We say nothing," said Jannes. "We give no counsel, unless asked. It's Pharaoh who is getting the whole blame for provoking this plague. Why in the world should we bring any part of that down upon ourselves?"

"That's one reason why I admire you, Father," said Jambres. "You always remember to keep first things first."

"I still think it's unwise of Tuthmose to keep letting people see him with Moses. The contrast is painful."

"I don't know, Father. If they remember what Moses was, perhaps so. But Moses is no longer the powerful general or the wise ruler."

"No, he's a priest now," said Jannes. "And to tell the truth, my son, I don't much like having people see the contrast between him and us, either."

❊

Miriam tried to be patient with the complainers, but as each day wore on, her temper wore out. "Yes, it's miserable having to dig new wells every day! Yes, the water is brackish and it still tastes like there are traces of blood in it! But try, *try* to remember two things: This is a miracle! It means that God loves us! And the Egyptians are having to dig wells just like us, and drink the same miserable fluid that we're drinking. They are feeling the mighty hand of God. Is there nobody who thinks this might just be a change for the better?"

❊

Now when Moses and Aaron entered the hall of judgment,

the courtiers were silent, sullenly respectful of the men whose god had the power to make their lives miserable for seven long days. Privately, many of them were impatient with Pharaoh for not killing these men so this nonsense would end. The other half, fearing the wrath of the Israelites' god, were impatient with Pharaoh for not letting the Israelites leave . . . so this nonsense would end.

No one said any of this to anyone else, however, for the words would surely be repeated to Pharaoh, cutting short a career at court.

Aaron's words were simple. "Pharaoh, will you let the Lord's people go?"

Pharaoh sullenly said nothing.

Jannes was all simpering kindness. "Moses, Aaron, what have the people of Egypt done to you, that you treat them so unkindly? Didn't Egypt provide succor for your ancestors when they were starving in the famine in Canaan? Haven't you enjoyed the best that Egypt had to offer for generations? And this is how you return thanks."

Aaron ignored him. "Speak now, Pharaoh, to permit Israel to go worship God in the wilderness, or frogs will cover the land of Egypt. There will be frogs in your house, in your bed-chamber, in your bed, and frogs also in the houses of all your servants and all the people of Egypt. They'll have to sweep frogs out of the ovens to bake, out of the troughs to knead, and shake frogs out of their clothing at every hour of the day."

Jannes chuckled. "The old frog trick," he said. "Look." A frog plopped out of his sleeve and into his hand. He tossed it into the air, and when it came down, there were three on the ground where it landed, hopping and leaping. "The Nile runs clear again. The frogs will also come and go."

"The wrath of God will only grow greater because of your mockery," said Aaron.

Aaron turned and led the way out of the hall. This time, though, many of the courtiers slipped out after him, and outside the palace a large crowd waited. Many groaned when they saw that Moses and Aaron seemed angry. And when Aaron reached the bank of the Nile, there was a crowd of many hundreds gathered to watch.

"Please! Not blood again!" cried someone in the crowd, and many murmured their agreement.

Moses spoke. "Stretch out your hand, Aaron, over the waters of Egypt, and bring forth a plague of frogs."

Aaron stretched out his hand. "Frogs," he cried. "Serve the Lord God of Israel!"

At once the water seemed to bubble and froth. But the bubbles streamed toward shore, and soon thousands of frogs were jumping out of the water. Nor were these timid animals—they jumped up onto the people, then climbed higher, tangling themselves in hair, plunging into clothing. Many tore their clothing off rather than have frogs inside it. In moments, the crowd had dispersed and fled. The frogs moved on like a green sea over the surface of the ground.

Moses and Aaron were also covered with frogs, but they made no effort to remove them. "Aren't you just a little disgusted to have these things crawling on you?" Aaron asked quietly.

"These frogs serve the Lord. I'd rather have their company than any number of rebellious or wicked people."

"May I pluck a few from me now and then, without harming our mission?" asked Aaron.

Moses chuckled. "I think the question of how to deal with the frogs is an individual one. I don't recall any scripture that says the righteous must lie down with frogs." As if to demonstrate, Moses pulled one off his beard and tossed it lightly to the ground.

"Miriam won't like this," said Aaron, pulling frogs out of his robe and shaking them off his staff. "She bears the brunt of the complaining. Isn't there some way to make the plagues strike only the Egyptians, and leave the land of Goshen alone?"

"When Israel submits gladly to the will of God, the Lord will no longer need to afflict them with the plagues."

"Are the frogs going to make them *gladder* to submit?" asked Aaron.

"I think this number of frogs is rather an impressive sight," said Moses.

"Oh, *I'm* impressed," said Aaron. He made a disgusted sound and bent down to pull a crushed frog from between his sandal and the heel of his foot. "I hope it's all right that some of them die."

❉

Ptahmose cried all night, terrified of the frogs. Hundreds of servants kept watch all around his room, but even when every frog had been found and the bed made afresh, Ptahmose still wept in fear and kept feeling frogs on him; and though sometimes no frog could be found, other times a frog had somehow gotten in between the sheets. Finally Ptahmose fell asleep in his father's arms, as the Pharaoh of the Two Kingdoms walked the floor late into the night with his first-born son.

It was still dark when, sleepless and despairing, Pharaoh sent servants to fetch Moses and Aaron. This late at night, there was no public meeting in the hall of judgment. This time they were brought into a small room, one that Moses remembered well, for it was here that he and Hatshepsut had counseled with each other about the government of Egypt. He was surprised that, except for some nostalgia for the woman who had been his mother and teacher, he had no regrets about leaving this place. He hadn't realized it at the time, any more than Pharaoh understood it now, but in these rooms in the palace there could be no vision. The world was small here, and the decisions made within these walls were also small. It took the Lord to drive Moses out of this narrow pen into the wider world of God's creation, but he was glad now that the Lord took such care for him.

Pharaoh came in almost as soon as Moses and Aaron arrived. There were no intermediaries now—Jannes and Jambres followed him into the room, but they were silent.

"Moses," said Pharaoh. "Ask your god to take away the frogs from me and my people."

But it was not Moses who answered him. "That will be easy," said Aaron, "when you let the children of Israel go out to offer sacrifice in the wilderness."

Pharaoh's mouth set hard when he saw that Moses was not going to speak to him directly. "When the frogs are gone, I'll let your people go."

Aaron turned to Moses, waiting for an answer. Moses put his hand on Aaron's shoulder, and spoke directly to Pharaoh. "The Lord knows how much it cost you to make this promise," he said. "When do you want me to ask the Lord to rid the land of frogs?"

"In the morning," said Pharaoh.

"It will happen at the time you said."

Many sleepless people saw Moses and Aaron emerge from the palace, and they saw that the prophet and his brother were smiling. "Will the frogs be taken away?" they asked.

"Pharaoh has promised that when the frogs are gone, the children of Israel can also go," said Aaron.

But Moses whispered to him, "Of course you know that once the Lord takes away the frogs and he can get a good night's sleep, Pharaoh won't feel the same sense of urgency about letting us go."

"Pharaoh will go back on his word?"

"I know he will," said Moses.

"Then why remove the frogs?" asked Aaron.

"Because he hasn't broken his word yet. We must treat him as a man of honor until he proves he doesn't deserve it."

As the first light of dawn came up on the sleepless people in the land of the Nile, the frogs in their houses and their fields, in the streets and in their clothing, became sluggish, then inert. They were dead, killed by the light of day.

But the problem wasn't over. There were all those dead frog bodies to dispose of. Huge piles of the corpses were gathered, far too many to be buried, nor was there fuel enough to burn them. By nightfall the whole land smelled of decomposing frog bodies. But at least there were no frogs in their beds, and the people could sleep.

The next day, Moses was awakened by the shouting of people arguing with the overseers. "The frogs are gone," the chief overseer declared, "and there are bricks to be made!"

Moses came out to find Aaron and several of the tribal elders arguing with the man. "Pharaoh promised," Aaron said.

"I have my orders. My most *particular* orders that the Israelites are to make a double tally in the next week to make up for the time wasted by these plagues."

Moses intervened. "You may tell Pharaoh that the people of Israel will gladly obey him. There's no quarrel between the

Israelites and Pharaoh, only between Pharaoh and God. It is the Lord God who will act."

"Well, don't go thinking you can bother Pharaoh any longer," said the overseer. "I'm to bar you by force from leaving Goshen. You won't be at the palace again."

"But I have no need to go there," said Moses.

"I'm also to keep you from going to the river," said the overseer.

"All right," said Moses. "Not the river, and not the palace."

The overseer glanced around to see who was listening, then spoke quietly. "Please, I'm only doing what I was commanded to do. Don't bring back the frogs."

"You can tell Pharaoh that if his word isn't kept, there are worse things than frogs that the Lord can send."

No sooner had the overseer gone, than Moses took Aaron with him and began walking a circuitous path along the outskirts of Goshen. The Egyptians saw that Moses was on the move, and that soldiers were watching him. Soon a crowd fell in step behind him, and by noon there were so many thousands of Egyptians crowding around him that the soldiers could not come near, and a cloud of dust arose from the shuffling feet on the dry soil. The people kept calling out to Moses, sometimes pleas, sometimes threats.

Aaron was uneasy. "Moses, these people are angry at us. Are you sure we're safe?"

"We're as safe as the Lord needs us to be," said Moses. "And we need witnesses." Then, loudly, so all could hear him, he said: "Because Pharaoh broke his promise to let the children of Israel go, the Lord commands you: Aaron, stretch forth your hand over the dust of Egypt, and the Lord will bring lice onto the bodies of all the beasts and human beings in the land."

Grimly Aaron stretched out his hand, turning a full circle as he did. Even those who hadn't heard Moses' words soon learned what he had said, as the dust was transformed into lice. The people, immediately covered with the tiny creatures, inhaling them with every breath, ran shouting from the place—raising more dust, and more lice, as they ran.

❋

Tuthmose paced up and down in the room as a slave combed lice out of the Queen Sakhmet's hair. "Do you think I cause these things?" he said. "Do you think I had the priests conjure lice out of the dust of the ground? Jannes and Jambres took such pride in making snakes from sticks, blood from water, frogs from their sleeves—I told them to make lice, and all they did was scratch themselves and say, 'If you want more lice, these were made by the finger of the Israelite god.' They were on the edge of mockery, those baboons."

"You're the one," she said, "who came railing to me about Ptahmose crying all the time. All I said was, I didn't make the lice." She never raised her voice at him. She knew—everyone knew—that after Tuthmose's lifetime of experience with Hatshepsut, he did not want any hint of a strong-willed woman around him now.

"But what you *meant* was that I *did*."

"You are a god," said Sakhmet, "but as far as I know, not a lice-making god."

"You think I should let them go!"

"All I think about is, what strange new marvel will happen next?"

"Well I can't let them go. And even if I could, I wouldn't!"

"Then don't complain to me when the child cries because there are bugs crawling all over his head."

"I won't see them. I won't talk to them. They can't make more demands if I cease to listen to them!"

Sakhmet looked down at the pile of nits, lice, and lice eggs that was building up on the floor behind her stool. "All this from my hair," she said. "Who could imagine."

Tuthmose stormed out of the room.

*

On the day Moses declared that it would happen, the lice died off as suddenly as they had come. But when Moses and Aaron came to Pharaoh's door, they were turned away with a threat of imprisonment if they ever came again. Aaron smiled and said, "Pharaoh will hear the message of the Lord, even if it sounds like the buzzing of flies. And this time, the Lord will make a division between the Israelites and the Egyptians. Every Egyptian will see that among the children of Israel there is no plague."

And so it was that the fourth plague came, flies swarming everywhere. Within a day, every bit of meat and bread was crawling with maggots. The grain had to be sifted before it could be ground into flour, and the flour sifted again before it could be made into bread. Through the open doors and windows of every Egyptian dwelling the flies came, until the entire land was corrupted with maggots. But among the Israelites, not a fly buzzed, not a maggot hatched and crawled.

On the third day of the flies, a messenger came to Moses and Aaron. They followed him to the palace.

"Pharaoh has no quarrel with your god," said Jannes. "Like all the gods, he *should* be worshiped. We'll give you a feast day, right there in Goshen. Sacrifice all you want."

After a brief conference with Moses, Aaron answered, "In Goshen we live under the eyes of the Egyptians. Our sacrifices are an abomination in their eyes. Israelites have been stoned before, for offering sacrifice here in Egypt. There would be riots, and some of our people would be killed. We must go three days' journey into the wilderness."

Jannes returned and knelt before Pharaoh, who refused to speak, or even meet his gaze. Finally the priest stood and glared at Moses directly. "All right, you can go a little way into the desert. Just ask your god to get rid of these flies while we still have any stores of grain left."

"We've heard such a promise before," said Aaron. "And yet on the morrow, we were held again to our tally of bricks."

Jannes leapt into the fray. "Pharaoh didn't break any promise—that would be unthinkable! He is a god! He promised that you could sacrifice, but he never said when. He waited for a more convenient time."

"Tomorrow the flies will be gone," said Aaron. "So tomorrow we will expect to go out and offer sacrifice."

In the morning, the flies were dead, but Pharaoh refused to see Moses, and though the overseers did not come to insist on the tally of bricks, there were soldiers on watch, to warn if there were any attempt by the Israelites to leave. The sight of the soldiers made the people afraid, and many of them pled with Miriam and Aaron to intercede with Moses. "He's going to get us all killed," they said. "He's got to stop."

"Moses isn't doing this," they answered, again and again. "God is doing this, and he promises that if Israel obeys, not one soul of you will be lost."

But the people would not consider preparing to leave, with the soldiers standing watch.

※

Moses stood at the border of Goshen, where a mob of Egyptian herdsmen, armed with clubs and hoes and makeshift spears, clamored and howled. "You killed our cattle! You poisoned our herds!"

Aaron's voice roared above the tumult. "You have seen the power of God! I warn you not to set a single foot beyond this point, for God will not allow you to harm his people!"

That stilled them, for they had learned, even if Pharaoh had not, to fear the power of Israel's god.

"Moses!" called an old man. "I was a captain under you in Ethiopia! You've made me a poor man, half my cattle dead this morning, the rest dying! What did I ever do to you, except serve you loyally!"

Moses answered, "If Pharaoh had kept his word, my friend, your cattle would all be alive. How can I restrain the anger of the Lord, when Pharaoh promises one day to let us go out and offer sacrifice, and the next day breaks that promise?"

"But *I* never broke a promise!" the man said. "And it's my cattle that died! While we know perfectly well that a lot of Israelites aren't faithful to your God—they worship our gods, or the calf of the Hyksos. Yet even the most openly rebellious of your people still has his entire herd today. Is there no justice in your god's heart?"

"These are questions that only Pharaoh can answer," said Moses. "If it were up to me, no harm would come to anyone in Egypt. But look at you—armed to attack my people! If God had not made you afraid of his power, how many Israelites would you have slain today? If you don't want the punishment of God to come upon you, look to your own hearts, and see how much harm your hatred has caused to the people of the Lord."

And the Egyptian mob dispersed to their homes, bowed down by the consciousness of God's justice.

✳

The fires that burned the bodies of the dead cattle had no sooner subsided than Moses had Aaron take ashes from the furnace where they burned, and together they went to wait on the road where the Lord told them Pharaoh would pass. Pharaoh commanded his men to ride on, but the horses drawing the chariots would not obey, and Pharaoh was forced to wait and watch as Aaron scattered the ashes toward heaven.

At once painful boils and sores broke out on the skin of man and beast. The horses were crazed by it, and had to be unhitched from the chariots. Pharaoh's chariot was drawn back to his palace by his soldiers, all of them suffering greatly. In his house, his son wept and scratched himself until his body was a mass of scabs and bloody sores, and Pharaoh was filled with hatred for Moses and Aaron and the god they served.

When Moses and Aaron came to the palace again, no one barred the way. Jannes and Jambres weren't there—the slave who painfully carried a tray of food told them that Jambres was caring for his father's awful sores at home. "Has Jambres no sores of his own?" asked Aaron.

"As I have mine," the slave said. "I am not your enemy, but look at my body."

"But see how the Lord has blessed you," said Aaron. "Clearly you're not suffering as badly as Jannes and Jambres, because they can't even rise up and come serve in the king's house—but here you are, serving in spite of your pain."

The slave smiled at the irony. "Yes, now that you put it that way, I see that my case is much lighter than theirs."

"Whom is that food for?" asked Moses.

"For Pharaoh and his queen," the slave said. "And their little boy."

"Then let us help you," said Moses. "As you can see, we have no sores, and I know the way."

Gratefully the slave handed the tray of food to them. "If I thought you meant harm to Pharaoh, I would die before I let you touch his food. Even now, he won't eat it unless I taste it first. And normally I'm watched by guards the whole way."

"The only food that Pharaoh does not have to fear," said Moses, "is the food he takes from my hand."

Moses carried the tray himself, leading the way, until they came to the inner chamber where Tuthmose and Sakhmet watched over their son, who slept fitfully. Tuthmose leapt to his feet when he saw Moses and Aaron, preparing to fight; but Sakhmet saw that they had brought the food, and she laid her hand on her husband's arm to restrain him.

Solemnly Moses took a taste from every dish and put it in his own mouth. "The cooking here is better than ever," said Moses. "And under the trying circumstances today, that's remarkable."

"Speak quietly, please," said Sakhmet. "Ptahmose gets so little sleep."

"The sores will heal now," said Moses. "And the itching will stop."

Sakhmet nodded; any word of gratitude she might have said would have infuriated her husband.

Tuthmose reached out and seized Moses by the arm. "Come," he whispered, "look at what you've done!" He drew him roughly to where the child lay. The sores were indeed pitiable, and the child winced even in his sleep. "Your god makes war on children!"

Moses looked at the child and remembered his own sons, how tender-hearted they were when they were young. He remembered other children, too, and spoke of them—softly, so

Ptahmose would not be wakened. "I've seen thousands of Israelite children working all day in the heat of the sun, making bricks because you decided to punish them for no crime at all. And yet even though I've seen far greater suffering than this, I also know that this child was born to a house of comfort and power, and he was not prepared to suffer anything at all. The Lord loves little children, Tuthmose, and blesses them with forgetfulness. His suffering is but a moment, and the Lord promises him eternal joy."

"You defile my son even to look at him," said Tuthmose.

"Seeing such a beautiful child," said Moses, "it's hard to believe that any child would ever grow up to murder his father."

Tuthmose recoiled as if he had been struck. "Get out of my house. Out of my child's bedchamber!"

Aaron stepped between Moses and Tuthmose. "Softly now, please. Let the child sleep."

"Give Pharaoh the Lord's warning," said Moses.

"You have nothing to say that interests me," said Tuthmose.

"Your kingdom has already lost a large portion of its cattle to the murrain," said Aaron. "Any cattle or other animals, and for that matter any man or woman that you wish to have survive, bring them in to shelter before morning. For tomorrow any living thing out in the open will be crushed in a storm of hail."

"Why do you tell me this!"

"To show your people the mercy of God," said Moses.

"And to show you how your own people believe in the power of the Lord God of Israel, even if you don't," said Aaron.

During the rest of the day, Moses and Aaron warned anyone who would listen, and the word spread throughout Egypt. The boils and sores were healing; the pain was gone. But there was no time to celebrate. Flocks and herds were brought under shelter, and families provisioned themselves so there'd be no need to go outside.

Ten thousand stars glowed brightly through cloudless night. But no one doubted the power of God to make it hail, even out of a clear sky. The only reason many herds and many servants were left outdoors was because many wealthy and powerful men feared to let Pharaoh see them heed Moses' warning, showing their belief in the power of Israel's god. And the hailstorm couldn't be *that* bad, could it? The frogs, the lice, the boils, the flies, even the blood in the river—none of them had killed anybody. Even with the murrain that afflicted the cattle, those beasts that didn't die of it at once soon recovered. Thus they talked themselves into disaster.

The hail, when it came, was brutal. Stones the size of a man's head fell among the thousands of smaller chunks of ice. The wind bent ancient trees and then tore them from the ground. And lightning started fires all over the kingdom.

But in Goshen, no hail fell.

Moses and Aaron stood in the threshold of the house of Pharaoh, waiting . . . and sure enough, he sent for them. Thunder roared outside, and cold wind howled through all the windows and doors of the airy building. Pharaoh paced fretfully in front of his throne when Moses and Aaron entered.

"Yes, I admit it!" cried Tuthmose. "I sinned when I didn't let your people go. The Lord God of Israel is righteous, and my people and I are wicked. Please, make this storm stop before the entire crop of Egypt is destroyed."

Aaron cocked his head, calculating for a moment. "I'd say

it's too late to save the barley and the flax," said Aaron. "But the wheat and the rye are still green. They'll probably recover."

"I don't need your crop assessment," Tuthmose hissed at him. "I need you to stop this storm. I'll let your people go and sacrifice."

"Keep your word this time," said Aaron, "or the disaster that will fall upon Egypt will make all these plagues look like a holiday."

"Stop the storm!" roared Tuthmose, but his voice was swallowed up by a clap of thunder far louder than any human voice could hope to overpower.

Moses and Aaron went outside, and Moses spread his arms before the Lord, supplicating him. As suddenly as it had begun, the storm ceased. The clouds dissipated, the air stilled. The ice on the fields melted, and where the fields were still green, many plants rose up, healing themselves from the damage of the storm. But in the fields where the ears of grain were already set, the destruction was nearly total.

All the rest of the day, Tuthmose and his officers, now healed of their boils and sores, labored to calculate how much grain and linen they'd have to import to make up for this damage, and how this would deplete the treasury. "They cost us too much, these Israelites," said Pharaoh when the meeting ended. "They can go when their labor has repaid the losses, and not before."

His officers heard this decision with fear and anger, but they had long schooled themselves to let their faces show nothing of what they felt. So Pharaoh heard not one word of opposition. Until Sakhmet spoke from the doorway. "Which will cost more? To let Israel go? Or to keep them here and face even more terrible damage tomorrow?"

"You don't understand affairs of state," Tuthmose snapped. "You don't understand anything."

But then he looked around the room, and saw that his men all thought as Sakhmet did.

"Is there no loyal man left in Egypt?" said Tuthmose. "Has Moses stolen all your hearts?"

"Pharaoh accuses when he has no enemy," said Jambres. "We want only good for you and for your kingdom. But how much more devastation can the people endure?"

"Why do they turn against me?" demanded Pharaoh. "Why don't they put the blame where it belongs, on Moses! He was always a traitor, yet they loved him; and now he brings destruction down on Egypt and they still love him!"

Jambres rose to his feet. "We have served Pharaoh badly. He has charged us to give wise counsel, but we have all been so fearful of the wrath of Pharaoh that we have given foolish counsel, or none at all. Now I'll say what we all think, even those who deny it, and if Pharaoh kills me for saying it, me and all my family, then I would still say it, for I would rather die with truth on my lips than live as a man who lied to his king."

"Say what you have to say!" shouted Pharaoh.

"We have seen the river run with blood. We have been covered with frogs and lice, with flies and maggots, and finally with boils and sores on our bodies. Our cattle have died of a sudden disease and our crops have been pounded into the ground by hail or burned by lightning. In all of these, the forces of nature have been arrayed against us. Our prayers to the gods have gone unanswered. Clearly the Lord God of Israel has taken over the land of the gods and all of them bow before his power. We are helpless to defend ourselves against these plagues, and it will take years to recover, years in which we'll deplete the treasury, divert our soldiers to labor in the fields, and become an easy target for the enemies of Egypt. And we endure all this so that lazy, rebellious slaves can make our bricks for us?"

"Does Pharaoh rule in Egypt or does he not?" cried Tuthmose.

"I waited for Pharaoh to stretch forth his hand and stop the hail," said Jambres. "All my prayers to Amon couldn't do it. So I waited for you. All the people wait for you. One way or another, we all wait for you to end these plagues, because you are the god we trust in to care for *us*. We pray to you: don't make us endure any more. Kill the messenger if you want, but hear the message."

"Tomorrow," said Tuthmose, "you'll see what answer I give."

The next day, Moses and Aaron returned to the palace. "Your soldiers still keep watch," said Aaron. "They still bar the way."

"They won't bar the way," said Pharaoh. "All your men can go out to the desert to sacrifice. But leave behind the women and children, and all the old men. You don't need them. We'll keep them safe here in Egypt, waiting for your return."

Aaron conferred with Moses for a moment. "We will go with our sons and our daughters," said Aaron, "with old and young, male and female, and with all our flocks and herds. We will be feasting in honor of the Lord, and we are forbidden to leave any of our people behind."

Pharaoh almost screamed his answer. "I will never let you take your little ones out of Egypt!"

"Then prepare for a plague of locusts," said Aaron. "See if any green thing grows in Egypt after they pass through."

❊

The wind blew from the desert, all the rest of the day, all

that night, and into the morning. And before noon, there appeared a low cloud on the horizon, growing and growing, dark and threatening. Only it didn't cover the sky. When the cloud came nearer, the people could see that it covered the ground and filled the air only thirty cubits or so above the earth. And when it was closer still, they could see the individual locusts leaping, flying, bouncing off the ground and soaring again.

They covered everything, swarming through the houses, over the fields. Where they lingered, every leaf was eaten, every blade of grass, every stalk of wheat and rye.

In the midst of the devastation, Pharaoh called for Moses and Aaron. "I confess my sin!" he cried. "My officers warned me and I didn't listen. Forgive my sin, only this once, and I'll let your people go!"

So Moses once again prayed to the Lord to remove the plague. A west wind came up, as strong as the wind that brought the locusts, and swept them all toward the east until all of them had plunged into the Red Sea.

But when Moses and Aaron returned, they were met only by Jannes and Jambres. "Pharaoh commands us to tell you," said Jannes, "that with the entire year's harvest destroyed, it would be an affront to the people of Egypt to let the Israelites go out and feast as if there were still plenty to eat. Pharaoh says that it isn't enough for your god to send away the locusts, he must restore what they consumed or he'll never let your people go."

"Jannes," said Moses kindly, "I know that you counseled against this."

Jannes held his tongue, neither affirming nor denying.

"Pharaoh is like a blind man," said Moses. "So let the world be as dark as his own vision. For three days, no light will be seen in the land, not of sun or moon, not of stars or any fire made by man."

Tears flowed down Jannes's face. "Moses, why doesn't your god soften Pharaoh's heart? If he has such power, why doesn't he make Tuthmose feel compassion for Egypt?"

Moses shook his head. "The Lord God treats no human being as a slave. We are all his children. He would see all his creation brought to ruin before he would take free will away from even the most rebellious of men. Men must bear the consequences of their choices, and they can choose only what is within their power. But choose they may, now and always. This world was created for humankind to dwell in it; if humans lose the freedom of choice that separates them from the animals, then this world has no purpose."

"Let God have mercy upon the innocent," said Jambres, catching Moses by the hand and gripping it in supplication. "Let the punishment fall only on those who rebel."

"It was the people of Egypt who goaded Pharaoh into mistreating the Israelites. Should they now be spared the consequences of *their* choices?"

"Darkness!" said Jannes. "Who will care for the sick and dying? What if a child wanders from its parents in the dark?"

"Give warning, then," said Aaron. "Let the people block their doors to keep their little ones inside. Let them gather food and water for three days, as quickly as they can. Tomorrow the sun will not appear in the sky, and no light will be seen in all of Egypt."

"Except," said Moses, "in the land of Goshen where the people of the Lord are waiting for Pharaoh to let them go offer sacrifice."

Jannes's voice fell to a whisper. "Then go in the dark of night. Sweep the soldiers away before you."

"No Israelite will raise a hand of violence against any Egyptian. When we have our freedom, it will be because Pharaoh bent to the will of God and gave that freedom to us."

"Tuthmose does not bend," said Jambres. "Especially he doesn't bend to you."

"Let him bow to God," said Moses. "I never asked a soul to bend to *me*."

"Or let him break," said Aaron.

"You've made new Pharaohs before," said Moses quietly, "and swept away old ones."

"Do you think I don't repent of my part in that?" said Jambres. "Do you think all of Egypt hasn't wished that Hatshepsut were still alive? *She* would have let your people go, simply because it was you, her beloved son, asking."

"Did she still love me, even after I went into exile?" asked Moses.

"She never spoke of you again," said Jannes. "But I believe she thought of you all the time. Whenever she got a sour look on her face, watching Tuthmose, we knew she was thinking: If Moses were here, it would all be different."

"I'm here now," said Moses, "too late for Hatshepsut, but not too late for Egypt. God is my only parent now, and I obey him like a son."

"Do you want us to overthrow Tuthmose? Because you know we can't. Look how young his son is. Who would be regent? All the obvious candidates are dead."

"Let Pharaoh serve God, and all that you have lost will be restored."

Jannes and Jambres looked at each other. "It's cheap to make a promise that you know you'll never have to keep," said Jambres. "You might eventually bend him to your will, but he will never serve God."

✻

The next morning there was no dawn. People awoke in dark houses. No fire would light, no lamp, no spark. Farmers heard the cattle complaining in the barns, and had to go out and feed them and milk them by feel, as their wives and children cowered in their pitchblack houses.

In Goshen, though, while the sky was dark, lamps could be lit, and fires; food was cooked, chores were done, all by the flickering light of burning oil.

When the three days were nearly up, Moses and Aaron made their way out of Goshen, carrying lamps. As the road led them past Egyptian villages, their light drew the attention of the villagers, who came out of their houses weeping for joy at the sight of even such a feeble light. A multitude jostled along behind them, all of them blind as before, except for the few near the front who were close enough to see by the light of Moses' and Aaron's lamps.

In the house of Pharaoh, Tuthmose saw the light and cried out. "Moses! Lamps will light for you!"

Moses laughed. "A lighted lamp? After all you've seen, and this is what amazes you?"

"I'm ready to keep my word," said Pharaoh. "Go, all of you, every Israelite. But leave your cattle behind, as an assurance that you'll return."

"We're going to feast and offer sacrifices," said Moses. "We will take our flocks and herds."

"Why do you still lie to me?" said Pharaoh. "You complain that I don't keep my word, but what about you? Saying that you just want to go out and sacrifice, when you know that your plan is and always has been to leave Egypt and never come back. My informers have told me everything—the promises about Canaan, the land flowing with milk and honey! Shame on you for a liar!"

"I never promised that we'd come back," said Moses. "All I promised was that one way or another, the Lord God will send his people out of Egypt into the wilderness, and we'll offer sacrifices when we get there."

"You're the same man as me," said Tuthmose. "I learned everything you taught!"

"You don't have the slightest inkling of the things I learned while I was gone. The knowledge I taught you was of another time and place."

"I have the blood of Pharaohs in my veins! I will not have it said that the kingdom of Egypt was diminished during my reign!"

"These plagues have diminished Egypt far more than the departure of the Israelites ever would. Keeping a nation bound in slavery diminishes Egypt, also. What I ask you for is largeness of soul, greatness of heart. God will forgive you even now, if you turn to him. You can be a great Pharaoh, if you submit yourself to the Lord God of heaven."

"My greatness does not depend on your god," said Tuthmose coldly. "My greatness depends on what *I* do."

"That's true enough," said Moses. "As long as you understand that how you respond to the Lord is the most important of your choices."

"Here is how I respond. I will never let Israel go. There is nothing you or your god can do to me to make Pharaoh bow down before a sheep-herding slave. Now get out, and trouble me no more. The day you see my face again, you'll die."

"You're right," said Moses. "You'll never see my face again, though you spend your whole life searching. What God does now will close the door on your heart forever, even as it opens the door to set Israel free."

"Your god can do nothing!" shouted Pharaoh. "He has no power over me! Your people are my slaves forever!"

His cries echoed through the palace. Servants and courtiers, officers and priests all peered from doorways or knelt in the corridors, eager and fearful to see Moses and Aaron with their lighted lamps. Pharaoh's desperate cries were plainly audible to all; more affecting, however, were the tears that streamed down Moses' face. They knew then that after nine plagues, the Lord had lost patience. To the people that they passed, Aaron spoke softly. "Ask for the news of what you must do to save yourselves. When we tell Israel, ask for word of what to do. God will spare all those who obey him."

❄

"From now on," Moses told the elders, "this month will be the first month of the year, and on the tenth day of this month, let every man take a lamb without blemish, and kill it on the eve of that day. Take the blood of the lamb and smear it on the doorpost of your house, to show the angel of the Lord that here is a household of faith."

Miriam listened beyond the firelight, where none could see her, or if they saw, they tolerantly said nothing. She knew what Moses was telling them, knew it because she had seen it again and again in dreams.

"Then roast the lamb, and eat it with bread. But the lamb must be roasted quickly with fire, not boiled and not raw. And the bread cannot be given a chance to rise, but must be made in haste. Eat everything; leave nothing for the morning, and anything that remains uneaten, burn it in the fire. And eat it with your traveling clothes on, your sandals on your feet, your staff in your hand, and eat in a hurry, for you are about to begin your journey."

This was Miriam's dream: Everyone in traveling clothes, eating in haste. She knew that it was important every time she saw it. But not until tonight did she understand. This is how Israel will eat on the night before they leave Egypt.

"On this night," said Moses, "the angel of the Lord will pass through the land of Egypt, and will take the life of every firstborn in the land of Egypt, both man and beast. But where the angel sees the blood of the lamb, he will pass over that house, and spare the firstborn who are inside."

The elders murmured. The Lord was taking terrible vengeance on Egypt for the slavery of the chosen people. But if they had let Israel go, this last plague would not have come upon them.

"Not only this night, but from now on, forever, Israel will keep the feast of the Passover. For seven days you will eat unleavened bread, and on the first and the seventh day Israel will meet in holiness. For you must never forget that for the sake of the blood of the lamb your lives are saved, and that God had mercy on his people and brought them out of bondage into the land of promise."

So this is what began when Mother labored to bear her son, and had me follow the ark she made, to see where God took the boy. This is what God planned: A night of dire judgment; a morning of bright deliverance.

It was Aaron's turn to speak. "Let no household go unwarned. In every tribe, let no man or woman say that they didn't know what God expected of them. Nor will you keep it a secret from any Egyptian. For now is the day for anyone who will serve the Lord to join with Israel."

Moses spoke again. "Generations from now, in the land of

promise, as you kill the lamb and mark the door with blood, as you stay indoors all night, as you feast on the unleavened bread, wearing traveling clothes, your children will say, 'What does this mean?' And you'll say to them, 'It's the sacrifice of the Lord's Passover, for the Lord passed over the houses of the children of Israel in Egypt, when he took the lives of the first-born of the Egyptians and set Israel free from bondage.'"

The elders rose to their feet, then, and obeyed Moses and Aaron, and spread the word of the Lord's commandment throughout the land of Goshen. Word of the warning spread also among the villages of the Egyptians. But Pharaoh warned that anyone marking his house with blood would be considered a slave, and would be forced to serve with the Israelite slaves in making bricks.

As the day of preparation began, Miriam heard the chatter of the women, hushed at first, in awe of what had already happened, at what was about to happen. But soon the familiar task of grinding the grain and making the dough brought back familiar conversations, and she heard their light laughter, the meaningless jokes that passed the time.

For a moment Miriam was resentful. Couldn't they remain solemn on this holiest day in the history of the people of Israel? Didn't they know that tomorrow all dreams and prophecies would be fulfilled, and Israel would be led out of bondage by the power of God?

But of course they laughed. Of course they were giddy. Everything was going to change, and in strange ways. Yes, they had endured change before—from freedom to slavery, from homes scattered throughout Egypt to confinement in the land of Goshen, and from labor at every honorable task to the backbreaking work of making bricks. But with all these changes, they had remained in Egypt. Now they would be

going out into the desert, a forbidding place where no
Egyptian willingly went. The only life they knew was life
within reach of the Nile, and now they would leave the river
behind and go into the country of sand and stone and sun, of
brutal wind and killing heat and permanent drought. Yes, the
Lord would be with them, but they were afraid; and also they
were delighted that their long period of enslavement was over;
and so they joked with each other to cover their fear and contain their happiness.

Didn't Miriam's own hands tremble at the kneading
trough?

The afternoon waned into evening. Lambs were butchered. Blood was smeared on the doorposts. Every Israelite was
indoors and would not come out through all the hours of darkness. For the destroying angel was coming to Egypt, and all
that was in anyone's power now was to save himself and his
family, by obeying the Lord. Those who refused to take part
in the feast, out of fear or unbelief or stubborn rebellion
against God, had made their own choice.

⁂

Tuthmose found Sakhmet with the cooks, watching as they
butchered a lamb.

"What are you doing?" he asked coldly.

"Preparing supper," said Sakhmet.

"A lamb?" asked Tuthmose.

"That was the meat I fancied tonight," said Sakhmet.

"And was it without blemish?" asked Tuthmose.

"I would hardly choose less than the best for our supper."

Tuthmose raised his hand and struck her across the face,
struck so brutally that she fell to the ground and hit her head.
She lay there, moaning and writhing, curling herself into a ball.

To the terrified cooks, Tuthmose's orders were brief and

clear. "Burn this lamb. Pour its blood on the fire. If one drop of blood is seen on any doorway in the palace, I'll have you and your families killed."

By now, Sakhmet had struggled to rise to her knees. "Tuthmose," she groaned, "it's the life of our son!"

"I forbid this to happen!" cried Tuthmose. "I forbid you to speak of it!"

"Kill me then!" cried his wife. "Kill me now so I don't have to watch our sweet Ptahmose *die* because you were too proud and stubborn to bow before the power of the Lord God of Israel!"

"This isn't a god we're dealing with!" shouted Tuthmose. "It's Moses! I know Moses! He was always weak and merciful. Making and keeping promises to people so weak that it didn't matter whether he kept his word or not. All these other plagues, they killed no one who was careful."

"I was being careful," murmured Sakhmet. "I was trying to be careful for our boy."

"Power comes from the willingness to kill," said Tuthmose, "and that's why Moses lost his power, and that's why he still has no power in Egypt."

"No power! When he can blot out the light of the sun! Make the river run with blood!"

"Moses is no killer," said Tuthmose. "Our son will not die. His people will not go free. He has reached too far this time."

"No, *you* have! *You* have gone too far!" She was frantic now, screaming, her face dark with rage, tears flying from her eyes as she flung her head back to look her husband in the face. "When our son dies, I will say nothing to you," she said. "But every time you see me looking at you, you'll remember this: I tried to save our son's life, and you stopped me. You are the one who decided he would die. You are the one who killed.

And *that* is what you call *power.*" The contempt in her voice was like an iron blade.

"You're no queen," said Tuthmose. "You are not a queen!"

"I don't care about queen or wife or any other name you can give me. At this moment all I am is Ptahmose's mother. But you are not his father. A father keeps his child safe, a father does whatever it takes to save his child's life. You are not a father! You are nothing to me!"

The cowering cooks, trying to be invisible against the walls of the kitchen, thought for a moment that Tuthmose would take one of their bone-cutting hatchets and kill her on the spot. They saw him get control of himself. Instead of violence, he turned to the cooks. "Remember. Burn it all. Pour the blood on the fire."

*

Moses and Miriam ate their small feast together in her hut—there was no room for them in Aaron's tiny, crowded house. So no one but Miriam saw how Moses spent the night. He tried to sleep, and so did she, but as the night wore on, she awoke often, hearing some distant cry, some far-off wailing, and whenever she woke up she saw Moses, kneeling beside his pallet, praying, or lying on his bed sobbing quietly. Once she heard the words he prayed, though he whispered very quietly, trying not to waken her. "O God of Abraham, Isaac, and Jacob, take me instead, leave my children fatherless, but let me die in place of all these others. It's too hard a punishment for them to bear."

Miriam heard him, but knew that the Lord would not grant any such prayer. If God were to take Moses' life, it would be for his own sins and mistakes, and not for the crimes of others.

Would some firstborns die innocently tonight? Of course,

and Miriam didn't have a heart of stone, she knew that such losses were unbearable. But why did this bother Moses so much, and so personally? He knew that this was ordained by the Lord. Wouldn't the innocent ones be caught up joyfully to the beautiful heaven Jacob saw in the vision that came to him when he was fleeing the anger of his brother? While those who died with no such joyful hope had decreed their own end, and what difference did it make whether it was tonight or later?

She even thought of saying all this to Moses, but as she rehearsed the word in her mind, she knew that he already knew these things. It wasn't for the dying that he grieved, anyway. It was for the living. He grieved because he was a father and had children; she had none. So he could easily imagine the agony of a parent whose firstborn was taken from him, while for Miriam it remained a mystery. She had seen how parents became frantic when they didn't know where their little children were; how they worried, how they thought of nothing but their children, how unhappy it made them; and how they rejoiced unreasonably over even the slightest achievement of their children until Miriam was unutterably bored. And whatever the bond parents felt for children, it wasn't reciprocated. Children were an ungrateful, careless lot, Miriam believed. In the end, there was no rational way to comprehend what parents felt. You had to be one.

That's why she felt so little sympathy for the parents whose children were being taken tonight. There had been lambs enough for all, if they had wanted to obey. The parents made their choice.

Tonight was a night for rejoicing; tonight God was finishing the miracle and bringing Israel out of bondage. Miriam couldn't sleep because she wanted to dance, to sing, to parade all through Goshen. Instead she had to remain within the house, had to try to sleep or at least pretend to sleep, and because of Moses' compassionate grief, she had to pretend to be solemn.

His tears were holy, she knew. But so were the dances and songs she felt in her heart.

❈

Tuthmose and Sakhmet might be at war with each other, but neither could force the other to stay out of Ptahmose's bedchamber that night. Guards stood around the room, watching. Sakhmet, sitting rigidly in her chair, and Tuthmose, pacing up and down, circling the room, never took their eyes off the boy, never spoke to each other. All they saw was the peaceful look on his face as he slept—his first night without fear, without pain, since the plagues began. All they saw was the steady rising and falling of his chest as he breathed in and out, in and out.

And then, with no sign from heaven, no clap of thunder, no tumult, no cry, not even a sigh or whisper from the sleeping boy, nor a twitch of his finger to show that he even knew what was happening, he let out a breath . . .

. . . and never took another.

❈

They heard him before he found Miriam's house. The messenger from Pharaoh walked through the Israelite settlement in Goshen, calling out, "Where is Moses! What house is Moses in!"

Moses got up and arranged his clothing and smoothed his beard. Miriam half-rose from her bed.

"Stay," he said to her, "and when the people awaken, remind them that the Lord said they should go to the Egyptians and ask what they will give us, to offer to the Lord in the wilderness. Whatever gifts the Egyptians give them for the Lord's sake, they are to take and carry with them. Have the herdsmen gather their herds. When Aaron and I come back from the palace, we must be ready to leave at once."

So . . . it was done. Miriam got up and prepared to go out, house to house, rousing the people and telling them that the time was here at last, arise and make ready to go.

❈

When Moses and Aaron reached the palace, they could hear the distant wailing of women in grief. Was one of them the voice of Sakhmet?

Pharaoh was not in the great hall. Instead, Jannes met them, looking far older than they had ever seen him look before, as if he had one foot in the grave.

"Pharaoh says for you and your people to rise up, take your flocks and herds, go out and offer your sacrifices. Cover yourselves in blood."

Jannes turned away.

"Jannes," said Moses, "I would never have brought harm to your house."

Jannes turned back to face him. "Jambres chose," he said.

"To die?" asked Aaron.

"He was less afraid to face your God as a dead man, than to face Pharaoh as a living firstborn, on the night when Pharaoh's own firstborn son would die."

"Would that be your choice, now?" said Moses.

"Get out of Egypt," said Jannes. "Now, before his grief gives way to rage."

❈

Sakhmet wailed and wailed over the boy's body. She would not look at Tuthmose, would not bear his touch. Nor would Tuthmose leave the room. He kept looking at the body, remembering the voice, picturing the legs running, the hands grasping, playing, the lips smiling, laughing, jabbering, eating, the eyes angry, sleepy, alert, happy, mournful.

If he could picture Ptahmose clearly enough, would he come back to life?

If he was a god, why was the most useful of godly powers denied to him—to raise the dead?

He imagined his son speaking to him. Father, why is the sky so grey? And he would answer, A storm is coming. Father, his son would ask, why can't I open my eyes? And he would answer . . . would answer not at all. Father! he imagined his son saying. Father, why is Mother crying so bitterly!

Because I did not believe that Moses' god would kill a child.

Pharaoh left the bedchamber and walked out onto the steps leading down to the river. The night was clear. Perhaps the eastern sky was growing a little lighter; perhaps not. He could hear keening and crying from every nearby house, it seemed. A choir of lament. All grieving for my son. All other deaths were nothing compared to the death of my son. All Egypt mourns because my son, my beloved son, is dead.

# W a t e r

The bending and stooping, lifting and hauling of brick-making had been one kind of work. Driving animals through scrub and stone, getting farther and farther from water, from familiar scenery, from villages, and all the time one foot after another, again and again, endlessly moving toward a horizon that never came any closer—this was a different kind of work, making their backs and legs ache in different places, hurting their feet and ankles, and above all, filling their hearts with dread and a sense of loss.

And yet they were free, and they brought with them carts and pack animals laden, not only with a few personal posses-sions and tools of long disused trades, but also with the gold and silver ornaments almost thrust on them by their Egyptian neighbors. Moses had told them that they would leave with the gold of Egypt, but it was scarcely to be believed—the Lord was hardly going to command them to loot a land that, after all, had been their home for generations before their privileged station turned to servitude. Yet when they went to ask if they could borrow . . . what, they never got to say. Everyone reported the same thing. The rich gave them carts and took the ornaments off their own arms and necks, shoulders and ankles, ears and noses to fill them up. From their tables they took lamps and bowls of gold and brass. Egyptians of lesser station gave less, but it seemed to some Israelites that they were giving all they had.

There was much conversation about this in the early hours of the journey—better to talk about the treasure that traveled along with them than to think of the keening mothers and grieving fathers whose firstborn had died. Some speculated that the Egyptians gave their gold so freely because they would pay any ransom to get the Israelites to leave—though others answered them that freedom was all the treasure Israel had ever asked for. Some supposed the Egyptians gave up their gold because they knew how much wealth had been taken from the Israelites by force when the Hyksos were expelled and the leading Israelites were forced out of their influential offices and fine houses. But by the end of the morning, the consensus in most parts of the vast sea of people was that the gold had been given to Israel because the Lord wanted them to have it, and after Pharaoh's will was finally broken, no soul in Egypt would resist the Lord's desire.

When they crested the low swells and ridges, and could see the throng spread out before and behind them, the people could hardly comprehend how large they were in number. Even in the brickyards, the work had been done in shifts, and in many isolated yards along the Nile throughout the land of Goshen. They had not even known how large each tribe was, but now, traveling with each tribe separated from the others, they could see that each tribe was much larger than anyone had thought the whole of Israel to be. And the whole congregation of Israel seemed almost to fulfill the promise to Abraham, that his posterity should be as numberless as the stars in the heavens, or the sand in the sea.

Only a few of them knew enough about the geography of the land between the delta and the wilderness of Sinai to realize that they were being led along a strange path. Near the shore of the Mediterranean was the Philistine Road, where large armies were garrisoned. Therefore there was much water and feed for the animals, and plenty of supplies for the people, as well, and the road was smooth and well marked.

But they were heading for the border crossing at the head of the Gulf of Suez, an arm of the Red Sea. This road was rockier, with far less water and little food except whatever could be foraged in the surrounding countryside. No one had ever brought such a multitude by the southern route, for it led nowhere that a multitude had ever wanted to go before.

And none of them was familiar enough with this area to realize that they soon turned away from even the southern road, and were being led straight to the unfordable arm of the Red Sea. Yet even if they had been aware, what could they do but follow where they were led? For it was no mortal man leading the way. No scouts ran ahead and then came back to report. Instead their scout was the Lord, their guide, their pilot, and all could see where he wanted them to go.

For by day, a white cloud rose in the shape of a pillar before them, and at night, instead of a cloud there was fire in the sky, rising as a column of light. All could see it, so no one could be lost, and no one could forget even for a moment that it was the Lord who was choosing their path.

Moses must be doing something to cause the cloud and the fire, said the more skeptical and sophisticated among them, but when they camped that first night, the pillar stayed in the midst of the camp of Israel, so all could see that there was nothing under the fire that it could use as fuel, and nothing under the cloud in the morning that might cause smoke to rise. By the second morning, the skeptics were silenced by the scorn of the others, who laughed and said, After the frogs, the lice, the hail, the locusts, the three days of darkness, you think the pillar of fire is a *trick?*

Only at the head of the company, where Moses and Aaron led the tribe of Levi, were there two men who knew very well that they had been led out of any route that made sense. And of all the people around them, talking to them, asking them for decisions about things that anyone could have decided, or asking them questions that could be answered by anyone or no one—of all these people, only Miriam could see that there was something very wrong, which was worrying Moses and Aaron.

"The Lord knows what he's doing," was all that Moses would tell her—at first. But on the second day of the journey, he had no choice but to let her know, for soon all Israel would see. "We're coming to the Red Sea," he said.

"But why?" asked Miriam. "To get to Canaan, we have to pass north of the Red Sea."

"The Lord cannot have forgotten that people are not fish, and cattle even less so," said Aaron. "Whatever he plans, he'll let us know in good time."

"When the people come over the last ridge and see the water spread out before them, what will I tell them?" asked Moses.

"The truth," said Miriam. "That the Lord brought us here."

"I can't help but think," said Moses, "that Pharaoh won't be content for long with our departure. The Lord has already taken his firstborn—he may feel that now he has nothing else to lose. In fact, when he sent word that we could leave, it's quite possible that he always intended to bring an army out after us, to wreak vengeance."

"Do you speak as the prophet, or as a one-time general trying to outguess his opponent?"

"I know that Pharaoh will never look me in the face again," said Moses, "for the Lord gave me those words when I said them to him. And I know that all of Israel will join me in serving the Lord at the holy mountain. As for the rest, I know that the Lord has told me to be patient, manage what I can manage, and I'll see in good time how he loves the people of Israel."

"*Is* Pharaoh coming?" asked Miriam.

"I don't know," said Moses.

"Did it never occur to you that it's all right for you to *ask* the Lord?"

"Do you think I haven't?"

"But how have you asked?" said Miriam. "Just—what are you doing? What next? No, it takes some intelligence, some *thought*."

"Are you teaching the prophet how to pray?" said Aaron.

"I don't mind if she does," said Moses. "She's been praying and getting answers since long before I ever began to imagine I should."

"*You* should come up with a plan," said Miriam. "One that includes what the Lord is doing—leading us to the shore of the Red Sea. Propose it to the Lord and let him tell you yes or no."

"What if I come up with the wrong one?"

"This is a different kind of school," said Miriam. "The Lord isn't teaching you to read and write, he's teaching you to lead a nation of people. Only, unlike most leaders, you have the power of God to use for the benefit of your people. How did you think of the plagues?"

"I didn't. I mean, I said what the Lord put into my mind to say."

"Are you sure? Or did you think of a plague out of your own mind, and then the Lord made it true?"

"No, no, don't say that," said Moses. "I didn't . . . the plagues were not my doing."

"Why not?" said Miriam. "Were they wrong? Would anything less have done the job?"

"But they were terrible . . ."

Aaron laughed. "Yes, strange and terrible are the ways of God. But the people of Egypt had to see the power of God unfold before them. They had to see, clearly, that when you spoke the elements obeyed."

"Like Enoch," said Moses.

Clearly they were unfamiliar with the story.

"Before Noah. Before the flood, a great prophet named Enoch brought together all the righteous sons and daughters of God in a city called Zion. And because wherever the righteous are gathered, the wicked are filled with envy and resentment, armies were sent against them. But such was Enoch's faith that he commanded, and mountains moved from one place to another, to throw up barriers against the armies. Try as they might, whatever route they attempted became an impassable cliff."

"What the plagues did," said Miriam, "*was* compassionate. The slavery of the Israelites was destroying the soul of the Egyptian people. They were taking vengeance on us for what our grandparents did in all innocence, serving those who ruled Egypt at the time. To hate a whole people, not for what they're doing, or what they did, but rather what their ancestors did — that was a terrible sin, and the plagues woke the Egyptians up to what they were doing. If the people of Egypt had risen up in rebellion, to insist that Pharaoh obey the Lord, do you think he would have resisted?"

"No," said Moses at once. "Pharaoh is no fool. He knows

where his power comes from, even if he has no comprehension of the power of God."

"All I'm saying," said Miriam, "is that God has brought you between the desert and the sea, and you know Pharaoh well enough to know that he might send an army against us. What is your plan? Victory in war? Are the children of Israel soldiers? I don't think so."

"Wait a minute," said Aaron. "I'm still back on the previous topic. You mean Moses was just making up those plagues and when he gave me those commands, God hadn't told him to? The gnats out of dust? The flies with all their maggots?"

"The plagues came from God," said Moses. "Miriam wasn't there."

"The Lord gives us the chance to think," said Miriam.

"You mean all those offensive things you've said over the years came from *you?*" asked Aaron.

She glared at him.

"Not war," said Moses. "If Pharaoh comes, we can't fight him."

"Armies of angels?" asked Aaron.

"If Pharaoh comes again, it means he's found a way to pretend that God didn't do all that he has done. He'll need to see the power of God again, and in a way that cannot be denied. An army of angels is still an army. No, the Lord brought us to the shore of the sea."

"But in its narrowest part," said Aaron. "Do you think we can see the other side?"

"I don't know," said Moses. "But we know the other side is there, don't we? The Lord brought us here so we could cross the Red Sea."

Aaron laughed. "In the desert where we're heading, we'll be lucky to find a single fishing boat."

"That's the plan," said Moses. "We'll row across, five at a time."

"Two generations will have lived and died before we got across at *that* rate," said Aaron.

"No," said Moses. "We'll cross on dry land. On foot, as we came here."

"A long, long row of steppingstones?" asked Aaron.

"The Lord can move the water out of the way."

"Dry up the sea?" asked Miriam.

"Pile it up on the left hand and the right. Like opening a canyon through the mountains."

"Water doesn't pile up," said Aaron.

"Which is why it's such a miracle," said Moses.

"I know that," said Aaron. "That's why I said it, because it's a miracle."

"But this is *my* plan," said Moses, "not the Lord's."

"Is it?" said Miriam. "The Lord brought us here—he must have planned something. The point is, if you thought of it but the Lord carries it out, then it becomes his plan."

"Lead the people," said Moses. "I'm going on ahead."

"When you pray," said Miriam, "ask about the fact that we're already running out of food, and this desert isn't famous for its fresh water supply."

"I pray about it all the time," said Moses. "But isn't it your turn? While I'm gone, *you* come up with a plan about that."

"As long as you do the praying," said Miriam. "You're the Lord's prophet now."

Did her voice contain an undercurrent of resentment, or at least of loss? Moses took her hands. "You served the Lord where he needed you, and Aaron, you also, where you were needed. When the Lord prepared me and sent me back, I found that you two had already kindled in Israel a passion for freedom and an abiding hope in the power of God. Could the Lord have freed Israel without you? Of course — just as he could have done it without me. But what he asked you to do, you did."

Moses knew as he spoke that this was no answer at all, for it merely raised another question: Why was Moses needed at all? If the two of them were preparing Israel for freedom along with faithful obedience to the Lord, why did the Lord have to bring Moses back from the desert? Since it was a matter Moses himself did not understand, he made no attempt to answer their unspoken resentment. It would seethe under the surface, he knew. But that was between them and God. He hadn't asked for this task.

Taking his leave of them, he strode on ahead, walking on his shepherd's legs, far less fatigued by this journey than anyone else. He was not young, but even the young men were worn out by the day's journey. No one could keep up with Moses.

Not that there weren't some who wanted to try. Young Joshua, of Ephraim, seemed to find it impossible to stay with his own tribe, and was always traveling with the Levites and seemed to be within earshot of Moses whenever possible. And now, as Moses took off ahead, Aaron could see how the young man took a few rushed steps, wanting to catch up, and then realized that no one else was going with Moses, that he would be noticed following him, and then he glanced at Aaron, and Aaron shook his head. No, don't follow. Joshua smiled sheepishly and allowed himself to fall back to the slower pace of the rest of the tribe.

Aaron understood why Joshua didn't travel with the Ephraimites — Joshua was young, and while his eagerness and intelligence were appreciated, he wasn't taken seriously by the elders of Ephraim. Moses, on the other hand, answered his questions, asked what he thought, treated him as a companion worthy of noticing. And Moses, after all, was the prophet of God.

Not that Joshua was ambitious. After all, the trust of God was bestowed by God himself, not by any man. Joshua wanted to be with Moses because he wanted to help with the most important work. Which, now that Aaron thought of it, *was* a kind of ambition. The bad ambition that led Pharaoh to poison Hatshepsut and at least go along with the murder of his own father, that was the ambition for personal power and prestige. Joshua had no scrap of that. His ambition was the good kind, to find where the most important thing was happening and then help to understand it and bring it to pass. There were others like him, though none so young. Hur, of Levi, was emerging as a trusted man whose loyalty was to the Lord and not to his tribe. Caleb of Judah bore watching. Others, with too much of the wrong kind of ambition, were soon given modest assignments that kept them far from the counselors Moses gathered around him.

Aaron couldn't help wondering: Which kind of ambition is mine? Or Miriam's? How much of our passion for freeing Israel was because we wanted Israel saved, and how much because we each wanted to be the savior? Until this moment, Aaron would have told anyone who asked that the distinction didn't matter. As long as you were there, helping, working constantly for a good cause, who cared whether your motives included a little hope that someone would recognize your efforts and reward you with honor or even entrust you with power?

But maybe it does matter. Maybe you don't have to be completely corrupt. Maybe a little bit of personal ambition could corrupt you a little bit. Maybe out in the desert, Moses was stripped of the last shred of personal ambition, and when it was gone, then the Lord could use him as his prophet. Maybe that was what Moses saw in Joshua, so that he allowed this—this mere *boy*, after all, however nicely his beard might be coming along—allowed him to take part in discussions that even the elders of the other tribes were not invited into.

Maybe the Lord is going to find a way to purify Miriam and me before this journey is through.

Or maybe the Lord has already given up, and doesn't think I'm worth purifying.

※

"Wait for your son's body to be embalmed," Sakhmet said.

"The embalmers know their business," said Tuthmose. "My son was killed by the Israelite god. He took away what I loved best! Now I'll show him how it feels."

"Go then," she said. "Show him, and see what he shows you."

"Is that a threat? A challenge? Or a warning?"

"You are Pharaoh," she said. "Your kingdom is in ruins. We have no crops, our herds are depleted, the people are grieving and dispirited—and you want to take the one remaining pillar of the kingdom, the army, and throw it against a god who can do the things we've seen him do!"

Tuthmose looked at her in fury. "Now the mask comes off and I see how I was deceived. You were so mild, so virtuous, but now I know you for what you are."

"And what is that?"

"Hatshepsut," he said, as if the name were a curse.

"We lost our son," she said. "It changed me. Being quiet

and obedient to you cost me my son! So now I speak, and you get angry at *me*."

"I didn't marry you to hear your advice."

"You married me to produce heirs," she said. "I produced one, a fine one. Where is he? What have you done with the child I made for you?"

Tuthmose roared with rage and grief. She cowered, expecting another blow. But this time her voice was not stilled. "Yes, hit me! Show the power of Pharaoh! The same power the lowliest slave has — to beat his woman! Oh, you're the mighty one! Oh, Egypt is proud of you!"

"I'm done with you. I divorce you."

This caused her far more fear than the threat of violence had. "My body has more children in it. Ptahmose was perfect; we can have another, and another."

"I never married you," said Tuthmose. "You never lived in this palace."

"If you strike out my name from all the inscriptions, you will have to strike out the name of Ptahmose, too!"

"Yes!" cried Tuthmose. "I will do that! A child who dies in his sleep might as well be a miscarriage! I need a man who will live, and for that I need a real wife, not a complaining woman who thinks she rules Egypt!"

"Do you repudiate Ptahmose?" she said, stricken as she had never been before, even by the death of her son. "Do you deny him?"

"I never had a son. I never had a wife. When I marry it will be for the first time, and whoever is born to that marriage will be my firstborn. Moses and his god took *nothing* from me! I was not defeated."

"This is beyond madness," said Sakhmet. "You have given your heart to evil."

"When I come back from slaughtering the leaders of the Israelites and dragging the rest back to Goshen to begin their slavery in earnest, you will not be in this palace. And that son of yours, the one who was so feeble that he died in his sleep, I will not have his body embalmed like a son of Pharaoh! He was never my son. My son will be Pharaoh someday, and Pharaoh is a god. Gods are not killed by the spells cast by escaped slaves."

She wept bitterly, and wailed at him as he stalked from the room, "You loved him! He is your son and you loved him!"

Out in the great hall, Jannes stood with several priests. Clearly they had heard the argument; there was no privacy in the palace, if you shouted, for the stone walls would carry the sound to every corner of the building.

Jannes and the priests said nothing to Tuthmose. Just looked at him.

"What's wrong with you?" demanded Tuthmose. "What are you looking at?"

"I'm looking at the king-god who rules Egypt," said Jannes.

Was there irony in his voice? "I need a priest to bless my six hundred chariots before I take them out to destroy the power of Moses. I should have done it the moment he returned to Egypt."

"I pray that Amon will bless Egypt with all good things," said Jannes. "But I will not say a blessing on your chariots."

"High priests can be replaced!" roared Tuthmose.

"As you wish," said Jannes. "But I cannot give blessings today, for I'm in mourning. Unlike you, I lost a son." And with that, Jannes headed for the door.

Tuthmose looked around at the men gathered in the great hall. There was one, a soldier, a man who was crisp in his obedience and submissive in his advice. "You," said Tuthmose. "You are now the high priest of Amon at Karnak."

The great hall fell silent, and Jannes stopped in the doorway, waiting.

"Go take the vestments of the priesthood from that old traitor and put them on. You will bless my chariots today."

Without question or complaint, the man walked briskly to Jannes, who surrendered immediately every scrap of priestly garb and decoration. Jannes walked naked from the hall, his old hams sagging, his skin hanging on him like old clothes, his back bent. No wonder the kingdom was in such trouble—the high priest of Amon had been this pathetic old impostor! Now there was a new high priest, and there would be a new queen, and new heirs. Egypt would rise from the setbacks of recent weeks, and Tuthmose would show the world that Pharaoh bowed to no man, and no god but the gods of Egypt.

At some point today, he would need to make discreet inquiries in order to remind himself of the name of the man he had just appointed to the highest religious office in the land. It wouldn't do for people to find out that Pharaoh's memory was less than perfect. Though with so much on his mind, a lesser man than Pharaoh would probably have forgotten his *own* name.

*

By the time the pillar of cloud led the people to the shores of the sea, Moses was ready for them, and from his smile, Aaron and Miriam knew that he had received his answer.

"The Lord is merciful to Israel," said Moses. "For the heart of Pharaoh is harder than anyone but God could ever have guessed. Even now he is coming with six hundred war chariots with their archers and swordsmen."

"Tell us about the *goodness* of God," said Miriam dryly.

"There is our highway," said Moses, pointing to the sea.

"And who will hold the chariots at bay while we cross?" asked Aaron.

"The Egyptians will know that the Lord is God," said Moses.

As the last of the Israelites came down to the shore of the Red Sea, Moses summoned the elders of the tribes. "Tell your people we will encamp here tonight."

"The people will ask where we are going from here," said Hur. "And why we came to the sea."

"Tell them this," said Moses. "The Lord will fight for Israel, and protect the children of Israel. Trust in the Lord, and not one soul of us will be harmed. Tomorrow the Lord will show forth even mightier miracles than the plagues. For there were flies and frogs and lice before, and darkness and blood and death. But what you will see tomorrow has never been seen on earth, and only the power of God could accomplish it."

"Pharaoh is coming, isn't he?" said one of the men of Naphtali. "The army is coming against us."

"Yes, Pharaoh comes in triumph, thinking his chariots have trapped us, hemmed us in against the sea," said Moses.

"Will the Lord make us mighty in battle?" asked Joshua. He said this with so much eagerness that it was plain to Moses the boy had never seen war. But then, none of the young men of Israel had fought in battle. Only the oldest men remembered the days when, under Hyksos Pharaohs, Israelites had been trusted with minor command. If Israelites younger than Moses had ever practiced battle, they had done it with sticks.

"The Lord will defend us against Pharaoh by his power alone. Our job," said Moses," is to walk from here . . . to there."

And he pointed out to sea.

"I'm looking for the boats," said an elder of Dan.

"I said we would walk," said Moses. "By the power of the Lord God, we will cross on dry land. Now go to your people and prepare them to move tomorrow at dawn, tribe by tribe, in the order of march."

They dispersed, except for the few who were emerging as part of Moses' inner council — Aaron, Miriam, Hur, Caleb, Joshua, a few others. Moses spoke to them as if he had asked them to stay. "Hur," he said, "tomorrow you will stand at the shoreline to keep the people moving. Caleb, Joshua, you will circulate among the tribes in the rear, and reassure them when Pharaoh's chariots come that not one Israelite will be harmed today. The three of you will be the last to cross. Aaron, Miriam, I want you to lead Israel across. They have to see you go first, because many will be afraid to believe the evidence of their own eyes."

"And you?" said Aaron.

"I will cross when I cross."

"Moses," said Aaron, "Israel needs you. Don't stand alone against Pharaoh."

Moses laughed, but touched his brother's arm affectionately. "It's good of you to worry about me, Aaron, but I've seen enough of war to know that the best battle is the one you don't have to fight. Now go, make your camp for tonight. Tomorrow you'll see what the Lord will do."

Joshua spoke up again. "Shouldn't we post guards, to watch for Pharaoh's army?"

"Why should we watch?" said Moses. "They'll follow our trail easily, and they'll find us when they find us."

"But what if they come tomorrow before we cross?"

"They will come tonight," said Moses. "They're almost here right now."

"And we're making *camp?*" said Joshua, incredulous.

"So young, to be losing his hearing," said Moses. The others laughed. But he could hear that they, too, were nervous, that Joshua had given voice to everyone's fears. "I said the Lord will protect us, and we will not do battle."

Even as he spoke, cries of fear came up from the camp, a tumult of noise. For there at the crest of the ridge, where only recently the last Israelites had come down on their walk to the sea, chariots began to appear, spreading out as if to attack. Archers could be seen nocking their arrows; the glint of swords in the last sunlight of the day brought screams from the people.

And then, before the people could panic and begin to flee, the pillar of cloud that until now had stood out over the water moved rapidly over the camp of Israel, changing shape as it did. Now the pillar became a thick cloud that blocked Pharaoh's chariots from view.

It took a while for the people to calm down and get back to making camp. They had got better at pitching their tents, those who had them; many just laid out blankets or robes on the ground. They would all have tents soon enough, refashioning robes or blankets, or making new cloth from wool as they traveled, for the nights in the desert could be bitterly cold, and the wind could blind them. But so far on the journey, the nights had been warm, the air still. Of course, for the weather belonged to the Lord and did his will.

All through the evening, as the sun set, the people kept looking at the cloud, waiting for a chariot to burst through. Instead, the cloud gave off a glow that brought light to the camp. And by the time the sky was fully dark, the people had finally come to trust that the Lord really was protecting them. Many of them even slept.

✿

"What can I do about the fog?" answered an officer. "I try to drive my chariot into it, but the horses stop in terror. And what does it matter? Morning sun will clear this fog away, and they'll still be there. Where can they go?"

Pharaoh didn't like hearing opposition to his orders, but the truth was the men *had* tried to obey, and the horses would not go. No doubt some of them were saying this fog came from the god of Israel, and that didn't help them find any new eagerness to plunge into the mist. Many of the soldiers had lost siblings, and some had lost children, and some of their own company had died, being firstborn. But these troops were the elite, and they would obey with courage and vigor. The officer was right. Tomorrow would be soon enough.

And Moses was wrong. Pharaoh *would* look at his face again. As Moses' corpse lay on the ground, his severed head between his feet, Pharaoh would see his face, with Moses' eyes finally downcast in obedience to his Pharaoh, who was the only god with any real power in Egypt. The time for tricks and spells was over. This was war, and while Moses had a vastly larger force, in no sense could it be called an army. Tuthmose's six hundred chariots would slice through the Israelites like sickles through wheat. Then the women of Israel would keen and mourn like the mothers of Egypt had mourned, as all the males of Israel died before their eyes, and then the women and girls would be raped and then sold off into slavery, dispersed throughout Egypt. There would be no Israelites then, only slaves in Egyptian houses, and the only children they would ever have would be fathered by their Egyptian masters. Thus Pharaoh would extinguish a rebellious people, and all the world would acknowledge his irresistible power.

✿

Before dawn the spirit of the Lord whispered to Moses that it was time, and he began to rouse the people. By the light of the cloud that protected them, they dressed, they loaded their burdens, and they gathered into marching order, tribe by tribe. Moses made only one change. "Today we pass beyond the border of Egypt. Therefore I charge the tribe of Ephraim to be first to follow Aaron and Miriam across to the other side. Ephraim! You are the bearers of the bones of our father, Jacob, called Israel. He prophesied that one day Israel would leave Egypt and return to Canaan, and today the prophecy begins to be fulfilled, for his bones will be carried at the front of our march."

A ragged cheer went up from Ephraim, but since no one could see how they were going to cross the water, it was hard for them to work up much enthusiasm.

Moses walked to the edge of the water. The camp of Israel was fanned out on the sloping beaches, and many could see him. "O Lord," said Moses softly, "show them your mercy."

Then, as the Lord had commanded, Moses stretched out his hand over the sea.

At once the sea began to roil as the water fled from the beach in front of the place where Aaron and Miriam waited. Immediately they walked boldly out onto the ground that moments before had been covered with water. "The ground is dry!" cried Aaron. He and Miriam strode on, as the water continued to recede before them. But it receded only where they walked; on the right hand and the left, it stayed up against the beach, lapping the shoreline normally. The water simply moved out of the way, making a path through the sea.

The farther Aaron and Miriam walked, the higher the walls of water stood on either side. Yet no drop of it fell on them, and the ground was a smooth highway under their feet.

Behind them, the company of Ephraim began to march down that road, bearing before them the carven box that held the remains of father Jacob. They marched in silence, some not daring to look right or left, others unable to look anywhere else but at the canyon of water that loomed silently over them.

Hour after hour, they passed down into the sea. When half the tribes had passed, Moses joined them and walked across. He walked quickly, overtaking them, walking among flocks and herds, among pack beasts and carts, among families with little children, companies of young men and women, old people leaning on their staves or on the arms of younger ones. And where he passed he saw some people laughing, others praying, some weeping—in awe? in relief? in fear? He could not guess. He spoke to many as he passed. "See how the Lord loves us," he said. "See how his power makes all things possible."

It seemed a lifetime ago, or perhaps it was another man's life, when Moses had passed down the Nile in a barge. Then he had heard the cheers of the multitudes, but those cheers meant nothing, and within a few days his name had been obliterated from Egypt, his life and works extinguished. He thought his life was over. Now he passed again through water, surrounded by multitudes, and none of them were calling his name. But *this* was triumph. This was the love of God made visible to his children. Moses had served Hatshepsut before, and in a larger sense had served the kingdom of Egypt, and therefore the people—but he had nothing to give Egypt except what little wisdom he possessed of himself. Now the gifts Moses had to give had real value, for they were not his own gifts, but rather the bounty of a loving God, and so Moses served the people of Israel, because he served God, and God loved this people and wanted them to be righteous and filled with joy.

When he reached the other side, he looked back and saw that the last of the Israelites were beginning to move down into the road through the sea. Still the cloud stood in place to protect them. And Aaron and Miriam were both weeping with joy as they embraced him on the other side.

*

The morning passed, and then it was noon, and then afternoon, and still the fog did not disperse. The soldiers waited patiently, but the horses needed to be fed and watered; they could not stand all day in harness. Pharaoh allowed them to unharness a hundred at a time, so that five hundred chariots stood continuously ready. His only consolation through the long delay was that on the other side of the fog, the Israelites must be in terror, regretting bitterly that they had ever followed Moses out to be caught between Pharaoh and the depths of the sea.

Then, at last, a cry from one of the men, with words that no one needed to hear because all could see with their own eyes: "The fog is gone!"

It was true. Just like that, the fog gathered itself up into a single pillar and fled before them, rushing out over the water. Only then could they see from the ridge down to the shoreline.

They were gone. All the Israelites were gone. Their footprints were visible, the ashes of their cookfires, the traces of their animals. Where had they gone?

That, too, was visible. For as Pharaoh's chariot led the way down the slope, all could see that the footprints led like a funnel directly down to the edge of the sea. But where the footprints crossed the shoreline, there was no water. Instead, a rift had opened in the sea, and the Israelites had obviously passed down into this impossible highway cut through water that held its shape like stone.

"What are you waiting for!" Tuthmose demanded of his men. "Follow them! Destroy them!"

These were good soldiers. They did not hesitate. Though the horses whinnied their misgivings, they too obeyed, and soon five hundred chariots had plunged down the road into the Red Sea.

Tuthmose waited on shore, impatiently signaling for the remaining hundred soldiers to get their horses back in harness. Tuthmose would ride with this last contingent through the carnage. The battle would be bloody and there would be no glory in it, cutting down unarmed men and women. The triumph would come when Tuthmose, his chariot wheels red with the blood of Israelites, came out of the sea to take Moses captive before the eyes of his surviving people—before the eyes of his miserable, vicious god. There Tuthmose would have Moses watch the execution of all the remaining males of Israel, a matter that should have been completed at the time when Moses was born. Only then would Tuthmose grant Moses' fervent plea that he, too, be allowed to die.

Not more than two hundred yards down the road through the sea, the chariots stopped. From shore, Tuthmose raged, but he could see the problem. The chariot wheels had become mired, and in trying to drive on, some of the wheels had broken. "Ride on!" Tuthmose screamed, though no one could hear him. "Leave the broken chariots and ride on! Don't let them get away!"

※

Caleb, Hur, and Joshua came up out of the sea.

"You are the last?" Moses asked them.

"Not one straggler was left behind," said Hur. "All of Israel has crossed. But Pharaoh's chariots have come down into the sea after us."

"Even now, those brave soldiers still obey him," said Moses, marveling. "The Lord will honor their obedience, and take it into account when he judges the worthiness of their lives."

Then he raised his hand again over the sea.

*

The soldiers struggling with their chariots hardly had time to realize what was happening. One moment the water was a wall on either hand. The next moment the crushing weight of it collapsed on them from above, from both sides, snuffing out their lives in an instant. They hadn't even the time to curse or pray.

On the shore, Pharaoh was just assembling his triumphal party of a hundred chariots when the road disappeared, and the sea returned to its former placid lapping of the shore. Now the Israelites' footprints and the tracks of Pharaoh's chariots seemed to lead nowhere at all.

Out on the water, there might have been crushed remnants of the wooden chariots, floating. But from where Pharaoh stood, there was no sign of his soldiers.

He stood in his chariot, gazing in silence over the water. But not for very long. After a few moments he wheeled his chariot to face the surviving men. Their faces were filled with horror, but he was their Pharaoh, so they looked at him and listened to what he would say.

"As you can see," Tuthmose said, "today we have destroyed Israel. We drove them into the Red Sea. And though we lost five hundred brave men, it does not diminish the value of our victory. Moses is dead, forsaken by his god and by his people!"

Then he fell silent and looked from man to man, the whole

company of them, to see if anyone would dare to speak or even think to the contrary. There was no will to rebellion there. Indeed, they all had to be thinking: If I told the truth, who would believe me? So when Tuthmose commanded his horses to go forward, they fell in behind him and this fragment of his army began the return journey to the Nile.

Within weeks, all record of the Israelites in Egypt had been wiped out — not that there had been much, since they were first servants of the Hyksos, whose monuments had long since been destroyed, and then were slaves, who are never worth mentioning. No one was permitted to write of the plagues, or even that the harvest was bad that year. Nor was there any mention of Sakhmet as the wife and queen of Tuthmose III, or of a child named Ptahmose. They had never existed.

But in Tuthmose's heart, they had once lived, and he had lost them. Lost them utterly because he could not bear to have any public admission of his defeat by Moses and his god. He could never grieve for them, never speak of them.

What he could do, however, was search for Moses and the Israelites. As soon as he could recover from the devastating losses of the plagues, he began to launch campaign after campaign, plunging ever deeper into Canaan, searching for the place where Moses and his people had settled. But in forty years of campaigning, he never found them or heard even a rumor of them. When he lay on his deathbed, waiting to turn his kingdom over to a son who had never known his father's approval or even the name of the perfect child against whom he was perpetually measured, he took some small satisfaction from the obvious truth that Moses and his people must have perished miserably in the wilderness. They probably starved. Or ran out of water and found no well. And as they realized they were all going to die, they must have turned on him and torn him limb from limb. Moses, who thought he could be Pharaoh, but never had the strength of will, the hardness of heart, to do the job.

*

The sea was flat and still.

Miriam turned to Moses. "Were they caught? Did the army of Pharaoh drown in the sea?"

"Whatever Tuthmose does," said Moses, "there is always more grieving in Egypt."

"What of Tuthmose himself," said Aaron. "Was he also drowned?"

"The Lord will never let Tuthmose trouble Israel again," said Moses. "Now come with me, and assemble Israel where I can speak to them."

Moses had no idea what he was going to say. Even when he climbed to the outcropping of rock and had the thirteen tribes spread before him, he had no speech in him.

What he had instead was song. In his years as a shepherd, he had learned to pass the long hours of watchfulness the way the daughters of Jethro did, the way all shepherds did, it seemed, in all lands of grass and stone: he sang. Moses found that what he could not say easily in words would sometimes flow from him in song, and at times he did not know what he truly felt or thought until he heard his own music.

The people of Israel had not forgotten the old tradition of shepherd song, though they had long ago become more accustomed to the rhythmic drumming and clapping of Egyptian music. But they had left that behind. It felt right to hear the prophet open his mouth in a shepherd's psalm, and they understood the message deeper than words: This is a new age, and we are a new people, but also a very old people, who are at last returning to our homeland, to our folkways, to our faith, to our God.

"I'll sing to the Lord," he sang.

> The Lord is my strength and song.
> He is become my salvation.
> He is my God.
> I'll make a place for him.
> My father's God,
> I will exalt him!
> Your right hand, Lord,
> Is glorious in power.
> Your right hand, Lord,
> Can break your enemy.
> Who is like you
> In holiness and glory?
> Who is like you
> Among the mighty ones?
> Like a young tree,
> You carry Israel
> To the land of planting,
> To the walled garden.
> Israel is the joy of your orchard.
> This young people,
> The jewel of your crown!

And the people joined him, singing the words he taught them. And there in the desert, on the Sinai shore, Miriam took out her timbrel and led the women of Israel in dancing for joy. For their freedom, for their deliverance, for the love of the Lord God, in whom they trusted now, and to whom they would be grateful and obedient forever.

I'll sing to the Lord!
The Lord is my strength and song.
He is become my salvation.
He is my God.
I'll make a place for him.
My father's God,
I will exalt him!

# M e n   a n d   W o m e n

For the long months that Moses was gone, Zeforah's only word of him came from the Lord, who told her little, but it was enough. She knew that he was on the Lord's errand. She knew that the Lord would bring him back safely. So when she led the children in prayer for their father, and for their people, the Israelites, the answer she received was a feeling of peace in her heart. All was well with him and with his work. She could be patient with that.

Gershom was not satisfied, however. "Why is Father bothering with slaves?" he asked one day. He had seen slaves, with the occasional traveler that passed by—they seemed to be treated like animals, less sturdy than camels, but more dextrous. Zeforah had to explain to him that slaves were people just like any other, who had been unfortunate enough to be captured in war. She didn't know enough about the Israelites in Egypt—or about Egypt itself, for that matter—to explain much more about their slavery than that they had been taken into captivity in Egypt and Father was going to tell them that the Lord would set them free.

"Then they must be happy to see him," said Gershom.

"I hope so," said Zeforah.

"Why wouldn't they be?" continued her inquisitive first-born.

"Because when your father lived in Egypt, he wasn't a

slave like the rest. He was adopted by Pharaoh's daughter and lived in the palace and commanded armies and was very famous and powerful."

"Why didn't he set the Israelites free himself?"

With Gershom, the questions only got harder. "Because he wasn't the Pharaoh, he was only the adopted son of Pharaoh's daughter." No use trying to explain how Pharaoh's daughter became Pharaoh, including the shocking behavior of dressing as a man. Especially since Zeforah didn't understand it herself.

"Didn't Pharaoh like him, then?"

"Pharaoh's daughter loved him, Gershom, because he was her only son and he was good and wise. But he still had to obey her, and not her him. I don't obey *you*, do I?"

"I don't always obey you, either," he answered.

"But you're sorry when you don't."

"Not always," he said. "Sometimes I'm right and you're wrong."

"Yes, that's true," she said. "But I'm always your mother. Besides, there was more to it than that, when your father was in Egypt." She did her best to explain that Pharaoh could not lead the people where they didn't want to go, that it was all Moses' Egyptian mother could do just to stop the Egyptians from killing the Israelites' boy-children.

By the end, though, she knew she must have made a muddle of it, because Gershom's response was to nod wisely and say, "So Father *was* a slave, after all, just like the rest of the Israelites."

"What? Why do you say that?"

"Because he had to do what other people told him all the time, and never got to choose for himself."

"No, he *wasn't* a slave, or else all adults are," she said. "Think about it, Gershom. When do I get to *choose* what I'm

going to do? Every day I have to provide a meal for you and
the other children. There are duties to take care of with
Grandfather's flocks. I have to watch the little ones all the time
so they don't play with snakes and scorpions or tumble off
cliffs. When during the day can I do what I want?"

"When you read the scriptures," he answered promptly.

"Your father had moments like that, too," she said, "when
he could be himself. But the rest of his life was filled with
duty."

"I don't want to grow up," he said. "I don't like chores."

"But when you're older, you understand the purpose of
your work, and so you take joy in it. That's why I'm *not* a slave,
because when I married your father I knew I was making the
choice to have wonderful children and care for them, and
work hard all the days of my life."

"You didn't know we were going to be wonderful."

"Yes I did. Gershom, slaves work because they're afraid of
being punished. I work because I rejoice in the lives of the
people I serve."

"I don't rejoice in Eliezer's life," said Gershom.

"But you will," she said, "when he gets older and he's the
most fun person to play with."

"Am I an Israelite?" asked Gershom.

"Yes," said Zeforah.

"But you're a Midianite, like Grandfather."

"I was until I grew up and married your father."

"So I'm half Israelite."

"It doesn't go by halves," said Zeforah. "Because the
Israelites are the chosen people of the Lord, you either serve
and obey the Lord, or you don't."

"But Grandfather serves the Lord and he's *not* an Israelite."

Zeforah despaired of making things clear to a child. "Then

I guess you have to grow up and adopt Grandfather as your son, so he can be an Israelite, too."

It took a moment for Gershom to realize she was joking. For that moment, his eyes wide, she knew he was imagining blustery old Grandfather as his own little boy. Then he got the joke and laughed and ran off to tell Grandfather that he would have to call him Father from now on, so he could be one of the chosen people, too.

Sure enough, within a few minutes, Jethro came charging into her tentyard. "What's this I hear about you planning to become my grandmother?"

"If I *were* your grandmother, I'd get you to bathe more often."

"I'm willing to become an Israelite," said Jethro, "but I'm not willing to become an Egyptian."

"I hope it's not dirt that separates Hebrews from Egyptians," said Zeforah.

"Dirt *and* water, as a matter of fact," said Jethro.

"What is *that* supposed to mean?"

"They're coming."

"Who?" And then she realized. "Moses?"

"And a horde of Israelites. They've been seen on this side of the Red Sea, heading toward the mountain of the Lord."

"So they did come out."

"And the stories that are being told about them are so fabulous as to be irresponsible. I won't even repeat them."

"Yes you will," she said.

"You need to show more respect for your father."

"You need to tell me."

"It's utter nonsense," said Jethro. "Supposedly the Israelites not only left Egypt, but they're bringing half the gold of Egypt with them, which was *given* to them by the Egyptian people as presents! I'm sure that one's likely to be true, Egyptians are always giving gold to departing slaves. And then they supposedly didn't go *around* the Red Sea at all, or even across it, they went right *through* it. And they don't carry grain with them, they find bread on the ground in the morning every day and just gather it up, and when they need meat, flocks of quail come and land among them, waiting to be knocked in the head and cooked for supper. I know the Lord is with them, but people should keep some degree of reason about the rumors they spread."

"The Lord's power is great," said Zeforah. "Maybe it's all true. Such a large number of people must be eating somehow, and there's not much food to be found here in the wilderness of Sinai."

"Yes, well . . . but bread on the ground like dew! Well, it doesn't matter. Time for you to pack up. The day is young, and we can reach the camp of Israel before noon tomorrow."

"Do you know where it is?"

"It isn't two tents and a dozen shepherds, Zeforah. It's a million people, more or less. And all their herds and beasts of burden. We'll smell them before we see them, and we'll see them from many miles away. They can't exactly hide, at least not from those of us who know this land."

"But . . . Moses hasn't sent for me."

"A husband doesn't have to send for his wife. You know he wants you there. You belong there at his side. And his children need to see their father being the Lord's servant and the leader of this multitude. They need to learn what it means to be Israelite."

"But it's not safe for a woman and her children to travel alone."

"Who said anything about alone? I said *we* would reach the

camp of Israel tomorrow. Do you think I'd miss this? Moses needs me to tell him what he's doing wrong."

Zeforah was horrified. "Father, you aren't going to criticize him in front of everybody, the way you used to do here!"

"Give me credit for a little tact," said Jethro.

"I would if I'd ever seen you use any."

"I was joking. I've been priest for this village most of my life, and the one thing I've never lacked was villagers willing to provide me with long lists of my faults and failings. The one thing Moses *won't* need is one more person telling him what he's doing wrong." Jethro made a show of suddenly thinking of something awful. "Oh no! A man who doesn't need criticism, and I'm bringing him his *wife?*"

"Very funny," said Zeforah. "We'll be ready in three hours. Two, if you can get any of my sisters to help me with the tent."

※

Visitors came to the camp of Israel every day, on foot, mounted, alone, with company. It bothered Joshua that no effort was made to secure the boundaries of the camp. He brought this up with Hur and Aaron, and both of them looked at him with some puzzlement. "The Lord watches over Israel," said Aaron.

"Well, shouldn't we try to do some things for ourselves?" Joshua asked.

"Like what?" asked Hur.

"There's gold in this camp," said Joshua, "and people make no effort to hide it. And since it belongs to no one in particular, no one has even tallied it so if half of it was stolen we wouldn't even know."

"Who would steal it?"

"These strangers! Gold has value, even here in the

desert—and if they had enough gold, a good number of these people might well *leave* the desert."

"If it can change their lives," said Hur, "then aren't they welcome to it?"

"No, Joshua has a point," said Aaron. "A man in need is not helped by becoming a thief. We shouldn't be tempting people."

"And it's not just the gold," said Joshua. "There are children who've lived in trust of their neighbors all their lives. What's to stop some desert vagabond from kidnapping one or two and selling them into slavery? Things can be bad enough in Egypt for slave children, but there are worse places, I've heard."

"These are all good points," said Aaron. "I'll take it up with Moses, as soon as I get a chance."

"No," said Joshua.

"No?"

"I don't want to wait until Moses has time to talk to you. He never has time, he spends every waking moment judging disputes and answering questions."

"He's the prophet," said Hur. "He can't help it that he's busy."

"This won't wait," said Joshua. "You're his brother, Aaron. You give me permission, and I'll organize the young men in every tribe into boundary patrols."

"Soldiers? What do you know of soldiering?"

"Nothing," said Joshua. "Neither did Adam. Somebody had to be the first soldier. We have all these young men who spent every day hauling clay or bricks or water, and now they have nothing to do and they're getting quarrelsome. I bet half the problems laid before Moses come from some stupid dispute because people are irritable and feel useless. So I'll give them something to do—walking the boundary, two by two, questioning all comers and escorting them to you, so they never get to wander the camp without someone watching them."

"Sounds like you thought it all out," said Aaron.

"No," said Joshua, "I'm making it up as I go along. But I think it's a good plan anyway."

"Go ahead and begin," said Aaron. "I'll check with Moses, and if he wants to make changes later he can. I think the Lord put this idea in your mind."

Joshua laughed. "I'm no prophet," he said. "I'm just as bored as any of the other young men. Moses used to have time to teach us. Now I spend my days wandering around, trying to think of some reason why a woman would want to marry me when I have no land, no wealth, no trade, and no future."

"You have a great future," said Hur. "What are you talking about?"

"*We* have a great future. Israel has a great future. But what makes *me* worth noticing? Women don't want to marry a man, they want to marry a man who's going to provide for them and be a good father and husband, and I have no way of showing them I'm worth anything. *That's* when I came up with this idea."

Aaron and Hur broke up laughing.

"It's serious to *me*," said Joshua. "*You're* already married."

So it was that Joshua began to distinguish himself in the camp of Israel. In a single day he got more than two thousand recruits, and instead of picking among them, he took them all. He divided them into four shifts to cover the four watches of the day and night, and the division was not by tribe, but arbitrarily, so that each shift contained older and younger men and the eager boys who insisted on being included. The boys were used as messengers between the patrols and the elders of each tribe, and the young men who weren't on duty would train together, practicing with such weapons as were included with the wealth brought out of Egypt, as well as clubs and tools, stones and slings. They had all seen Egyptian soldiers and had some idea of what soldiers had to do—they all mastered the swagger and brag of a soldier from the first.

His patrols had been on duty not many days when a particularly rude and surly group of armed men showed up at the camp. The leader proclaimed himself to be Amalek, and he declared that the land where the Israelites were camped belonged to him and his people. Instead of arguing, the patrol was cheerful and began to lead the men to Moses, meanwhile sending messenger boys to assemble all the off-duty soldiers and alert Moses to what was happening. By the time Amalek and his men reached Moses, all two thousand of the patrol were gathered around, armed and watchful, and clearly well-organized into companies that obeyed their officers promptly and completely. Amalek's tone remained belligerent, but his men didn't have the same contemptuous grins they had worn when they arrived.

Moses explained that Israel was here on the Lord's business, heading for the holy mountain. "We aren't eating your food, our animals are grazing only a small portion of your land, and the spring we're drinking from didn't exist until the power of God broke it out of the rock that confined it. We're causing no harm and we mean to move on peacefully. So I can't think of a reason for there to be a quarrel between us."

Amalek was surly but he agreed to tolerate the Israelites' presence. Most of the patrol surrounded his men and peacefully escorted them to the borders of the camp. Moses turned to Aaron and said, "I didn't know we had an army."

"Joshua asked me if he could organize a patrol for the boundaries of the camp. I thought it was a good plan."

"I don't know what the Lord plans," said Moses, "but this Amalek is plain enough to understand. He's going to come back with a large group of armed men, intending to raid this camp. He's the kind of man who lives by raiding, we're the richest prize that's ever come through here, and he saw that our soldiers were young and untrained."

"I doubt his men are particularly well-trained either," said Aaron.

"But they think they are. And they aren't used to seeing civilized self-restraint. We look weak to them — numerous but weak. So they'll be back."

"What will the Lord have us do?" said Aaron.

"I don't know," said Moses. "I only know that whatever we do, the Lord's people will prevail. But in the time we have left before they return, it would be foolish if we didn't train these men in battle."

As soon as Moses took a personal interest in the training, the number of soldiers swelled to nearly four thousand, but Joshua took this in stride, and as he learned what Moses wanted them to do, he drilled the soldiers ruthlessly until they had a kind of rough skill. The few swords they had, they passed around until everyone had some skill with that weapon; the plan was that anyone who fell, Israelite or Amalekite, his sword was to be taken up and used. In the meantime, they had the more boyish weapons — staves, slings. They had the massive strength they had built up during their slavery in Egypt. And they had faith that God would deliver them from these ruffians as he had delivered them from Egypt.

One morning the early watch reported that armed men were picking their way more or less secretly among the rocks near the camp of Ashur. Immediately Moses gave his instruction to Joshua. "These Amalekites will fight with no subtlety at all—man to man, by brute force. But they'll be determined, and won't give up easily, and they have more skill than any of you. So tell your men that I will stand on that hill, where all can see me, and as long as I hold my hands high, Israel will prevail in battle by the power of God. It wouldn't hurt if you made sure the Amalekites knew this, too."

Joshua went to his men at once, and within minutes their officers had passed Moses' words along to the whole army. Then, with their ragged arms and unskilled awkwardness, they advanced to meet the Amalekites on open ground.

Amalek laughed aloud at the sight of them, for though they outnumbered his force greatly, they were young, lightly armed, and lightly dressed. "What do you girls plan to do, spit at us until we drown?" he taunted them.

Joshua answered calmly but in a voice that all the ruffians could hear. "The prophet of God stands on that rock. As long as he holds his hands high, the power of God will be with us and we will prevail."

And so it happened. The Israelites with swords fought at the front, but behind each of them were at least two men with staves, who watched closely and jabbed low and poked high and swatted down at the Amalekite so that he could never aim well at the poorly trained swordsman facing him. It was almost comic, but the Amalekites became angrier as the battle wore on and they seemed to make no headway against these dancing lightweight boys. More and more they began to cast their eyes up toward Moses, seeing that his arms remained high. It must be the power of God thwarting them, they realized, and their attack became less confident, more timid, and they gave ground. Some even threw down their swords and ran—and when they did, on the instant there was a young Israelite with a blade in his hand.

Up on the hill, however, Moses was becoming almost frantic as he called in vain for Aaron, for Hur, for someone to come help him. Finally Miriam heard him and summoned his two closest counselors, who hastened up the hill. "My arms are growing tired," he said. "I didn't expect Amalek to fight so stubbornly, giving ground so slowly, and when they see my arms grow slack, they take courage and attack and our men fall back."

Immediately Aaron and Hur brought a large stone for Moses to sit on. Then they stood beside him and each held one of his arms, keeping it high, so both sides could see that God was still with Israel. The battle lasted a good while after that, but finally the power of the Amalekites was broken. A large group of Israelites threatened to cut them off from their line of retreat into the hills, a good number of their comrades had been killed while hardly an Israelite was even injured, and it seemed like a good idea to go somewhere else seeking easier prey.

Finally they were gone. The Israelite soldiers were better armed, better trained and more experienced than they had been before, and while some of them had taken painful wounds, not one was killed, and even among the wounded none would be maimed. Moses knew enough of battle to recognize a miracle when he saw it. Yes, his arms in the air, that had been a device to terrify the enemy and give confidence to his own men; but the fact that the Amalekites hadn't been able to stop one Israelite from journeying on to meet the Lord at the mountain—that was only possible because of the intervention of God.

He said as much to the soldiers when he addressed them

by the light of the pillar of fire over the camp. "You did fight bravely, and you learned something of war today, but what you did *not* see was the horror of having your comrades die or be maimed beside you, because the Lord protected you. As long as you're faithful to God, his power will be with you. But when you rely on your own strength, or when you fight in wickedness, your strength will be no different from any other man's, and what happened to those dead Amalekites can then happen to you. Don't ever come to love war, you sons of God. Love your Lord, the God of heaven and earth, and fight only in his cause, when he fights beside you."

But he could not keep his voice from showing how proud of them he was, and they couldn't keep from smiling back at him, so he dismissed them with thanks and joined with his closest counselors inside his tent.

This time, though, there was a difference. Joshua didn't lurk outside the tent, hoping to get invited in — Aaron and Hur practically thrust him through the door. He had earned his place at council.

A few days later, Hur had occasion to notice Joshua practically fleeing from a young woman of Gad. "What's the matter, Joshua? I thought you wanted to distinguish yourself in the eyes of the young women."

"I get no peace," said Joshua. "I have fathers and mothers practically throwing their daughters at me. I have women talking to me as if we were planning to have children together. I never get a chance to have a normal conversation with any of them. How can I possibly choose a wife when they're all acting like that?"

Hur couldn't answer, he was laughing so hard. Joshua gave up in disgust and fled the scene before two more young women converged on him, each trailing a chaperoning relative behind her.

❖

Joshua avoided his new popularity by immersing himself in duty, working three shifts a day, walking the perimeter with team after team, getting to know the young men, asking them for ideas, listening to their experiences. Some of them had been quite shaken by the experience of fighting, and not just the ones who had killed or drawn blood. Some worried, Am I a coward? Others asked, Will God forgive me for having killed a man? Some thoughts were more random: I wonder if my father might have looked like him, if he had lived long enough for me to know him. Were these men married? Why did they want to kill us? Joshua didn't pretend to have answers, though sometimes he promised to pass a question along to Moses. What he offered was his attention, proof that their thoughts and observations, their questions, their lives mattered to someone in authority. Perhaps more than anything else, more even than the battle experience, it was Joshua's attentive leadership that kept the peace among these men. Everything else could be borne if they knew that their lives had meaning beyond the moment.

After all, that was what Joshua needed, too.

Sometimes, though, he walked the perimeter alone, and sometimes walked out beyond, into the trails made perhaps by animals, perhaps by marauders, perhaps by shepherds. Maybe Moses walked here with his sheep one summer, thought Joshua. Maybe the Lord spoke to him here, or heard his prayer. He even thought of praying here himself, but then scorned his own thought. Was it the stones he knelt on that made a man a prophet? Not likely. It was the purity of his heart. And Joshua knew his heart was not pure, that it was filled with such a mixture of desires and dreams, not all of them noble, that he doubted the Lord thought much of him at all. Instead of trying to become like Moses, the best he could do was try to be useful to Moses in trying to accomplish his work. If only Joshua could understand what, exactly, that work was supposed to be. Israel was out of Egypt, yes, but what now? Why were they going to the holy mountain? The Lord had obviously chosen the Israelites as his people, but was that an end in itself, or were they supposed to accomplish something in his name?

He was on one such contemplative, self-doubting walk when he came across an old man, a middle-aged woman, a donkey bearing a tent and supplies, and a flock of children, the oldest of whom was a twelve-year-old boy.

"Peace be unto you," said Joshua.

"And to you," said the old man, "peace."

"My name is Joshua, the son of Nun, of the tribe of Ephraim in the house of Israel."

The old man's smile broadened considerably. "Israel!" he cried. "Then we're here!"

These didn't look like ruffians—indeed, they looked like people who needed protection from men like Amalek's crew. "You haven't told me your name, friend."

"Jethro. I'm a priest, a Midianite. I serve a village not far from here as the crow flies, but several days' journey when you take back trails to avoid the robbers who prey on travelers."

"You're not a half-mile from the camp of Israel," said Joshua. "I can lead you there."

"Do you know Moses ben Amram?" asked the old man.

"We all know him," said Joshua. "He's the prophet of the Lord God of Israel. He leads us and judges us in the name of God."

The old man and the middle-aged woman exchanged smiles. "Well, Joshua, son of Nun, I'm bringing you some stray children of Israel."

"Of Israel? Israelites, already here in the desert?"

"Israelites who have been waiting for their father to come home, and now he's here, and they've come to join him."

"Who is he? I can take you directly to him, if I know his tribe."

"Levi," said the woman.

"Then I can take you to Aaron, he knows everyone in Levi."

"No," said the woman, "I think you should take us directly to my husband."

Joshua was about to protest that he couldn't be expected to know every member of every tribe, when it finally dawned on him whose family would have been waiting here in the desert for him to return from Egypt.

"Are you Zeforah?" he asked her. "Are these the children of the prophet?"

"I *am* Zeforah," she answered, "but these are merely the children of shepherds."

The oldest boy spoke up. "My father *is* the prophet!"

But a stern look from his mother silenced him. "What he means is that his father, a shepherd, was given a message by the Lord, which he took to Egypt several months ago. Will you take us to him?"

And as Joshua led the way back along the trail to the camp, he heard Zeforah, with gentleness but great firmness also, tell her children that while their father was doing important work in the camp, this did not make his children more important than any other children. "You are the most important children in the world to your father and to me," she said, "but to other people, you're simply the children of shepherds."

"Father's a shepherd *and* a prophet," the boy said. "Aren't we just as much his children?"

"But a shepherd, just like a king, can pass his possessions on to his children. A prophet, on the other hand, teaches what he knows of the Lord to everyone, for it doesn't belong to him or his family, and those who are faithful become the heirs of God, not of the prophet."

"So Father doesn't love us any more than any other child?"

"Father loves you more than life itself," said Zeforah. "But if you are ever to join him in his great work, it has to be because of your own faithfulness in serving the Lord. It's between you and God, not between you and your father."

"But if somebody asks us, Is the prophet Moses your father, are we supposed to lie?"

"Gershom," she said sharply, "you understand me perfectly. You're just being contrary."

Sheepishly the boy said, "Oh, I know. You don't want us strutting around acting important."

A younger brother piped up. "Gershom doesn't know how to do anything *else.*"

"See how I'm not hitting him, Mother?"

"Let me not hear of you punishing him later, either. As for you, Eliezer, I'm ashamed that I heard you speak ill of your own brother in front of a stranger."

Joshua realized, with amusement, that he was the stranger.

"Sorry, Mother," said Eliezer. "Sorry, Gershom."

"I forgive you," said Gershom, but in deep round tones that made it a joke. "I forgive, I forgive, I forgive you."

Zeforah only sighed, while Jethro chuckled. "How much

farther?" he asked Joshua quietly. "I've already spent two days hearing the conversation of children."

Despite old Jethro's wry comment, Joshua had heard enough to know what the prophet's children were being taught, and what kind of woman Moses had married. He resolved then and there that if he could not do as well, he would not marry, for he would never be happy with a woman who lacked such wisdom and patience.

❊

In front of Aaron's tent, in the scant shade of the awning, three women sat together, carding wool and gossiping. "I was embarrassed for her, the poor thing."

"I suppose it's the way all the shepherd women dress, but—such coarse cloth!"

"Not that we'll have fine looms to work with this wool."

"The children were dirty."

"I saw that."

"Of course, out here in the desert *all* the children are dirty, since there's not enough water for bathing."

"But I'll bet those children have never bathed in their lives. They must have dirt on them that's as old as they are!"

"Well, if we didn't know it already, seeing his wife and children made it plain as day that Moses is just a man like anybody else. He was in the desert, he had his needs, and so he married what was available. I'll bet it isn't long before he takes other wives, much more educated and sophisticated women, out of Israel."

"Aaron says that Moses told him his wife *is* educated. That she taught him to read Hebrew."

"Reading Hebrew isn't reading. Hebrew's just the language we *speak*. All the books are in Egyptian."

"Well, do *you* read?"

"No, but I know the manners of Egypt. I know how to speak Egyptian, and very high-class Egyptian, too. I'll bet she doesn't know a word of it."

"I know you have to defend her, Elisheba, because she's your husband's sister-in-law, but we'll just take it for granted that you said all the nice things. It'll save time."

They laughed.

"I'm sure she's a sweet girl," said Elisheba. "I haven't had much chance to talk with her yet. Her children are modest enough, though the oldest boy *is* a talker, speaking right up in adult company as if he expected his opinions to be heard."

"Well there you are, no discipline."

"I suppose it's natural for the son of the prophet to be full of himself."

"Well, just because somebody's related to the prophet doesn't mean he should lord it over other people."

There was a moment's stunned silence, and then the woman realized her mistake. "But you can't think I was referring in any way to your husband Aaron! Why, he earned his own place in Israel long before Moses came back from the desert—in fact, before Moses even left the palace."

"I think Aaron would have been important in Israel even if his brother *hadn't* been a prince of Egypt and then the prophet of God. He *earned* his place."

"Now, please, don't worry that you've offended me," said Elisheba. "I know my husband's true worth."

"And so do we. So does everyone! In fact, some of us have been saying it's quite shameful the way Moses has to do everything and Aaron is just there to run errands for him."

"I never thought of it as errand-running," said Elisheba.

"Well, no, I was only repeating what others have said, who don't understand how important Aaron's work is . . ."

"In fact, many of us feel that Aaron has been shamefully neglected. Does Moses think he's the only one the Lord has ever spoken to? Didn't Aaron's own staff turn to a snake?"

"Aaron doesn't care about who gets the credit," said Elisheba. "All the glory belongs to the Lord."

"Well of course he'd feel that way."

"Not everyone does. Some think Moses takes too much upon himself."

"Setting himself up as a judge. As if just because he grew up in the house of Pharaoh he has some special wisdom."

"Or pretending that God gives him every judgment he makes! Why, it's well known that he plays favorites. If you just talk piously enough and bow *down* then he'll decide your way—"

"Honestly, Elisheba, we don't know how Aaron keeps his patience. Aaron's the one who shared Israel's burden all those years while Moses was getting flies fanned away from his face. And while Moses was out in the wilderness herding sheep and making babies with his little shepherd girl, Aaron was there in the brickyards, bearing the burden of slavery. It just makes my blood boil sometimes, to see Aaron put in second place—"

"It was all well and good for Moses to lead us while we were escaping from Egypt. But now it's just Israel, and we should be led by a *real* Israelite who understands us."

"And the way Moses puts the tribe of Levi last all the time. When a man has some authority, he's supposed to use it to help his kinfolk, isn't he? He simply has no sense of how things are done in Israel."

"I tell you, Elisheba, Israel would be better off if Aaron were the one in charge of things."

"Now, please, I don't think I should hear things like that," said Elisheba.

A fourth woman emerged from the tent. It was Miriam.

"Oh," said Elisheba. "Miriam. Did you have a nice sleep?"

"Yes, I did," said Miriam.

"I didn't know you were inside the tent," said one of the women.

"Clearly," said Miriam. "But you *did* know that the bright cloud of the Lord's presence stands almost directly overhead."

The women glanced up. "Well, if a person can't speak her mind . . ."

"Perhaps a person should clean up her mind before inviting others in to see it," said Miriam.

"I'm not going to apologize for a thing I said."

"Certainly not to me," said Miriam. "I'm not the one you were stabbing in the back."

"I think you're a fine one to talk. It's not as if *you* haven't said some pretty nasty things about people. Everyone knows that the reason Miriam hasn't married is because she has a tongue that leaves bloody wounds."

"If my tongue is a knife, it makes its wounds on a man's face, not on his back," said Miriam. "And you have never heard me speak against the Lord's anointed."

"Oh, pay no attention to her. Everyone knows she's besotted with Moses every since he was a baby. He can do no wrong."

"Moses knows that I don't always agree with his decisions," said Miriam. "And Aaron is my brother as much as Moses is."

"That's not how it looks to anybody else. Is it, Elisheba."

Elisheba put up her hands. "I've hardly said a thing in this whole conversation and I'm not starting now."

Miriam turned on her sister-in-law. "Yes, that's right, you *haven't* said a thing. For instance, you might have said, 'I won't hear such disloyalty against the one the Lord God of heaven chose to be his prophet.' Or you might have said, 'My husband serves the Lord exactly as the Lord has asked of him, and desires nothing more.' Or you might simply have said, 'It's not appropriate for me to hear opinions like these.'"

"I did say that!" protested Elisheba.

"Not until after you had sat quietly and listened to everything they had to say, which gave them the clear impression that you agreed with their envious backbiting."

"We didn't get any such impression."

"You certainly seem malevolent toward your own sister-in-law, Miriam. It's a wonder she still lets you in her tent."

"But she'll always want *you* to visit," said Miriam, "because you save her the trouble of finding her own words to express the disloyalty in her heart."

"I am loyal to my husband," said Elisheba icily.

"If you were loyal to your husband," said Miriam, "you wouldn't encourage the envy and resentment and ambition that have been his weakness all his life."

"I should think," said Elisheba, "that you would be the last to criticize envy in others."

Now that the quarrel had shifted to Elisheba and Miriam, the others were quick to make their simpering apologies. "I think we should let you two have this conversation privately."

"Next time let us know when you have a listener in your tent, Elisheba."

"I didn't know she was there," said Elisheba sweetly.

"Of course she didn't," said Miriam. "Or hypocrisy would have required a very different sort of pretense than she was giving you before."

"I see that you truly *are* loyal," said Elisheba. "For instance, you would never dream of speaking ill of your brother's wife."

The women, wide-eyed and full of the best gossip of the week, quickly headed off to begin spreading it, knowing they could end their tale with the truthful claim that "Of course I left right away, so I don't know what they said when they *really* got into the fray."

They couldn't guess that as soon as the audience was gone, silence settled between Miriam and Elisheba. And when the silence was broken, it was with a very different tone. "I hope you won't tell Moses what was said today," said Elisheba.

"Shouldn't he know?" asked Miriam.

"I really *don't* agree with what these women said. You don't understand how it is, Miriam. Most people avoid me because they think I'm too proud to want to speak to them, since I'm Aaron's wife. I feel as though I've lost all my real friends."

"These aren't real friends either, Elisheba. You know that if I hadn't spoken, they would have gone to *their* friends and told them, 'I was talking to Aaron's wife Elisheba, and I really think she's upset at how badly treated Aaron is.'"

"But I never said that," said Elisheba.

"You don't have to say it. It was said in your presence."

"And I denied it. You heard me."

"Elisheba. You know. You *know* that's not the story they intended to tell."

"Well, now they have a better one. You and me fighting like cats."

"If it's any consolation," said Miriam, "I'm the one who'll come out looking like a demon, while you're the sainted suffering loyal wife."

Elisheba burst into tears. "Miriam, Aaron really *is* unhappy, and I don't know why. He won't talk to me."

"Maybe he's ashamed of what's making him unhappy."

"He has the thing he always said he wanted," said

Elisheba. "Israel is out of Egypt. God dwells among us. And yet instead of facing every day with joy, he gets up as if he were already weary and comes home as if his life were nothing but grief. He hardly speaks to me or the children."

"I don't know," said Miriam. "I don't know what passes between a husband and wife."

"Please don't say that," said Elisheba. "You say that and it makes it impossible for me to talk to you because I feel like everything I say about Aaron will hurt you because you're unmarried. I know perfectly well that you had your chances to marry and you made your choice. And I also know that God speaks to you and you're very wise and Miriam, I need wisdom."

The tears flowing down her face belied any notion of hypocrisy now. Miriam put a hand on her shoulder. "Elisheba, all I know is this. You can't make a man happy by comforting him. He'll only be happy when he feels right with the Lord. So maybe all you can do is treat him like the prophet in your own home. Don't sympathize with him, because your sympathy will only diminish him in his own eyes."

"Don't sympathize with him?" asked Elisheba. "But if I don't, who will?"

"No one should," said Miriam. "What he needs is your high expectations, to help him become the kind of man who is filled with joy. Your sympathy only encourages him in his belief that he's somehow being mistreated."

"Are you sure he isn't?"

"If he is, it's the Lord doing it, not Moses. And that's the real reason why he's unhappy, Elisheba—because he knows, deep in his heart, that for some reason the Lord is not fully satisfied with him. Only when he's right with the Lord will he be happy."

"Then there's nothing I can do at all."

"I've told you what you can do," said Miriam.

"But I think you're wrong," said Elisheba. "I think a man should have a place where someone loves him even if he's not perfect yet. I know that's what *I* need sometimes, and he gives that to *me*."

Miriam chuckled dryly. "Well, it's certainly helped *you* be a better person."

Elisheba recoiled as if she had been slapped. Her back straight, she spoke to Miriam coldly. "Forgive me, Miriam. I forgot, for a moment, that I was speaking to a judge."

"You weren't, Elisheba. I'm sorry, I shouldn't have—"

But Elisheba was on her feet and disappeared at once into her tent, drawing the flap closed behind her.

Miriam was left alone in the shade of the awning. She looked around at the camp of Israel, tent after tent. Some of the gold they carried had gone to buy more tents from the traders who now flocked to them; nearly every family had a tent of their own now. They were adapting to the pastoral life, to the rhythms of the camp. They were also adjusting to a life surrounded by miracles. They gathered their bread like dew every morning, a direct gift from God, and yet because it happened every day they forgot what a miracle it was. Human beings are too adaptable, Miriam concluded. We lose too quickly our ability to be surprised. We forget too quickly that everything we have is a gift, and who gave it to us.

And I need to learn how to speak the truth to people in a way that doesn't make them see me as their enemy.

※

It was well after dark when Moses returned to his tent, and even then, there were two more conversations at the tent door.

When he came inside, Zeforah was just putting the youngest back to sleep.

"Did I wake her?" he whispered.

"Does it matter?" she said with a smile. "You do your work, and I do mine."

Moses knelt before her and kissed her. She threw her arms around his neck and kissed him back wholeheartedly. "Talk to me," she whispered in his ear.

"We're both tired," he said. "And we shouldn't wake the children."

"Walk with me outside. Just for a few minutes."

So they walked among the tents, his arm across her shoulder, their heads bowed so their soft voices wouldn't carry to other ears. "What did you want to talk about?"

"Nothing," said Zeforah. "I just wanted the sound of your voice, talking to me. We used to talk all the time, about everything. About scriptures, about the children, about Egypt, about the whole world. Now . . . everything I know about what happened in Egypt has been told to me by others and I'm not even sure which parts of it are true. I miss you, Moses."

"And I miss you. You have no idea how frustrating it is, day after day, but they give me no peace. It's maddening to know you and the children are here in the camp and then I never see you and when I get home I'm so tired I just . . ."

"You need to sleep. It was selfish of me to . . ."

"No, Zeforah, no, really. It feels so good just to be alone with you."

Then they both looked up, glanced around at the thousands of tents spreading as far as the eye could see in every direction, then up at the pillar of fire only a little way off, and they both dissolved in silent laughter at their own predicament. "Zeforah," Moses finally said, "the best I can say is, in my heart I'm with you all the time. When I sit in judgment, I hear your wise voice in the back of my mind, telling me the sensible, fair thing to do. Reminding me of this scripture or that."

"Trust me, you're just imagining that," said Zeforah. "Because what I'm really doing is stopping children from hitting each other and trying to keep Gershom and Eliezer working on their reading and—but here's the funny thing—I feel like I have *you* there with me. As if everything I say to them, I'm storing up to show it to you later. To say, Moses, you should have heard what Gershom said, or Eliezer, or any of the others, what a man he's becoming, what a woman she'll be. It's all done for your eyes. Or no, not really, it's all done as if you were there watching, that's the truth. Because we *are* together, aren't we?"

"We became one person together, there in the hills, watching the sheep," said Moses. "When I stood before Pharaoh, he told me once that he knew everything I knew because I had taught him, and I wanted to tell him that he had no idea who I was, because I wasn't the same person he knew. And do you know what the difference is? You. Because you were there, inside my mind, inside my heart. You were my teacher. I prayed as you taught me to pray. I learned about God with you at my side, guiding me. I learned about life because you loved me and gave me these children. So the man Pharaoh was looking at—he couldn't possibly see me or understand anything about me because he didn't know *you.*"

She held him tightly then. "Is that true? I want it to be true of you, because it's how I feel."

"God knows it's true," said Moses. "When God wanted to make me into a prophet, he took me out of Egypt and put me in your hands."

"In my heart."

They clung to each other there among the tents of Israel. Then they went back to their tent, back to their children, and gratefully slept the few hours they had for sleeping before dawn.

✵

The line of people waiting for judgment was already long when Moses got to his judgment seat soon after sunrise. His heart sank when he saw them. Didn't anybody learn from what the previous decisions had been? Of course not. Everybody was absorbed in his own life and had no idea what other decisions were needed. What Moses should be doing was copying out the scriptures for other people to read, so they could learn God's teachings for themselves. Or teaching people directly. Or writing down the story of the Lord's dealings with Israel during his own life. But instead his life was consumed by the need of the people for judgment. He kept thinking that soon things would calm down, that he'd have more time. But he could see no end to it, and he was close to despair.

Of course, he knew that at any time he could send people away and tell them to come back tomorrow. That was what Pharaoh did, hearing only a few cases that were most interesting. But Pharaoh had other institutions to depend on. The priests handled much of what the people needed — but who were the priests in Israel? That's what he needed, a priesthood to teach the people. He'd have to ask the Lord if he could have priests, the way Jethro had ordained him. Then he'd ask the Lord for a couple of spare years in which to train them as Moses had been trained. . . .

No, he was dreaming. There was nothing he could do. The whole burden fell on him, and he couldn't get it off his shoulders long enough to even think about training somebody else to help him.

"Moses!"

The voice sounded angry. Well, it wouldn't be the first time some angry petitioner had tried to cut ahead of his place in line.

"Moses, you're going to talk to me right now!"

He knew that voice. He looked up to see Jethro pushing his way through the crowd, ignoring complaints and curses from the people in line.

On impulse, Moses rose to his feet. "It's my father-in-law," he said with a sheepish smile to the people whose stories he had been listening to. "You know how it is. I'll just be a minute." And without waiting for the people to protest that he could certainly finish *their* case first, Moses bounded from the judgment seat to meet Jethro, take him by the shoulder, and let the old man's momentum carry them both away from the crowd and into Moses' tent.

"What are you doing, Moses? Don't you love these people?"

"I'm doing my best, that's what I'm doing."

"No you're not. You're doing your worst. Wearing yourself out!"

"I can't help it that there are so many people here."

"Right, and you think they're grateful for your hours of service? At the back of the line there's nothing but complaint about how long everything takes and did you bring them out into the desert so they could die in line?"

"We try to keep things moving smoothly and they don't *have* to wait, we take names and—"

"Foolishness. The problem isn't the process here. The problem is *you*."

"I can't do justice if I don't hear the case."

"No, you can't do justice at all because there's no possibility of this ever ending and you're going to die of exhaustion and *then* what will happen to my neglected daughter and her neglected children? You see! I put a lot of effort into raising Zeforah and you're going to waste all that by dying and leaving her a widow thrown back on *my* resources."

"You didn't have to put any effort into raising Zeforah. She mostly raised herself."

Jethro paused and thought about that. "Well, that's true. So I'm back to my claim that you're not serving Israel well. You need to set up other judges to hear the lesser cases. Aren't there elders in every tribe? Let them do the judging and then you hear only the hard cases. For an hour or two a day."

"Well of course I want to do that, Jethro. But when will I *train* them? When will I teach them the scriptures?"

"Oh, I see. You're doing such a good job of that *now*."

"I invited them all to watch me giving judgment so they could learn."

Jethro rolled his eyes. "I'm sure they all sit there avidly, listening to every word."

"Nobody has lasted more than half an hour, except Aaron, and his patience seems infinite. And Hur, but he's not listening, he's managing the line."

"Good. Those are your first two choices as judge. In fact, they should stand beside you as general judges of Israel, so they only hear appeals, too."

"You still haven't solved my problem of how to teach them when I don't have time to breathe!"

Jethro laughed incredulously. "*This* is why I say *you're* the problem. First, do you think you're the only man with a sense of fair play and decency? And isn't that what you rely on in most of your judgments?"

"No, I base my decisions on the scriptures."

"You base your *explanations* on the scriptures, but you make your decision first. That's how you decide which stories from the scriptures to tell to buttress your case."

"Does it matter?"

"Call men to serve as judges, get them busy so they take this load off your shoulders. Each one of them will have only a small fraction of this burden, and so they'll have time enough during each day for you to gather the judges and teach them And since they'll actually be judging people, they'll have questions for you. They'll have experience. They'll even suggest things that you never thought of and *you'll* learn."

"It sounds wonderful, but I don't know these men well enough."

"One man never knows another man completely anyway. If you want advice, doesn't your brother Aaron know them all? That's the impression I get. And besides, it doesn't have to be up to you. Ask the Lord! Suggest the people you want to have as judges, and let the Lord tell you what he thinks!"

"I thought if he wanted me to have help in the judging he would have—"

"He would have wanted you to think for yourself. Moses, I think you're a wonderful boy, but didn't Hatshepsut teach you anything about good government?"

"She taught me to rely on *highly trained* people to share the burden of—"

"Exactly! That's what she did! And what good was all their high training? Where were they when Tuthmose came to kill her?"

"What's your point here, Jethro?"

"My point is that training is no substitute for faithfulness, and training can come while doing. You weren't ready to be a prophet either, when the Lord called you. But you trusted in him to give you what you lacked, because Israel needed you to have it. Do you think that process was only for you? The Lord will do that over and over again. He'll help you choose the men to do the job, and he'll also help them do it, if they ask him."

Moses was about to offer another argument, when he stopped himself and laughed wryly. "You know what I was doing? I was explaining why *I* was the only one fit to do the job."

"Yes, I *knew* that was what you were doing."

"And yet when I was thinking of praying for help, what idea popped into my mind? Priests! I needed a priesthood to help me."

"There you have it. But don't wait until you have people willing to devote their lives to the priesthood. Appoint judges now, and make them priests later. Tell me you agree."

"I do agree, now that you've helped me see it."

"Good. Then it was a good thing I came here."

"Stay, then! Be the first of my judges! Train the men who will be my priests!"

"I trained *you.* That was hard enough. And if you need my advice, ask your wife. She knows everything I ever knew, and a lot more besides."

"It would be nice to have time to talk with her."

"Well then. It's decided. Now go out there and tell the people you're through with judgment for the day."

"They'll be angry!"

"So let them go find *another* camp with the pillar of the Lord's presence and manna on the ground every morning!"

Moses laughed. "Everything seems so clear when you explain it, and so muddy when I try to see it myself."

"That's what old people are for! We speak our minds! Besides, the spirit of God tells you that what I'm saying is true—that's why it seems so clear. Now I'm going to go take a nap while you send that lovely line of people home."

Jethro strode out of the tent and Moses came out at a more thoughtful pace right after him. From the shocked looks on the faces of people nearby, he realized that they had heard every word of the conversation—not surprising, since Jethro's voice could carry across a valley. The more they heard, the better they'd understand that this wasn't his idea.

Moses stood in front of his judgment seat and addressed the crowd. "I will hear no more cases today."

A moan of disapproval and disappointment rose from the crowd.

"From now on, the first thing you do is try to settle your problems peacefully between each other. And I mean *try.* If you can't bring witnesses who can prove that you have tried to reconcile the case, it won't get heard. Second, I'm going to appoint judges in every tribe. If you don't like their decision, the council of elders in that tribe will decide whether you should have the right to appeal to me. And then, the Lord has given me two trusted counselors who will hear cases at least as often as I do—Aaron and Hur. If they are your judge, it has the same force as if I were giving judgment." Moses looked at Aaron and Hur. "I hope neither one of you is going to argue with me about it?"

"I don't have your knowledge of the scriptures," said Hur.

"Then you'll enjoy coming to the school I'm starting. A school for priests and judges." He raised his voice again to the whole group. "Go home now! If your matter really is important, you'll remember it in a few days!"

Without waiting for questions or arguments, Moses walked away from the judgment seat, saying as he went,

"Aaron, Hur, come help me choose the first of the judges in each of the tribes."

By the next day at noon, messengers were going to every tribe and elders were being called in to receive their appointment from Moses. By the day after, there were at least two judges in every tribe, and Moses was teaching for hours a day.

He also got home just at sundown and spent the evening talking and playing with his children, and after they went to bed, he and Zeforah talked and talked into the night.

"I knew what to do," said Moses. "Why couldn't I do it?"

"Maybe you needed permission from someone else," said Zeforah. "Or maybe you couldn't bear to let go of the responsibility for fear the people would stop needing you."

"And yet I know perfectly well that the most important work ahead of me is to get Israel to a point where I'm *not* needed. Where everyone is hearing the word of the Lord in their own hearts, and obeying God out of pure love for him and all his works."

"Do you think you can accomplish that?"

"Before I die, I swear I will."

"Good. Then you'll live forever." She laughed and kissed him.

He kissed her back, but he didn't laugh. The people had seen God's power so clearly—how could she doubt that they were ready to become the Lord's people in fact as well as name?

# C o v e n a n t s

W hen the camp of Israel formed at the base of Mount Sinai, the pillar of cloud grew to envelop the entire mountain. This was the place to which God had brought his people, the goal of the journey.

On the day they arrived, Moses returned from the cloud with a simple message from the Lord:

"You have seen what he did to the Egyptians for your sake, and how he bore you on eagles' wings, and brought you to him. Now, Israel, if you will obey his voice and keep his covenant, you shall be his own dear treasure, beloved above all other people, and you will serve the whole of God's earth as a kingdom of priests, as a holy nation."

Led by the judges of every tribe, the people answered: "All that the Lord has asked, we will do."

At the Lord's command, Moses told the people to wash themselves and their clothes, to make themselves clean and holy, ready to receive the Lord on the third day. Strict bounds were set about the mountain, so no one would stray inadvertently too close to the presence of the Lord.

At the beginning of the third day, thunder and lightning came from the cloud, and the clear sound of a trumpet, and the people trembled at the coming of the Lord. Moses led the people out of the camp, and brought them up to the boundary marked for them, as the cloud roiled down the mountain and stood before them. The trumpet sounded longer and louder. Moses cried out to the Lord within the hearing of the people, and then in answer they all heard the voice of the Lord:

"Moses, come to me at the top of the mountain."

Alone Moses walked into the cloud, and the people waited. When he returned, a few hours later, he reminded them again to respect the boundary, for the danger to mortal bodies unpurified by God was great. Then he stretched forth his hand to Aaron. "Come with me, my brother," he said. "The Lord wants you with me to receive his law."

So Aaron walked with Moses into the bright thundering cloud of the presence of the Lord.

When they returned that night, they taught together the law that the Lord had given them, repeating God's words to the people. "I am the Lord your God who brought you out," said Moses. "You shall have no other God to set against me. You shall not carve images or bow down to any God but me, for I will hate whoever hates me, and the sons of his sons. But I will love whoever loves the Lord."

"Once you take the name of the Lord upon you," said Aaron, "you shall be bound by it, and your oath shall not be in vain."

"Remember the Sabbath day," said Moses, "to keep it holy."

"Honor your father and mother," said Aaron, "that you may live forever in the land that I will give you."

"You shall not kill, or commit adultery."

"You shall not steal, or witness to a lie."

"You shall not covet what your neighbor has."

As they spoke, the thunder and lightning behind them punctuated their words, affirming to the people that it was the Lord's words they were repeating. The people became afraid, for they knew that they had already sinned against some of these commandments, and they begged Moses and Aaron: Let us hear your words, gladly, but don't let the voice of the Lord come to us, or we'll die.

So Moses and Aaron continued to teach them, elaborating upon the law. The old desert law of vengeance was swept away. Where once a man would answer a word with a blow, a blow with a wound, a wound with a murder, and murder with two or three or five murders in the family of the wrongdoer, now the Lord set strict bounds. Vengeance would come, not from the individual or his family, but from the law and the community as a whole, and it would not be heavier than the offense, but would be exactly proportionate. An eye for an eye, a tooth for a tooth, and nothing more. And the people recognized the mercy of the Lord, setting them free from the blood feud of anarchy on the one hand, and from the arbitrary rule of tyrants on the other. The law would be fixed and the judges would carry it out with the consent and help of the community, and neither ruler nor any individual would have the right to set it aside and exact more or less than justice. It would be the foundation of peace and freedom in Israel.

They were also taught that they must share the bounty of the earth with the poor, and when lending to the poor they were not to profit from it, but to take their repayment without interest. And they were taught how to build their altars, and how to choose the animals they would offer as sacrifice.

And if they made a covenant to obey these laws, and kept that covenant, the Lord would give them the land of Canaan from the Red Sea to the Sea of the Philistines, and from the desert to the river. They would be charged with the duty to drive out the inhabitants of the land — Amorites and Hittites, Perizzites and Canaanites, Hivites and Jebusites — for they had once known the name of God and rejected him, worshiping Baal and Astarte in their high places and their groves, and the land would no longer bear their abominations. The people of Israel must make no treaty with them or permit any of them to remain in the land, for if any of them remained it would be a constant temptation and snare to Israel.

Moses wrote down the words of the Lord and caused them to be read again to the people, and again, until all had heard and knew the covenant they were about to take. And when Moses asked them, they declared with one voice, "We will do all that the Lord has said."

Moses called young men to bring the animals for sacrifice, and upon altars they killed the beasts and burnt them to the Lord, and Moses took half the blood and put it in basins, and half the blood he sprinkled on the altars. And with the book of the law in his hand, he walked among the people and sprinkled on them the blood from the basins, saying, "Here is the blood of the covenant which the Lord has made with you concerning all these words."

With the blood of the covenant fresh on the people, Moses and Aaron took Aaron's two eldest sons, Nadab and Abihu, and seventy of the elders of Israel, and led them into the cloud. There with their own eyes they glimpsed the God of Israel, the terrible bright beauty of his loving face, his body as clear and pure as heaven, and it seemed to them that the ground under his feet was paved with sapphires. And when the elders returned to the people and told them what they had seen, the people wept and rejoiced at the mercy of God.

"This is only the beginning," said Moses. "The Lord has called me to go up into the mountain again, and receive from him a higher law and commandments, written on stone by the hand of God, to bring down to you, and teach to you."

And this time he took with him only Joshua, leaving Aaron behind him to govern the people, to be their judge and teacher and priest until Moses returned.

*

"Why me?" Joshua asked, as he followed Moses along the steep and challenging path up the mountain.

"I don't know," said Moses. "Why not you?"

Wavering between the thrill of having been chosen and terror at what might be expected of him, Joshua could have listed hundreds of reasons, but he distilled them all into one. "I've sinned."

Moses answered with laughter. "If the Lord used only perfect men as his servants, he would go unserved."

It was strange to Joshua, to hear the prophet laugh here in the midst of the cloud of the presence of the Lord. Ahead and behind they could see no more than a few yards, though the cloud also was light, and illuminated the rocks where they placed their hands and feet. "The Lord doesn't laugh at sin," said Joshua.

"Every sin is grief to the Lord," said Moses. "I laughed at your thought that your sin made it impossible for the Lord to choose you as his servant. Do you recognize that your sins were sins, or do you try to make them into virtues?"

"No, I name them for what they are."

"And do you pretend to others that you are not sinful?"

"I've never tried to pretend such a thing."

"And when the law was placed before you, and I called on Israel to make the covenant, did you reject your sins and put them behind you and promise to commit no more of them?"

"I did, Moses, but I fear that I won't have the strength to obey all the commandments!"

"And yet did you overcome that fear and follow me into

the cloud? Do you even now obey the Lord and climb this stony path, rather than hang back and let fear rule you?"

"How could I say no to the Lord?"

"And how could the Lord say no to you? Your heart is pure at this moment, and as for the sins in your past, the price will be placed upon a willing sacrifice and paid for you, as long as you hold fast to your repentance."

"Then I owe every step I take up this mountain to that sacrifice," said Joshua.

"As do I," answered Moses.

❖

Joshua? He took Joshua with him? Aaron was stunned. What could this mean?

Miriam, of course, had an answer at once, when he made the mistake of asking her that question. "You've already seen God," she said. "Joshua didn't."

"So why didn't the Lord include him among the seventy elders?"

"The Lord didn't include me then, and he didn't include me now, either," said Miriam. "But that doesn't undo all the gifts the Lord has given me up to now."

"And you don't feel even a trace of . . . surprise?"

"I'm always surprised by the Lord," said Miriam, "and so I'm never surprised at being surprised."

"I don't resent it," said Aaron. "I'm just puzzled."

"Do you have to have it all?" asked Miriam. "He brought your two eldest sons with you to see the face of God. Isn't it plain he intends to give you gifts that you will pass on to your children? You went with Moses to receive the law and came back and the two of you taught the words of the covenant side by side, because your ears heard the same things that Moses' ears heard. He set you beside the prophet and made you his

equal in giving the law to the people. And when the Lord
called Moses to the mount again, he left you to govern the
people. Explain to me how Joshua's going with Moses somehow hurts or diminishes you."

"It doesn't, it doesn't," protested Aaron. "I don't know why
it worried me. But I heard that Joshua was going and it made
me afraid."

"I'll tell you why," said Miriam.

"Oh, you know why I feel what I feel?"

"You're afraid that the Lord will notice that you're unworthy after all."

"The Lord is perfect. He already knows my weakness."

"Ah," said Miriam. "But do you?"

"And what does *that* mean?" Aaron demanded.

But she was already walking away from him. Elisheba
took her place at Aaron's side. "I don't know why you even
listen to her. She just resents you because at last the Lord has
lifted you up to put you beside Moses where you belong, and
now you govern the camp of Israel, and the Lord hasn't given
*her* any of the authority she so obviously craves."

"I don't need to hear this, Elisheba," he said.

"Yes you do," she said. "You are finally in your rightful
place, as the leader of the Israelites."

"Moses is still the leader, Elisheba."

"Moses is up on the mountain. You're the judge who rules
Israel here on the ground." She squeezed his arm. "I'm proud
of you, Aaron."

Elisheba could not know it, but her words stung Aaron
deeply. He did not want her to be proud of him because he
was judge. He wanted her to be proud of him because he was
righteous and strong and good. Why should he be proud of
being judge? He was terrified. Until now, he had had Moses

beside him, and everything he said and did, he knew Moses could correct it if he was wrong. And while he resented the corrections when they came, he also felt safe knowing that when his best efforts fell short, Moses would keep his mistakes from doing harm. Who was there now to fall back on? Moses was with the Lord.

And Joshua was with Moses. That ambitious boy had somehow hurtled over Aaron and now *he* was alone with Moses as he went to get whatever it was the Lord intended to engrave on stone tables. Why did the Lord choose Joshua over Aaron at this moment? Having made Aaron a judge in Israel, were Moses and Joshua going to be raised higher yet, leaving Aaron behind? Had he been judged and found, if not *un*worthy, then less worthy?

How could Elisheba be proud of Aaron when the Lord placed him no higher than third among the children of Israel?

No, that was an unworthy thought. The Lord loved this people and had placed them in Aaron's hand. And *that* was what should worry him, that he might do something wrong and lose them. To be in a position of leadership, with all the Israelites looking to him, that was what Aaron had longed for in his heart of hearts for all these years. Now he had that position, and he had no idea what to do with it. Was he expected to do no more than handle judgment from day to day, and mark time until Moses returned? Would Moses then return and look at him in disappointment and say, You were given the trust of the Lord, and this is all you did? Or worse, Moses would look at him in horror and say, Aaron, didn't you understand anything? How could you fail so miserably? And Aaron would look around him and have no idea what he had done wrong. His humiliation would be complete.

I can't be the leader of Israel, he realized. I have no idea what I'm doing.

And yet, within the hour, he found himself sitting in the judgment seat, speaking calmly and making decisions in the cases that had been appealed from the tribal courts. Later in the day, he taught the elders and judges, and found that he knew the answers to their questions, or knew when he should say, Let's ask Moses that one when he returns. And in the evening, when, with knife in hand and his sons beside him, he slit the throat of a sacrificial goat and led the people in prayer, he realized that yes, he could do these things, and if they were enough to meet the needs of the people, then he must be good enough to lead them.

＊

Moses stopped abruptly. "Joshua," he said.

"I'm here."

"This is where the Lord wants you to wait."

Wait? Joshua had thought that, like Aaron, he would participate in the entire experience. But he was going to be set aside, at the last moment! Why, then, was he brought? "How long?" asked Joshua.

"Until I come back."

How long is *that*, Joshua wanted to ask. But he did not ask. He merely nodded and sat down in the midst of the fog and watched Moses as he climbed on out of sight.

＊

"What have I done to offend Elisheba?" asked Zeforah.

"Nothing, as far as I know," said Miriam. "Why?"

"She avoids me. When she can't, she speaks to me quite abruptly, as if we had quarreled and not made up yet. But we didn't quarrel. I only just met her."

Miriam chuckled, and it sounded as though there were malice in it. "Believe me, Zeforah, you and Elisheba *have* quarreled. Only you never knew it, and Elisheba knows the wrong is entirely on her side. So she's waiting for you to forgive her."

"But how can I forgive her, when I don't know that she's done me any wrong?"

"That *is* a quandary, isn't it?" said Miriam. "From my experience, this is how it will go. Right now she still feels guilty when she sees you, which makes her surly. Her surliness will make you shy. Your shyness will seem to her like aloofness, pride, even arrogance. This will make her resent you, and so her guilt will turn into anger. Thus, before more than a few days have passed, it will be all *your* fault. So my advice to you is to wait a few days, and then apologize to *her.*"

Zeforah listened to all this in silence. But then, after a few moments, she burst out laughing.

"So you see the humor in it?"

"You've just described my life with my sisters."

Miriam sighed and smiled wanly. "I wish I had had some sisters."

"Will you take volunteers?"

"What, a shepherd girl like you, entangled with babies, who doesn't even speak Egyptian?" asked Miriam.

Zeforah's shock only lasted until Miriam roared with laughter. "Oh, my. Is that how sisters do it? Tease each other?"

"Only if they're willing to get doused over the head with a bucket of water. Or worse."

"Oh." Miriam grew a little more sober. "So there are physical retaliations?"

"Beware the insects in the blankets."

"Mud in the underwear?" asked Miriam.

"That might be popular near the Nile, but in my country we wouldn't dare waste the water."

"Isn't it a shame we have to pretend to be adults?"

"Still, don't you wish more people would?"

Miriam smiled at that. "Nice to know Moses didn't marry a fool."

"Apparently you weren't willing to, either," said Zeforah.

"Actually, the men who were interested in me weren't fools," said Miriam. "They just weren't prophets."

"Neither was Moses, when I married him."

"There you are," said Miriam. "I had brothers, so I had no illusions about men. You had illusions, and so, by the grace of God, your dream of him actually became true."

"Moses suggested that you might want to learn to read Hebrew."

"You really do know how?" asked Miriam.

"I learned out of the scriptures, with my father's help."

"Teach me from the same books," said Miriam. "I'm getting old, but I'd like to read the scriptures for myself before I die."

*

Moses.

"Lord, how is it I can see your face without dying?"

My glory is upon you and sustains your life. I am the Lord your God, and Endless is my name, for I am without beginning of days or end of years. You are my son.

Your life has been shaped to be a shadow, a harbinger of the life of my Only Begotten Son. A child prophesied, a son under sentence of death, born to be at once a king and a servant, who grew to manhood and went out into the wilderness to meet his God and accept the mantle of his authority. A man who returns to his people and brings the power of God to bear against all the powers of the world, and delivers the children of God from the hands of the enemy by bringing them through the water to a safe place. A man who saved them from death by the blood of the lamb, a lawgiver, a just and merciful judge, a high priest, a prophet, at whose command water and bread are given to the people. Because of your work, there will be a people ready to recognize the Only Begotten of the Father when he comes, and obedient enough to receive the higher law that he will bring. For my Only Begotten is and shall be the Savior, full of grace and truth.

"The son in the nameless book. In whose name Zeforah prays. The sacrifice for sin."

I will show you what I have created. Not all, for you could not receive it or understand it, but I will show you the world you dwell in. See how it began.

✳

"You have no idea how hard it is on the people to wait, not knowing what will happen. If *anything* will happen."

Aaron smiled wanly. "Harubel, you seem to forget that I am also waiting, and I also don't know what will happen."

"Every other time Moses went up the mountain, he came back in the same day. Now it's been three. How do we know he didn't fall and break a leg? Or his neck?"

"God wouldn't let that happen."

"Do you *know* that, Aaron? The people need something to distract them. Something to comfort them, to take their minds off the long waiting, the fear."

"The presence of the Lord is comfort enough for anyone."

"For you, perhaps. Maybe no one will tell you the truth about what they feel. That's the loneliness of the ruler, that he never knows what anyone truly thinks."

"Please, Harubel, I'm not Pharaoh, I'm just an Israelite like any other."

"You saw the face of God, Aaron!"

"Harubel, you obviously have something in mind, so what is it?"

"I was trying to help you understand the mood of the people. I *could* come up with some kind of plan, I suppose, if you wanted."

"Plan for what?"

"To keep them from quarreling with each other. From fleeing the thunder and lightning from the mount."

"Their faith in God should be enough."

"Most of them haven't seen him."

"They don't need to see him to have faith!"

"They're not as strong as you. Don't you have any compassion, Aaron? Don't you understand what it's like for them? They're like children."

"And you and I are not?"

"Perhaps we are too, but slightly *older* children. We have to look out for them."

"Harubel, the plan we have is to teach the law to the people."

"And what do they do the rest of the day? Sit around and fret!"

"No, they have you to do that for them."

"Ah. Humor. I'm glad to see you still have your wit."

"Harubel, you don't represent the people. You represent your own scheme, and whatever it is, I don't want any part of it."

"But you *have* to be part of it! Aaron, you're the only one who *can* help them."

"Help them what?"

"No, I can see you aren't ready. Talk to me later, when you see chaos and terror among the people. When you see quarreling and stealing, oath-breaking and adultery, all because they live in constant fear and without a leader who is willing to fill them with joy and hope."

"Go on, get out of my tent. The people have made covenants and I expect them to be kept, which means no stealing, no oath-breaking, no adultery, and I'll thank you not to try to drum any up just to prove yourself right."

"Time will prove me right, Aaron. Moses will come down the mount, find the people fighting or fled, and he'll look at you and say, Couldn't you have done something?"

"Not another word, Harubel. Out."

✳

The whole sweep of the world's past moved past his eyes. So much of it made little sense to him. The plants arising from the ground, the animals appearing, first the lesser ones, then the greater, and finally the coming of human beings, and through it all the constant awareness of the will of God, speaking, calling forth the future out of the present. Let me hold onto some part of this, let it remain in my memory, let me have some understanding, he prayed, and prayed again, and even as the prayer was granted he cried in his heart, More! Let me hold more of this in my mind!

All your mind can hold, it will have, said the Lord.

The sweep of human history, the wanderings upon the earth, Moses saw them man by man, woman by woman, child by child. He saw them as God saw them, as individuals, each infinitely precious to the Lord, yet each burdened by his or her own contrary desires. And he felt God's agony of love, as his children, offered so much, kept turning away from the inheritance of joy in order to pursue the life of animals or the pride of rule over one another.

"O Lord, how do you keep your patience with us?"

In answer, the Lord showed him the prophets, each given as much of the truth as his mind could hold, his language could express, or his people could hear. They all knew more than they could say, and all said more than their listeners could understand or obey. Yet even among those who understood, there were always more than a few who saw the faithful as a flock to be sheared. These were not the weak and fallen children of the Lord, these were the willful rebels against the power of God.

"Why do you permit them?"

They must have their chance to show their brethren who they are.

"But what about the suffering they cause?"

The sufferers also show who they are, by how they respond to their grief and pain.

"But don't you already know all our hearts?"

What I know must be known by those of less perfect understanding. In every soul is goodness that might be, and evil that might be, and even though I know how much of each will come to be, the child must have his day to choose and show himself and all around him which he loves more: his appetites? his power? his safety? or the leap out of the self into service in the kingdom of God?

"Yet it is only there that the soul finds its greatness."

But they must choose it because they love the works of God, not because they seek their own greatness. So I hide the greatness from them, so their choice can be made for love alone.

"May I not tell them, then?"

You must tell them. But only the great-hearted will believe and act on what you tell. It is the downfall of evil, that it never sees far enough ahead. The enemies of God steal what pieces of power they can steal, not realizing that in the stealing, they destroy what they try to possess. When at last there is nothing left, they will wail to heaven, being in torment at their nothingness, envying the righteous who possess all things; but the law is irrevocable, that nothing can be owned forever unless it gives itself freely, and no one can rule forever except him who serves utterly.

And there in that moment, Moses saw how all time before and after pointed to the meridian of time, to the one who gave himself completely, and then arose perfect and received the ownership of all things, for all things gave themselves to him, trusting him to use his power only for their good. And together, creator and created, organizer and ordered, servant and served, ruler and ruled were united in perfect joy.

"Is this the Son?" asked Moses.

You were named for him, Moses, for the one who, brought low, will be lifted up.

And Moses saw the Son of God in all his glory, and recognized his face, and knew that he had known him before he was born, and loved him then; but now he loved him even more, for he understood the pains and temptations of mortal life, and the agony of sin and loss, and could feel the value and the cost of the gift the Son would give him. It was more than his mind could bear. He fell to the stones, weak, spent, unable to move, but filled with a sweetness that left him without tears enough to vent his joy.

For hours he lay there before he could summon strength enough to move.

"Moses."

He looked up, and a man stood in the air just beyond the edge of the cliff. The man's robe billowed in a wind that Moses could not feel. His smile was beautiful and seemed kind. He stretched out his hands toward Moses, and dazzling light fell from his fingertips. "Son of man," he said, "worship me."

"Who are you?" said Moses.

"Don't you know me?" The sweet face grew a little sad. Moses felt regret tug at his heart.

"I know who *I* am," said Moses. "A son of God, like the Only Begotten of the Father. Where is your glory, that I should worship you? For I could only see the face of God because his glory filled my body and sustained me, transfiguring me before him. But whoever you are, I can see you with my natural eyes. And this light that you scatter, it feels like darkness to me."

As if in answer, the light that flashed from the man grew brighter and brighter, until Moses had to avert his gaze.

"I can judge between you and God," said Moses. "You blind me with your light, but God enlightened me. I made my covenant with God that I would worship only him. Get away from here, Enemy, and stop trying to fool me. I'm here to learn from God, I have more questions I must ask him, and you're wasting my time when I need to be calling upon the Lord."

Still the man stood there, waving his arms, scattering light. Moses was tempted for a moment to pity him, but then remembered seeing in the vision of the Earth how this one hated the children of God and tempted them with lust for power and majesty. You are the one, Moses realized, who led Tuthmose away in his childhood, and taught him to kill for his own benefit and glory. You are the one who undoes all the good works of God, if you can find proud souls willing — eager — to believe your lies.

"Get away from here," Moses said with loathing.

Suddenly the kind face was gone, and in its place was the

face of scorn. "I am the Only Begotten of the Father," said the man. "Think of what you owe to me, and worship me!"

Now the light in the man's hands became fire, and he loomed larger and darker, and Moses felt the weakness of his body and he was afraid. "O God," he cried, "give me strength against our enemy." And in answer, he felt warmth flow through his body, and he rose to his feet. "Leave me, Enemy, Satan, for there is only One whom I will worship, the God of glory."

For a moment he was tempted to taunt Satan about how pathetic he was, compared to God, to heap scorn on the feebleness of his imitation of glory—tricks with light, when real glory was seen, not just with the eyes, but with the whole soul, body and spirit together. The moment he thought of spewing contempt upon Satan, however, he knew that this was just another way to serve Satan, by imitating him, and to the degree that he answered hate with hate and scorn with scorn, he became more like Satan and less like the Only Begotten of the Father. So he held his tongue, and spoke no poison with it. Instead, using the priesthood he was given under the hands of Jethro not so many months ago, he spoke the command that could not be disobeyed by any being of spirit:

"In the name of the Only Begotten, I command you to depart, Enemy."

The man wailed and wept, as if his body were being torn in pieces, and he writhed as if in agony; but as he did, he also shrank, and drew himself farther off, and farther, and finally he was utterly fled from Moses' presence.

As soon as Satan was gone, Moses felt his body filled again with the light of the Lord, and strength flowed into him. He stood upright, and heard a voice speak to his soul: You are blessed, Moses, for I have chosen you, and you shall be stronger than the sea, for it will obey you as if you were God.

I am with you, Moses, to the end of your days. For you will deliver my people, Israel my chosen, from bondage.

"But Lord, they are already out of Egypt."

Out of Egypt, but not yet free, for the one who fled from you just now is still their ruler, for they have not yet broken the shackles of sin and pride, and his whip falls heavy on their hearts, and his daily tally cannot be borne.

And for one moment, Moses' vision was utterly purified. He beheld — did not merely see but *saw* — every particle of the Earth he stood on, and every soul that dwelt on it. He saw it all as God saw it, comprehending it completely in the moment, knowing every being, great and small, and how they all fit together into one great whole, obedient to God, and of all these beings, only the humans, only the children of God, unable to comprehend how they all belonged together, and who they really were, and who God was; and so only the children of God rebelled against him, and lived in darkness though light was all around them and through them. The light shone in the darkness, but those blind of heart did not see it, did not know that it existed, and so staggered and stumbled and were injured and knew not why.

Even this was not enough, for suddenly Moses' vision was enlarged, and he comprehended with the same clarity not just Earth and all who dwelt on it, but all the other worlds that God had made, and all who dwelt on them, each calling their own world Earth, and all together forming an even greater whole, which existed only to bring joy to each being comprised in this great creation, as much joy as each was capable of receiving, according to the degree of service that each could deliver to the whole. And on all these worlds, the only ones who sorrowed were the children of God who had not yet given their hearts to him.

With his whole heart, Moses yearned to cry out to them, to show them what he could, in this bright moment, see.

But he knew that their eyes were shut to such a vision, and that if he shouted to them each would hear only the faintest whisper of his voice, and no two would hear the same; if he showed them what lay before their very eyes, they would see only the dimmest of shadows, not comprehending how much light was made invisible by their vanity, and no two of them would agree on what it was they saw.

"How did you make all this, and why?" Moses asked.

By the word of my power I made them; by the Son I created them, worlds without number. More than you can see, for many worlds have already finished their history and completed their work, and uncountable worlds are yet to be created, and even those you see now would be uncountable to men. But I count them all, for they are mine and I know them. As one world passes away, another comes to be; there is no end to my works, as there was no beginning. For this is my work and my glory, Moses, to bring to pass the immortality and eternal life of man.

To you it is given to write only an account of the world you stand on, for only the story of your world will help your brothers and sisters to know who they are and what they might become. Only the prophets who have dwelt upon your earth have spoken words that your sisters and brothers need to hear. And even many of the words you will write shall be withheld from those who would not be helped by hearing them.

"O Lord, may I not tell my wife and children? My brother

Aaron and my sister Miriam? May I not tell Joshua, who is only a little way off?"

In the hour when you speak to them, you will know how much it would be good for them to hear, and you will say only as much as would do them good. When they are ready for more, more will be given to them. But you may be sure that whatever you write will someday be had again among the children of men, for in the day when they have need of it I will raise up another like you, to write again what you have written.

✻

A spirit of darkness had descended on the camp of Israel, Aaron could feel it. He knew that most people were still keeping their covenants, waiting patiently for Moses to return; and they trusted in the Lord, for didn't they see the cloud of his glory on the mountain? Didn't they gather his manna from the ground every morning?

Yet it almost didn't seem to matter that most people meant well, and did well, for they were not the ones who did the talking, they were the ones who passed each day peaceably, without contention. What Aaron heard, what he saw, was the constant parade of complainers, quarrelers, faultfinders, telling him what other people were doing wrong, or demanding that he tell them what could not be known, or do for them what could not be done.

Even at home there was no respite, for Elisheba had her own catalogue of tales to tell, of people who regretted ever leaving Egypt. "You just need to take charge, Aaron. Get control of things. Let them see that things really *are* going to be better."

"How can I show them what should be obvious to anyone who's been awake at all for the past months?"

"This is your chance to make a difference, Aaron. Are you going to let it slip by and just mark time while Moses is on the mount? Isn't there something you can do to make them happy? Isn't that what God expects you to do?"

Leave me alone! "I don't know what God expects, except that he gave us laws and I'm supposed to teach the people how to live by them."

"Fine, you're teaching, but it's not enough, is it, because people just aren't happy!"

"You keep talking about 'people,' Elisheba, but who are these people? Are you one of them? Are you not happy?"

"How can I be happy until *you're* happy? And how can you be happy until you finally take your rightful place as the great benefactor of Israel? All the years you served Israel day and night. Even now, Moses is gone again. Show them who it is who really loves them!"

"*God* loves them, Elisheba."

"God they can't see. You they can."

"I can't talk about this anymore, Elisheba. You don't understand me, and I don't understand you."

"You're just afraid to offend Moses."

"I'm not afraid to offend anyone but God."

"But that's just my point! How could it offend God, for you to—"

"What's your plan, Elisheba?"

"Not *my* plan, Aaron. Simply what the people need, something visible, something they can *see*, to make them feel the greatness of the power of God. To make them feel like they have something comfortable and familiar—"

"All of this talk of yours, and it comes down to this," said Aaron. "You've become Harubel's message-bearer in my own home."

"Who is Harubel?" It was clear she honestly didn't know the man.

But it didn't change the fact that she was acting out his plan. Or someone's plan. "Tell me then, Elisheba, what particular visible thing would make the people feel comfortable?"

"I don't know, Aaron. Certainly none of the gods of Egypt—those were symbols of our slavery. But perhaps something from the glorious days when the Hyksos pharaohs ruled, and Joseph was remembered as the great vizier, and the Israelites were held in honor throughout the lands watered by the Nile!"

"Why are you giving speeches to me?"

"Because it's the speech you should give. I dream of it, Aaron, of you standing before the people raising a standard in the name of God. When we next go into battle, this is what would be raised up! When we offer sacrifice, the people would see it as the symbol of the Lord and gather to it!"

"The Hyksos bullcalf."

"The calf of sacrifice."

"Do you think for one moment that anybody would take it to be a symbol of the God of Israel?" said Aaron.

"They would if you told them so," said Elisheba. "Symbols mean what we choose to make them mean. The Hyksos called it a god but only because they didn't understand the truth the way we do."

"Do you know what rites are performed where this bullcalf is worshiped?" Aaron asked.

"Well, they certainly won't happen here—you'll see to that."

"Stop listening to whoever it is that tells you this nonsense," said Aaron. "It's unbearable to me that I have to hear such things in my own home."

"Oh, I'm wrong to want you to give the people what will keep them happy while they wait for Moses to finish whatever he's doing up there?"

"You took the covenant, too," said Aaron. "We are forbidden to make graven images."

"I know that," she said.

"So why are you asking me to make one?"

"Because . . . because. . . ."

She stood before him, confounded.

He gathered her into his arms and held her. "Elisheba," he whispered, "don't you see what they're doing to you? Using you to try to get me to do evil in the sight of God."

"They don't want evil, they're just trying to think of ways to heal the dissension and trouble among the people."

"They *are* the trouble, Elisheba. They're the ones quarreling and complaining, and then they come to you pretending to be benefactors willing to *heal* the quarreling and complaining, if you only give them what they want."

"Well what do *you* think they want, then?"

"They want to dance before the bullcalf, Elisheba. These people, the plagues taught them to fear the power of God, but they didn't lose their yearning to do the obscene things that pass for worship among those who danced before the calf."

"No!" said Elisheba. "You don't know these women, they would never. . . ."

"*You* don't know these women," said Aaron. "I can promise you, they already have, many times, and all they're trying to do is use *you* to get *me* to permit their abominations in the camp of Israel, right here where we can see the cloud of the presence of the Lord. They know if they did it themselves, most of the people would rise up in fury and stone them to death, which is what they would deserve as blasphemers and oathbreakers.

But if *I* give them a calf, with some nonsense about it being a symbol of the God of Abraham—"

"You're leaping to conclusions about people you don't even know."

"I know them," said Aaron. "I knew them in Egypt. I wish they had stayed there and hadn't come with us."

"You think you know them but these are my friends."

"They are not your friends. Speak to me no more about this."

"But—"

"Not another word."

❈

The goldsmith heated the wooden frame over a low fire. Within the frame, the hard-baked clay grew warm, and out of the vent at the bottom, melting wax slowly dripped, then faster and faster, collecting in the pan.

"All of this is useless, you know, unless you can get your hands on the gold," said the smith.

Harubel laughed. "Oh, we'll get it. In fact, Aaron will melt it down and pour it into the mold with his own hands."

"That'll be the day."

"You have no idea how unsophisticated these people are. It's like they're all children, clinging to these rules they've been taught, not even knowing what the *real* game is. They don't know what passion is, or pleasure, or even worship. All of this effort, and for what? The most boring god, the most boring worship, just standing there watching somebody go *swip* with a knife and then sprinkle blood around and say prayers. Why not just lie down and everybody have a nap."

"Aren't you a little worried about what God might do? Look what happened to Pharaoh when—"

"We aren't rebelling! We aren't interfering! Isn't there

room for more than one way to worship? We're doing it all in the name of their God, aren't we? Is Aaron's way the only way? Isn't there room for a little variety? Is everybody supposed to come out of this *exactly* like everybody else? What did we get our freedom for, if not to be a little *free?*"

"You don't have to persuade *me.*"

"I'm just saying, God is the one who made us the way we are, isn't he? I mean, isn't that the whole point? The God of Israel is like Ptah, he made everything, so didn't he make *me,* complete with all these needs and desires? And if he put these desires in me, then how can it be wrong to satisfy them? In fact, I'm worshiping him more fully than these pious people are, because I'm using my whole self in my worship."

"Have you tried that argument on Aaron?"

"He hasn't had a desire in fifteen years. Have you seen his wife? This is an old man's religion they've got here."

"You're going to persuade Aaron to gather the gold, melt it down, and pour it in?"

"Watch me."

❊

The angel sat across from Joshua and opened the book again.

"The more I read," said Joshua, "the easier it gets."

"This is the book of the days of Noah," said the angel.

"Has Moses read it?"

"A fragment. With most of the plainest truth lost from it. Even the name was lost. And yet it still opened a door in his heart, because his wife read it and taught him from it."

Joshua had only read a few words when he stopped. "Why am I never hungry or thirsty? I've been here for days, but I never even think of eating."

"You thought of it now."

"I just read this verse: The fruit is given to man to eat, but he lets it ripen and fall to the ground, while he gnaws on old bones and grows thin."

"The glory of God is on this mountain," said the angel, "so you have no need of food or drink."

*

Aaron heard the tumult before the messenger reached him. "Quickly!" the boy shouted. "At the boundary of the Lord's land!"

Aaron leapt from the judgment seat, Hur behind him, and rushed as quickly as he could to the foot of the mountain, where the line had been drawn that the people could not cross. Hundreds had gathered there. Many were onlookers, but most were a group that was shouting and cursing at the young men of the patrol, who looked sick at heart at the prospect of striking out with weapons against their own people.

"Let us by!"

"The Lord has forgotten us!"

"Moses is dead!"

"He's not coming back!"

"Moses is dead!"

It became a chant. Moses is dead. God has forgotten us. Moses is dead. God has forgotten us.

Aaron strode at once into the space between the soldiers and the crowd. He held up his arms for silence, and because the staff that had become a snake was in his hand, the people recoiled a little, and relative quiet settled over the crowd.

"Moses is alive," Aaron said.

"You haven't seen him either!"

"The Lord has much to teach us. Be grateful at how long he's been up the mountain! It means the gift he'll return to us is that much greater!"

"How do you know he didn't fall and die!"

"Because the Lord that gives you manna every morning is also the Lord who led him up the mountain. Do you think the prophet's foot could slip when there are angels to bear him up?"

"But nothing changes! Day after day!"

"Go home!" Aaron said. "Back to your tents. Don't defy the Lord by crossing this boundary line. It would be death to you if you tried! Go to your families!"

They obeyed him, straggling away. But then, to his chagrin, one group of them began chanting again as they walked among the tents: "Moses is dead! God has forgotten us!"

"Do you want me to take some of these men and go silence that chant?" asked Hur.

"And then what?" said Aaron. "Send soldiers wherever people say things we don't like? Is that what these young men entered into this service to do? Is that why we came out of Egypt?"

"We didn't come out of Egypt to have troublemakers tear the nation of Israel apart, either," said Hur.

"They'll quiet down soon enough," said Aaron. "Most people will know that the whole idea that Moses might be dead is ridiculous. Or that the Lord has forgotten us. They have only to look at the cloud over the mountain on a day that's completely clear. The Lord is with us."

"Well, technically, the Lord is with Moses," said Hur, "and we're on our own down here."

Aaron glared at him. "You, too?"

Hur smiled uncomfortably. "I think I was joking."

"I think I'm relieved to hear it." Aaron held up his hand, listened. "Hear that?"

"What?" asked Hur.

"The chant has already stopped."

Hur grinned. "Well, what can I say? You were right."

But later that day it began again, somewhere among the tents of Manasseh. And in the darkness, it began in Gad and went on for an hour before people in neighboring tents pulled the stakes on the tents of the chanters. It became a fistfight and Aaron had to come and arbitrate, and the result was a new rule against loud noises at night. But the chanters bruited it about that Aaron was now trying to make them be quiet because he *knew* Moses was dead but was afraid that if the camp of Israel knew it, they'd divide up and each family would go to Canaan or back to Egypt or wherever they wanted. "And then who would have Aaron as ruler and judge?" It was a vicious rumor, but it was repeated often enough that some people started to believe it, a little, and wonder aloud about whose interest was foremost in Aaron's heart.

At least at home Aaron finally had some peace. "You were right about them," Elisheba said. "They're no friends of mine."

"What happened?"

"I overheard them telling somebody else that there was another army of Egyptians coming to attack us and take us back into slavery, and you knew about it but you weren't going to tell anybody because you kept hoping the Lord would make you a prophet like Moses only the Lord doesn't love you like Moses so you'll try to stop the Egyptians yourself and—oh, it goes on and on, I can't believe anybody was listening to it!"

"But they were?"

"When I challenged them on it, then everybody said that it was just speculating, and there was no harm in wondering about things, was there? Aaron, they really *are* vicious, trying to stir up trouble."

"If you can see that, maybe others will see it, too."

"But think how long it took me. I feel like such a fool."

"Honest people are easiest to fool, Elisheba. It never occurred to you that they might be flattering you, because you don't lie."

"So much of what they said to me sounded true, and I still don't—I can't even sort out what I think now."

"Then hold fast to the Lord, and wait. These are his people. He'll open the door for us and make it clear what we must do."

❊

As Moses watched, the rough face of the stone crumbled and slid down, leaving a smooth surface. Then small bits of dust formed on the face of the stone. When he brushed them away, he could see that letters had been incised in the stone, deeper than any tool could have engraved them. He read, brushed away more dust, and read again.

What emerged was the order of the priesthood of the Son of God, and sacred rituals that would bind husband to wife and parents to children through every generation of the world. He read the pattern for ceremonies that taught the dead how to enter heaven, and knew that the Books of the Dead in Egypt were but a weak echo of what Melchizedek had known, and Noah, and Enoch, and the great prophets and patriarchs of the earliest age of man. Following this pattern, Moses would be able to ordain all the men of Israel who chose to live worthy as high priests after the order of Melchizedek, the great king of Salem, to whom Abraham had paid his tithes. A nation of high priests, all of them linked to the Lord and to their families by the holiest of bonds. And in the deep places in his soul, where he held memories that he could never fully bring to consciousness again, he felt how the order established by the writing on the stone fit in with the order of all the earths and all the heavens, so that instead of human beings being cut off from knowledge of the creations of God, they would know their place and gladly serve within it, and receive the joy that the Lord had in store for them.

He knelt and prayed, even as the writing went on, thanking God for his mercy and praying for the wisdom to know how to bring Israel to the point where all could receive these blessings.

❖

It was a fullblown riot now, the chanters tearing down tents wherever they roamed. "Moses is dead! God has forgotten us!"

The captains of the guard waited for Aaron to tell them what to do. Hur, Caleb, and other elders of the tribes kept urging him to take action, that this could not go on, everyone was becoming frightened.

Harubel appeared at his side. "Aaron, what can I do to help you?"

"As far as I know, you're the one behind all this," Aaron snapped.

"What *I* want is peace and quiet," said Harubel. "We won't make a god, we won't dance, but we'll make an emblem, a visible sign that the people can gather around. Something to see—isn't that what they're calling for? Something to *see.*"

"This is what you wanted all along," said Aaron.

"Yes, of course," said Harubel. "I want Israel to be content. But this—it's descending into chaos, and when Moses comes back and finds the whole camp in an uproar, what's he going to say to you?"

"I'm not afraid of my brother, he'll understand that—"

"He'll understand that Israel *has* no leader when he isn't here."

"Spare me the sniping," said Aaron. "I have plenty of people doing that already."

"Let's put it in the Lord's hands," said Harubel. "I know a smith, he'll make a clay form with a hollow place in it. Gather the gold we got from Egypt, melt it down, and pour it in—and ask the Lord to make it into whatever shape he wants the people to see. That way *we* aren't making a graven image, God is. It'll be a miracle! The people will see that the Lord is with them!"

The chant was growing louder and louder, and so were the shouts and screams of the people who were fighting.

A miracle would be helpful at this moment.

"Whatever comes out of the clay," said Aaron, "there'll be no dancing. None of the rituals from the worship of the calf."

"Of course not," said Harubel. "The people wouldn't stand for it anyway."

"Not any of the hand-clapping music of Egypt, either."

"Oh, suddenly that's evil?"

"Nothing that sounds like the worship of other gods. Or that looks like it."

"I agree completely," said Harubel. "I wouldn't have it any other way. It's the Lord who'll do this."

But when the smith and his assistants carried the wooden frame and the clay within it to the judgment seat, Aaron grew suspicious. "You already have a shape inside that, don't you?"

The smith looked at him in puzzlement. "How could I? The gold pours in and burns away the clay and makes its *own* shape. I have no control over it."

"Smiths shape things all the time." If only he knew anything about how smiths did their work, but those were closely guarded secrets, and Aaron could only guess whether he was being told the truth or not.

"Yes, we shape things," said the smith, "but not when the form is already enclosed like this. How could I? Am I supposed to reach in with teeny-tiny tools and carve something down in the hole?"

Aaron looked at him and knew that he was a liar but didn't know what the lie was. He also knew that the chanting was growing louder, and so were the cries of those trying to silence the chanters.

What should I do, Lord? Can I believe these men? Will you make the gold come forth in some shape that will help to still this riot?

He heard no answer.

Aaron turned to the leaders of the patrol. "Go tell the chanters to come and see that God still remembers Israel."

Moments later, the patrol headed off to find the chanters. In the meantime, Aaron had the elders of the tribes bring the carts filled with gold booty from Egypt and bring them to the large clay melting pot that was being set up before the judgment seat.

When the chanters fell silent, it was almost more frightening than the noise had been. The fire under the melting pot grew intense, and Aaron let the smith choose the ornaments of the most pure gold and put them in the pot to be melted down.

"What are you doing?" demanded Miriam.

"Trying to stop the rioting," said Aaron.

"Harubel is a calf-worshiper," she said. "So is that smith he's working with."

"The smith, also?"

"He's not even an Israelite, Aaron. He's a Hittite."

"Then what is he doing here?"

"Maybe he came along on the journey so he could get his hands on some of that gold. And now you're giving it to him."

"The Lord will make it turn out all right."

"The Lord has nothing to do with this, and you know it!"

"As the Lord did with the plagues, he'll do now."

"Not the way you think!" cried Miriam. "Aaron, the Lord won't do anything with this. Whatever it is, it'll be a graven image. Why would the Lord *ever* help you create the very thing he forbade us to have?"

"But it won't be graven, it'll be—"

The smith's assistants ran their rods through the slots at the top of the melting pot, so that four long handles emerged from it. Then they picked it up by the handles and carried it to the form.

Zeforah and Elisheba ran to Aaron. "Husband!" cried Elisheba. "Don't do this! It's a trick!"

"Elisheba, I can't stop now," said Aaron.

Zeforah spoke up. "Aaron, I have said nothing about the governing of this camp, but you must listen to Elisheba, this will bring you nothing but shame."

"What will bring me shame is standing before this crowd and letting them see that my wife and Moses' wife and my sister Miriam are the real rulers of this camp. I've made the decision, and it will stand."

"Aaron, please!" cried Elisheba. "God will destroy us!"

"You're the one who was telling me we needed this," said Aaron.

"But not like this. Look at them—those aren't the children of Israel, those are devils!"

The faces of the chanters were all intently focused on the gold as it poured out of the melting pot and into the form.

"It's in God's hands now," said Aaron. "Whatever forms in the mold, that's up to God."

"God has no part in this," said Miriam.

"I was charged with governing Israel," said Aaron. "By *God* I was assigned. The crisis is upon us! I have to act."

"Act to stop them then," said Zeforah. "Don't surrender to them!"

"I'm surrendering to no one."

"Moses would not do this," said Zeforah.

Aaron whirled on her. "Should *you* govern us then? You're his wife, so you know what he *would* do. I can't believe I've lasted this long without your advice."

"That's not fair," said Elisheba. "Zeforah has *never* tried to give advice before."

"But you have," said Aaron.

"I was wrong," said Elisheba. "I'm glad you didn't listen to me—then."

"What I needed from you, then and now, is your support, not your criticism."

"I am trying to support you in the righteous resolve you had before," said Elisheba. "What happened to change that?"

"Look around you," said Aaron, indicating the crowd of one-time chanters, now intently watching as the smith and his assistants carried the form on their shoulders. Inside it, Aaron imagined the gold changing shapes, growing into something. Whatever the Lord wanted it to be. O Lord, please make the gold take the shape you want it to have!

"Never mind," said Miriam to the women. "He's not going to listen. Get back to your tents and keep your children away from this."

"I am keeping Israel safe!" cried Aaron as the women left.

"Of course you are," said Harubel. "What do they know? Now we get a chance to see a miracle come from Aaron *without* Moses there."

"The miracle, if it comes, will come from God."

"What do you mean *if?*" said Harubel, laughing. "Have some faith!"

It was then that Aaron realized he had been deceived, that he had succumbed to flattery as surely as Elisheba had the week before. Harubel knew what was inside the form. It had been planned from the beginning.

"Don't break the form," said Aaron.

"You can't be serious," said Harubel.

"I forbid you to break the form."

"Forbid? You *forbid?* Do you have any idea what would happen then? Look at these thousands of people, waiting, watching for the sign from God. If you refuse to break the form, what do you think they'll do?"

"They can do what they want. I forbid you to break the form."

Harubel responded by stepping in front of Aaron. "Aaron the prophet says, It's time to see what God has given us!"

He turned around and leered into Aaron's face. "As you were to Moses, now I am to you. Spokesman!"

When Harubel turned back around, Aaron could not bring himself to rush forward, for the people were now pressing close, frantic in their excitement. He could never silence them, could never push his way through that crowd to stop them, and even if he could make himself heard or seen, he knew they would not obey him now. They all knew what the gold would be. Some of them were already tearing off their clothes, to dance naked for the god the mold had shaped for them.

"This is not from God!" cried Aaron. But his voice was lost in the tumult from the crowd.

The wood frame was gone, and the clay stood alone. The smith's hammer tapped at the baked clay. Pieces chipped off. More and more of them. The gold glinted underneath, lustrous with firelight, perfect, new. Four legs. The triangular head. The bull calf.

They clapped hands, in the rhythmic music of Egyptian worship. The naked men and women began to dance, and more, before the calf. More and more threw their clothing aside or laid it on the fire so it would burn more hotly. The calf seemed to sweat as much as the dancers from the heat.

"O God," cried Aaron, "strike them down now, and me with them. We are all worthy of death."

If God heard his cry, he was the only one, for no one else even noticed Aaron in the frenzy of the music and the dance.

"Here is your god!" cried Harubel. *His* voice was heard. "Here is your god!" And no one thought for a moment that he meant the Lord God of Israel.

❊

"Mother," said Gershom. "What's all that clapping?"

"I've never heard such a sound before," said Zeforah.

"Its the way the Egyptians make music when they worship their gods," said Miriam.

"But who would be worshiping an Egyptian god?" asked Gershom.

"People who want to die for their blasphemy against heaven," said Miriam.

❊

The writing was finished, four columns of it. A fine line appeared all the way around the writing. Two tables of stone, each with two columns of writing, slid down the face of the rock. Moses caught them, gathered them into his arms, and rose to stand straight, ready to bear the stone tables down the mountain. Only then did he see that the tables were written on the reverse side, too—writing that he had not yet read.

He was about to start reading the back of one table when the voice of the Lord came to him.

Go, get down the mountain, for the people have corrupted themselves. They have turned aside quickly from the covenant they made with me. They worship a golden calf, and sacrifice to it. Get down, and see how I will destroy them.

"No, Lord, please!" cried Moses. "Did you bring them out of Egypt to destroy them? Did you make your promises to Abraham, Isaac, and Jacob, only to end them here? Destroy those whose fault it is, but not the innocent. There are surely many who are innocent!"

Go, then, and separate the guilty from the innocent. By your judgment I will be bound. Whomever you condemn on earth, I will condemn in heaven.

※

Joshua stood on the path, listening to the tumult coming up from the camp. He was torn between his duty to wait for Moses and the urgency of the need to get down the mountain and join with his soldiers.

Then he heard stones clatter, and Moses came into view, carrying two large tables of stone.

"Moses," said Joshua. "There's a noise of war in the camp!"

"I don't hear anyone shouting in triumph, or screaming in terror," said Moses. "What I hear is the sound of singing."

Only then did the voices resolve in Joshua's ears; only then did he understand what he had been hearing.

"After all we've seen," said Joshua, "how could they?"

Moses didn't answer as he passed Joshua and began the long walk down the mountain.

"What is the writing engraved on the stone?" asked Joshua.

"A temple, and a nation perfect before the Lord, with no poor among them, each man a priest and prophet to his family, and Holiness to the Lord written in the door of each house and the windows of every soul. A nation where angels minister to every household, as the angel ministered to you."

So he knew. And the Lord meant to give the same gift to all. But now? "What will the Lord do now?"

"What good will it be to enter the promised land, if we carry Egypt with us?" said Moses. "It will take longer than I thought. For myself, I pray only that I live to *see* the promised land. When the people are ready to enter it, then my work is done."

"If I had been down there," said Joshua, "my soldiers might have—"

"No," said Moses. "The wicked had to have the chance to declare themselves. The lines are drawn. Now help me get down the mountain."

# S t o n e

Aaron stood beside the judgment seat, looking down at the sea of frenzied bodies demanding pleasure from their god. He wanted to pray for God to strike them all down, but he was sick at heart with the knowledge that when the Lord took his vengeance on these oathbreakers, Aaron himself would be the first to die. So it was not for him to call down punishment on the sinners. It was for him to see what he had done, so when he suffered the torments of hell his sin would be fresh in his mind forever.

He was aware of someone behind him, climbing up to the judgment seat. He did not look. There was no one whose face he could bear to see.

Joshua stepped forward to the edge of the outcropping of rock on which the judgment seat rested. He sank to his knees, weeping.

Moses stepped forward, looking tired, grief-stricken. In his arms were large tables of stone, closely written in Hebrew on both sides. He looked out over the dancers. A few of them noticed him and stopped dancing; a few of the hand-clappers and singers fell silent. Most, however, were oblivious to the judgment standing over them.

Moses leaned his head back and spoke to heaven. "As they have done to their covenant, do so to them."

Handing one table to Joshua, Moses raised the other high

above his head. The dancers at the foot of the judgment seat saw the movement, realized what he was doing, and dodged out of the way, shrieking, just as Moses flung down the stone. It hit the ground and shattered into a hundred shards, many of which hit the naked bodies of the revelers, drawing blood, making bruises. Moses took the second stone table, and threw it down after the first.

Not from the dancers, but from the crowd of angry onlookers, a chant began. "Moses! Moses! Moses!" The faithful began to push their way forward, forcing the dancers together. A few judges climbed up to stand with Moses on the judgment seat, Hur and Caleb among them. Moses turned to them now. "Take that calf," he said. "Grind it into dust and put it in water."

The revelers parted to make way for Caleb and Joshua as they strode to the calf and pulled it down from the platform that had been set up for it. Other judges brought them a mortar and pestle; they hammered the calf into pieces, then ground the pieces down to dust.

Hur led several young men in filling the melting pot with water, into which the gold fragments were now poured. Around them, dancers searched frantically for any item of clothing they could put on.

"Give it to them, every one of them, to drink!"

Sobbing now, frightened of the prophet who had brought such terrible plagues to Egypt, the dancers recoiled. Some tried to flee, but the crowd surrounding them would not let them through.

"All of you who danced before the calf, all who clapped your hands, all who sang, drink!"

Weeping or sullen, babbling excuses or silent with shock,

the revelers came forward and drank from the basins the judges were filling and refilling with gold-dusted water.

While they filed to the water, Moses turned to Aaron and spoke quietly. "What did they do to you, Aaron, that you let them sink to such a sin as this?"

Aaron knew he had done enough to be condemned, but he also could not bear to let Moses think he had consented to the worship of the calf. "Moses, don't be angry with Israel. You know how these people are, set on mischief. When you'd been gone so long, and no one knew when you'd be coming back, or *if* you ever would, they demanded a sign, something they could see, to prove God was with them. They promised not to dance, so I took the gold and put it in the fire and they poured it in the mold and the calf . . . came out."

Moses looked at him wordlessly for a long moment, then turned his back.

This was not at all how Aaron had meant to say it. He wanted to start over, to explain that some of the people had lied to him, and some had flattered him, and many had goaded him with their chanting that Moses was dead, that God had forgotten Israel. He wanted to make Moses realize how frightening it had been, to have rioters in the camp, quarreling and fighting. But that would sound like an attempt to excuse himself. Even what he *had* said sounded like a pitiful attempt to put the blame on someone else. And he wouldn't do that. God had left him to lead and judge the camp of Israel, and he had failed so spectacularly that he wanted only to die now, for he could never bear to stand before the people again. He sank down to his knees, head bowed, waiting for the end.

Casting his eyes over the assembled people, Moses flung his arms out. "Who is on the Lord's side!"

Hur pointed to a large group of the men of Levi, whose camp was nearest the judgment seat. "There is Levi!" he cried.

"Put swords in your hands and come to me!" shouted Moses.

The dancers shrieked and screamed, wept and begged for mercy, but the surrounding crowd held them and let none of them escape. The Levite men who had swords brought them; others took swords out of the hands of the young soldiers. This was not a matter for these young protectors of the people to deal with. This was for men who were fathers and grandfathers, who knew that in this bitter work today they would be saving their children and their children's children from the destroyer.

"What is the penalty for idolatry?" Moses demanded. "What is the price of adultery? What happens to the oathbreaker?"

A complete hush fell over the people.

"Death," said Hur.

"Levites," said Moses. "Send the idolaters and oathbreakers to face the judgment of God."

With sword in hand, Hur leapt down from the judgment seat and struck deeply into the neck of the first dancer he came to. The other Levites plunged into the crowd; the swords rose and fell. They set about the business grimly, methodically, taking no pleasure in it, but sparing no one. Screaming, pleading, shrieking, cursing, many of them denying they had danced or clapped or sung, even some who stood naked and covered with caked-on dust and sweat, they faced the sword and then fell, their blood making a viscous mud out of the dancing ground.

Elisheba and Miriam came briefly to the judgment seat, their eyes averted from the grisly scene below them, as they raised Aaron to his feet and led him away to his tent. Zeforah arrived with them, but did not leave. Instead she watched her husband as he stood and oversaw the slaughter, his presence keeping the Levites from losing the courage to continue.

Beside him, Caleb turned to Joshua. "What was written on the stone he broke?" Caleb asked.

"All that the Lord can give was there," said Joshua.

"Can we ever have it back?" asked Caleb.

Moses heard them, and answered. "The Lord will carve new stone tables, and write upon them, but what we'll have now is a lesser law, a law for schoolchildren." A cry of agony tore its way from Moses' throat. "O Lord!" he shouted. "The sin of your people is great! Forgive them, Lord, or blot my name from your book!"

The voice of the Lord came into Moses' heart: I will blot the sinners from the book of life, but those who have chosen me, I choose forever.

As if she had heard the Lord's voice, Zeforah came forward then and put her arm around Moses' waist. He held her there beside him until the killing was done.

"Let each tribe's elders come and search for their dead," Moses told them. "Before the sun goes down, put all these bodies in the ground." The gold of the calf would be buried with them, scattered among so many graves that no one would ever shape it into anything again.

As the work of identifying and burying the dead began, Moses finally turned to Zeforah. "Go comfort the children without me," he said to her. "My brother is the one who needs me now."

※

Aaron looked so small, sitting hunched over on the rugs inside his tent. His children were gone, taken by Elisheba to another tent; they did not need to see or hear what would pass between the sons of Jochabed.

Moses stood at the door, coming no closer to his brother than that.

Aaron looked up at him. "I have no excuse. I should have been killed with the others."

"Did you worship the calf?" asked Moses.

"I ordered them to bring the gold, to pour it into the mold. I told them the Lord would form it into the shape he wanted. I led them to evil."

"Did you know the smith was casting it to be a calf?"

"I should have known. They only deceived me because I wanted to be deceived."

"Why would you want that?"

"You have to do something, Aaron!" he said, mimicking Harubel. "Are you the leader or not? Can't you do anything without Moses to tell you what to do?"

"So you believed him."

"I believed his promises. I didn't understand that the people rioting were the same ones telling me how to stop the riots. But I should have. I should have guessed."

"You were alone."

Deep, bitter sobs wracked Aaron's body as he bowed his back over the carpet.

"You were alone but you didn't have to be," said Moses. "Did you consult with the judges?"

"No two of them gave the same advice," said Aaron. "They were as frightened and confused as I was, and someone had to act!"

Moses roared back at him: "No one had to *act!* There is never a time when it's better to do something terrible than to do nothing at all!"

"I know that now," said Aaron quietly.

"You can't govern the people alone," said Moses. "I always had you and Miriam. Didn't you ask Miriam?"

"They mocked me if I listened to women," said Aaron.

"Did you pray?"

"I asked God to form the gold into the shape that he desired."

"Did you pray *first* to know if that was right?"

"I had to decide then, in that moment, and—"

"Why not the next moment? Why not the moment after you prayed?"

"God doesn't talk to me!" cried Aaron. "I'm not like you, I don't pray and get answers in the same moment. God gave me a dream—*once*. Everything else came because I was standing beside *you*. It all came to you, never to me. So no, I didn't pray first, because God never speaks to me anyway! He leaves me on my own, and on my own I'm nothing. I'm nothing all the time, I've never been anything, you've always been the one that God was looking out for. You never should have left me in charge. The people needed a prophet and all they had was me."

"You would have been enough," said Moses. "The Lord gives me what the people need to have. He would have shown you the way."

"How do you know that?" demanded Aaron. "You've never been *me*. You've never heard that stony silence from heaven!"

"How do you know what I've had from heaven?" said Moses. "How do you know the agony I went through, learning how to pray? The years of patience when I had lost everything in my life and I heard no explanation out of heaven, but I learned to pray and keep the law as best I could, and I studied the scriptures and loved my wife and raised my children. Were you there, so that you can judge me now and say that my life was easy, while yours was hard?"

"All right, yes, I'm sure that you faced heroic challenges and overcame them all," said Aaron bitterly. "And the silence of heaven was my own fault. My own unworthiness. But that's what I had from God—nothing! For you he writes on stone and hands it to you. For me, the stone is always blank and I can't pry it away from the mountain. But yes, I'm sure it's my fault! So let me die now. Bury me with the idolaters. I also broke my oath and defiled the law."

"You never took an oath not to be stupid," said Moses.

Aaron looked up at him with deep anger. "Is that what I am?"

"It's what we all are," said Moses, "until the Lord teaches us."

"I'm not stupid now," said Aaron. "I'm wise enough to see the blood on my hands. The ones who died today—if I had been the leader Israel needed, they all would be alive."

"Like a poisoned man needs to vomit, Israel needed to have those idolaters out of their belly and spilled on the ground."

"So now you tell me that I did *well?*" said Aaron nastily.

"I tell you that the will of God was not thwarted by your mistakes," said Moses.

"Because Moses is always there to fix everything. Do you think any of this is comfort?"

"I'm not here to comfort you!" Moses shouted. "I'm here to wake you up! You take upon yourself guilt that belongs to others, but the guilt that really does belong to you, you refuse to recognize—you put it all on me!"

"What guilt is that! Name my sin for me! You're my judge,

aren't you, Moses? Just like with that Egyptian innkeeper you killed—you always know who deserves to live and die, who is worthy and who is not!"

"That's the sin, Aaron," Moses said.

"What is? Daring to speak impolitely to God's chosen one?"

"Listen to yourself! What if it were one of your sons, saying these things to his brother? Wouldn't you know *then* what was wrong?"

"The same thing that was wrong with Cain and Abel," said Aaron bitterly. "One son was loved by God, and the other son was evil and despised."

"One son was broken-hearted and offered his life to the Lord," said Moses, "while the other son was consumed by envy and nursed the wound of his injured pride until it destroyed him. Is that what you want to be? You see that your brother's sacrifice is accepted by the Lord, but instead of letting your own heart break, you brood upon your injuries and hate your brother—as if my service to God made yours impossible, as if my meekness before the Lord required you to remain proud!"

Aaron leapt to his feet and shouted, "I am not proud!"

"Never prouder than at this moment!" Moses roared back.

"I heard Israel crying!" Aaron said. "I prayed to God: Let my arm free Israel! But he never heard me."

"He heard you. He was waiting for you to say, Make of me whatever you need me to be. You didn't want to serve the Lord, you wanted him to serve you."

"I loved my people and I wanted to lead them to freedom!"

"Then why didn't you free yourself so you *could* lead them?"

"I couldn't free *myself,*" Aaron answered. "It took God to do that."

"It always does," said Moses. "Aaron, the greatest blessing God has for us is not to astonish the world with our achievements, but to be his hands, and do whatever he needs his hands to do. Do you think the Lord didn't need you in his service? He sent you to me in the palace again and again, goading me until I finally walked out among the people and what I saw there transformed me. *You* were God's hands that blessed me then, even though I was angry at you and didn't understand what was happening. You and Miriam, you were serving God even then. You were doing what was needed, the first steps to bringing Israel out of Egypt. Your prayer *was* being answered, if you had only been willing to see it. Aaron, you have always been as strong as you dreamed of being, a pillar I have leaned upon through every step of this journey. *You* are the only one who doesn't understand how God chose you and favored you and loved you all along."

The anger fled from Aaron's face, as he was stricken with the knowledge of what he had not understood about his own life, until now.

"Yes, your sin is grievous," said Moses. "Yes, your heart will break. You have things to repent of, and by the gift of God you can be forgiven if you give yourself wholly to the service of God. Live to save his children! Live to teach his word! Every longing of your heart·has been heard in heaven and even now the Lord holds out his hand to you and offers you the life you long for. You are already what you always longed to be. You already have the love of your God. And of your brother."

Moses embraced him, held him close. Aaron could not respond, could hardly move as thoughts raced through his mind and feelings swept through his heart. He felt Moses withdraw his arms and wanted to cry out, No, don't leave me alone again! But he said nothing and Moses left the tent.

Aaron sank to his knees and prayed as the words rushed into his mind.

"O Father, turn your ear to the cry of my heart, for my soul is full of troubles, I have no strength. I'm as dead as the dead, and I'm laid in my own soul's grave. Your hand has cut me off and my brother's heart is far from me, you've laid me in the pit and closed it, I can't escape from myself."

Yet even as he said it, he knew that it wasn't true. The Lord had not cut him off; his brother's heart was closer to him than ever, and he could escape from the grave he was buried in.

"Can your loving kindness be felt in the grave? Will you do a miracle for the dead? Cast away my soul, and hide my face, I'm ready to die, from my youth I long for death. Your wrath flows over me, your floods have come to cut me off. The man I was, dies now in the flood. Here is the sacrifice you most desire, the broken heart, the bending spirit, fire instead of flesh, all these in me are yours."

He trembled and wept as he felt the Lord touch him in every part of his being. How can I bear to have you touch me! And then, as the sweetness flowed into him, he thought, How can I bear to ever have you stop?

"Make me know wisdom," he prayed. "Purge me with hyssop, and I will be clean. Oh, wash me and I'll be whiter than snow! Put a new heart in me, your spirit in me, and then my old bones will rejoice, my eyes will sing, my words will dance, and I'll write your law in my life."

For the first time in his life, the joy of the Lord filled him and he knew what it was. He rose to his feet, looked upward into heaven.

"I'm the man who didn't make the Lord my strength. I trusted in my arm and in my words. But now my ancient tree is fallen, now I'm a sapling branch that's green within your house. I root myself in you for ever and ever, I drink from you, for you have forgiven me."

# The   Promised   Land

There were trials and pitfalls in the road ahead, and for
many years the camp of Israel moved from place to place
in the desert of Sinai, fed by manna, watched over by cloud
and fire. Moses brought new tables of stone down from the
mountain; few guessed and fewer knew that it was not the
same law that had been shattered into shards at the judgment
seat. Aaron was ordained high priest, and his sons would succeed him as priests. The whole tribe of Levi would serve as a
priestly clan, which removed them from consideration for a
land of inheritance in the promised land. There would be
twelve tribes again, with the Levites as a tribe apart, ministering to all.

They built an ark to hold the stone tables of the covenant,
topped by the mercy seat on which the Lord would sit when
he came to visit his people. They built a tabernacle as well,
which served as a movable temple, and when one day a king
in Israel built a temple it was modeled after the pattern of the
tabernacle. As the years passed in the wilderness, those who
had known Egypt became accustomed to the new life, and to
the worship of the Lord, and a new generation grew up that
did not remember Egypt.

There were trials for Moses' family, as Miriam had her
time of grief and rebellion, and as Aaron watched his two
eldest sons struck dead as, defiantly or stupidly, they treated

the rites of the tabernacle with contempt. And the people were also tried, with disease, with temptation, with their own fear to enter the promised land.

Through all these years, Moses' labor was to teach. He felt his responsibility, not just to the Israelites who gathered to listen to him, but also to the generations yet unborn. So he wrote, or dictated for others to write, and trained many to be scribes in the Hebrew language and make copies of the scriptures so that they might be preserved. When Zeforah's children no longer needed her, she took on the project of assembling many accounts of the lives of the prophets and patriarchs into one account, to which Moses added a small part of his own vision of the creation. Aaron taught the order of the Levites and his regulations were written down. Joshua wrote Moses' own story, as Moses told it to him, so it reflected Moses' own reluctance to include the details of his life before the Lord awakened him and brought him to the desert.

Miriam and Aaron both died before the journey ended, but they died knowing their work had been well done, their sins forgiven them, their people prospering and growing in their knowledge of the Lord. Aaron's two eldest sons were gone, but the younger ones had grown to be faithful and responsible in their service as priests, and the people worshiped as before.

At last the day came when the Lord told Moses that this next journey would take them into the promised land. They came through the desert up the east side of the Dead Sea, and when they were within sight of the prosperous Jordan Valley, Moses called Joshua to him.

"You're the one who will lead them now," he said.

"It should be you," Joshua answered him.

"That's not for us to decide. Don't forget I never asked for this work."

"How will I know what to do?"

"The man who talked with an angel for all those days on the mountain—you're asking me?"

"The people of this land will not be glad to see us."

"The Lord raised you up to be a man of war, because the people of this land are ripe in their rebellion, ready to have their inheritance taken away from them. But the war is in the name of God, and not for any lust for blood. I know that you, by nature, are a man of peace."

"So why does God give this task to me?"

"Because you didn't ask for it, and don't love it, and will gladly set war aside when the need has passed."

"Moses, will the people follow me? No matter what I say or do, they'll whisper to each other, Joshua means well but he's not Moses."

"Then you'll be doing better than me," said Moses, "because they didn't always give me credit for meaning well."

"The Lord gave you signs to show them when you were first called."

"You'll have the sign of the parting of waters," said Moses. "When the time comes, your people will cross the Jordan on dry land."

Joshua bowed his head in gratitude. "Then the Lord is good to me, and to this people."

"Go and tell the others that I will bid them good-bye. But send my son Gershom to me first."

Joshua left, and after a little while, Gershom came into his father's tent. He was a grown man now, with full-grown children of his own.

"What a wise and patient man you grew to be," Moses said.

"As best I could," said Gershom.

"All these years, you watched as Aaron's sons became priests, and I prepared Joshua to lead the people as their prophet. Today I'm giving Israel to him, and taking leave of everyone, and yet in all these years, you have never said to me, Father, what about my inheritance?"

"My inheritance," said Gershom, "is to have you and Mother as my parents, and the love of my wife, and my honorable children, and to feel the love of God in every morning and evening of my life."

"All that," said Moses, "and yet there's one thing more."

Moses took two scrolls out of a cloth bag and showed them to Gershom. "These books are not to be had among the children of Israel."

"What are they?"

"The account of my vision on the mount, and of all I learned there. The higher law, the prophecies of the meridian of time, and of the fullness of time. This is what Israel lost when they allowed the dancing before the calf, not as punishment, but because they weren't ready yet. Even the law they have now, they'll forget again and again until they finally learn to obey; even the promised land that will be given to them now will be lost again, two more times. This law was too hard. But someday the Lord will see fit to give these books to his children. For now, though, they are to be kept as a secret treasure by you and your children, as long as the Lord allows or needs."

"The book will decay," said Gershom.

"You must open it and copy it," said Moses, "and each new generation after you. But no one can ever know that it exists, or what it contains, until a time that the Lord reveals to you. If any of your descendants disobeys this rule, an angel will come and take the book. But the labor will not be lost. The Lord remembers every word that is written."

"Then my duty is to become as obscure as I can," said Gershom. "And to think I've been practicing for that all my life, without knowing it."

Moses laughed, then kissed and embraced his son.

Legends grew up about Moses, that perhaps he didn't die, and in one sense he did not, for there was no fear of death, nor was there pain in his passage out of mortality. On the mountain, looking out over the promised land, one moment he was alive in the body, seeing with the eyes of flesh, and the next moment he saw with his whole spirit, and rose from the old shape that had contained him all those years. He was not surprised to find Zeforah at his side, for he had felt her there through the long years of separation after she died.

As Joshua stopped the waters of Jordan and the children of Israel crossed over, Moses was with them. And Aaron and Miriam were both weeping with joy as they embraced him on the other side.